S. Sylvan Simon

**Clockwise from left: Director S. Sylvan Simon
with the cast of _I Love Trouble,_ including
Donald Curtis, Janis Carter and Janet Blair.**

S. Sylvan Simon, Moviemaker

*Adventures with Lucy, Red Skelton
and Harry Cohn in the
Golden Age of Hollywood*

DAVID C. TUCKER

McFarland & Company, Inc., Publishers
Jefferson, North Carolina

ALSO OF INTEREST BY DAVID C. TUCKER
AND FROM McFARLAND

Pine-Thomas Productions: A History and Filmography (2019)
Gale Storm: A Biography and Career Record (2018)
Martha Raye: Film and Television Clown (2016)
Joan Davis: America's Queen of Film, Radio and Television Comedy (2014)
Eve Arden: A Chronicle of All Film, Television, Radio and Stage Performances (2012)
Lost Laughs of '50s and '60s Television: Thirty Sitcoms That Faded Off Screen (2010)
Shirley Booth: A Biography and Career Record (2008)
The Women Who Made Television Funny: Ten Stars of 1950s Sitcoms (2007)

All photos, except where otherwise noted,
are from the author's collection.

LIBRARY OF CONGRESS CATALOGUING-IN-PUBLICATION DATA

Names: Tucker, David C., 1962– author.
Title: S. Sylvan Simon, moviemaker : adventures with Lucy, Red Skelton and
Harry Cohn in the golden age of Hollywood / David C. Tucker.
Description: Jefferson, North Carolina : McFarland & Company, Inc.,
Publishers, 2021 | Includes bibliographical references, filmography,
and index.
Identifiers: LCCN 2020057297 | ISBN 9781476682198 (paperback : acid free paper) ∞
ISBN 9781476641744 (ebook)
Subjects: LCSH: Simon, S. Sylvan (Samuel Sylvan), 1910–1951. | Motion
picture producers and directors—United States—Biography. | Motion
pictures—United States—History—20th century.
Classification: LCC PN1998.3.S5335 T83 2021 | DDC 791.4302/33092 [B]—dc23
LC record available at https://lccn.loc.gov/2020057297

BRITISH LIBRARY CATALOGUING DATA ARE AVAILABLE

ISBN (print) 978-1-4766-8219-8
ISBN (ebook) 978-1-4766-4174-4

Front cover: Producer/director S. Sylvan Simon with Lucille Ball, who credited him
with encouraging and developing her flair for comedy (author's collection).

Printed in the United States of America

McFarland & Company, Inc., Publishers
Box 611, Jefferson, North Carolina 28640
www.mcfarlandpub.com

To the memory of my sister,
who accomplished much
in a life that was too short.

Contents

Acknowledgments

This book could not exist without the support and encouragement of the late S. Sylvan Simon's children, Susan Granger and Stephen Simon. When I contacted them with the idea, both immediately agreed to cooperate in making it a reality. Susan and her son, film producer Don Granger, went above and beyond the call of duty when they put into the U.S. mail their father's fragile, leather-bound copies of his movie scripts, a great display of trust that I much appreciated. Susan and Stephen also gave me candid interviews about their beloved father. I think he would have taken great pride in Susan's latter-day acclaim as a syndicated film reviewer and Stephen's credits as a movie producer, which include *All the Right Moves* (1983) with Tom Cruise and the cult favorite *What Dreams May Come* (1998). Sylvan's grandson Don Granger carries the family tradition into a new generation as a producer and studio executive whose films include *Mission: Impossible—Rogue Nation* (2015) and *Jack Reacher* (2012).

Of my other interviewees, a special thanks goes to Margaret O'Brien for her vivid recollections of making *Bad Bascomb* (1946) under Simon's direction. I'm also grateful to the indefatigable Richard Simon, Sylvan's nephew (still alive and kicking at the age of 98), and to Richard's son Ken, who facilitated that interview. It was a privilege to speak with Jane Powell, a lovely lady who spoke warmly of her first Hollywood director. Melissa Greene, daughter of lyricist and comedy writer Mort Greene, had intriguing thoughts about her father's friendship with Sylvan. Arlene Dahl, offering her second contribution to one of my books, answered a key question concerning the making of *A Southern Yankee* (1948), while Terry Moore graciously shared her recollections of making *Son of Lassie* (1945).

As with my previous books, archives and archivists were critical to uncovering information. Barbara Bogart Allen, a fine researcher who helped me with *Pine-Thomas Productions: A History and Filmography* (McFarland, 2019), once again mined the holdings of my favorite archive, the American Heritage Center at the University of Wyoming, doing so with skill and care. Stephen Frug likewise did yeoman's work at the Rare Manuscripts Collection of Cornell University, sifting through a small mountain of material and helping me interpret the idiosyncratically scrawled (but fascinating) correspondence of actress Aline MacMahon, Sylvan's cousin. Others who located and retrieved significant material were Caroline Cubé of the Special Collections Department at UCLA, William C. Daw, curator of the Curtis Theatre Collection at the University of Pittsburgh, and the reference staff of the Bentley Historical Library at the University of Michigan. As for the one and only Ned Comstock, from the Cinematic Arts Library at the University of Southern California, I asked him to look for one item from that library's holdings; his response, which will surprise no one who has been lucky enough to work with him, was to send that piece of information and quite a bit more.

Susan Swan and Dr. Sondra Thiederman, daughters of the late character actor Arthur Space, are enthusiastic keepers of their father's legacy, and they made available to me correspondence that passed between him and Sylvan Simon when both were young men building their careers in Hollywood. I learned more about the history of the Simon clan (and of the Markowitzes, his mother's family) from genealogist Rhonda McKinney-Bullard and through Eric S. Lidji, director of the Rauh Jewish History Program at the Archives of the Heinz History Center. Wes D. Gehring, acknowledged for his expertise on classic film comedy, spoke with me about Simon's collaboration with Red Skelton. Elias Savada made available to me vintage copies of the *Chronicle*, a publication of the Schroon Lake Camp, where Sylvan Simon was both camper and, later, faculty member.

Alan Weltzien, professor at the University of Montana, talked with me about author Thomas Savage, whose novel *Lona Hanson* nearly became an S. Sylvan Simon film. I also appreciate the assistance of author and historian Susan Warrender and the staff of the British Columbia Aviation Museum, who identified the dignitaries seen in photos taken on location during production of *Son of Lassie*. I gratefully acknowledge baseball historians Peter Morris and Gabriel Schechter, who pitched in when I was writing about Simon's film *Whistling in Brooklyn* with its cadre of real-life Dodgers.

As always, I appreciate the two most important people in my life, Louise Tucker and Ken McCullers, whose love and support went a long way toward completing yet another book project.

Preface

I am not sure when the name S. Sylvan Simon first crept into my consciousness. It may have been, in part, thanks to repeated viewings some years ago of the 1950 film comedy *The Fuller Brush Girl*, starring Lucille Ball, which he produced. As a dedicated Lucy fan, I enjoyed it thoroughly, and so did my then-young nephews, who demanded several replays of "that silly movie." (This was a compliment.) The unusualness of that alliterative name may have also helped call it to my attention.

The common wisdom has often been that Lucy's 18 years in movies prior to *I Love Lucy* represented the motion picture industry's foolish blindness to what she did best. Yet, *The Fuller Brush Girl*, coming near the end of her pre-television career, is a hilarious slapstick comedy that could easily have been a Lucy Ricardo adventure. In fact, some of its gags and comic ideas would be reprised on her classic sitcom. As several sources confirmed, Miss Ball herself readily acknowledged the debt she owed to Simon, who was a personal friend as well as a valued colleague.

Curious, I looked into the man who put together such a film (as well as produced Miss Ball's comedy *Miss Grant Takes Richmond* and directed her in the underappreciated *Her Husband's Affairs*). I soon learned that Mr. Simon had also been a strong contributor to the film comedy of another zany redhead, Red Skelton, who considered him his favorite director. With a lifelong affinity for comedy, Sylvan Simon was at the helm of two classic Abbott and Costello comedies and twice directed films teaming Wallace Beery and Marjorie Main. He even shot a memorable line for the Marx Brothers' film *At the Circus* (1939) and was initially slated to direct their film *Go West* (1940). Anyone who contributed that much to the world of motion pictures—and the above examples represent only his accomplishments in comedy—is surely worth remembering. So why could I find out so little about him?

One obvious answer to that question is that S. Sylvan Simon, born in 1910, died on May 17, 1951, at the age of 41. At the time of his sudden death, he was serving as Vice-President in Charge of Production at Columbia Pictures, where he had already produced the film adaptation of *Born Yesterday* (which won an Oscar for star Judy Holliday) and had just begun preparations for quite a different type of film, *From Here to Eternity*. Simon, who'd taken the executive position in 1949, was being groomed to step up whenever Columbia's irascible founder Harry Cohn, already in his late 50s, might be unable to continue. It was a job that, in the opinion of Simon's wife and several of his friends, substantially shortened his life.

Though he worked hard—perhaps too hard—as a studio executive, Simon had in fact been an overachiever from a young age. In the course of his 15 years in Hollywood, he directed more than 30 films. He made his first one at the age of 27, only a year after arriving in California. Starting his directorial career at Universal, he was soon stolen away by the more prestigious MGM. Though he loved comedy, and made many films in that genre, he was no one-trick pony: he could and did direct mysteries, war films, and more. With his lifelong love of live theater, he compiled five books devoted to that field, first becoming a published author at the age of 24. Several of his books are anthologies of plays, chosen with an eye toward meeting the needs of amateur theatrical groups. Some of the plays within those pages he also wrote. (These literary efforts are outlined in the book's appendix.) Truly a man ahead of his time, Simon even played a key role in a startup venture that promised to send movies streaming into viewers' living rooms—in 1947!

After deciding that Sylvan Simon's legacy merited a full-length study of his life and films, I then had to find out whether giving him that tribute, more than six decades after his death, was even possible. Not only was there little published information about him, some of what there was happened to be wrong. During his decade as a contract director at MGM, that studio's publicists seem to have either embellished, or flat-out invented, some aspects of his biography, and several of those inaccuracies found their way into print for years afterward. Wheeler W. Dixon's *The B Directors: A Biographical Directory* (Scarecrow, 1985), says, "Upon graduation he became director of dramatics at the University of Michigan from 1918 to 1931." If he indeed held that particular position on the Michigan faculty (which my research did not confirm), it's unlikely he did so in 1931, when he was an undergraduate student pursuing a degree there. It's even less likely that he did it in 1918, when he was eight years old.

Other errors seem to be attributable largely to human error. The distinguished stage and film actress Aline MacMahon, whom Simon would direct in *Tish* (1942), was not his real-life aunt, as is frequently reported; they were cousins. Even when accorded proper credit, he was sometimes slighted, as when one of James Jones' biographers mangled his name in print: "Cohn assigned Jones to work with his assistant Sylvan Sidney," wrote Frank MacShane in his book *Into Eternity: The Life of James Jones, American Writer* (Houghton Mifflin, 1985).

Luckily, Sylvan Simon's professional legacy was matched by one that surely meant as much or more to him as his career achievements—his daughter Susan and son Stephen. Susan Simon Granger, the older of the two siblings, had more distinct memories of her father, as well as his mother and other family members, and was refreshingly candid and straightforward in recounting them. She also played small roles in several of his 1940s films and shared her memories about those experiences. Stephen, who wrote movingly about the father he lost when he was four years old in his book *Bringing Back the Old Hollywood*, provided additional recollections in an interview.

Sylvan Simon's own bound copies of scripts for more than 30 movies, which I was able to consult in preparing this book, proved a treasure trove. Tucked in between script pages were a multitude of never-published photos of Simon on the sets of his films. The scripts themselves typically contained an original draft interspersed with rewrites and changes on pink sheets. Although he was not much given to making notes on the scripts, he frequently sketched diagrams to help him block scenes and occasionally reminded himself of what camera angle he wanted to use. It was also interesting to note those occasions on which, up to the days of shooting, some lines were crossed out in the script and replaced by new ones written in by hand. (This was true, for example, of one of my favorite lines in *Whistling in the Dark*.) Also bound into these volumes were cast and crew lists (usually listing home addresses and phone numbers for the entire company, including stars—imagine that today!), occasional pieces of correspondence, and other memorabilia he had wanted to keep.

I managed to locate, often with Susan's help, some of the actors who worked with her father, including Margaret O'Brien, Jane Powell, and Terry Moore. Naturally, not everyone I contacted could remember work they had done so long ago, in most cases when they were children. Billy Gray, when asked about *Father Is a Bachelor* (1950), succinctly replied, "Can't think of a thing," while Dwayne Hickman, in a polite response, admitted he retained no recollections whatsoever of his minor role in *Her Husband's Affairs* (1947).

In due time, I learned of two men who had been protégés of Mr. Simon. Character actor Arthur Space first worked with Sylvan before either of them made it to Hollywood in a theatrical troupe circa 1935. It was Simon who offered the little-known Space his first film role and subsequently cast him in almost every picture he made from that point forward, helping to launch a career that continued well beyond Sylvan's early demise. Though Space passed away in 1983, he left behind letters and journal entries that shed light on his early experiences in Hollywood and his memories of working with Simon. Another Simon mentee was his frequent assistant director Earl McEvoy, and I was pleased to speak with Mr. McEvoy's daughter Dusty Burke, who remembered the gratitude her late father felt for the man who took him on as a protégé.

Tucked away in the papers of architect Clarence Stein at Cornell University was a boxful of correspondence from his wife, actress Aline MacMahon, in which she talked about her cousin Sylvan and the film they made together, *Tish* (1942). Another fascinating discovery in the Simon family tree was journalist and social reformer Sophie Irene Loeb, Sylvan's (and Aline's) aunt. Her memories of the Simon clan's struggles in the late 19th century inspired a public campaign for reforms that would keep the children of young widows out of public institutions. Production records for several of Simon's Universal films, housed in the Cinematic Arts Library at the University of Southern California, were valuable as well.

This book opens with a biographical section tracing the course of Sylvan Simon's short but eventful life, beginning with his family background and his boyhood in Pittsburgh, Pennsylvania. Though he attended law school, he soon abandoned that field, making his way to Hollywood in the mid–1930s after initially following a career in the theater. All told, his time in the motion picture industry, first at Universal and later at MGM, was fairly short—just under 15 years—yet he completed nearly 40 feature films. Aside from the names already dropped, major stars such as Milton Berle, William Holden, and Ida Lupino were Simon colleagues. Also included is information about the preparatory work he did on *From Here to Eternity* in the last weeks of his life, conferring with his houseguest James Jones on the initial screen treatment and brainstorming the idea of casting Sinatra in a key role.

Part Two of the book is an extensively annotated filmography of the pictures directed and/or produced by Sylvan Simon. It provides background information on the making of each film, critical commentary, and excerpts from reviews published upon their release. Whenever possible, I have drawn on his annotated scripts. However, a few of his films were not represented in that collection, a fact sometimes telling in and of itself. If the filmography lists more entries than you'll find in online sources such as the Internet Movie Database, it's primarily because Simon, on at least two occasions, had his name removed from the credits of films on which he worked. This book offers substantial evidence that he produced the film noir *Shockproof* (1949), starring Cornel Wilde, and directed the majority of the Red Skelton comedy *A Southern Yankee* (1948), attributed onscreen to Edward Sedgwick. In several instances, it also lists crew credits more extensive than found in the film's opening titles or in online sources. These were taken from the documentation that appeared in Simon's bound scripts or studio production records and are set aside with brackets for clarification.

To write a book about a man nearly 70 years after his death is a task fraught with peril. It may be inevitable that what results is an unfinished portrait. It was, nonetheless, one done with respect and admiration, and I hope that it shines some overdue light on a filmmaker whose accomplishments deserve to be remembered.

PART I

Biography

"Laughter was a great part of his life."
—Susan Simon Granger, on her father Sylvan

1

Early Stages

Though it appeared on movie screens across the country throughout the 1940s and into the early 1950s, S. Sylvan Simon (the first initial standing for "Samuel") was not a household name. Yet his abilities as a filmmaker, and his solid instincts for what audiences wanted to see, consistently made money and won acclaim for the studios that employed him. His movies advanced the careers of such notable Hollywood players as Lana Turner, Red Skelton, and perhaps most notably, Lucille Ball, who played some of her best film comedy roles in Simon pictures. Not given to self-aggrandizement, Simon mostly let his work speak for itself, according to his cousin Richard Simon: "He liked to stay in the background most of the time."[1] His death at an early age not only cut his flourishing career short, it allowed his accomplishments to be overlooked in the years since.

In recent years, when the films he made and the stars he directed are lauded, his name is too often omitted. The rightly-acclaimed documentary *Finding Lucy* (2000), written by Thomas Wagner and directed by Pamela Mason Wagner, which aired as a segment of PBS' *American Masters* series, both recognizes Simon's contribution to Miss Ball's career—though his name is never uttered—and simultaneously distorts it. Over footage of the hilarious secretarial school scene in *Miss Grant Takes Richmond* (1949), which Simon produced, the narrator comments, "The future Lucy Ricardo is slowly emerging, like a photograph in a developing bath. But no one was paying any attention." (Which rather begs the question of who wrote, produced, and directed the film.) The montage continues with clips of brilliantly executed slapstick from *The Fuller Brush Girl* (1950), also a Simon production.

While the documentary producers used these two films to illustrate her breakthrough moments in film, they are dropped into a segment intended to convey how unsatisfactory and frustrating her movie experience was. The viewer is left with the implication that her comedies for Simon came earlier in her career than they did, when she was tagged "Queen of the Bs." Later, when the evolution of *I Love Lucy* is discussed, the focus is placed squarely on her radio show *My Favorite Husband*. There's no question that producer Jess Oppenheimer merits every bit of credit he's given for launching her as a radio and television comedienne. However, it would be difficult to tell from *Finding Lucy* that the radio show existed alongside her stint starring in films for Columbia Pictures, where producer-turned-studio executive S. Sylvan Simon was casting her in roles that drew heavily on her gift for physical comedy in a way that radio could not really do.

Author Cindy De La Hoz, in her study of Miss Ball's motion picture career, emphasized the importance of these films, if not the man who made them. Discussing

Miss Grant Takes Richmond, she wrote, "The character was a precursor to Lucy Ricardo."[2] Of *The Fuller Brush Girl*, she added, "Lucille was in top form as the loveable bungler Sally Elliot and again, Lucy Ricardo is clearly in bloom."[3]

Though film historians haven't always acknowledged his contribution to Lucy's career, the actress herself did, according to Simon's daughter Susan, who knew Miss Ball over a period of some years. "She always got teary when she talked about my dad," said Susan, and called him "one of the best comedy directors," noting "how instrumental he was about her going into comedy."[4] A biographer who interviewed Lucy in the 1970s likewise reported that the mere mention of S. Sylvan Simon's name, long after his death, caused the star to tear up. "How could you know that name? It was he who

MGM studio portrait of contract director S. Sylvan Simon, circa 1940.

inspired the crazy comedy that led to *I Love Lucy*. No one ever gave him credit for it."[5]

As anyone who knew Simon could tell you, he loved comedy, having a special fondness for slapstick and physical comedy. His response to a funny scene went beyond a considered and analytical approach. He often struggled to maintain his composure while his favorite comedians performed scenes, not wanting to spoil a take by bursting out into audible laughter. Knowing the value of a hearty laugh, he once explained, "Its secret lies in the fact that it reduces human relations to the ridiculous. It appeals to the urge in us to throw an oozing pie in the wholly unprepared and grievously surprised person—swish, swoosh, smack!"[6] Aside from Lucy, Simon counted among his close friends another cinematic redhead of note, comedian Red Skelton. Like Miss Ball, he hadn't always been well-served in his film career, and his collaborations with S. Sylvan Simon would remain highlights of his somewhat checkered tenure at MGM.

He was never the type of director who ruled over sets with swaggering authority. Over the course of his nearly 15-year motion picture career, Simon developed a reputation as not only a gifted director, but a man who made friends with many of his cast and crew members. Actress Margaret O'Brien was only a little girl when he directed her in *Bad Bascomb*, but retained vivid memories of him nonetheless. "He was a wonderful director," she said. "I was just sorry we had to lose him so soon."[7] Among his prime assets on the set, as Miss O'Brien saw it: "He had a wonderful temperament."

During Simon's heyday as a producer and director in the 1940s and early 1950s, the Simon family—Sylvan, wife Harriet, and their two children—occupied a luxurious house on Sunset Boulevard, complete with a swimming pool and a private screening room. They regularly opened their home for Sunday afternoon barbecues attended by his coterie of show business friends and colleagues, among them Lucille Ball and Desi Arnaz.

One might imagine that Simon was in front of his television set, cheering for Miss Ball, when *I Love Lucy* debuted on October 15, 1951, becoming an overnight sensation. About a month earlier, his friend Red Skelton had also begun a weekly series. But in fact Sylvan Simon's life had came to a tragic and abrupt end some five months earlier, on May 17, 1951, when he died unexpectedly at the age of 41.

While Simon's sense of humor was never far from the surface, his own life had moments that, like anyone's, were nothing to laugh at. The future motion picture director and studio executive was born in Chicago on March 9, 1910, the only child of David and Eva Simon, married three years earlier. The complete name that film fans would see onscreen wasn't yet established. As recorded on his birth certificate, his name was Samuel Simon, the same as his paternal grandfather. However, as he told the story some years later, Eva soon amended it. Columnist Maxine Garrison, interviewing Simon, wrote, "His mother, not caring for the Samuel with which he was to be christened, added 'Sylvan,' after the name of the street on which he lived."[8] Good story, although the 1910 census, taken only weeks after his birth, placed the family on Prairie Avenue.

David Simon was a naturalized American citizen, born in the Russian Empire on June 9. The year of his birth is most often reported as 1882; however, his 1918 draft registration card shows it as 1881. Though at least one source referred to him as "David J. Simon," he put only a dash in the space for a middle initial on that draft card, and there is likewise no middle name or initial given on his death certificate. He was the fourth of six children born to Samuel and Mary Carey Simon, and the last to arrive before they emigrated to the U.S., settling in Pennsylvania. Both parents were in their mid–20s when they arrived, having been born a few months apart in 1856— Samuel on March 15, Mary on September 14.

According to one history of Pittsburgh's Jewish population, "The assassination of the Russian Czar, and the resulting pogroms of 1881, sent Jews fleeing the Russian Empire to the safety of America. Thousands came to Pittsburgh."[9] For the Simon family in particular, "Samuel and Mary Carey Simon immigrated to Western Pennsylvania from Ukraine about 1882. They had six children, Sophia, Jennie, Abraham, David, Israel and Celia. The four older children were born in Ukraine while the younger two were born in Pittsburgh. The family later moved to McKeesport, Pa., and lived on May Street."[10] Samuel Simon was a jeweler and watchmaker who shared with his family a "frame house across from the big iron-pipe mill."[11]

For reasons that are uncertain more than a century later, Samuel and Mary Simon went their separate ways in the late 1880s, around the time their daughter Celia was born. By 1890, Samuel had taken up residence in Fresno, California, where he again opened a jewelry store. It could have been an effort to make a better life for his family. However, Sylvan's nephew Richard Simon recalled: "Their father abandoned the family ... my father [Israel] hired a detective agency or some individual to try to trace him."

Samuel Simon's new life on the West Coast was a troubled one. His store went up in flames on Christmas Day in 1891. Only a few weeks later, he was dead. An item in the *Pittsburgh Press* (February 11, 1892) reported, "The many friends and acquaintances of Miss Sophia Simon, of McKeesport, will be grieved to hear of the sudden demise of her father at Fresno, Cal. on Tuesday last [February 9]. He was formerly in business here and in McKeesport and was well known and respected."

As recorded in newspaper reports, Simon ended his own life. An unsigned article in the *San Francisco Examiner* stated, "Simon had been in deep financial trouble for more than a year, due to outside speculation and bad management.... [He] was to-day threatened with arrest on a charge of arson unless he refunded $1,000 insurance paid him for damage by fire in his store Christmas morning. He could not raise the money, and rather than be disgraced took his life with a pistol bought only an hour before." The reporter added, "There is considerable feeling here against the insurance people for offering to compound a felony and driving a man to suicide."[12]

According to another report, "Simon, the Fresno jeweler who committed suicide last week, was engaged in several shady deals with Max Gutter in West Side lands.... Several of the parties who were swindled were preparing to make it lively for Simon and Gutter, which in fact no doubt drove Simon to his desperate deed."[13]

The death of Samuel Simon left his widow Mary Carey Simon to support their large family (three daughters, three sons) alone, with kids ranging from teenagers to toddlers. She had few resources with which to do so. As a biography of the Simons' daughter Sophie told it, Pittsburgh neighbors said sadly when he died, "He didn't leave a cent. It all went into that California jewelry store that didn't pay."[14] Samuel Simon's estate, when probated, reportedly consisted of little more than a series of promissory notes, listing unpaid debts, and a set of watchmaker's tools.

Sophie, who grew up to be a newspaper columnist and social activist, later dedicated her book *Everyman's Child* to her mother, saying that Mrs. Simon had been "reared as a delicate, beautiful flower; whose prospects were so bright as to exclude any possibility of poverty, yet who suddenly faced the firing line of not only fostering but financing her family of six children, when she became a widow." Sophie said it took her mother "Herculean effort" to raise her family successfully.[15]

The older Simon children went to work, helping to support the family. Sophie took a job clerking in a store, and later went on to become a public school teacher. When she was 19 years old, the *Pittsburgh Press* (March 10, 1896) announced her engagement to local merchant Anselm F. Loeb, "one of McKeesport's most popular and enterprising business men." They were wed the following spring at the home of her mother, Mary Simon.

Despite the difficulties caused by Samuel Simon's death, his family survived and prospered as one century drew to a close and the next one began. Two of his daughters would go on to build successful lives for themselves in New York. In 1898, daughter Jennie married William Marcus MacMahon, who would serve as editor of *Munsey's Magazine*, and hold an editorial position with the Associated Press in New York. The following year, Jennie gave birth to daughter Aline, who would become an acclaimed stage and film actress. Brother Abe attended law school, and in the early 20th century began a long career as a practicing attorney in McKeesport. By the age of 18, when the 1910 census was recorded, David Simon was clerking in a clothing store, while youngest siblings Israel and Celia were still in school. The family also took in roomers at their home on May Street.

While Jennie's marriage succeeded, her sister Sophie's ultimately did not, ending in divorce after 14 years. One of her students would later recall that Sophie had cautioned her, "Bessie, don't you marry young. You have too much to you."[16] Unhappy in her marriage to Mr. Loeb, David Simon's elder sister Sophie (1876–1929) would go on to make a name for herself, first in Pittsburgh and later in New York. From a young age, she demonstrated a talent for writing, placing poems and articles in local publications such as the *Jewish Criterion*, and then the *Pittsburgh Press*. She eventually landed a job as staff writer for the *New York Evening World*. By 1906, her articles were syndicated to newspapers nationwide. In 1910, the independent-minded Miss Loeb (as she chose to call herself after divorcing) wrote in her column that many women were too quick to marry men they didn't really know well: "She goes to the altar with him, sometimes little dreaming that she is putting a HALTER around her neck.... Let us make a marriage a DIFFICULT proposition instead of an EASY one, and we will alleviate the divorce courts working overtime."[17] That was the year that her own marriage to Mr. Loeb came to a close.

Though much of Sophie Irene Loeb's copy touched on issues of home and family, she also had a passion for social reform. Said one writer, "Born of Russian parents who had been steeped in the tyrannies of a bad monarchy, the child was filled with a great urge to help the down-trodden."[18] Her earliest efforts focused on her own community. "A school attended by the children of poor working people in the downtown section of McKeesport was congested, illy [*sic*] ventilated and there was no place for the children to play," noted one account. "Through Miss Loeb's efforts, a fine modern building was secured.... Then was born the idea of devoting much of her time to such welfare work."[19] As she advanced in her journalistic career, she found it provided an ideal platform to crusade for social change: "She was the social worker first, the newspaper woman second, but she managed to combine both phases of her career.... Her newspaper work was merely the expression of her strong social interests."[20]

Once settled in New York City, she found even more problems in need of attention, as later noted in her obituary. "She obtained pensions for widowed mothers. She inaugurated the penny lunch in New York City schools. She helped draft laws demanding that moving picture houses be sanitary and fireproof. She asked that taxicab drivers bond their drivers so that the victims of accidents might have protection. She worked for housing relief in the slums and built playgrounds for the children of congested districts."[21] Author Maxine Schwartz Seller explained, "Remembering a childhood in which her widowed mother was barely able to keep the family together, Russian-born Sophie Irene Loeb Simon [*sic*] helped create New York's Child Welfare Board and pioneered outdoor relief as an alternative to the institutionalization of children."[22]

She was passionate in her belief that children born into disadvantaged circumstances should not be penalized for what their families could not provide. She believed that it was preferable to keep children in their own homes, with state or municipal governments providing financial assistance to widowed mothers, rather than farming them out to institutions. Her philosophy was expressed in the epigraph carved on her tombstone: "Not charity, but a chance for every child." Though she became renowned for championing people living in poverty, Miss Loeb rarely made

Sylvan Simon's aunt, Sophie Irene Loeb, was a social reformer and activist who understood the difficulties that widowed mothers, including hers, faced.

her point by invoking for public consumption her own family's struggles. By 1915, she was reportedly earning $15,000 a year, though she never accepted payment for her service on charitable boards.

The tenacity and drive that would lead the Simons forward was echoed in the maternal branch of Sylvan Simon's family tree. Sylvan Simon's mother, Eva Markowitz, was born in Chicago, Illinois, on April 14, 1887, the second daughter of Max and Rosa Phillips Markowitz. Rosa was born in Germany, while Max hailed from Austria. Eva was the second of four daughters, arriving less than a year after the birth of her sister Etta in May 1886. Shortly afterwards, the family relocated to Pittsburgh, where daughters Sadie and Pearl were born, and son Samuel. By the time the 1900 census rolled around, Eva and her family lived in Pittsburgh, where her father's place of employment was recorded as "notion store."

An account drawing on archival materials noted, "The family owned a five-and-dime store on East Carson Street on the South Side in the early 1890s before moving to the Midwest. They returned to Pittsburgh about 1912, when their daughter Pearl married a local man named Alfred Hirsch. The family opened a millinery shop at 1926 East Carson Street and lived next door. Over the years, the Markowitz family acquired several lots and buildings on both sides of the block around the store."[23]

At the age of 20, Eva accepted a marriage proposal. An item in the *Pittsburgh Press* (April 16, 1907) stated, "Mr. and Mrs. Max Markowitz of Sylvania Avenue, Knoxville, announce the engagement of their daughter, Miss Eva Markowitz, to David Simon, of McKeesport, which will culminate in a June wedding." (The Knoxville in question was a small Pennsylvania community, not the Tennessee city.) A few weeks later, the *Pittsburgh Daily Post* (June 4, 1907) reported that the couple had taken out a marriage license. (More than a decade later, the two families would intertwine yet again when David's brother Israel married Eva's sister Sadie.)

At the time of the 1910 census, David Simon was said to be employed as a commercial traveler in the glass industry. He and his bride relocated to Chicago, where their neighbors followed such occupations as painter, nurse, stenographer, and railroad conductor. The Simon family was sufficiently affluent to employ a live-in servant, Annie Hansen. Like his elder sisters, David Simon seemingly possessed an entrepreneurial spirit, a gift for speaking effectively, and the willingness to work at success. However, that didn't always pan out, and his best efforts were sometimes met with setbacks. As the public face of various business enterprises, he frequently found himself at odds with his employers.

A few months after his son's birth, David Simon applied his salesman's skill to a new arena, making deals for the establishment of new theaters in various cities. In the fall of 1910, newspaper articles from various cities and trade-paper items described his efforts. The November 1, 1910, issue of *The Nickelodeon* carried two separate column items about him: "David Simon of Chicago, representing a large and independent theatrical syndicate of New York and Chicago, closed a deal in San Antonio for the erection of a modern theater." Likewise, Simon "will probably lease a building on Baronne Street, New Orleans, and remodel for theater; cost of improvements, $25,000."

Variety's reporter, savvy about show business matters, was openly skeptical of the glib sales talk. "David Simon, claiming to represent Chicago capital, blew into [New Orleans] Sunday. Monday he had built a new burlesque circuit almost from Chicago to the Coast." The uncredited reporter admitted, "There seems to be no doubt that Simon did close for the lease and construction of a new house on Canal [Street]." Simon claimed he had come directly from Montgomery, Alabama, where he had likewise made a deal, and was headed next for Houston, Texas. Noting that another company had, with difficulty, opened some 30 theaters over the course of four to five years, the reporter questioned how the company Simon represented could do so virtually overnight, and pointed out, "He would not tell who the Chicago capitalists were or whether showmen were behind the move."[24]

A few months later, Simon was in San Francisco, telling a local reporter, "I represent a trio of Eastern financiers. We have already established houses in sixty-six cities in the United States. We plan to build two in Los Angeles and one each in this city and Oakland. We will book any show in our houses until the chain is completed, and then we will play burlesque exclusively."[25] An item a few days earlier in the same publication noted, "Mr. Simon refuses to divulge the name of the corporation he represents, but says they have operated in the larger cities for years."[26]

That venture not proving his claim to fame and fortune, David Simon moved on to a new one a few years later, involving the Robyn-Kander Company's "Universal Movie Tickets." The product allowed customers to shop at particular stores, and by doing so earn points toward movie tickets. As one merchant's advertisement put it, "We Honor Robyn-Kander Universal Movie Tickets.... As Good as Cash to Us.... We Give Green Trading Stamps and A GOOD SHOW."[27] Robyn-Kander periodically advertised for salesmen "on liberal commission basis," but Simon's role went beyond that. In 1916, he was one of the applicants filing paperwork to form the "Moving

Picture Ticket Corporation of Delaware," along with Allen Kander of New York and Franklin L. Mettler of Wilmington.[28] A trade paper item noted, "David Simon, manager of the Universal Moving Picture Tickets ... was in Cincinnati last week [and] established a branch office to take care of the Southern Ohio trade. He also made arrangements with the Cincinnati Star [newspaper] to give the stamps."[29]

His tenure representing movie tickets came to an unhappy end. In 1919, he sought $65,000 in damages from the owners of the Universal Film Manufacturing Company. "The complaint alleges that in September, 1915, the parties made an agreement by which the plaintiff was made agent for three years for Western Pennsylvania for the sale and distribution of moving picture tickets for the Robyn-Kander Movie Ticket Corp. ... The plaintiff alleges that he organized a corporation for the sale of these tickets and disposed of stock in the corporation.... He alleges that the defendant in the transaction broke the contract ... he was deprived of large profits." The outcome of the case, however, gave him little satisfaction. "In a suit of David Simon ... Justice Giegerich has granted judgment for Universal dismissing the first cause of action for $73,583 for the alleged loss of profits and for the purpose [*sic*] price of stock in the Moving Picture Ticket Corp. of Delaware. The plaintiff has permission to file a new complaint."[30]

By the late 1910s, Simon and his young family had returned to the Pittsburgh area, where he accepted a position with the Leader Film Service. A blurb in *Moving Picture World* (June 30, 1917) explained, "The Leader Film Service, formerly operated by E.A. Wheeler, in the Sauer building, Pittsburgh, has been taken over by A. Cole, formerly of the Liberty and Pathe exchanges here, and David Simon, formerly manager of the Universal Movie Stamp Corporation." According to a column item in *Motion Picture News* (March 2, 1918), David Simon, treasurer of the organization, "arrived in New York last week to look at the offerings current on the independent market" and, while visiting the trade journal's office, "shook hands with old friends."

When he registered for the draft in September 1918, Simon reported that he lived at 23 Forbes Terrace, near the intersection of Forbes and Murray Avenues, in Pittsburgh's Squirrel Hill community. He was employed as general manager of the Mina Transfer Company, a firm that a stock offering published in the *Pittsburgh Post-Gazette* (August 31, 1919) said, "owns and operates the LIGHTNING PACKAGE EXPRESS, successfully delivering packages for over 250 of the LEADING MERCHANTS of the City of Pittsburgh." Physically, Simon was described in the draft paperwork as short in height, of medium build, with black hair and brown eyes.

According to the 1920 census, he, wife Eva, and their young son shared the home on Forbes Terrace with Eva's sister Etta, her husband David Berman, and a servant, Anna Beck. Squirrel Hill, on the eastern side of Pittsburgh, was a thriving community with a substantial Jewish population; historian Barbara Burstin later described it as "the cultural, religious and institutional capital of the Jewish community in Pittsburgh."[31]

Built only a few years earlier, the homes on Forbes Terrace were advertised in the *Pittsburgh Post-Gazette* (April 25, 1915) as "the most modern, up-to-date houses in the city—7 rooms and 2 baths each; artistically decorated.... The houses all face a beautiful private park." A later newspaper account added, "Forbes Terrace was a desirable address in its day.... There are built-in bookcases, large ceiling beams defining the first-floor rooms and other elements typical of the Craftsman style."[32] In 1923, the homes rented for $115 to $150 per month. Extensively refurbished and renovated, they still stand in the 21st century.

In Pittsburgh, young Sylvan Simon's activities were occasionally noted in the pages of the *Jewish Criterion*. The April 20, 1917, issue reported that the seven-year-old attended the Sabbath School of the Rodef Shalom Congregation, supplementing his regular education with religious training. He also spent time with the illustrious women of his family. A social note in the *Criterion* (August 3, 1923) stated, "Master Sylvan Simon, of Forbes Cottages, is visiting his aunt, Miss Sophie Irene Loeb, at her summer home, Harmon-on-the-Hudson."

While all seemed to be well on the home front, a familiar pattern soon resurfaced in David Simon's business affairs. In 1922, he "entered suit in Common Pleas court against the new owners of the Penwick Distilling Co., Cheswick, to recover $34,350, claimed to be due to him in commissions." The company had apparently been sold at a fire-sale price following the implementation of the Eighteenth Amendment in January 1920. Simon reported that "he was employed as an agent in August, 1920, to dispose of whisky held by the distillery ... and that he was to receive $1 a case commission. He said he handled the sales of 4,350 cases under this arrangement, and that under another agreement, entered into in 1921, he obtained purchasers for 20,000 cases of whisky and was to receive a commission of $1.50 a case."[33]

Once already the Simon family had been traumatized by the loss of a father at an early age. It happened again in 1924, while Sylvan was still attending public school. David Simon died at the family home on Forbes Terrace on the morning of September 4, the circumstances of his death ominously recalling his father's demise more than 30 years earlier. Though Eva Simon was, as her granddaughter remembered her, rarely at a loss for words, there was one subject on which she remained reticent for the rest of her life. "She never talked about him," Susan Granger said of her grandfather David.

What little can be known about the end of David Simon's life comes mostly from the coldly blunt terminology of his death certificate, which stated his cause of death as "Gun shot wound through mouth. Probably suicide." According to a brief news item in the *Pittsburgh Daily Post* (September 5, 1924), Simon "was found dead in his room yesterday morning when members of the family went to awaken him." David Simon's obituary in the *Pittsburgh Post-Gazette* described him as "proprietor of a mail order business in the Curry Building." Listed as survivors, aside from wife Eva and son Sylvan, were his mother Mary, brothers A.M. and I.A. Simon, both of Pittsburgh, as well as his sisters, Mrs. Jennie MacMahon, Mrs. Cecilia Weiss, and Mrs. Sophie Loeb, all of New York. A memorial service took place the day after his death at the family home.

Though the subject of David Simon's death remained closed, Eva nonetheless did not allow him to be forgotten by their son. "She made him go to the graveyard and put flowers on his grave," Susan Granger said. The young boy found the task upsetting; as an adult, Sylvan Simon gave explicit instructions that he was to be cremated when his time came, expressly to prevent his own children from having to do this. He also, Susan said, "rebelled against organized religion," adding, "He had such an aversion to organized religion that going to temple was not a part of his life." Sadly, some 25 years later, Eva Simon would find herself in a similar position where her son was concerned, surviving him by many years and working to keep his memory alive.

In the late 1920s, the widowed Eva Markowitz Simon took up residence in a large apartment at the recently opened Morewood Gardens community, sharing it with her sister Etta and brother-in-law David Berman. Eva's brother-in-law I.A. Simon was president of the corporation that had constructed the complex. The complex's owners boasted in newspaper ads that it was "situated in the most healthful, distinguished and aristocratic section of Pittsburgh."[34]

Sylvan Simon's ability to limn distinctive and intriguing characterizations of women in his films could only have been inspired by the example of his own mother, who Susan Granger described many years later as "quite a character in Pittsburgh," adding, "She only had a slight knowledge of what the truth was." Her brother Stephen Simon concurred, saying, "His mother was a character out of Damon Runyon."[35]

"Eva was a gambler," said her granddaughter Susan. "A brilliant card player. Gin rummy was her specialty. I think she had ESP because she *knew* what cards to play when. She taught me how to play and would slap my hand if I made a stupid discard. She told me that, if I was a good enough player, I could always have a way to make money at cards." Mrs. Simon also taught her granddaughter how to drink and smoke.

In November 1929, Eva, her sister Etta, and Etta's husband David applied to incorporate as "David, Inc. of Pittsburgh," for a business "buying, selling and dealing in ladies' ready to wear suits, dresses, millinery, hosiery novelties and other wearing apparel."[36] There could hardly have been a less auspicious time to go into business, as they were doing so on the eve of the stock market crash. Booking passage on an ocean cruise, Eva Simon gambled throughout the trip, doing so with sufficient expertise to earn thousands of dollars that she used to stock the shop in Pittsburgh.

The William Penn Hat and Gown Shop, as their business was called, introduced its clients to clothes by Christian Dior, Coco Chanel, and other acclaimed designers. A fixture in the Alcoa Building downtown, the upscale store catered to affluent clients, including the wives of Pittsburgh steel magnates. Eva continued to make buying trips overseas as the shop prospered. She also made frequent visits to New York City, becoming friendly with her colleagues, among them Elizabeth Arden and Helena Rubenstein. Described in advertisements as "Pittsburgh's most exclusive ready to wear shop," the Simon-Berman family's business prospered. When Etta died in December 1964, her obituary claimed that its illustrious clients had included Katharine Hepburn, Fanny Brice, and Marion Davies.

As Susan Simon Granger pointed out, "Eva was also unorthodox in her personal life—for a Jewish woman in that era. She refused to marry after David Simon died. However, she 'kept company' with a pharmacist, Isador Gorenstein, for many years. I always called him Uncle Gorey. When I asked her why she didn't marry him, she explained, 'If we were married, I couldn't say, "Gorey go home."'" Gorey lived in a nearby apartment.

While his mother had a pronounced dramatic flair, Sylvan Simon too was, from childhood, stage-struck. As a teenager, he experienced at close hand the ascents to fame and acclaim of two strong women in his family.

Throughout the 1920s, Aline MacMahon worked almost constantly in Broadway shows, making a name for herself as she appeared in a variety of genres, including comedy, drama and musical revues. She won acclaim for her imitations of Gertrude Lawrence and other notables in *Grand Street Follies*, Lewis Mumford noting, "Her takeoffs on a series of Broadway stars were sometimes better than the original exemplars."[37] Her performance in a revival of Eugene O'Neill's *Beyond the Horizon* was lauded as well. Mumford commented, "The Shuberts would recognize Aline's abilities with a handsome Broadway contract, without having enough sense later to pick out a play that would do justice to her ripening talents."[38]

In 1925, she married architect Clarence Stein, who would later be described by his friend and peer Mumford as "one of the three or four influential architects and civic designers of our time."[39] According to author Kristin E. Larsen, "Attracted to her stunning presence, talent, and intelligence, Stein courted her for six years, although she later laughingly commented that Stein had asked her to marry him within the first few months of meeting."[40] As they both progressed in their chosen careers, the Steins were able to move into a top-floor New York apartment on West 64th Street, which he dubbed their "sky parlor." Kermit Carlyle Parsons later remarked, "In this home they entertained their friends with sustained elegance."[41] (Later in life, Aline's mother, Jennie Simon MacMahon, also took up acting, appearing in several Sylvan Simon films. She died in Beverly Hills on December 29, 1984, not long before her 107th birthday.)

Sylvan Simon's daughter commented, "He adored Aline, who really introduced him to theater. She was a major influence for him." As his cousin's career was going full speed ahead, Simon took his own first steps into the theatrical world, moving beyond his early appearances in camp and amateur shows. As told in an interview with hometown journalist Maxine Garrison, "It was with the George Sharp Players here in Pittsburgh that Simon got his first whiff of the stage" when he was given a small role in a play, Ralph Thomas Kettering's *The Clutching Claw*, which starred Ann Harding. He recalled appearing just after the curtain rose, playing an old man who's throttled and falls, dead. "On hearing the housekeeper's scream for the first time on opening night, the 'corpse' leaped off the floor in terror, and brought down the house with laughter instead of terror."[42]

Though the George Sharp Players were active in Pittsburgh for only about five years, the stock company was extremely popular with local audiences, presenting "a rotating mix of contemporary hits, melodramas, mysteries, and musical comedy revues."[43] With movies encroaching on the success of many stock companies, Sharp shrewdly advertised his product as "Spoken Plays at Picture Prices," also telling the local press, "People want the drama in three dimensions, not merely flickers and shadows."[44]

In a later interview, Sylvan dated the embarrassing mishap to 1926. He shared this anecdote with little variation at least twice in the early 1940s, drawing on recollections then between 10 and 15 years old. However, it would seem that the passage of time had caused a few memory slips, perhaps attributable to having played small roles in other Sharp productions. Kettering's play opened on Broadway in February 1928, closing after only 23 performances. Only a few weeks later, the Sharp Players staged their Pittsburgh stock production. Although Ann Harding did work with the company on at least one occasion, contemporary newspaper coverage makes no mention of her being in the cast of *The Clutching Claw*, and credits stock players Anne Forrest and Mabel Kroman with the leading female roles.

The *Pittsburgh Press*' Karl Krug panned the show vigorously in his mid–April review, but if he attended the particular performance Simon recalled with such embarrassment, the critic made no mention of the gaffe. His criticism instead focused on Kettering's script, saying that it wasn't hard to see why the play had failed in New York. In later years, Krug would be a good friend and booster to Simon, mentioning him frequently in Local-Boy-Makes-Good items in his column.

As a teenager, Sylvan also appeared in plays put on by or at the Young Men and Women's Hebrew Association of Pittsburgh. In the spring of his junior year, he joined the ensemble cast of "Council Gaieties," a musical revue and fundraiser staged by the local chapter of the National Council of Jewish Juniors. As described in the Y's weekly newsletter (April 22, 1927), the show featured "tuneful musical numbers, skillful dancers, costumed male and female choruses trained to perfection, pleasing voices, clever sketches, and a number of novel features." Though his exact role was not specified, Sylvan was listed along with nine other featured cast members. Some 30 chorus members took part as well.

The following month, he served in both the cast and the crew of "a fantastic melodrama," "R.U.R." by Karel Capek. He contributed to the "remarkable scenic effect[s]" and appeared onstage, cast as a robot. Already sporting the bow tie that would be one of his sartorial trademarks in Hollywood, Sylvan was pictured with other cast members on the front page of the Y's May 20, 1927, newsletter. That fall, the organization presented a production of Leo Tolstoy's posthumously published play "The Man Who Was Dead," and that too found him in the cast.[45] On the verge of his high school graduation, he was cast in "Sun-Up," a play by Lula Vollmer that the *Y Weekly* (March 23, 1928) termed "a rather powerful drama about folks' ways in the Carolina mountains."

Meanwhile, Sylvan attended Pittsburgh's Schenley High School. Opened in 1916 at a cost reported to be around $1.5 million, Schenley had received attention both positive and critical for its then state-of-the-art facilities and furnishings. "The Schenley," said one article, "from science laboratory equipment, such as very few of even the great universities of the country can boast, to lockers, showers, and rest rooms, is the last word in educational institutions."[46] It was built to accommodate a student body of 1,800.

There, too, Sylvan seized on theatrical opportunities. During his senior year, he was in the cast of Schenley High's class play, "Bab." A write-up in the school yearbook, the *Schenley Journal* (June 1928), said the April production, "delightfully performed, with fashionable costumes and artistic settings, left a sweet taste and burdened the mind with no disturbing afterthought." Young Mr. Simon was singled out for his performance "as 'Bab''s synthetic lover, Guy Grosvenor," the blurb saying he "carried himself with professional poise." Also noted among his school achievements were serving as vice-president of the school's Camera Club, as well as being a member of its Thespians group. In June 1928, when he graduated, *The Schenley Journal* offered a piece of poetic doggerel to commemorate each member of the senior class. Sylvan's read: "In history class he argufies/Till Mr. Straitiff's wild/He doesn't know just what to say/To that persistent child."

While his cousin, 10 years older than he, was on her way to Broadway success, Sylvan was playing on a much smaller stage. Since he was a child, he had regularly spent part of each summer at the Schroon Lake Camp in the Adirondacks. Initially a camper, he returned during his teenage years as a counselor. Established in 1905, the camp described its mission of raising young men in the 1930 issue of its *Chronicle* yearbook: "Self-reliant, well trained—a Schroon Lake Camper of today is the staunch citizen of tomorrow." Camp director Eugene F. Moses, in the 1931 *Chronicle*, added,

"The summer camp is an open air school-room where the molding of character and experience receives definition from association with carefully trained and sympathetic directors."

The boy campers could play golf, baseball, or tennis, explore the lake by canoe, or take part in dramatics. The staff employed as camp counselors were known to their young charges as "uncles." Uncle Sylvan Simon was, by 1930, the camp's "Director of Dramatics," gaining valuable experience that he would incorporate into his first published book, *Camp Theatricals*. "Under his guidance," said that season's yearbook, "the Sunday Night Shows came to be an outstanding attraction at camp for our visitors and campers." The last of those, it was said, "fittingly ended a season that had thrilled and entertained the Camp from the rising of the first curtain, in July. Uncle Sylvan Simon had arranged all of the stars and entertainers of the season in a burlesque on our Big Show.... The actors seemed inspired, giving deep feeling to their parts, and when the curtain finally came down, it was unanimously agreed that the dramatic season at Schroon Lake Camp was just the biggest ever." As was often the case in later years, Simon's sense of humor found its way into his productions; one of the skits, "Airedale Drummond," was a parody of the popular Bulldog Drummond character.

In the 1931 *Chronicle*, Simon wrote, "It is my firm conviction that of the 13 summers I have spent at Schroon Lake Camp, the dramatic season of 1931 stands forth as being the one most resplendent with brilliant and successful performances. This was accomplished in the main by the unprecedented enthusiasm and cooperation that the boys displayed, and it is noteworthy to mention that every boy in camp ... participated in at least one Sunday night show." The yearbook also noted, "The stage effects produced by Uncle Sylvan Simon were the most complex and sensational ever witnessed upon our stage. Not content with conventional camp scenery effects, Uncle Si managed to find plays of a nature where the unusual was emphasized rather than the ordinary. With a battery of flood lights and spotlights, it was possible to reproduce the crow's nest of a sailing schooner, the interior of a coal mine, and a typical dug-out behind the German lines during the World War."

As per the 1934 *Chronicle*, Simon had by then been the camp's dramatic coach for seven years. His faculty profile summarized his credentials: "graduated University of Michigan, 1931, with a B.A. Degree ... recently published first dramatic handbook for camps, 'Camp Theatricals,' which went into second edition six weeks after publication ... written from sixteen years' experience at Schroon Lake Camp ... every Sunday night is a 'triumph night' for Uncle Si.... He makes instruction in dramatics dramatic!" Not afraid to make bold choices, he even staged a production of Eugene O'Neill's *The Emperor Jones*, a drama about the hardships of African American life. His riding skills also proved useful, the yearbook noting, "Horseback riding has always been a favorite camp activity. Horses are easily available to those who wish to ride, and there are competent instructors to teach the novices. Under the direction of Uncles Sylvan Simon and Frank Meyers, both of whom are experienced riders, the campers enjoyed a successful season."

Even after relocating to the West Coast, and launching a successful Hollywood career, Simon maintained fond memories of the Schroon Lake Camp, and was in frequent contact. The 1939 *Chronicle* reported that the Dramatics trophy for which campers vied was "a beautiful cup donated by S. Sylvan Simon, former camper, never-to-be-forgotten dramatics counselor at Schroon Lake Camp, now a Director with Metro-Goldwyn Mayer studios in Hollywood." The following season, campers staged Simon's playlet, "Too True," published in his book *Easily Staged Plays for Boys.* The 1941–42 issue of the *Chronicle* reported, "An outstanding event was the return of S. Sylvan Simon, to direct his own show, 'Trouble in Tunnel Nine,' at Schroon Lake Camp. 'Sy,' former camper and counselor is now a director for Metro-Goldwyn-Mayer. His visit from Hollywood to our camp—a distance of about 3500 miles—will long be remembered by all of us."

Not all of Simon's connections to the world of show business came from his father's side of the family. His mother's younger brother, born Samuel Markowitz, also entered the field, renaming himself Sid Marke. Born in 1896, Sylvan's uncle would outlive his nephew by more than 30 years. Upon his death in 1985, obituaries described his varied career, noting, "Mr. Marke was an assistant director and actor in silent movies." Going on to work as a theatrical agent, working out of Pittsburgh, Marke "booked fairs and banquets nationwide for 68 years. He scheduled vaudeville acts into local theaters [and] also booked many of his acts on Broadway and the old Ed Sullivan Show."[47] It was, apparently, something of a hand-to-mouth existence. Susan Granger remembered that "he always seemed to be out of money," adding, "He looked pretty seedy to me."

In the fall of 1928, Sylvan entered the University of Michigan as a freshman, pursuing a Bachelor of Arts degree. Easing his transition into campus life was the B'nai B'rith Hillel Foundation, a social and cultural organization that "sought to convince incoming freshmen that it offered plenty of attractive activities as well as a welcome environment for Jewish students of all stripes."[48] The society's publication, the *Hillel News*, put out a special "Freshman Issue" around the time of his arrival, "offer[ing] the incoming freshman the promise of belonging to a cohesive, and growing, community."[49] Hillel encouraged members' involvement in a wide array of activities, encompassing dramatics, athletics, debating, and others of a purely social nature.

His interest in the stage as potent as ever, Simon was disappointed to learn that, as a freshman, assignments to direct University-sponsored plays were not open to him. However, he soon found a venue with the Hillel Players, where his experience and enthusiasm made him a leader in the group. He took whatever opportunities presented themselves, initially making his mark acting and writing. According to the *Hillel News* (December 5, 1929), he played the role of Wellyn, an "easy-going, impractical artist" who's nicknamed the Pigeon in John Galsworthy's *The Pigeon Awaits.* Reviewing the production in the *Michigan Daily* (December 12, 1929), Charles A. Askren wrote, "Perhaps outstanding in the cast were Sylvan Simon as Christopher Wellyn and Marshall Schutz as Ferrand, both of them handling their lines and indeed carrying the play off with distinction." He wrote for the stage as well. In the spring of his freshman year, as reported in his hometown newspaper, "S. Sylvan Simon of Morewood Gardens, a freshman at the University of Michigan, recently won honorable mention in a play contest conducted by the university. His play, 'Skeleton Mine,' was the only play submitted by a member of his class in the three-act play contest."[50]

For all its satisfying moments, his freshman year was marred by the February 1929 death of Sylvan's aunt, Sophie Irene Loeb, after a lengthy illness. By then a well-known public figure, Miss Loeb left an estate valued at some $100,000, an amount that would be equivalent to a seven-figure sum in the 21st century. Her will specified bequests to her two sisters, Jennie and Celia, with the remainder of the estate earmarked for her nephews and nieces after the death of Miss Loeb's mother Mary, who would survive her by four years.[51] (Sylvan's grandmother Mary Simon died in the Coconut Grove neighborhood of Miami, Florida, on August 6, 1933.) In New York City's Central Park, the Sophie Loeb Fountain, "etched with characters from Lewis Carroll's Alice in Wonderland" commemorates her "tireless work for orphans."[52]

Back at Michigan for his sophomore year, Simon began directing plays for the Hillel Players, with the *Michigan Daily* (March 7, 1930) announcing that "Sylvan Simon, '32, is in active charge of rehearsals." That spring, he oversaw the group's production of Arthur Goodrich and Rose A. Palmer's *Caponsacchi*, a poetic drama which had played on Broadway during the 1926–27 season. The show had not yet been licensed for production by amateur groups. However, the campus newspaper noted, "After several recent communications with Sylvan Simon, '32, Arthur Goodrich, the author of the play, became interested in the work of this new campus group and approved their desire to present the show in Ann Arbor."[53] A few months later, the *Daily* reported that Simon was serving as "student president" of the group, which was staging a series of one-act plays, and considering a more ambitious project: "An attempt to produce a very rare manuscript of 'The Golem,' a dramatic legend, will be undertaken if a sufficient number of capable actors and technicians are available during the early productions."[54]

For a time, Simon had to give up his work with the group, the *Hillel News* (October 30, 1930) reporting that Simon had resigned as president of the Players due to "ill health," adding, however, "He will continue to act in an advisory capacity and also as technical director." Indeed, his activity with the Hillel Players continued throughout his undergraduate career. During his senior year, he directed and performed in a production of Albert Costello's *Death Takes a Holiday*, which the *Michigan Daily* (April 20, 1932) noted would benefit the University Loan Fund. A few days later, that same publication panned Simon's show nonetheless, suggesting that the Hillels had bitten off more than they could chew: "Last night's production can only be judged as fair.... Sylvan Simon, who directed the production, is not particularly meritorious in the part of the sometime rejuvenated Baron Cesara [sic] and at times was a bit boring. His direction, however, was somewhat better."[55]

Simon's college years also provided an opportunity to explore the potential of radio broadcasting, still a fairly new medium, on Detroit station WJR. He served as an assistant to Professor Waldo Abbot on a weekly hour-long radio program "broadcast every Saturday night from the campus." As described in the college newspaper, "The alertness of at least five men is responsible for the smoothness with which a program comes to the listener." Those men included Abbot, as well as one responsible for conducting musicians, and the technicians who oversaw microphones and sound. "Over all of this hovers Sylvan Simon, '31, Professor Abbot's assistant, who is ready for any emergency."[56]

He also stepped in front of the microphone when circumstances called for it, as in a December 1929 broadcast featuring, along with the usual music, a speech by a law school professor on "Lawlessness and Its Causes." "Simon will announce for Professor Abbot who is convalescing in the University Hospital...."[57] He did so again when WJR provided live coverage of the University's "Junior Hop" dance, the program "pick[ing] up the music from the ballroom."[58] A few weeks later, the *Michigan Daily* (March 28, 1930) noted that Simon played host when "song hits from the 1930 Junior Girls' Play, State Street" were broadcast.

By the following year, his radio work was rewarded with a new title and growing responsibilities: "Sylvan Simon, a third year student from Pittsburgh, is Assistant Director [of the U of M's Broadcasting Service], by action of the Regents. Simon announces many of the programs and also aids in preparing the productions and in securing speakers and entertainers. Before entering the University he was connected with KDKA in Pittsburgh..."[59] In later years, Professor Abbot said of his protégé, "Sylvan worked in broadcasting neither for credit nor pay. He was one of the hardest working assistants I have ever had.... He had everything that makes for success. I don't think that I did anything to hurt him and possibly the only thing I did that might have helped him was to make him shave every morning. I'll bet he has a beard now."[60]

Not all of Simon's collegiate activities were devoted to the arts. The University of Michigan's 1930 yearbook showed that Simon, then a sophomore, was a member of the Kappa Nu fraternity, a social organization for young Jewish men. Scholar Marianne R. Sanua explained, "The constitution limited membership to Jews only, and Hebrew words and Biblical and liturgical references predominated in their secret initiation rituals."[61] He also taught horseback riding at the University of Michigan, an avocation he would continue to follow for years to come. "My dad was an excellent rider," Susan Granger recalled.

Sylvan received his Bachelor of Arts degree from the University of Michigan in 1932. He had received a broadly-based liberal arts education that would serve him well in years to come. Much of his coursework spoke directly to his theatrical interests; he completed classes in stagecraft, advanced drama production, contemporary dramas, Greek drama in English, and acting.

He also studied English literature, journalism, creative writing, and the Spanish language. One credential, however, nearly stymied him. In later years, he recalled, "I needed just one course to become an instructor in dramatics. It was called 'The Art of Direction,' but the professor advised me against taking it. He said I couldn't possibly pass, and he was about right. By great perseverance I managed to get a D, which meant 'barely passing.'"[62]

Simon was one of more than 800 students to be conferred a B.A. at the university's 88th graduation ceremony, held on Monday, June 20, 1932. Some 15,000 spectators were in attendance as Professor Wilber Ray Humphreys, Assistant Dean of the College of Literature, Science and the Arts presented the graduates in that discipline. There were 2,133 diplomas conferred that day, in what the *Detroit Free Press* (June 21, 1932) described as one of the largest classes in the university's history.

Even after graduation he continued to take an interest in his alma mater. In 1940, Simon, from Hollywood, responded to an interview request from the *Michigan Daily* about the Michigan Union Opera's upcoming all-male production, "Four Out of Five." He cheerfully denied having appeared in a previous production while a student, and "observed that a mixed cast would present more opportunity for everybody involved." He joked that he could imagine "nothing more discouraging than walking home arm in arm with a fraternity brother who played the leading lady."[63]

After receiving his undergraduate degree, Simon did not enter the workforce immediately, but instead continued to pursue his education, having been accepted to

Michigan's law school. For a time, he remained in Ann Arbor, where he began graduate school while maintaining his interest in theater. With the Hillel Players, he staged
a production of *The Dybbuk*, adapted from the Jewish legend about a young woman
possessed by a malevolent spirit. Praising his leading lady Vivian Cohen, he commented, "Few women have ever attempted to take this part because it necessitates a
person who has both a high speaking voice and who also can give a low range of tone
with full dramatic expression."[64] As his hometown newspaper stated, the show was
a success. "His activity with the Hillel Players of the university in an English transla-
tion of a Yiddish play *The Dybbuk* has resulted in praise for the production from many
sources.... Encouraged by the acclaim, the Hillel group plans to send Mr. Simon and
the leading actors of the group on a road tour."[65]

In later years, it was frequently said in studio publicity that "Simon was left an
income so long as he attended college." A biographical sketch published in MGM's
Lion's Roar (April 1943) claimed, "It was at this point [upon graduation from college]
that his father offered to make a deal with him. He was to enter Columbia University
and his allowance would continue as long as his academic career did. Sylvan accepted
the offer as a practical means for earning a living—and he spent his spare time in the
sedulous pursuit of a job as a stage director." But his father had been dead for eight
years. Another explanation for his continued studies was offered by daughter Susan,
who noted, "His mother insisted that he have a profession."

His transfer to Columbia University in New York City put him in closer proximity to the world of professional theater. As per one account, "He enrolled in Columbia Law School so that the income would continue, and haunted producers' offices
between college work until he was established in stage work."[66] The move indeed
proved beneficial, though perhaps not for the expected reasons. A Pittsburgh-based
columnist later wrote, "We advised him to enter Columbia Law School even though
we suspected that he would not be happy there and would never practice at the bar.
How horribly we misdirected him we did not appreciate until he went west and gave
full expression to his remarkable imagination and latent skills."[67] Indeed, not even the
rigorous environment of studying law at Columbia could squelch his interest in the
theater.

No snob when it came to live entertainment, he enjoyed it in various forms and
venues. He later noted, "My avocation while doing serious plays was going to burlesque shows. Whenever I had time to spare I'd beat it across the street to a burlesque
house.... I went to see the comedians. They never failed to amuse me and their originality was so striking that I began to study them."[68] It was in that world that he first
enjoyed the antics of Bud Abbott and Lou Costello, a comedy team that would figure
significantly into his motion picture career.

In the summer of 1934, Simon further broadened his horizons when he took a
trip to Europe. He returned to New York aboard the *Ile de France*, which departed
from Plymouth, England on June 27. While on board, he composed a letter, only a
portion of which, unfortunately, has survived. To his correspondent, Simon wrote,
"With all the scurry about London, I even had time to take your suggestion and have a
real tweed suit made for me. And even my mother liked it—which was a distinct revelation." To the unidentified recipient of the letter, Simon wrote, "You've completed
my preliminary training for me, and I shall never forget it." More than likely he was
writing to his cousin Aline MacMahon, by then juggling a noteworthy career in both

film and stage work, as a handwritten note in the margin alludes to her mother, saying, "Love to Aunt Jen."

An already eventful summer was made more so when Simon became a published author, his first book, *Camp Theatricals: Making Your Camp Entertainments More Effective* being issued by Samuel French. Favorable notices soon appeared in the *Brooklyn Daily Eagle, Boston Globe, Hartford Courant,* and the *Oakland Tribune.* Though it didn't pan out, the *Jewish Criterion* reported that further literary efforts were expected: "This fall, a mystery novel of his is to appear."[69]

Like any good play, Simon's life story called for the introduction of a romantic interest by the end of the first act. His arrived in the person of Harriet Lee Berk, a lovely young woman some six years his junior. Born January 20, 1916, to Benjamin A. Berk and Jeane Hartstein Berk, she and her family lived on 54th Street in Brooklyn, where her father, a native of Hungary, was a dress manufacturer. Her mother was born in New York of parents with Hungarian ancestry.

Their first meeting may have taken place in the Adirondacks, where the summer of 1934 found him once again a counselor at Schroon Lake Camp. Harriet, still a teenager, attended the adjoining Camp Rondack. Many years later, Harriet took part in a reunion of women who had attended. "Today I am a Rondack girl," she told a *New York Times* reporter in 1982. "Very few people are privileged to go back in time to a happy part of growing up. This is the first time in 40 or 50 years we've gotten together; still we have emotional, warm ties."[70]

Living in New York City, opportunity knocked with some regularity for Sylvan Simon, and he was always eager to answer when it did. The *New York Evening World,* the newspaper that had employed his Aunt Sophie, regularly featured theatrical reviews by columnist Bide Dudley, who also offered his commentary on radio, with a program called "Theatre Club of the Air." Dudley's show, heard at midnight six nights a week on station WMCA, critiqued the play he had seen that evening, adopting the slogan, "Dudley Points the Way."

As *Radio Digest* described the setup, Dudley "attends all Broadway openings, rushes to the studio after the final curtain and goes on the air at midnight with his review before any of the newspapers are off the presses." Of his approach to reviewing, Dudley explained, "I make it my creed to offer only constructive criticism, not to use wise-cracks and other alleged humor and never to attack the players personally. Mine is an honest opinion of the new offering, free from personal likes and dislikes and as fair otherwise as I can make it."[71]

Dudley's multi-media exposure brought him to the attention of many young aspiring actors and directors, among them Sylvan Simon. In his newspaper column, Dudley wrote that his readers frequently asked him if there was an amateur dramatic society they could join. While seeing the value of such an organization, Dudley noted that the chief problem in forming and maintaining one was the need for a capable director. Presenting himself at Dudley's newspaper office, Sylvan Simon told him he was the man for the job, and the columnist concurred. While the ambitious young man made a favorable impression, he readily admitted that being the nephew of the late "Sophie Irene Loeb helped me get that director job, though."[72]

Like the actors he took on the task of mentoring, Simon was looking for a little exposure. "Struggling to be an actor may be tough," he explained, "but at least if you get a part, there's a chance that some one [sic] may see you. A director's task is much harder because he has to gather a lot of actors around him."[73] Once the formation of such a group was announced, some 300 to 400 applicants, the majority of them women, wanted to join. One of them was his girlfriend Harriet Berk, their relationship growing more serious. The story their daughter Susan was told had Harriet, a student at Barnard, being expelled for climbing into a dormitory window after a late date with Sylvan.

Also captivated by Dudley's radio announcement of the group was a young aspiring actor named Arthur Space. "I heard over a New York radio (which was only twenty miles away) that a group of actors was being formed and that it was open to all. This was my start toward the profession…. Here was where I met the man that seven or eight years later was going to be responsible for my coming out to Hollywood."[74]

Plans for the new group came together quickly under Simon's guidance. "The Players Guild, organized by Bide Dudley, is planning to give an opportunity for young actors and actresses employed during the day to rehearse a series of plays at night and show Broadway managers what they can do," reported the *New York Daily News* (November 23, 1934). "In January, the group will produce 'Night over the Mall,' by J. Leon Burdo, 'Freedom's Detour,' by Van Sims, and 'Dog Watch,' by Dudley." A few weeks later, the same publication (December 27, 1934) added, "Bide Dudley's Players' Guild, headquarters 150 Riverside Drive, will revive two classics as their first presentations, namely a new English version of 'The Dybbuk' and Maurice Donay's adaptation of 'Lysistrata,' retitled 'Ode to a Grecian Urge.'"

The organization was described as "the only co-operative playhouse in the world having six complete companies functioning within it, and, according to Mr. Simon, many of the members have never been seen upon the professional stage in this country."[75] As the Guild's Milton Roseburn told it, "The Players Guild is actually the largest amateur dramatic group that ever existed. We have five groups in rehearsal under the direction of Sylvan Simon and Ernestine Minciotti."[76] In March 1935, Simon's company, by then known as the Players' Group of New York, announced that *Ode to a Grecian Urge* would open shortly. A newspaper profile of cast member Arthur Space pointed out that, before going into production with *Urge*, he had been able to work on various plays in class exercises, which "proved invaluable. He portrayed roles of an old English lord, a rabbi and a boxer," and in the new production "takes the role of a warrior."[77]

Simon and his troupe staged their productions at the Heckscher Theater, a large venue with seating for nearly 600 audience members. As journalist Kate Taylor later reported, "Built in 1921 and located on Fifth Avenue between 104th and 105th streets, the theater … is like a small-scale Broadway house, with a proscenium arch, an orchestra pit, and wall murals depicting fairy tales." The building was originally constructed to serve "as a shelter for abused or neglected children who had been taken from their families…. The philanthropist August Heckscher and his wife, Anna, wanted the building to be a happy home for the children, and the theater was one of its much-touted features." During the Depression, it housed shows staged by the Federal Theatre Project, and was occasionally booked for tryouts of prospective Broadway shows. Taylor noted, "In the late 1950s and early 1960s, Joseph Papp's nascent New York Shakespeare Festival had its offices and performed there."[78] The spacious facility allowed Simon to stage productions with dozens of cast members.

A society column item in the *Jewish Criterion* (March 22, 1935) noted that Mrs. Eva Simon would attend the New York opening of *Ode to a Grecian Urge*, "produced by her son, Mr. Sylvan Simon, who is attending Columbia Law School when not on the set." A scribe for the *Barnard Bulletin* (March 29, 1935), catching the show later the same week, commented that the audience contained "what seemed to be a fair representation of students and friends of the Columbia Law School, possibly due in part to the fact that Mr. Sylvan Simon, of that part of the university, directed and staged the presentation." The reporter also spotted Aline MacMahon in attendance, "looking very nice in an Alaska Seal coat and obligingly autographing programs for admiring little girls."

The routine of law school plus his theatrical ventures kept Sylvan on the run. One journalist wrote of busy Mr. Simon, "If you should ever want to get in touch with him, you must either call him at seven-thirty in the morning or, as I did, try to talk with him in the few minutes preceding rehearsal." Sylvan explained that the group catered to the many young people who came to New York in search of acting opportunities, but found most producers unwilling to give them the break they were seeking. "The producer hasn't anything against these young people, you understand—they may have been great guns back home. But the producer of a big Broadway show can't afford to take a chance; there's too much money tied up in the show business. So he tells the aspiring young actor to go out and get in a show, to prove his or her talents.... Most of these young people try to stay in town; they get jobs in restaurants, department stores, hotels and so on. These are the ones who compose our organization. What we are endeavoring to do is put on plays so that the young actors and actresses will get a chance to appear before the public."[79]

Though Simon's troupe was off to a promising start that spring, the onset of hot summer months meant that theater in New York City would soon be at a low ebb. Undaunted, he took his theatrical company to other venues, including the summer resorts. An item in the *New York Daily News* (May 16, 1935) noted, "Sylvan Simon has organized a stock troupe to play 'Accent on Youth' on one-night stands in the Adirondack resorts, including Sarasota Springs and Lake Placid."

Their efforts were soon concentrated on one site in particular, the Brown Swan Club at Schroon Lake, New York. "Occupying a commanding site overlooking Schroon Lake, it commands a view of the surrounding country not obtainable from any other resort," boasted one account of the club and its facilities. "Decidedly unique in its appointments and most attractive in design, it is possessed of features so far removed from the ordinary that it is indeed an ideal playground for vacationists and tourists."[80] Guests of the Brown Swan Club could enjoy swimming, dancing, and live entertainment in rooms that cost $5 or $6 per day, with meals included. The club was marketed to prospective visitors as "large enough to be excellent, small enough to be personal."[81]

Settling in for the summer with a troupe of a dozen or so players, actor Arthur Space among them, Simon promised the club management that guests could look forward to a new production every week. "The Broadway Players Company, under the direction of S. Sylvan Simon, will present Broadway shows every Friday, Saturday and Sunday nights at the club."[82] Players at the Brown Swan Club received only room and board for their efforts. "They don't go out much. By the end of the day, they are usually too tired to do anything but go to bed. A swim, perhaps, or a stroll out onto some mountain trail, is their only recreation."[83]

Reporter Don Finkelhor opined, "Whatever success the group has experienced or will experience in the future is due directly to the efforts of S. Sylvan Simon. You will find the players themselves the first to acknowledge it. They're his; the whole group is his, and in most everything they do you can see his guiding hand. Together, they're going places; anyone who sees the group in action can't doubt it."[84]

The group's repertoire that summer encompassed a variety of comedies and dramas, some well-known, others less so. Noël Coward's *Hay Fever* was presented, as was a melodrama, *Blood Talks Too*, and a comedy, *All Girls Don't*, by Maurice Marks. Of the latter production, one source reported, "Once again Schroon Lake's capable and competent Players' Group scored another hit ... staged in the ever-inviting auditorium of the Brown Swan Club. The comedy, an amusing one moved with fast pace, holding the attention of the audience in a firm grasp, while the players went through their slang-laden breezy roles to the welcome volleys of laughter raking the theatre."[85]

"Troupe members 'bring to their performances wide stage experience, and a varied and modern repertory,'" reported *The Post-Star*'s review (August 12, 1935) of Samson Raphaelson's *Accent on Youth,* which included Arthur Space in the cast. Operating on the model of a stock company, the group debuted a new show each week; all told, Simon and his cast offered nine productions that summer. For the last, "The Players Group, under the direction of S. Sylvan Simon, will produce Francis DeWitt's new adaptation of the Flaubert novel, 'Madame Bovary,' at the Brown Swan theatre, Schroon Lake, beginning August 29." The column item noted that the Players hoped to take this show to other resorts during the month of September, with the idea of "bringing it to New York early in October under their own auspices."[86]

It proved to be a busy summer personally as well as professionally. On June 3, 1935, Sylvan eloped with Harriet Berk, the couple marrying in Manhattan. According to their daughter Susan, only the family doctor knew of the couple's plans to wed, because he had done Sylvan and Harriet's blood tests as required by New York law. As she later said, "I married the boss." Oddly, several months after they were wed, columnist Ed Sullivan posted an inaccurate announcement in his *New York Daily News* column (October 11, 1935), which read, "S. Sylvan Simon, at Warners, will announce his engagement to Harriett Herk [*sic*] Nov. 10."

Although Simon's proud mother Eva had regularly submitted items on his personal and professional milestones to Pittsburgh newspapers, she apparently did not do so in the case of his impromptu wedding. According to Susan Granger, Harriet Berk Simon and her new mother-in-law could not be described as simpatico. "There was no love lost between them," she said, noting that the free-wheeling, unconventional Eva rarely saw eye-to-eye with Harriet. "My mother was far more straitlaced." The wedding and subsequent relocation put a stop to Harriet Simon's education for the time being, though after their move to the West Coast she completed a degree at UCLA.

At the conclusion of a successful summer, plans were evolving for the Players' Group to go south for the winter, staging performances in Florida and other warm climes. An item in *Motion Picture Herald* (September 28, 1935) noted that incorporation papers had been filed for The Players Group, Inc., New York, "theatrical business with a capital of 7,500 shares $1 preferred and 125 shares common..." Listed as officers in the filed application were "Julian Lieberman, S. Sylvan Simon, Jean Berk, Max R. Less and Benjamin J. Goldman." Before those plans could go forward, though, Simon's skill at staging summer theater led to an unexpected job offer—the kind both he and his players had always hoped their work would bring.

2

Go West, Young Director

Any remaining ideas of a law career for Sylvan Simon fell by the wayside when he went to work at a major film studio's East Coast office in the fall of 1935. As journalist Naomi Bentan later explained, "One day along came a Warner Bros. talent scout who hired Mr. Simon as a test scout," his job to seek "possibilities" in the New York area.[87]

In an interview some years later, he said that he had parlayed the job as "a combination office boy and talent test director" into something more. Some men of that era might have balked at admitting they possessed secretarial skills, but Simon explained that his shorthand and typing helped him get a foot in the door. "Being a steno is the way to learn all about making pictures—from script to final product," he explained. "It's a strategic position. From stenographer to writer, director or producer is just a series of steps."[88] Operating from his New York base, he sought talent not only there but elsewhere, including his hometown. One column item noted, "S. Sylvan Simon, a former Pittsburgher now scouting talent for Warner Brothers, is flying to town next week to catch a couple of performances of 'The Distaff Side' at Carnegie Tech."[89]

While working at Warners,' he released *Easily Staged Plays for Boys*, his second book and the first of four published anthologies of short plays. Two more volumes followed in 1937, with the fourth and final one appearing in 1938. Though he was about to move into a new medium, his enthusiasm for live theater was carried forward as the plays in his books continued to be performed regularly by amateur groups.

Simon's affiliation with Warner Brothers lasted only about a year. In the summer of 1936, *Variety* (July 29, 1936) reported that Simon "has resigned his position [with Warner Brothers] on doctor's orders. He goes to California for a rest and to cure a sinus complication.... For the past year he has been with the talent department under Macklin Megley, having been transferred from the play bureau." Capitalizing on his East Coast experience, Simon had little difficulty landing a job at Universal. *Daily Variety* (September 17, 1936) reported, "Sylvan Simon, former Warners test director and talent scout, has joined Universal in same capacity working under supervision of Rufus Le Maire, executive assistant to Charles R. Rogers."

Sylvan and Harriet Simon were soon joined on the West Coast by several members of her family. Said Susan Granger, "When my mother moved west, my grandfather, Benjamin Berk, sold his business in New York ... and moved to Beverly Hills. He opened a small clothing shop in Burbank, near a jewelry shop owned by my aunt and uncle, Margery and Martin Slaton." Of Harriet's mother, Jeanne Berk, Susan noted, "I remember her very well. She was very kind to me—and she loved to cook Hungarian delicacies."

Whether in New York, Hollywood, or elsewhere, aspiring actors often found it difficult to break into the industry—or even attract the attention of those in positions of power. As Eve Arden's character in *Stage Door* (1937) memorably comments when trying to get an appointment with a prominent producer, "Imagine opening a great big office like this just *not* to see people." Simon, however, emphasized that he took pride in being approachable. "Anybody in the world can get into my office," he said. "They don't need to have influence, or an agent. If they write me a note, I'll give 'em an appointment.... There never was a time when it was easier to get into the movies."[90] For those unable to appear in person, he was even willing to review 16-mm home movie tests mailed in from elsewhere.

Though some were surprised by his accessibility and supportive approach, Simon told syndicated columnist Paul Harrison (February 13, 1937) said, "It's hard for them to understand that I'm for 'em 100 per cent. Naturally, I'd do anything to improve their appearance or their voices. We need players." Discussing the requisite physical attributes for close-ups on a huge motion picture screen, Simon told Harrison, "The most frequent fault of women is their teeth. With men, their eyes. Lots of handsome men have deep-set, narrow eyes. Just looking at them you'd guess they'd photograph perfectly, but on the screen they seem to squint, and appear a little sinister."

He explained, "I interview between forty and fifty people a day, week in, week out. From them I choose perhaps two a week of whom to make tests." Each test cost the studio between $500 and $800. Those lucky individuals so chosen would be assigned scenes to study from current Universal films, and given access to professional makeup and costuming. The test itself would find them playing scenes opposite one of the studio's established actors. For those fortunate enough to be offered a contract, they began with small assignments. "In every picture where their type can possibly be used, they function as extras and as they become more experienced, they get a line or two to speak, always coming under the tutelage of our capable and experienced directors."[91]

In an interoffice memo dated September 14, 1936, Simon advised studio executives, "I want to make the following tests on Thursday: Jack Dunn with Nadiene Dale, Marjorie Deane, Elain Shepherd, in a scene from *Fresh Fields*. The scene is a living room very well furnished." Planned for the next day were "Alan Handley with Ethel Sykes in a scene from *Merrily We Roll Along*. The scene is a living room." That same day, "Joan Kaufman with Ann Graham, scene interior radio station with piano and accompanist, songs to be sung on set." Simon's proposed tests were initialed "OK" by William Koenig.[92]

As he gained the respect of his studio colleagues, Simon's duties grew to encompass help with casting current Universal films as well. He reportedly interviewed five thousand young men for *The Road Back* (1937), a long-delayed adaptation of Erich Maria Remarque's follow-up to *All Quiet on the Western Front* that featured a number of prominent male roles.

Successful in his job as Universal's talent scout, Simon was a logical choice to direct when the studio captured a somewhat glamorized view of the process in a short film, *Hollywood Screen Test* (1937). At first, the idea was for Simon was to play himself onscreen, but he soon had to bow out of that role; a recent Screen Actors Guild ruling had clamped down on giving acting assignments to people that were not union members. *Variety* (July 14, 1937) described the finished product, and the process it depicted: "Short showing steps taken in bringing out best in potential candidate for acting role follows closely actual Hollywood procedure without revealing everything. Kay Hughes, now on Universal's player rolls, portrays candidate for screen job, with Cesar Romero spotted in for informal scene and actual test enactment. ... Possibilities of the short as a means of arousing interest in local talent quests understood to have attracted exhibitors and circuit that figure in a search-for-talent contests [*sic*]."

From there, Simon's career took a leap forward with the announcement, after a year on the Universal payroll, that he had "been promoted to a full-fledged feature director."[93] *Film Daily* (August 2, 1937) reported that Simon would make his feature film debut by directing *Prescription for Romance.* Almost before the ink was dry on that trade-paper item, however, there was a change of plans, when his fellow director, Lewis R. Foster, fell ill. Foster had been set to direct "Mightier Than the Sword," but Simon was pressed into service to take his place. Word of his career advancement soon reached his hometown. "Salutations to my friend, Sylvan Simon, who is reminding the tycoons of the film industry on the coast that Pittsburgh is more than a hamlet. He has been made a director on the Universal lot.... And not so long ago it was the legal profession or bust."[94]

On Monday, August 16, 1937, cameras rolled on "Mightier Than the Sword," a newspaper drama starring Wendy Barrie and Walter Pidgeon, which would ultimately be retitled *A Girl with Ideas.* Simon was about to undergo a trial by fire, with studio executives watching closely to see if he had the mettle to be a director. He had been allocated 18 shooting days and a $139,000 budget to get the job done.

By the end of the first week, studio production manager Martin F. Murphy wrote in an interoffice memo, "On account of a novice director we were somewhat skeptical about his ability to maintain this apparent tight schedule for a rather long script. We are most encouraged over the progress made during the first five days of shooting." In order to keep costs down, it was important that the film was completed by Friday, September 3, 1937, so as to avoid extra pay for keeping actors on salary over the Labor Day weekend. Despite what he characterized as "a little rough going" during the final week, Murphy wrote, "We are most happy to report the picture will finish today right ON SCHEDULE—and the probable final cost will be ... $5,000 under our estimated budget."[95]

But it was not only the bean-counters who found Simon's work praiseworthy. A visitor to the set of his first film commented, "Simon is a young director, who goes about his business and gets what he wants from his players as if entirely unconscious of the fact it is his first picture." After each take, he was careful to praise his cast members, but usually said something like, "Let's do it once more, and this time...."[96]

In his review of *A Girl with Ideas* (November 6, 1937), the *Motion Picture Herald*'s William R. Weaver wrote, "It is the first picture directed by S. Sylvan Simon. Some of the more veteran troupers appearing in it were inclined to scoff at his methods of procedure in the making of the film but experienced a swift change of heart for the better when press and public let go roar after roar of laughter as the picture unreeled." Weaver added that, when the film was screened for a preview audience at the Hollywood Pantages Theatre, "a mixed audience manifested unmixed pleasure in frequent sustained and healthy laughter."

Directors of B movies rarely had time to rest on their laurels, though. The assignment to direct *A Girl with Ideas* didn't preclude his doing *Prescription for Romance*;

The laboratory set from *The Crime of Doctor Hallet* (1938), with a slate board bearing Simon's name visible at left (Universal Studios Collection, USC).

he shot them both in rapid succession, and they were in theaters before the year was out. A melodrama with a jungle setting, *The Crime of Doctor Hallet*, soon followed.

His output continued to please studio executives and moviegoers alike. As per a studio production report (April 9, 1938), Simon, completing *Nurse from Brooklyn* on a $125,000 budget, was paid a $500 bonus. Shortly afterwards, Simon's stature at Universal had grown to the point that he was considered to direct one of the studio's biggest moneymakers. "The fight out at Universal over who is to direct Deanna Durbin's next vehicle may mean the break of his life for Sylvan Simon, the young Columbia University graduate," a trade paper reported.[97] Henry Koster, who had made her first two films, balked at doing a third, leery of being pigeonholed. Ultimately, however, that directorial assignment went to Norman Taurog.

Though he wasn't entrusted with Miss Durbin's latest picture, his association with another singer-actress would be critical to his career advancement. Simon's career took a step in the right direction when he worked with actress-singer Hope Hampton on a Universal comedy called *The Road to Reno*, with leading man Randolph Scott. Making her motion picture comeback after an absence of some years, Miss Hampton underwent a thorough screen test under Simon's supervision before signing on for the role. The result won her a studio contract, and she gifted the young director with a diamond wristwatch to express her gratitude.

Having worked well with Simon on the test, she wanted him to helm the film as well. "She insisted on him as her director," said Susan Granger. "She just thought he was wonderful." With the film's budget projected at $350,000, it was by far the most expensive and ambitious one Simon had been given at Universal. Production began in June 1938, following a research trip to Reno. One column item claimed that he had declined to take Harriet along. By Simon's account, "I told her that it was just a business trip and that I would have to work hard and that, anyhow, taking a woman to Reno would be like taking coals to Newcastle."[98] However, there was also the fact that Harriet was pregnant with their first child.

Back in Hollywood, filming continued apace, though by mid–July, production manager Martin Murphy was complaining, "Over-shooting on the part of the director is extending the shooting period on this production longer than we anticipated."[99] Nonetheless, the film neared completion by the end of July. Late that month, there was cause for celebration in Simon's personal life, when Harriet gave birth. He was hard at work on a Universal soundstage when the big event finally took place. As a column item told it, "The baby, to be christened Susan, was born during the lunch hour, which permitted Simon to leave his set at Universal to go to the hospital without causing any delay."[100]

The movie itself, while garnering some good reviews—"a surprise from the low-budget division," proclaimed the *Brooklyn Daily Eagle*'s Herbert Cohn (October 4, 1938)—made no great waves, and Miss Hampton's film resurgence was short-lived. However, the screen test also attracted the attention of other industry people, including MGM's Mervyn LeRoy (who, according to Susan Granger, became "a good friend and a great supporter" of her father). Viewing the footage, he reportedly said, "I don't want the girl but I do want the director." Consequently, Simon was offered and accepted a contract to direct at Metro-Goldwyn-Mayer, a step up in both pay and prestige from Universal. *Film Daily* (August 4, 1938) noted that Simon finished *Road to Reno* on the Universal lot, and then reported to MGM the following day.

Given that Simon was still only 28 years old, MGM thought the youthful director was just the man to direct its films centering on young characters. His first assignment was "Spring Dance," a story of college life, which before release was retitled *Spring Madness*. Reaction to his work was strongly positive, with his hometown paper reporting, "Metro-Goldwyn-Mayer lifted the option of Director S. Sylvan Simon, the Pittsburgh lad, the day after his first picture there, *Spring Madness*, had been previewed."[101]

Simon celebrated the holiday season in late 1938 with a two-week vacation trip to Pittsburgh, taking wife Harriet and their new baby daughter Susan for a visit with her grandmother. While there, *Spring Madness* opened in local theaters. Interviewed during his vacation, he was asked about making the switch from the theater to motion pictures, and said, "The enormous scope of the screen as a medium for portraying drama so completely eclipses the stage that, in my opinion, there is no ground for comparison.... You can really stretch your arms and go places as a director of pictures."[102]

From early in his career, Simon wanted not only to direct the films he was assigned by studio executives, but to develop his own projects. In February 1939, he was said to be interested in making a film about Joseph Lister, known as "the father of modern surgery." As a column item explained, "S. Sylvan Simon has submitted the idea for the picture, based on the story by J. Charles White, to M.G.M. Simon has

A young director assigned to work with MGM's younger players, Simon reviews the script of *Spring Madness* with Maureen O'Sullivan.

ambitions to direct the subject."[103] Though that project didn't pan out, he continued to keep an eye out for ideas and literary properties that showed promise.

As Simon became not only an increasingly prominent director, but also one recognized for his skill at developing young talent, aspiring actors sometimes went to extreme measures to catch his eye. Said columnist Read Kendall, "A young chap, trying to get ahead in pictures, purposely drove a golf ball at Director S. Sylvan Simon on a local course, to secure an introduction. But the chap got cold feet taking advantage of this kind of a meeting when the ball hit the megaphonist."[104]

One young MGM player who would benefit from Simon's guidance was Lana Turner, whom Mervyn LeRoy had brought to the studio. She and Simon would make three films together; the first being *These Glamour Girls*. Originally he was scheduled to do *Dancing Co-Ed* first, but in short order *Variety* (May 31, 1939) announced that the order had been reversed, noting, "*Glamour* starts late this week." Simon described their working relationship: "A little more than a year ago Lana came into pictures from high school. She had never acted before in her life and she admitted that she knew nothing about it.... So she placed her fate wholly in the hands of the directors. With an entirely open mind she allowed herself to be molded into the characters she played and the result is that her success has been phenomenal."[105]

Seeing that she lacked confidence in her own abilities, Simon set out to teach her while at the same time being protective. When Lana messed up a take, one account noted, "Simon found a way out of this by bawling out his crew when Lana faltered. Suffering grips and cameramen hung heads and said, 'Yes, sir, I'm sorry,' when Lana blew a line. But she never saw them wink."[106] For all her lack of formal training, he predicted major stardom for her within a year. Lana's early promise, as a Hollywood scribe told it, had "director S. Sylvan Simon and four studio veterans frantically combing through" material envisioned for Jean Harlow before her death because "Metro believes it has found a girl to take Harlow's place." Said that journalist, "It was Simon himself who first told the studio of the girl," calling her potential to the attention of studio colleagues though she was already under contract.[107]

Box Office Digest (August 16, 1939), in its review of *These Glamour Girls*, noted, "This Sylvan Simon, who showed a few tricks at Universal, has something on the ball. So far he has been limited to these short-budget pictures, so it is always rather difficult to decide [whether] he is one of our comers, or just a short-budget flash in the pan. But to date, he has managed to squeeze in the touches that give indications of being able to go to town with a few days extra time." The boundless energy he applied to his work was commemorated with an anonymous gift Simon received, apparently from an actor he'd directed. It was a loose-leaf folder personalized to read "S. Sylvan Simon, We Never Sleep."[108] That summer, *Daily Variety* (June 29, 1939) announced that his director's contract at MGM had been extended.

Explaining his techniques for bringing out the best in young, inexperienced actors, Simon said, "You can't treat them as grownups and you can't direct them as you would children. They're all at that romantic age when the latest date is likely to be much more on their minds than what you happen to be telling them about the script, or their lines or what was wrong with the last take."[109] On the set of his third film with Lana, *Two Girls on Broadway* (1940), Simon explained that, when working with younger players, he preferred to use the first take whenever possible.

"I try to follow several easy rules," he wrote of directing Miss Turner. "I aim to keep her pepped up and to make the first take a good one." Though she might not be letter-perfect the first time out, Simon explained, "If there is a muffed line, and it is not too serious, I will use it nevertheless, because the enthusiasm often outweighs the proper choice of words." When possible, he liked to rehearse young actors prior to the start of production, often in a casual atmosphere such as their own homes. Though he admitted that the challenges presented by working with actors not fully trained could be "profoundly irritating," he added, "Give the kids a break. They're your box-office stars of tomorrow."[110] For her part, Miss Turner said in an interview, "I do thank Mr. Simon for the hard work—he showed me that youth is no excuse for laziness."[111]

Though he never directed one of their films in its entirety, Simon also worked, however briefly, with MGM's star comedians, the Marx Brothers. Columnist Hedda Hopper (October 6, 1939) joked that, after his accomplishments with Lana Turner, "they've given him the Marx Brothers to glamorize." One report explained, "S. Sylvan Simon, the Pittsburgh director, piloted the retakes on the Marx Brothers' 'A Day at the Circus.' He was assigned to the job because M-G-M has him in mind to direct their next comedy, 'Out West,' and wanted to see how Simon got along with the comedians."[112]

In that capacity, he captured on film one of the film's funniest lines, quoted for years afterward. When Peerless Pauline, played by Eve Arden, tucks a wad of cash into her bosom, attorney J. Cheever Loophole (Groucho Marx) makes an aside to the audience: "There must be some way of getting that money without getting in trouble with the Hays office." When Brecher pitched this joke, Groucho liked it, but director Eddie Buzzell put the kibosh on it, saying, "Are you kidding? What kind of shit is this? Nobody knows the Hays Office." He dug in his heels and refused to shoot it. As screenwriter Irving Brecher subsequently told it, LeRoy, who liked the line, went in search of another director on the lot, and came back with Simon in tow. "Simon loved the line and quickly shot Groucho saying it," Brecher wrote. "A month later at the sneak preview, it got the biggest, longest laugh in the movie."[113]

Simon's time with the Marx Brothers went swimmingly enough that *Boxoffice* (October 14, 1939) announced that he would be directing their next picture, *Go West*. However, the film's start date would be pushed back by several months—as Groucho wrote to his pal, screenwriter Arthur Sheekman, "*Go West* is being constantly postponed. I read the script and I don't blame them."[114] By the time it finally went before the cameras, Simon was occupied with other projects.

Away from the studio, he helped his friend Milton Berle compile a book of jokes and comic routines called *Laughingly Yours*, published by Samuel French in 1939. A review in *Variety* (November 22, 1939) offered praise for the volume, saying, "Bright reading and good amateur stuff are the comedy dialogs." A newspaper review was decidedly less enthusiastic, saying, "S. Sylvan Simon, the film director, apparently has a great affection for the humor of Milton Berle, which means that he has a great affection for the warmed-over jokes of other comedians." Although Berle admitted in his introduction that some of his material might have originated with others, and been around for a while, the reviewer thought that was putting it mildly, snapping, "Some of his jokes were hacked out in hieroglyphics."[115]

Having benefited greatly from mentors in his own life, Simon paid it forward whenever he could, not only to actors but to other colleagues as well. One he took under his wing was Earl McEvoy (1913–1959), who worked on numerous Simon films at MGM, going over time from script clerk to assistant director. "Sylvan sponsored my father," said Dusty Burke, McEvoy's daughter. "My father thought very highly of him. I heard his name very often."[116] Later, when Simon left MGM for Columbia, McEvoy did likewise, functioning as Simon's assistant on *I Love Trouble*, and then Associate Producer of *Lust for Gold*. "They respected each other's abilities," noted Burke. Like his mentor, sadly, McEvoy died young, at the age of 46.

Another Simon pal was William Parry O'Brien, who worked in the electrical department at MGM. O'Brien's son, Parry, Jr., later became an Olympic champion shot-putter, winning gold medals in the 1952 and 1956 games. Simon's daughter Susan remembered, "Parry Jr. was a few years older than me, so he would often 'baby-sit' me on the set. Actually, he'd throw me up in the air and catch me, clowning. Little did I know that he would become a famous athlete."

Simon's success at MGM enabled him to provide a more-than-comfortable life for his young family. In the late 1930s, the cast and crew list for *The Kid from Texas* showed Simon's address as 312 South McCarty Drive, in Beverly Hills. However, the Federal census of 1940 recorded Simon, wife Harriet, and their young daughter living on Camden Drive, with cook Lottie Sharp also part of the household. Just a few doors down was producer Orville O. Dull, a longtime MGM employee who would later produce Simon's films *Tish* and *Bad Bascomb*. Supplementing his horseback riding and other leisure activities, he took an interest in sailing as well. A column item reported,

"S. Sylvan Simon, the director, told Edgar Selwyn he was thinking about buying a boat and Selwyn said, 'Just so you can call it the S.S. Simon, I suppose.'"[117]

In the summer of 1940, Simon and his wife Harriet embarked on a Hawaiian vacation. They left Los Angeles aboard the S.S. *Monterey* on August 31, returning on the S.S. *Lurline* a week later. The destination had been suggested by Robert Young during the making of *Sporting Blood*, who by one account "has talked of nothing but his recent trip to Hawaii since returning to Hollywood."[118] While on vacation, Simon shot film footage with his own camera, and said that he hoped to make a picture there.

In the meantime, however, MGM assigned him to direct Wallace Beery in a project then known as "Get a Horse," which would reach movie screens as *The Bugle Sounds*. Beery could be a handful for a director, and was initially dubious about one a generation younger than he. But Simon managed him well enough that they would ultimately make three films together. Pittsburgh-based columnist Karl Krug, to whom Simon sent an autographed copy of his newest book *Let's Make Movies*, reported that his friend's prospects at MGM seemed bright: "Mr. Simon ... is the apple of Louis B. Mayer's eye, and if he continues his present pace, within a very few years will be one of the most important men making pictures at Culver City."[119]

Sylvan turned 31 years old in the spring of 1941. His cousin Aline, in Los Angeles to fulfill a film assignment, wrote home to her husband Clarence, "We had a whole suckling pig by way of celebrating.... It was done at a very good new restaurant."[120]

One of Simon's most important collaborations began when he was assigned to direct comedian Red Skelton in *Whistling in the Dark*. After several years as an MGM contract player, the redheaded funnyman was being given his first opportunity to carry a film on his own. Skelton's biographer, Arthur Marx, remembered Simon proclaiming, "Red is probably the greatest living comic. The funniest sequences in all the pictures we've done together have come as a result of

Simon (right) lends a helping hand to comedian Red Skelton (Simon Family Collection).

his split-second inspirations. He's the only comic I know who can get laughs and heart-tugs from the same audience."[121] A set visitor during production of the first *Whistling* film noted, "Simon directs with the light touch, making a suggestion here, a correction there, always as if he were consulting instead of giving orders ... the feeling of a fun fest carried right into the shooting and the finished product."[122]

He later explained, "Directing Red Skelton is like packing a trunk. You always have twice as much stuff as you have room for.... To make it more complicated, Red doesn't always give warning when he is about to throw in an impromptu bit of business. He does it right in the middle of a 'take' and the cast, trying to keep from laughing, misses cues. Then we have to rehearse, retime, relight, and often reset the camera to allow for the new business."[123]

Although *Whistling in the Dark* was unquestionably Skelton's vehicle, it afforded Simon the opportunity to give a family member a career break in a minor role. Aline MacMahon wrote to her husband, "Sylvan has a little part of a lady who is in a spiritualist['s] office, trying to get in touch with her husband, and he wants Jennie Mac to play it." Aline's mother, apprised of the opportunity, said, "No, I put all that behind me, I just can't take the discouragement if it doesn't go through." But Aline was more confident, writing, "I think it will go through. Won't that be something..."[124] Indeed Simon's aunt did appear as one of the denizens of Joseph Jones' cult.

Whistling in the Dark was a hit that paid off for both star and director. A sequel was soon ordered up, with *Whistling in Dixie* released the year after its predecessor. Having worked well with Red Skelton, Simon was a logical choice to direct two more top comedy stars when Abbott and Costello made the first of two films at MGM. Though under contract to Universal, the studio made a loanout deal with their competitor to resolve a longstanding complaint of Louis B. Mayer that the rival studio had "stolen" them. The studio gave *Rio Rita* a much higher budget than was the norm for the comedians at Universal.

Like Skelton, Bud and Lou took a freewheeling approach to creating comedy. Simon said he didn't object in the slightest to the improvisational approach of the comedians who starred in his films. "As a comedy director, I like their sparkle and spontaneity, especially on a set where pace and exuberance are important." Of Red Skelton and former burlesque comedian "Rags" Ragland, with whom he would make three "Whistling" comedies at MGM, Simon said, "Keeping them from ad libbing in front of a camera is tougher than bringing in a four-horse parlay."[125] Similarly, he recalled one sequence in *Rio Rita*, starring Abbott and Costello, which went through 18 takes, as the boys tried out every variation they could dream up.

Simon was a captive audience, and an admittedly easy target, for comedians who delighted in making the director lose his composure. Many years later, Ann Rutherford commented, "My greatest memory of working with him [Skelton] was watching the director out of the corner of my eye while we filmed. He was sitting beside the camera, stuffing his handkerchief into his mouth as tears streamed down his face, to keep from laughing and ruining the take."[126] He later explained, "Players can't be entertaining unless they are entertained. A bored comedian or [an] angry one can't be funny."[127]

Wes D. Gehring, author of numerous books on film comedy, considered Simon "an atypical MGM director, with regard to the freedom he gave his comedians." Although there were certainly other important influences on Skelton's film style, among them Buster Keaton, Gehring credited Simon with directing what he considered the comedian's three best films—*Whistling in the Dark, A Southern Yankee,* and *The Fuller Brush Man.* "Simon knew funny," Gehring added, "and knew enough to let it happen—regardless of the script. This is no small talent."[128]

Simon's increasing success in Hollywood came to the attention of an old pal, actor Arthur Space. Wishing he could get his foot in the door of a film studio, Space wrote to his former director from the East Coast acting troupe, seeking help. Responding to his friend, Simon's letter (January 29, 1941) was friendly and encouraging, but made it plain that earning a steady living as an actor was chancy. "I'm really hesitant to give you any concrete advice," Simon stated, "because it's such a haphazard business and even more catch-as-catch-can than Broadway.... At the beginning, such a career is tough, so you must be prepared for a stiff grind, but as you have the ability, I think you can get somewhere and I, for one, will do everything in my power to help."[129]

His resources limited, Space nonetheless made the arduous trip West, reporting for work in September 1941. "Hello, Arthur! My, but you're looking well," Simon greeted him upon his arrival at MGM. "You haven't changed much since I last saw you." After being sent to meet the film's producer, Space returned to the soundstage, watching as Simon put Wallace Beery and Lewis Stone through their paces for a scene in "Steel Cavalry" (subsequently renamed *The Bugle Sounds*). The glamour of moviemaking was quickly dissipated as the newcomer observed: "Beery, I hear, is ill and has been missing lines all day and now has Stone doing the same thing."

Space admitted that he was nearly overcomes with nerves on the day of his film acting debut. "I died a thousand deaths that first day," he later wrote. Day Two proved a bit easier. "Sylvan took a considerable amount of this weight off of my shoulders by saying that he had seen the rushes of my scene the day before and that he was satisfied with them." From then, Space was a little calmer. He wrote, "Get this, Diary, this is not the average 'bit' part—I'm playing right up there with Beery and [George] Bancroft and the rest of the boys. Sylvan liked my death scene very much."

As the young actor explained, "This director has been responsible for my small success in Hollywood. He sees to it that I am in all of his pictures, no matter how small the part may be." Though Simon indeed gave his friend's career considerable help in the beginning, Space proved over the long haul that he was a proficient and reliable character actor. He would continue to be in demand for many years after Simon's death. Space also gave Simon credit for seeing him cast in *Random Harvest,* which according to the actor his friend was originally slated to direct.

Tish (1942), based on the popular magazine stories of Mary Roberts Rinehart, offered the opportunity to direct his cousin Aline MacMahon in one of the leading roles, that of Tish's sensible friend Lizzie. Her mother, Jennie Mac, was also offered a bit part. Writing to her husband Clarence, Aline noted good-naturedly, "We tested the clothes yesterday. Mine were too good. I told Sylvan to give my wardrobe to Marjorie Main, who is playing 'Tish.' Noblesse oblige 'yu' know."[130]

Shortly after *Tish* wrapped, however, Aline wrote worriedly, "Sylvan has a fearful cold, and is working entirely too hard. They are wearing him out at the studio, and he is doing B pictures, and trying to keep them down in cost.... He's a sweet fellow, gets on well with everyone, and is very conscientious. He needs some dreams."[131]

Hollywood newcomer Arthur Space (left) and his mentor Sylvan Simon (center) take a break to speak with a visiting reporter.

That fall, Simon began work on one of his biggest films yet at MGM, the wartime drama *Salute to the Marines*, a Technicolor epic that marked his second collaboration with Wallace Beery. In his *Los Angeles Times* column (September 11, 1942), Edwin Schallert reported, "There are nine prominent masculine roles to be cast, incidentally, and S. Sylvan Simon, director, has been making many tests with plenty of difficulties, considering the present shortage of male players." Production was delayed when the director fell ill. Hedda Hopper (December 2, 1942) reported that he was hospitalized for an unspecified complaint, noting that his colleague Norman Taurog was a patient in the same facility. The two, she wrote, "weren't allowed to talk to each other over the phone. So they sent notes back and forth via the sympathetic nurses, who censored them carefully to see that the boys weren't talking shop."

Andrew Marton, later to become a full-fledged director of film and television in his own right, worked second unit on several Simon films. At MGM, Marton said, "I did some occasional helping out in a few scenes that were either difficult to do, or in locations too distant to efficiently send the main director." Over the course of his career, Marton shot second-unit footage for a host of prominent directors, including Vincente Minnelli, George Cukor, John Huston, and William Wyler, for whom he captured much of the chariot race footage in *Ben-Hur* (1959). Of working with Simon, Marton recalled, "He wasn't sickly, but he had a record on other pictures of having had a few days when he couldn't show up during shooting. He died very young—unfortunately, because he really was just getting his stride."[132]

Interviewed by a Pittsburgh reporter, Simon noted that it had taken some nine months to complete *Salute to the Marines*, at a cost in excess of a million dollars. He pointed with pride to the screen debut of a promising young player—his daughter Susan, not yet five years old. Tongue in cheek, he described Susan's ambitions: "She insisted on being in a picture of mine, so I gave her a part to get it out of her system. But I don't know about that getting it out of her system business. Because she's not bad at all in the little she has to do."[133] He claimed Susan did one take of her scene in *Salute to the Marines*, then when told it would be shot a second time, said, "If my daddy's the director I don't see why I have to do it over."[134]

As an adult, Susan remembered, "It was great fun being on the set with him." He did away with any nerves or complications for her by presenting the scenes in the context of, "Let's pretend." Unlike some of the professional juvenile actors she knew, Susan said, "I didn't feel any of the pressure." Getting—or not getting—a job was paramount to them, she explained: "They had to support their families." Though she continued to act periodically into her teens, she was later counseled by her stepfather that acting was a hard life, and accepted his recommendation that she focus on her writing instead.

In Pittsburgh, columnist Harold V. Cohen called *Salute to the Marines* "the picture that definitely gets Mr. Simon out of the minors. His direction is sharp, solid and incisive, and he has not only charged a pedestrian narrative with a realistic mobility, he has likewise produced an acting [Wallace] Beery instead of a caricature."[135]

With *Salute to the Marines* released in the spring of 1943, Simon and his wife set out for the East Coast, their first stop being a visit with his mother in Pittsburgh. From there, he traveled to New York, where he supervised the filming of location footage for the upcoming Skelton comedy *Whistling in Brooklyn*. Situated at the Savoy Plaza Hotel, Simon took advantage of the opportunity to catch up on current Broadway shows, and attended opening night of the latest *Ziegfeld Follies*, with his pal Milton Berle as headliner.

Away from Hollywood, some challenges arose, Simon noted, explaining that he had difficulties "trying to get 500 extras where only some 200 are officially listed here. I solved it by having each regular extra bring a friend." Team manager Leo Durocher he described as "a sweet fellow. No temperament at all. He reserves his temperament for crowded ball parks…. The Dodgers are all as good actors as they are ballplayers—and that's saying a lot."[136]

Like his previous films with Skelton, *Whistling in Brooklyn* was marked by a loose approach to the material on the written page. One observer reported Skelton's ad-libbed dialogue during a scene that found him climbing a rickety ladder with co-star Jean Rogers. "Gee, what an old shaft!" Skelton said, to which she replied, "Beg pardon?" "I mean the elevator," Skelton said with a glint in his eye. Not missing a beat, "Director Sylvan Simon orders the dialog included in the scene."[137]

One project that didn't come to fruition during this period was a script called "Jennie Was a Lady," an original story by George Oppenheim and Charles Lederer, which MGM acquired in late 1943. Hedda Hopper (June 21, 1944) reported that Lana Turner, or perhaps Susan Hayward, would play the lead role, that of a 19th century woman reporter. Simon's name was attached to the project as the likely director. As

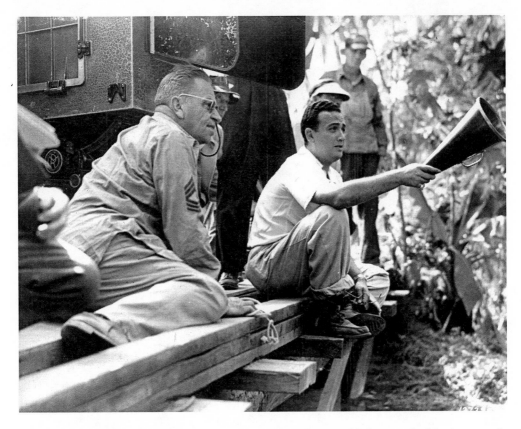

Wallace Beery (left) and Sylvan Simon, pictured on the set of *Salute to the Marines*, made three films together for MGM.

late as 1946, studio publicity stated, "An important new picture coming up for the M-G-M director is 'Jennie Was a Lady,' with a Rodgers and Hammerstein score,"[138] but any interested moviegoers looked for it in vain on their local marquees.

He did, however, embark on another musically-oriented project. In 1944, Simon was assigned to direct *Song of the Open Road*, a teen-oriented musical that marked the film debut of young Jane Powell. Miss Powell admitted that she "adored" her first Hollywood director. "I had a crush on him. He looked so much like my father. He had such kind eyes and was so soft-spoken." Like her father, Simon smoked a pipe.

While that project was being completed and others were underway, Simon was making his contribution to the war effort, organizing and training troupes of actors to put on shows for servicemen. Noted one account, "Director S. Sylvan Simon is just about the busiest guy in town right now. In the morning, he has been cutting, supervising, dubbing and scoring *Song of the Open Road*. In the afternoon, he works on his new Metro picture, 'Whistling in Hollywood.' And at night, he rehearses three camp show units of 'Kiss and Tell.'"[139] *Variety* (October 25, 1944) announced that the Hollywood Victory Committee's new troupe was at work on a production of *Girl Crazy* for GIs: "S. Sylvan Simon volunteered to produce and direct the show for Actors Lab, which has already sent two theatrical companies abroad."

Boxoffice (February 17, 1945) added that the Committee would follow that up with a production of "Flying High," noting, "S. Sylvan Simon, who piloted *Girl Crazy*,

On location for *Whistling in Brooklyn* with (left to right) star Red Skelton, director Sylvan Simon, and real-life Dodgers manager Leo Durocher (Simon Family Collection).

will pilot the new venture." Cast members would rehearse in Hollywood before going on a six-month tour overseas. Simon's fellow Pittsburgher Morton Beck, a young aspiring actor, was reported as "rehearsing in a USO unit of Bert Lahr's old Broadway musical, 'Flying High,' under the direction of S. Sylvan Simon."[140] Edwin Schallert, in the *Los Angeles Times*, noted that Larry Parks was "making a great hit in the Actors Laboratory production of the New York stage hit 'Kiss and Tell.' The Actors Lab has been presenting this before servicemen." Arthur Space was also in the cast, as were Ann Rutherford, whom Simon directed in multiple films, and his aunt, billed professionally as Jennie Mac.

Another effort on behalf of enlisted men found him among dozens of Hollywood notables who signed a petition circulated by the Hollywood Free World Association, concerning legislation affecting soldiers' rights to vote while serving. The document was reprinted in a large advertisement appearing in the *Los Angeles Times* on January 15, 1944, the headline reading, "I died for nothing.... If not the right to vote." Simon is listed on the "sponsoring committee," with many others of varying political stripes including John Garfield, Adolphe Menjou, Rita Hayworth, and Bob Hope.

Nineteen forty-five found Simon contributing two new films to the nation's movie screens, beginning with the April release of *Son of Lassie.* Playing a small role was young actress Helen Koford, who would go on to greater success under the stage name Terry Moore. Miss Moore recalled of Simon, "He was a wonderful director, very sensitive. I was crazy about him." Looking back over a career that encompassed dozens of film and television roles, and continued into the 21st century, the actress said she had only one truly bad experience with a director. However, she added, "After Sylvan Simon, who was so nice, no one would ever seem quite as nice as he did."[141]

She stayed in contact with the Simon family beyond the filming, and was a guest in their home. "I stayed there at least two weeks at a time," Miss Moore said, noting that Sylvan thought her a good friend for his daughter Susan. She remembered Harriet Simon as "so beautiful," Sylvan as "kind and fun," and commented, "He made everything so right for Susan and me." Susan later recalled that she enjoyed being "a kid who tagged along with Terry and her brother" Wally.

Later in the year, he was back at the helm for a second round of Abbott and Costello mayhem, when MGM assigned him to direct *Bud Abbott and Lou Costello in Hollywood*. Actress Jean Porter, cast as Lou's love interest, recalled, "Bud told Sylvan to keep them in line—don't let them get wild … let them know if they were going too far with something."[142] Despite his best efforts, moviegoers' response to the film was lukewarm, and that apparently brought to a close the studio's wish to borrow the comedians, who would continue making pictures at their home studio, Universal, for several more years.

Still, the privilege of making comedies never lost its luster for Simon. He relished the chance to be party to Abbott and Costello's creativity, saying, "It's a lot of fun directing them. When I go to work in the morning I never know what's going to happen. The script doesn't mean a thing."[143] Asked if Wallace Beery, whom he would direct again in 1946, belonged on the list of professional laugh-getters, Simon said, "Yes, Wally's a comedian definitely." Defining the varied working styles of his stars, he added, "Berry [*sic*] works from instinct, Skelton works from script, and Abbott and Costello work when they feel like it."[144]

Screen newcomer Jane Powell is happy to be working with Simon on *Song of the Open Road* (Simon Family Collection).

Whenever one film was in the can, another was always in the pipeline. Noting the breakneck schedule that he maintained as a matter of course, columnist Hedda Hopper (June 20, 1945) wrote, "Director Sylvan Simon jumped from *Son of Lassie* to Abbott and Costello, then skidded off to Jackson's Hole, Wyo., with Wally Beery, Margaret O'Brien and Marjorie Main to direct 'Maggie's Bandit' [subsequently retitled *Bad Bascomb*]. Because he'll stay there until Sept. 1, he's called it a vacation."

The Simon family lived in a Georgian-style house at 10456 Sunset Boulevard, on the corner of Loring Drive. Susan recalled, "Dad loved gardenias, so there were gardenia bushes everywhere and the scent permeated the air." The large living room, perfect for entertaining, featured a bar at one end, and "a grand piano which was always kept tuned for parties," Susan said. Prominently displayed over the mantelpiece was a portrait of the Simons' young daughter. "Beyond the dining room was a 'game room,' which my dad had equipped with two pinball machines and a slot machine. No money required to play."

She remembered, "My dad drove a station wagon with wood sides on which was printed TRIPLE S, like a ranch. He had horses which he kept at Leo Dupy Stables near Culver City." At that time, Sylvan and his daughter found opportunities for riding that have long since gone by the wayside. "Back in those days," she said, "there was a bridle path in the middle of Sunset Boulevard, believe it or not! We'd ride almost to the beach … sometimes, we'd ride to the Bel-Air Hotel, where Mother would join us for lunch."

On June 30, 1946, the Simon family welcomed a new member when son Stephen was born. The house on Sunset Boulevard was expanded to add a nursery for the new arrival; there was also a first-floor guest room, where Sylvan's mother Eva frequently stayed on her visits from Pittsburgh. Years later, Sylvan's son remembered, "My oldest conscious memory is sitting in my father's lap at the age of three watching 'dailies' in our house."[145]

At home, Simon adopted a daily ritual with daughter Susan. They would open the dictionary, and she would blindly point at a page. When she landed on a word she didn't know, she would read the definition, and then proceed to find every opportunity she could that day to put it to use. By the end of the day, it became part of her vocabulary. Though he spent his days immersed in a world where women were frequently valued for their looks, Simon had other ambitions for his daughter. He emphasized to her the importance of reading. When she went away to summer camp, "he would send me comic books," she said. His frequent comment to her was, "I don't care what you read, as long as you keep on reading."

For the rest of his life, he would be a strong believer in the importance of education, whether for himself, his children, or the young actors he took on the task of mentoring. Asked about education as a prerequisite for success as a performer, Simon said, "I know there is a tendency among young folks who are stage struck to look on college as a waste of time. I think that is dead wrong. Jumping directly from high school to Hollywood or New York is putting a tremendous lot of pressure on a youngster who is still immature and who, if he or she fails to make good right away, may carry a permanent emotional scar."[146] Interviewed for a Detroit newspaper, he elaborated on the theme: "You tell those students at Michigan or anybody else, who want to become actors or actresses, to get all the education possible. In fact, tell them to stress philosophy and psychology. Because, in this business, one always deals in the abstract. Besides, intelligence is actually the basis of competent acting."[147]

Columnist Louella O. Parsons (November 23, 1943) wrote, "Simon is known as one of the best dressed directors in Hollywood (he smokes a Sherlock Holmes pipe and dresses to the teeth at all times)." Her claim is somewhat undercut, however, by the numerous extant photos of him on the job, many of which of show him wearing nothing dressier than a short-sleeved shirt topped with a sweater vest.

Performers and others who worked on her father's films often joined his circle of friends.

A favorite part of his leisure time was the routine of cookouts, which took place in the Simons' backyard almost every Sunday afternoon. Hot dogs and hamburgers were served to the guests. Those who frequently attended included performers such as Lucille Ball and Desi Arnaz, Red Skelton, Abbott and Costello, Larry Parks and Betty Garrett, Donna Reed and her husband Tony Owen, Frances Rafferty, and Ann Rutherford. The guest list wasn't restricted to on-camera talent, though. Screenwriter Albert Mannheimer, a longtime pal, was often in attendance as well. As Simon's daughter Susan explained, "There was a familial feeling about a group that got together to make a movie."

Two of her father's close friends became Susan's godfathers—Skelton and Milton Berle. The latter she remembered "always had a cigar in his mouth." As a girl, she could count on being greeted by Berle on each visit with "big hugs and kisses." Though others sometimes found the comedian crude, and insensitive, she said, "I didn't know that side of him." While both made their names with broad comedy, and would do almost anything in pursuit of a laugh, their personalities were not altogether alike. Berle, Susan said, "was far more of a businessman than Red."

Songwriter Mort Greene (1912–1992) was another Simon friend who frequently attended the Sunday afternoon gatherings, with his actress wife Jan Wiley. Along with collaborator Harry Revel, Greene was an Oscar nominee for their song "When There's a Breeze on Lake Louise," heard in the film *The Mayor of 44th Street* (1942). "I think Sylvan was some sort of anchor for Mort," said Greene's daughter Melissa, who believes that her father aspired to climb the Hollywood ladder along the lines Simon did in the 1940s. "I know he liked Sylvan a lot. I think Sylvan was a nurturer."[148]

After Simon's death, Mort Greene transitioned from songwriting to a career as a comedy writer. One of his most prominent assignments was serving on the staff of Red Skelton's television variety show, where he was usually tasked with writing the comedian's "Silent Spot." Though his quick wit served him well professionally, Greene's relationship with the idiosyncratic comedian was not as congenial as Simon's had been. Greene, said his daughter, "was very stressed when he was working for Skelton. The comedy was all borne of stress."

Aside from the Sunday get-togethers, another form of relaxation Simon enjoyed was a parlor game he invented, which he dubbed "Comedians of Errors." With the works of William Shakespeare at the heart of the game, players would bring up a question about their lives. Other participants would then provide a relevant Shakespearean quote, and debate its accuracy as applied to the situation in question. Simon told a columnist, "The fellows I play it with most are Louis Hayward, Keenan Wynn, Melvyn Douglas, Lee Bowman and Allyn Joslyn, so you can see the meetings are mostly gag fests."

When Simon was contemplating a loan out to Columbia to direct *The Thrill of Brazil*, the logical Shakespearean reference was, of course, "Neither a borrower nor a

Star Evelyn Keyes consults with Simon on the set of *The Thrill of Brazil*.

lender be." "That line took an awful beating from the gang," Simon said. "They brought up everything from famous men who built fortunes from small loans to the fact that I was in a rut and out [*sic*] to try something new."[149] With that in mind, he agreed to take the assignment.

Many in the movie industry of the late 1940s were extremely nervous about the fast-growing popularity of television, which cut sharply into the sale of movie tickets. According to Susan Granger, her father, always fond of gadgets and electronics, was intrigued by the new medium: "We were the first on the block to have a television set." As the family watched at home, Simon told his wife and children, "This is the way we're going to see movies in the future." By 1947, he had entered into a startup venture that promised to make that vision come true, with a company called Radio Cinema Theaters Corporation.

The concept entailed streaming recent feature films into subscribers' homes via telephone lines, which he dubbed "phono-vision." Caught off guard when she was asked to comment by a Pittsburgh reporter who got wind of the venture, his mother Eva said, "It was supposed to be secret. I heard about it last year when I visited Sylvan in Hollywood. He'll be here in November and I'll find out all about it then."[150]

But within a day or so, Simon himself broke the news in a nationally syndicated interview. "In the first place there will be no commercials. We feel that the subscriber will be paying a nominal sum for the entertainment and they should not be required to pay for ballyhoo of some commercial product. It will be pure entertainment."[151] Each film would cost the subscriber $1, to be billed on his regular monthly phone bill.

In September 1947, he announced that the venture was nearly ready to go, after working on it for more than a year. He added, "As soon as final arrangements are worked out with the Bell Telephone Co., we plan to have 10,000 receiving sets installed immdiately [*sic*] in New York and Los Angeles homes. Later it will be nationwide."[152] Simon explained, "I'm called the president, but I'm only a minor official in the company. It's a closed corporation of top radio and television executives. I can't tell you their names, but I can tell you they're not trying to wrangle any outside money."[153]

Later stories indicated that Simon and his cohorts would also venture into original programming: "Rights to the George Harmon Cox[e] crime books have been acquired by Radio Cinema Theater with [Gene] Raymond in mind as film star ... the first picture will be shot under the title of 'Police Photographer.'" Coxe's popular character, Jack "Flashgun" Casey, was already the hero of a radio drama, *Casey, Crime Photographer*.[154] For whatever reason, however, whether technical or contractual, the plans for streamed movies into the home never came to fruition.

As time passed, Simon was increasingly eager to originate and develop his own projects. He began acquiring the rights to books and stories with his own money, in the hopes of persuading studios to bankroll the films he envisioned. It was a somewhat risky undertaking; some of the projects would never see the light of day. But in 1947, one of Simon's longstanding dreams came true when he reteamed with his friend Red Skelton for the slapstick comedy *The Fuller Brush Man*. Simon said the idea had first hit him some six years earlier. "Hundreds of jokes had been cracked about the various services these fellows render beside their standard chore of purveying mops, brooms, etc. to the American housewife. The Fuller Brushmen were as well known to the public as Superman...."[155] With the right script, and most importantly a top-flight comedian to star, Simon thought *The Fuller Brush Man* could be a box office sensation.

Simon and Red Skelton wanted to work together again, but when the director pitched the concept of *The Fuller Brush Man* at MGM, executives there turned thumbs down on it. One frequently heard objection, at Metro and at other studios where he subsequently tried to place the film, was the idea of using the name of an actual commercial enterprise in the title. As Simon dryly pointed out, MGM was then working on a film called *Week-End at the Waldorf*, but the application of logic didn't seem to help. Nor did he succeed in making a sale at Paramount, where he presented it as a potential Bob Hope vehicle. During wartime, when Skelton was enlisted, Simon thought a stage show might work, and he envisioned Milton Berle as the headliner. "Milton was anxious to do it," Simon wrote, "until his lawyers talked him out of it."[156]

Even after Louis B. Mayer personally nixed the project, Simon wasn't ready to throw in the towel. As producer Edward Small told it, "Simon came to me with the property and, after I read it, I told Harry Cohn I would like to make the picture."[157] If Mayer thought broad slapstick comedy was beneath the dignity of the august MGM, Cohn, who had made plenty of money at Columbia on the raucous antics of the Three Stooges, had no such reservations, and quickly saw the potential for a box office payoff.

A slightly unexpected collaborator on this and other Simon projects of the period was young mystery writer Roy Huggins, whose first novel *The Double Take* had been published in 1946. Simon bought the rights to the book, which was subsequently adapted into the film *I Love Trouble* (1948). With his help, Huggins was offered a well-paid screenwriting job at Columbia, but was dismayed at the workings of Hollywood. "My opinion was not something Simon felt compelled to deal with or give much thought to," he later complained.[158] Though his stint at Columbia was short-lived, Huggins' ideas furnished mystery elements that were incorporated into not only *The Fuller Brush Man*, but a later slapstick comedy, *The Good Humor Man*, as well. Before going into production with the film, Simon had to obtain clearance from A.C. Fuller, head of the Fuller Brush Company. "He was apathetic to the idea," Simon admitted. "Fortunately, Mrs. Fuller found my telling of the story funny. And she sold her husband the idea."[159] Simon wrote to producer Small in September 1947 to advise that the first draft script was complete, and copies being sent to executives at the Fuller Brush Company for their review, noting, "I have made all the changes suggested by them in my telephone conversations with both Mr. Peterson and Mr. Adams, so I do not anticipate any problems from that source."

He noted that the script of *The Fuller Brush Man* as it then stood did not incorporate all of the suggestions Small had made for improvements. "However," Simon wrote, "in view of the physical preparations necessary for this picture, I wanted to get the script out in this form for all the departments so we can get a budget and start the set and prop shop work...." He added that the screenwriters had been tasked with "doing a general polish job on the whole script, because I realize we are still over-length. In the polish, we will condense and consolidate to bring us down to the necessary page count."[160]

Now the difficulty was to persuade Mayer to loan out Skelton for a picture he had already rejected. "Red was absolutely the one man who should play the lead role," Small felt, and certainly Simon concurred.[161] Fortuitously, Small owned the film rights to Dumas' *The Three Musketeers*, a property Mayer coveted. After some negotiation, both sides agreed to the trade, with one unusual stipulation from Metro's end: Small and Simon were to tell no one that Mayer had nixed *The Fuller Brush Man* as an MGM picture. That allowed the studio head to save face, and avoid any suggestion that he had made a bad call. Skelton was enthusiastic about the prospect of being directed by Simon again. Noted Louella O. Parsons (December 16, 1947), "That Skelton is one of those rare people, few and far between, who is 100 percent loyal, and ever since Simon started him off as a screen star in *Whistling in the Dark* Red's been sold on him—even to taking him along for his loan-out to Columbia."

At the star's instigation, Simon made a guest appearance on Red's radio show, *The Kool Cigarette Program*. "I'd sure better have some good comebacks ready for the air show," he joked before the broadcast.[162] He appeared on February 24, 1948, in a skit titled, "Junior Gets into Motion Pictures, or The Perils of S. Sylvan Simon." On the air, Skelton crowed, "He lost a bet, and had to come on the show!" The script found Junior and Grandma (Verna Felton) going to Columbia Studios to audition for parts in *The Fuller Brush Man*. Junior, of course, proceeds to wreaks havoc. Simon appears on the scene:

> **SIMON:** "I'm really going to do everything in my power to get Junior a contract at Columbia Studios."
> **VERNA:** "Why, Mr. Simon, I don't think I realized you were so interested in Columbia."
> **SIMON:** "I don't think *you* realize I'm under contract to Metro-Goldwyn-Mayer."

Though he loved Skelton's high-energy, slapstick antics, Simon noted that he had helmed films that drew laughs through various types of comedy, including situational and that which derived from character. "No matter how you classify comedy," he said, "it is concerned with personalities and built entirely around them. Just as the punishment fits the crime, the situation must suit the comedian."[163]

While still under contract at MGM, Simon made two films on loan-out, partnered with actor-turned-producer Franchot Tone and his newly created production company, Cornell Productions. Both men wanted to exert more control over their professional destinies. Tone wanted more varied acting assignments, and Simon, after 10 years on the payroll, was concerned that MGM executives increasingly found him useful to loan out to other studios. Simon directed Tone in the comedy *Her Husband's Affairs*, which came out in 1947, and the detective drama *I Love Trouble* the following year. Both were released through Columbia Pictures, putting Simon once again in close proximity to Harry Cohn and the studio which had grown tremendously under his leadership. *Her Husband's Affairs* marked Simon's first chance to direct Lucille Ball in a lead role, following her cameo appearance in *Bud Abbott and Lou Costello in Hollywood*. They would ultimately work together on four films. Columnist Sheilah Graham (October 10, 1947) predicted, "Don't be surprised if Lucille Ball signs with Columbia to make one movie a year for them. She is simply terrific in their picture 'Her Husband's Affairs.'"

In the late 1940s, Sylvan and Harriet attended weekly square dance parties organized by Lucy, and held at her home. Others who regularly joined in the fun were Dorothy Lamour, Eve Arden, Victor Mature, and even Harry Cohn. "And guess what these movie people have as refreshment! Lemonade and soda pop!"[164] Indeed, Simon was once described in a column item as "a strict teetotaler who considers sarsaparilla [*sic*] hard-drinkin' likker."[165]

The Fuller Brush Man pleased audiences and critics alike, becoming a sizable hit in the spring of 1948. After attending a preview showing, Paul Manning of the trade publication *The Exhibitor* wrote to congratulate producer Edward Small and company on a "wonderful comedy achievement," saying, "This is without a doubt the most uproariously funny deal to hit the screen this year.... When a real live and tough Hollywood audience reacts as they did last night, literally rolling in the aisles, that, Mr. Small, is the pat on the back that really pays off!" Manning added, "After many years of utter waste at M.G.M. it took real showmanship to strike the mother lode bonanza of Red Skelton...."[166]

Simon's final directorial assignment at MGM reunited him with Skelton, but the experience ended unhappily, contributing to his exit from the studio. Metro executives, having belatedly acknowledged that Skelton could carry a film, assigned him to *A Southern Yankee*, a comedy with a Civil War background. The comedian knew exactly whom he wanted as director: "Skelton worked with Simon at Columbia on the recently completed 'Fuller Brush Man' and asked for him in the director's spot on 'A Southern Yankee.'"[167]

Simon was on his way out the door when studio executives decided that retakes were needed on his film, in response to reactions it received in previews. The job of shooting additional footage for *A Southern Yankee* went to director Edward Sedgwick. Seeing that his film had been tampered with, Simon asked to have his name removed from the credits. Upon its release that summer, the finished product was attributed onscreen to Sedgwick. However, leading lady Arlene Dahl later commented, "I only recall working with S. Sylvan Simon. I don't recall any retakes."[168] Simon's exit may have scotched another potential collaboration with Skelton; columnist Sheilah Graham (March 20, 1948) reported that the comic redhead had sparked to the idea of starring in a biopic about Harry Houdini, to be directed by Simon.

That spring, a newspaper item noted, "S. Sylvan Simon, who seemed to be gravitating toward a new affiliation because of three loanouts from MGM in a row, has secured his release from his contract to that studio which had four more years to go.... He is in Phoenix for a short vacation, and will announce future plans on his return."[169] The plans in question offered exciting new opportunities after a decade directing at Metro. But they also came with a substantial risk—in the form of the man who would become his new boss.

3

Mr. Simon Takes Columbia

Harry Cohn, head of Columbia Pictures, had liked *The Fuller Brush Man* quite a bit, especially once the box office receipts came rolling in. He saw the potential for more moneymaking hits if he could get the movie's producer-director on the studio payroll. Sylvan Simon, for his part, sensed an opportunity to make more films of his own choosing. On April 12, 1948, *Daily Variety* announced, "Simon checks in at Columbia today to begin work under a new long-term producer contract inked over the weekend." One industry observer commented, "It looks from here as if Sylvan Simon ... is due to become the white-haired boy at Columbia. Simon has been handed three important properties for his schedule as producer-director, all of which are being given high priority on the studio's schedule of pictures."[170]

Indeed, from his first days on the job, Simon had multiple projects on his plate, including some he had originated. *Showmen's Trade Review* (April 24, 1948) said his first production for Columbia would be "Superstition Mountain," based on the 1946 book *Thunder Gods' Gold* by Barry Storm, which Simon had optioned. Though it wouldn't be ready to go before cameras until the following year, it was ultimately released as *Lust for Gold*.

Simon believed that the success of *The Fuller Brush Man* proved that filmmakers should think outside the box, trusting their own judgment rather than being overly reliant on mimicking earlier hits. Though his new project had, on the surface, little in common with the Skelton comedy, Simon saw both as original concepts that would appeal to audiences. A thriller based on a real-life case, *Lust for Gold* presented characters that were not necessarily intended to attract audience sympathy. The film's draw was the puzzle itself, and the appeal of prospecting for a fortune. Simon described it as "a grand-scale detective story" that he expected would have viewers wanting to seek out the real-life treasure themselves. "In other words," he added, "the picture will appeal to the larceny of the audience.... I think theatre patrons will be as interested in the mountain-hero as they ever were in any flesh-and-blood hero or heroine."[171]

Another project at the top of his to-do list was "Lona Hanson," an adaptation of a bestselling novel by Thomas Savage, earmarked as a vehicle for Rita Hayworth. Simon was set to produce the film in the summer of 1948, with Norman Foster named as director. According to Louella O. Parsons (May 11, 1948), "S. Sylvan Simon took an option on the book and sold it to Harry Cohn and Beckworth Pictures." Author Savage was then an English instructor at Suffolk University in Boston, earning a meager salary, "and had just been turned down for a $500 loan he needed to buy furniture for his young family. His good fortune was duly recorded in the newspapers."[172] The novel, which told the story of a woman who inherits a ranch and falls in love with a hired hand, had won critical praise, one reviewer stating, "Savage writes a terse, warm, moving prose.... The man can write, tell an impelling story, force you to believe in him against your will, and he has written one of the few Western stories of ranching life wherein guns play a small part."[173]

For all the promise that his new job at Columbia held, it also meant working with a boss notorious for clashing with virtually anyone and everyone. As film historian Bernard Dick explained it, "There were two Harry Cohns: the womanizer and tyrant and the studio head who read scripts carefully, respected writers, and treated a select number of actresses as ladies and the rest as dames."[174] Author Rochelle Larkin wrote of Cohn's tyrannical reputation, "Despite it all, Harry Cohn commanded a fantastic loyalty from the people who worked for him. Some may have hated him, but they all respected him."[175] Actress Betty Garrett, who along with her husband Larry Parks worked at Columbia, concurred: "He was awfully hard to like sometimes, but he certainly knew how to make movies."[176] Although actress Terry Moore acknowledged, "He was very hard on people," she added, "He was really nice to me."

Ambitious as he was, Simon knew it would behoove him to appeal to Cohn's budget. As Hedda Hopper (July 6, 1948) recounted it, Simon shrewdly approached his boss to say, "I want to tell you about a terrific property," the title of which was (for the moment) "What My Next Husband Will Be." Cohn listened to Simon's enthusiastic sales pitch and liked the story: "Great. How much will we have to pay for it?" The answer—nothing—warmed the cockles of the studio chief's budget. "It's been on your shelf for four years," Simon explained. This became *Tell It to the Judge* with Rosalind Russell. Although *Miss Grant Takes Richmond* (1949) had been earmarked for Miss Russell, eventually Bob Thomas (July 28, 1948) reported that she and Lucy had switched film assignments—Miss Ball would play Miss Grant, while Russell was to do *Tell It to the Judge*.

For the second time that year (after the problems with *A Southern Yankee*), Simon refused credit on a film he made. Multiple trade sources confirm that, in the summer of 1948, he was producing "The Lovers," with Cornel Wilde and Patricia Knight in the starring roles. That misleading title masked what was to become a suspenseful *film noir*. *Boxoffice* (July 3, 1948) reported that Simon had "gunned" (i.e., begun production of) the film. But by the time it was released several months later, under the more fitting title *Shockproof*, it was officially produced by nobody in particular. *Variety*'s review (January 26, 1949) termed it "a front-office production."

In the fall of 1948, Simon set out for Arizona, with a twofold purpose. One was to select key locations for the upcoming Rita Hayworth film. "He will make an aerial survey of southern Arizona for a spot to film Columbia's next picture, 'Lona Hanson,' starring Rita Hayworth and William Holden. Simon seeks a large ranch for the location of the new film."[177] But the major task at hand was the making of the project initially known as "Superstition Mountain," and later "Greed," based on Barry Storm's gold-mining adventure. It had been rechristened again, as "Bonanza," when cast and crew arrived in Phoenix just after Thanksgiving, with shooting to begin by the end of November. Heading the cast of what finally became *Lust for Gold* were Ida Lupino and Glenn Ford.

Simon and leading man Ford had originally met in the late 1930s, and their shared history didn't bode well for a collegial collaboration. According to Ford's son and biographer, Peter, "The producer told the young Gwyllyn Ford that he lacked the looks required of a leading man. Their relationship never recovered from that awkward moment."[178] Glenn Ford later recounted the story to author C. Courtney Joyner: "Simon threw me out of his office after an acting audition 13 years before I made this film for him.... If Simon had his way in 1936, I'd be working with a lot of my classmates from Santa Monica High School at Douglas Aircraft on an assembly line by this time."[179]

Not exactly an unbiased observer, Peter Ford (recording his father's memories) wrote that Simon made a nuisance of himself during the early days of production back in Hollywood. "Simon had been a director for many years, and he could not keep himself from interfering on the set, buzzing around with suggestions and countermanding [director George] Marshall's directions with cries for extra takes or different camera setups."[180] Though Simon was arguably carrying out the function of a hands-on producer, he and Marshall clashed. Other accounts didn't place the blame with Simon. As columnist Hedda Hopper (November 1, 1948) told it: "George Marshall, usually the most co-operative director in town, didn't make friends on his loan-out to Columbia for 'Bonanza.' He took his own writer along and wouldn't discuss the scenes with Sylvan Simon."

Marshall soon left the project, and a few days later the party of the third part gave his version of the story, resulting in a follow-up comment from Hopper a few days later (November 8, 1948): "When George started directing, he realized that producer Sylvan Simon wanted to direct as well as produce. George, never one to stand in anybody's way, stepped aside for Simon, with Harry Cohn's blessing."

Watching Simon behind the camera as *Lust for Gold* was filmed on Arizona locations, a local reporter noted, "The scene would flicker for a few brief seconds on the screens of the nation's movie houses, but it took an entire morning to film it to the satisfaction of S. Sylvan Simon, producer-director. No detail was overlooked, scenery, lighting, sound, or acting.... Time dragged on as first one thing and then another was corrected, as director, stars, and other scores of men and women in the company struggled for perfection."[181]

While cameras were grinding on *Lust for Gold*, plans for "Lona Hanson" hit a serious snag when the leading lady, at the eleventh hour, made it clear she would not report for work as instructed. Reported Louella O. Parsons (December 6, 1948), "Miss Hayworth was supposed to leave Saturday for Nogales, Ariz., but she refused to go. S. Sylvan Simon, the producer, is already there working on locations, and the picture has been held up for some time waiting for Rita's return.... Columbia is looking for another actress to take Rita Hayworth's place."

Harry Cohn and his studio colleagues made no secret of the fact that Miss Hayworth had been suspended, and took care to see that her $4800 a week salary did not go unmentioned in newspaper accounts. Fighting insinuations that she was just another spoiled ingrate of a star, the actress defended herself, saying, "A script was handed me last Thursday. The part to be portrayed by me was not adapted to me and would be detrimental to me. I said so and was suspended."[182] Her biographer Barbara Leaming added, "Her new Beckworth contract entitled her to script approval, but Harry Cohn was anxious to overlook this important provision and proceed as in the past—with the studio assigning her projects."[183] Ultimately, "Lona Hanson" was abandoned altogether, and Simon moved on to other projects.

Less than a year after Simon signed on at Columbia Pictures, *Daily Variety* (March 17, 1949) reported that he had taken on a bigger role. He accepted a post as the studio's executive producer, making him second-in-command to Harry Cohn. As Bernard Dick explained, "Since Harry never knew how long an executive producer would last, he began grooming S. Sylvan Simon for the position in 1948. While Simon was not a writer, he had credentials Harry respected," among them his extensive education.[184]

Five forthcoming pictures were set to be made under his personal supervision: *Miss Grant Takes Richmond*, *The Good Humor Man*, *The Fuller Brush Girl*, *Pleasure Island*, and *The Petty Girl*. His responsibilities would include supervising the output of Columbia's A producers Alex Gottlieb and Buddy Adler. "Col's program of B pictures will take somewhat of a nosedive as result of the new regime, with company now aiming for improved revenues that go hand in hand with longer playing time." The *Pittsburgh Post-Gazette* (April 9, 1949) reported that he would collect a weekly salary of $2,500 in the post. Other films that soon came under his purview included *No Sad Songs for Me*, with Margaret Sullavan, and *The Killer That Stalked New York*.

That summer, Simon told a journalist, "We're proud of the pictures we're turning out now.... We're getting ready to come out with the best entertainment the world has ever known, and when better movies are made, we're going to make them." Though the rapidly growing popularity of television had some industry insiders worried, he declared, "There's nothing the matter with the movies that good pictures won't cure."[185]

According to Susan Granger, her father's new job, demanding though it would prove to be, allowed him to be home more than he had been as a producer and director. Location shoots out of town were curtailed in favor of time spent at the studio. Still, the demands were intense. "There was always a telephone on the table during dinner," Susan said. He took work calls at any time. "When you are involved in a project, it's 24/7." More than ever, of course, his new job hitched his professional wagon to Harry Cohn. While Sylvan's nephew Richard observed what he described as "a great personal relationship with his boss.... Harry Cohn," Stephen Simon saw it differently, describing it as "a contentious relationship."[186] As author Will Holtzman later put it, "Cohn thrived on conflict, and when none was to be found, he instigated it."[187]

Stephen Simon's most vivid memory of Harry Cohn involved the day the studio mogul, at one of the Simons' Sunday afternoon get-togethers, thought it would be funny to offer the little boy a shot of whisky. When Stephen began to gag after gulping the noxious drink, it was Red Skelton who noticed and summoned Sylvan and Harriet, while Cohn suddenly decided he had somewhere else to be. Stephen, who said he had never been able to abide whisky since, said, "It shows you what a jerk Harry Cohn was."[188] Susan Granger, who sometimes accompanied her parents to events at Cohn's house, concurred, saying, "I never found him to be a very nice man at all. He was rude, always very gruff and angry." However, Cohn's wife, Joan, she remembered as being gracious.

As Simon settled into his new job, his nephew Richard, newly married in November 1949, paid a visit. "As newlyweds my wife and I arrived in California on a Sunday morning," he said. "Sylvan and Harriet invited us to dinner at their house and from there Sylvan took the two of us to Harry Cohn's house to view an unedited version of a new movie.... Also there was Phil Silvers and Harry's wife Joan. Can you just imagine how wide-eyed my 22-year old wife was!" The Simons continued to socialize. "I spent most weekends at Sylvan's pool," Richard noted. "His closest friends were Ray Stark and his wife (Fannie Brice's daughter)." Stark (1915–2004), who would go on to become a renowned producer and motion picture executive, initially served as Sylvan's agent, but the men soon became friends as well, and would remain so until Simon's death.

Though *Lust for Gold* performed well for Columbia upon its release in the summer of 1949, one viewer who saw it promptly hit the ceiling. Barry Storm, who had sold Columbia the screen rights to his book, "is now shopping for a lawyer to fight a million-dollar damage suit against Columbia. Says he was falsely portrayed as a grandson of the murderous, seducing, gold squandering 'Dutchman' of the famed Lost Dutchman mine."[189] The author also complained that Simon's film contained "anti-mining propaganda,"[190] writing that it was made "during a time of critical war-born mineral shortages," but promoted the idea that "prospectors are murderous criminals to start with and unreliable stumblebums to end with."[191] He claimed that people in Phoenix supported the movie unquestioningly because it brought money into the community, employing dozens of people, and consequently harassed him for his views.

Storm fired off an angry letter to Sylvan Simon. The producer/director's measured response was tactful and kind, expressing regret at Storm's unhappiness while reminding him of a few salient points. Among them was the fact that Storm, present during much of the Arizona location shoot, had reviewed the script at that time:

> "As a matter of fact, it was to that end that I had you come to Hollywood during the writing of the story, and that was why I had my assistant, Earl McEvoy, give you the script in Phoenix. When I asked you for your comments on the script, when I arrived in Phoenix on Thanksgiving Day, you said you thought the story was just great.
>
> The script very definitely showed you as representing yourself as the grandson of Jacob Walz.... I believe you were on the set in Phoenix almost every day, about ten days of shooting. Prior to that you were with Earl every day looking for locations, and on none of these occasions did you ever bring up this point.
>
> As far as your reputation as a writer is concerned, Barry, I think that this picture will be invaluable for you because it will be seen by so many people who might be potential buyers of your forthcoming books. However, just between us, I don't think the picture is going to show a great deal of profit, if any, because of its high negative cost."[192]

Storm's presence on the set during production was confirmed by multiple sources, including a *Variety* column item (November 17, 1948) advising that he, having sold Columbia the story rights to his book, "is working for the company out of Phoenix as a technical advisor." He also traveled to Hollywood, spending a week there as a paid consultant for the studio.

The enraged author apparently rebuffed Simon's attempt to extend an olive branch. In addition to the lawsuit he filed, Storm put his version of the story on paper with a slender volume, more a pamphlet than a full book, called *I Was Swindled by Red Movie Makers*, published in 1954. His claims veered from the doubtful into the bizarre, including the alleged use of a "stage transmitter designed to brainwash him into compliance with communist movie makers and drugging with the hypnotic choral [*sic*] hydrate to make the brainwashing work."[193]

A few years later, his updated edition of his book *Thunder Gods' Gold* said, "The Columbia Pictures vice president, Lester W. Roth, who signed the movie rights contract to 'Thunder Gods Gold' was later identified by the California Committee on Un-American Activities (Fourth Report) as Chairman of an international communist front. S. Sylvan Simon, the Producer, and George Marshall, the Director, were identified respectively as a communist front Chairman and a hard-core Communist party liner."[194]

The California State Senate began investigating allegations of Communist activities in the late 1940s, with a committee under the leadership of Senator Jack Tenney. However, the committee's Fourth Report, which Storm referenced, in no way identifies Simon as a Communist, nor does he even appear prominently in its pages. His name appears precisely one time, in a document that runs 462 pages. On page 97, he's identified as a board member of the Actors' Laboratory, which the report painted as a Red front. Board officers Rose Hobart, Roman Bohnen, J. Edward Bromberg, and Will Lee were subpoenaed to testify in February 1948, and their answers did little to satisfy senators. Apparently because of this, CUAC created a card in its files for Simon, listing the address of the Actors' Lab. However, the card merely cross-references the committee's files on the Actors' Lab, which are notable mostly for the almost-complete absence of Simon's name in more than 100 pages of documentation. Storm's claims notwithstanding, there is no indication that he was ever the subject of any substantive investigation.

The sole basis for the Committee's awareness of Simon appears to be an undated theater program for an Actors' Lab-sponsored event called "An Evening for the Lab," on which he is listed as a member of the Executive Board. Investigators at the time likely didn't know that the event in question had been held some three years earlier, during the time that Simon was engaged in war work. The showcase in question featured short plays by Anton Chekhov, Sean O'Casey, and Howard Fast. *Variety* (August 4, 1944), reviewing the dramatic showcase, gave it a rave review, calling it "one of the finest evenings for an audience ever presented in a little theatre."

At that time, the Actors' Lab enjoyed a solid reputation as a training program for aspiring performers. Veterans were allowed to study at the Actors' Lab with financing from the GI Bill, and studios frequently referred their less experienced new hires there for additional training. One trade paper noted, for example, that new Universal contract player William Ching "will join the Actors Lab for schooling in line with studio procedure with new players."[195] The attention of the CUAC, however, quickly brought a reversal in fortunes for the group. As film historian Anthony Slide noted, "In 1948 the IRS revoked the tax-exempt status of the Actors' Lab, and the following year, the Lab was forced to end its involvement in the veterans' training program."[196]

Longtime Actors' Lab board member Phil Brown, aware of his colleagues' widely divergent opinions about almost any topic, scornfully dismissed the notion that they could have solidified plans for a Communist overthrow of America, much less carried them out: "They [the leadership] couldn't have taken over the house next door, let alone Hollywood, let alone the U.S. Government," he scoffed. "That was pure bullshit."[197] Roman Bohnen, co-founder of the group, died in February 1949, and the Actors' Lab was defunct by the following year.

Though Barry Storm probably never knew it, Simon had in fact tried more than once to bring an anti–Communist story to 1940s movie screens. In 1948, Louella O. Parsons (February 25, 1948) reported that Simon wanted to film a communist expose based on Willa Gibbs' "Tender Men." The author wanted a portion of the proceeds to go to the fight against Communism. Parsons noted that Simon "is negotiating for the book and if he gets it he will, of course, carry out the request of the author." A few weeks later, the columnist (March 16, 1948) wrote that Simon had purchased screen rights to John McFarland's "Portrait of an American Communist," which had appeared in *Life* Magazine, with Collier Young to produce the film for Columbia.

His daughter Susan described Simon as "very apolitical," though he was a registered Democrat, and it was surely an absurdity for anyone to think he was pushing anti–American propaganda through the likes of his slapstick comedies. However, his cousin, Aline MacMahon, who as a prominent actress had a higher public profile, came under attack when she was listed in the notorious *Red Channels: The Report of Communist Influence in Radio and Television,* issued in the summer of 1950.

Ultimately, Barry Storm's case against Columbia was settled out of court, though he apparently continued to stew about it for years to come. "According to Herbert B. Finn, Storm's attorney, Columbia paid the author $5,000 for any damage which may have resulted ... and agreed that no future use of Storm's name would be made in connection with the picture without his consent."[198]

A far happier result of Simon's affiliation with Columbia began in the summer of 1949, only weeks after his promotion to head of production, when Lucille Ball signed a contract to make one film a year there. They were friends of long standing, enough so that Susan Granger remembered the famous redhead telling her, "I carried you home from the hospital!" In years past, Miss Ball had shied away from signing on at the studio. Well aware of the boss man's reputation for butting heads with almost anyone in his employ, she once told Louella O. Parsons, "Harry Cohn and his wife are good friends of mine, and I wish to keep our friendship." Having first directed Lucy when she made a cameo appearance in *Abbott and Costello in Hollywood*, Simon was eager to collaborate more fully. Said his cousin Richard Simon, "I believe his success with Lucille Ball and Desi was because they were friends over and above working together."

When it came to comedy, Lucy had complete faith in Sylvan Simon's taste and judgment. In the fall of 1949, she nonchalantly told columnist Sheilah Graham (February 26, 1949), "I'm starting my new picture, 'Miss Grant Takes Richmond,' at Columbia this week. I haven't read the script yet. But I'm sure it's O.K.—Sylvan Simon is directing and producing." The results were laudable, with multiple reviews echoing that of the *Pittsburgh Press* (October 3, 1949), which said that *Richmond* "could very easily shoot Lucille Ball to the top of the Hollywood comedienne ladder."

Given the box office success of *The Fuller Brush Man*, it was no surprise that plans were underway for a follow-up, *The Fuller Brush Girl.* Said journalist Bob Thomas, "There'll be a search for the right 'girl,' but don't be surprised if a famous redhead lands the part."[199] Simon and his Columbia colleagues had hoped to retain Skelton's services again, to make another slapstick comedy, *The Good Humor Man*, which columnist Edith Gwynn (December 5, 1948) noted was "a natural for Red." However, MGM refused to loan him out a second time, and instead put him in a comedy on his home lot, *The Yellow Cab Man.* Ultimately, Jack Carson inherited the *Good Humor Man* role. Ideas for other broad comedies were sparking as well. Bemused, the *Los Angeles Times'* Edwin Schallert commented, "Tops in bizarre picture plans is Columbia's to produce 'Confessions of a Diaper Salesman,' which ran in Fortune magazine. It is about high-powered methods used by baby garment laundries." *Showman's Trade Review* (August 27, 1949) predicted that "Diaper" would be "another Lucille Baller."

Simon thrived on the chance to make movies audiences would want to see. Columnist Leon Gutterman expounded on his characteristics as a filmmaker: "He is [a] fearless experimenter; he is a skillful producer-director with a shrewd sense of manuscript values; he is always given to a fondness for easy, unforced and naturalistic playing.... Highly intelligent and very sharp witted, he believes in making movies for the universal audience, young and old alike." He quoted Simon as saying, "The influence of the movies on the mind and morals of the community is so great as to be incalculable.... Films make a peculiar appeal to children. Above such things as radio and even newspaper comics, the movies are without question the chief influence which enters into the life of youth."[200]

Other projects were somewhere between the drawing board and the screen as 1949 drew to a close. *Showmen's Trade Review* (October 8, 1949) noted that Simon was scouting locations in Jamaica, Virgin Islands for "Virgin Island," announcing a few weeks later that the project would star Glenn Ford and Terry Moore. Based on the William Maier novel "Pleasure Island," the project was delayed, eventually becoming a reality as *The Girls of Pleasure Island* (1953), after Simon's death. Another project was "The Flying Fish," which dealt with guided missiles launched from submarines. *Showmen's Trade Review* (November 5, 1949) noted, "Jerry Bresler will produce the film under Simon's supervision. The screenplay is by Harry Haislip and Richard Nash." When the finished project finally surfaced, it was called *The Flying Missile* (1950), and starred Glenn Ford and Viveca Lindfors.

Another top film had been in the works well before Simon's arrival at Columbia—the movie version of Garson Kanin's smash hit Broadway comedy *Born Yesterday*, for which Harry Cohn had impulsively agreed to pay $1 million to acquire the rights. It was no coincidence, the playwright admitted, that the uncouth, loud-mouthed businessman in Kanin's play was named Harry. Kanin had a healthy dislike for the head of Columbia Pictures, and while he was happy to base a character on him, had no intention of letting Cohn get his hands on the hit play. "I had informed his New York representative that although the play was for sale, it was not for sale to Harry Cohn.... Not for a million bucks."[201] But when Cohn agreed to pay that precise amount, Kanin capitulated.

Hollywood insiders were openly dubious that the hit show could be the basis for a successful film, with one trade-paper columnist saying that the purchase indicated "rank extravagance and poor judgement ... a funny play, but it should have been obvious to Mr. Cohn that it would need a thorough dry cleaning" to be adapted as a movie. "It will probably resemble something entirely different from the property that cost a fortune before a camera was ever turned on it."[202]

Interoffice teletypes from the studio's files in 1948 and 1949 showed that Cohn and his colleagues spent quite a bit of time spinning their wheels over the possible permutations of adapting Kanin's play. Various casting possibilities were bandied about, with notes about director King Vidor supervising a test for Marie McDonald, and the unavailability of Victor Mature, busy with *Samson and Delilah*. One lengthy conversation in August 1948 included the possibility of using MGM contract player Robert Taylor, to which an unidentified participant stated:

I HAVE DEF INFO FROM MY SPIES AT METRO THAT TAYLOR HAS BEEN A BUST FOR A LONG TIME ... UNDERSTAND TAYLOR HASN'T MADE A DECENT PIC IN YEARS WITH THE POSS EXCEPTION OF JOHNNY EAGER AND THEY VERY ANX FROM MY INSIDE INFO TO LET US HAVE HIM.

Brian Donlevy was considered, then rejected:

WHILE IT IS TRUE THAT I SUGG DONLEVY & U ACCEPTED HIM AFTER FURTHER CONSIDERATION THINK THIS WOULD BE TREMENDOUS MISTAKE. WE HAVE INVESTMENT OF ONE MILLION DOLLARS IN A PLAY & GE [sic] WOULD ONLY PULL THE PIC DOWN & CERTAINLY HAS NO BOX OFFICE DRAW.

The merits of James Cagney and Humphrey Bogart, and the salaries they might command, were heatedly debated across the wires, one of those present arguing, "I think the way to salvage Born Yest[erday] is to do it with Bogart," followed by the comment, "Think Bogart even without a gun is a much bigger draw than Cagney."

With Simon's star on the rise at Columbia, the prestigious project eventually fell into his lap. Announcing his assignment to produce *Born Yesterday*, one columnist noted, "That's the plum of the year at that studio."[203] Still, the casting conundrums continued unabated. Initially, Cohn expressed no interest in having Judy Holliday reprise her acclaimed stage performance. "I've got Rita Hayworth under contract," he purportedly said. "I've got Lucille Ball. Maybe I'll go for Alice Faye or Stanwyck."[204] In November 1949, the *Los Angeles Times* reported that Simon and Cohn were testing Jan Sterling, who'd played the role onstage.

Reports vary as to Lucille Ball's pursuit of the much-coveted role of Billie Dawn. Early on, Hedda Hopper reported (October 24, 1947): "Lucille Ball's fans have gone out on a rampage trying to get 'Born Yesterday' for the redhead. They call her 'Queen of Comedy.'" One source quoted Miss Ball herself as saying, "I'm not going to campaign for it: Columbia ought to realize I'm right for the role."[205] But after seeing Jean Parker play it onstage, the actress apparently reconsidered, telling columnist Bob Thomas (January 21, 1949), "It's not for me. I can't play a dumb role. People are used to my knowing the answers." By the summer of 1949, one columnist noted, "The million-dollar Broadway play has been in the movie mill two years, and so far the only thing anybody knows for sure is that Rita Hayworth won't be in it."[206]

Still dubious about casting Miss Holliday, Cohn finally offered her a test, though she later told Hedda Hopper (July 30, 1950) that it was done under inauspicious circumstances, while she was shooting *Adam's Rib*. "It happened to be Father's Day, and I could see that the crew was sore as a boil having to report to the studio at seven in the morning to test another dame," she recalled. "Charlie Vidor, who directed me, was in a hassle with the studio, and Brod Crawford, who was to play opposite me, had tested with so many girls he was weary of it. I couldn't have been tested under worse circumstances."

Used for the test was the gin rummy scene that, aside from being quite funny, also, as critic Ruth Prigozy has noted, makes clear the relationship between Billie and Harry: "Billie's single-minded concentration, her mockery of Harry's rage, her humming and singing ... and her determination to collect her winnings convey at once her character, the nature of their relationship, and the ultimate outcome of the plot."[207] It also demonstrated that the female lead role had complexities beyond playing a blonde of limited intelligence.

With Lucy out of the running for *Born Yesterday*, she was instead assigned to star in Simon's comedy *The Fuller Brush Girl*, under the direction of Lloyd Bacon. If not a vehicle that carried the prestige of playing Billie Dawn, it was nonetheless a milestone in her movie career. More than any other, this film would draw attention to her peerless expertise with physical comedy. As *Variety* noted in its review, "*The Fuller Brush Girl* is hardly more than a vehicle for Lucille Ball, and she makes capital of the situation. If ever there were any doubts as to Miss Ball's forte, 'Fuller Brush' dispels them. She's an excellent comedienne, and in this rowdy, incoherent yarn with its Keystone Kops overtones, she garners the major laurels."

After starring in the hit comedy *The Fuller Brush Man*, Red Skelton was greeted by this eye-catching display when he returned to play a cameo in *The Fuller Brush Girl*.

With Miss Holliday finally signed to reprise her stage role, Simon moved full steam ahead on his production duties for *Born Yesterday*. His tasks in that capacity included making arrangements for location shooting in Washington, D.C., opening up the play by showing Billie Dawn visiting some iconic national landmarks. Louella O. Parsons noted (June 24, 1950) that he also undertook a pleasanter task. "George [Cukor] and I put in a call for extras," Simon told the columnist, "and what answered were hordes of young beauties, some of whom could have walked right out of the chorus of a Ziegfeld Follies.... Most of these girls work for the government either whole or half time, and working in a picture is a big thrill in contrast to their regular job."

Production of A films was humming along at the studio, with one influential trade paper noting, "There is every reason to believe that 1950 may be one of the best [years] for Columbia" and the studio "might very well move into the ranks of the majors."[208] This despite the fact that the studio's biggest star was still AWOL; Louella Parsons reported (October 23, 1950) that Cohn is "sending S. Sylvan Simon to Europe with several scripts for Rita Hayworth, and among them is one in which she'd play a ballet dancer." With or without Miss Hayworth, though, Simon's tenure was clearly working out well for Columbia, which Cohn recognized.

Although the movie industry in general was suffering the impact of television, all indications were that Simon's first year as head of production was a successful one for the studio. By the end of 1950, reviewing data covering the previous fiscal year, "Cohn revealed an all time high record in profits for his organization." Moreover, morale was up, "...the spirit of cooperativeness which prevails on the lot, for the first time in many a year. From the front office right down the line, there is a new wholesome spirit that bodes well for the future of the company."[209] That fall, a Hollywood journalist reported, "S. Sylvan Simon has been signed to a new five-year producer pact. Considering their differences in the past, it seems strange that the two men could agree to another long term of it, but Cohn, badly in need of producer strength, must have made substantial concessions to hang on to Simon."[210]

Not that Cohn had passed any charm courses in the interim. Millard Kaufman recalled an instance in which he, Simon, and producer Buddy Adler teamed up to convince Cohn of a change needed in their current project. After making their case, Simon said genially to his boss, "We all think it would work. So you see, Harry, the vote is three to one." Unimpressed, Cohn snapped, "You're wrong. I'll tell you what the score is. It's one to nothing."[211] The grouchy studio head added, "Simon, Gower Street is paved with the bones of my executive producers. Now get the hell out of here!" If Simon was bawled out, Kaufman suffered a worse fate: he was summarily fired. Little wonder that, for all his professional advancement, Sylvan Simon was taking prescription medication for migraine headaches. Stephen recalled, "Worried that my father would actually work himself to death, my mother had actually begged Cohn to fire my father but he refused."[212]

In March 1951, Simon celebrated his 41st birthday, his hometown paper reporting that he "shared a triple birthday cake with Harry Karl and Albert Manneheimer [sic] at the Mocambo.... Took several waiters to bring it to the table."[213] Also cause for jubilation that spring were five Academy Award nominations for *Born Yesterday,* including Best Picture, Best Director, and Best Actress. The latter category in particular seemed like a long shot—as Judy Holliday's biographer Gary Carey later commented, "No one really expected her to walk off with the award—least of all Judy."[214] She was up against stiff competition that included some far better-known film actresses, Bette Davis (*All About Eve*) and Gloria Swanson (*Sunset Blvd.*) among them, and was aware that comedy rarely took home Oscar gold. Still, in the days leading up to the ceremony, more than one poll predicted she would be the winner, as did the trade paper *Daily Variety.*

The event, which was not yet being televised, was held on March 29, 1951, at the RKO Pantages Theatre in Hollywood. Miss Holliday, back in New York, attended a party hosted by fellow nominee José Ferrer; a coast-to-coast radio hookup would allow nominees back East to speak should they win. Sylvan Simon, accompanied by his wife and daughter, was in attendance at the Hollywood ceremony.

Broderick Crawford read the list of nominees for Best Actress, and then announced that Miss Holliday was the winner. Recalled Susan Granger, "Dad was ecstatic—and stunned.... Judy Holliday's win was quite an upset!" Before the actress, crowded by well-wishers, could make her way to the microphone in New York, her friend Ethel Barrymore accepted on her behalf on the West Coast. Praising her "radiant performance," Miss Barrymore commented, "I don't know exactly what she wants me to say, but I think it's safe to say that she's very happy, and very grateful." The film itself lost to *All About Eve*. A few days later, a hometown columnist wrote, "In all the excitement over Judy Holliday's Academy Award, everybody seems to have forgotten that it was Pittsburgher S. Sylvan Simon, producer of *Born Yesterday*, who held out for her to play the role from the very start when practically every other actress in Hollywood was either being tested or mentioned for it."[215]

In the wake of the Oscar excitement, however, it was full steam ahead on another project that showed promise of being equally prestigious and successful, if not more so. Simon was set to produce the film adaptation of *From Here to Eternity*, the controversial bestseller by James Jones. Columbia acquired the film rights to Jones' novel on March 16, 1951, only a few weeks after the book was published. One source noted in early April, "Jones ... returned to Fort Myers Beach last week from New York where he signed with Columbia Pictures for the movie rights to the novel...."[216]

As with *Born Yesterday*, Columbia executives had taken the risk of acquiring a property that might present considerable difficulties in adapting to films. Producer Simon took on the task of making a compelling film while adhering to movie censorship rules. Louella O. Parsons (April 3, 1951) wrote, "Rumors that the army is clamping down on Columbia and refusing to co-operate in filming ... are not true." She noted that the film adaptation of *From Here to Eternity* "will be without all its profanity and some of the troubles of the enlisted men when it reaches the screen. That's the outline S. Sylvan Simon gave the Department of Defense in Washington."

Though initial reports indicated that Jones had no intention of coming to California and working on the script, Cohn assigned the novelist to work with Simon and story editor Eve Ettinger "to write a treatment that would avoid problems of language and situation that might arouse the hostility of the Breen Office."[217] Jones traveled to the West Coast, and stayed with the Simons during his visit. Susan Granger remembered their houseguest as "very gruff.... He didn't talk a great deal." Jones and Simon met in the latter's home projection room, a separate building known in the family as the "Simon Bijou." Susan remembered peeking through its windows when Jones and Simon were meeting.

Though his novel would not ordinarily be considered fit reading material for a 12-year-old, Jones noticed that his collaborator's young daughter had taken an interest in what he and her dad were doing. He offered to let her read the story, promising, "I'll cross out the profanity." However, he soon realized this was a lost cause. Commemorating their collaboration, Simon gave the novelist a copy of his book *Let's Make Movies*, which he inscribed, "Sat. May 12, 1951. To Jimmy Jones, A hard-headed writer, with a conscience, composed of integrity, self-consciousness and respect. Best regards, S. Sylvan Simon."

To direct *From Here to Eternity* would be a plum assignment for the director lucky enough to be chosen. Vincent Sherman, whose films included two with Bette Davis (*Mr. Skeffington* and *Old Acquaintance*), had seen the possibilities of Jones' book, and tried to take an option on it, but was stymied when Columbia acquired it. He recalled phoning Simon to express his interest in helming the film, but was told, "I'm hoping to do it myself, Vince. I'm tired of being an executive and want to get back to the set."[218]

In the short time he worked on *Eternity*, Simon also brainstormed an idea that wouldn't come to fruition until after his timely death. Stephen Simon wrote, "In 1951, my Dad, who had been a huge Sinatra fan, had called Frank to his office at Columbia to tell him ... that there was a character in the film named Maggio that would be perfect for Sinatra and promised [him] the part."[219] Susan Granger concurred: "He wanted Sinatra to play Maggio," and "my father threatened to quit" when Harry Cohn nixed the idea.

Though it was not until after Simon's death that Sinatra won the role, a decision usually attributed to the intervention of Ava Gardner, the actor-singer would be kind in later years to both kids, repaying a debt he felt he still owed. "Your father died before I could properly thank him," he told Susan. To her brother, he proclaimed, "That part changed everything for me, Stephen. After Maggio, people took me seriously as an actor. Without your dad, that might have never happened."[220]

While his work environment was demanding, Simon's personal life had also developed complications. "They did not have the happiest marriage," Susan acknowledged of her parents' life by the early 1950s. She didn't recall fights, per se—"My father never raised his voice"—but described her mother as "very narcissistic ... always a hysterical personality." At some point, according to Stephen Simon, his father sought out other companionship; he "kept an apartment in another part of town for assignations with a series of girlfriends."[221]

Still, despite the pressures Simon faced, no one could have predicted the denouement that took place on May 17, 1951, when he died at his home, only 41 years old. As Hedda Hopper told it (May 21, 1951), Simon "was playing with his 12-year-old daughter Susan before putting her into bed when he was seized with a heart attack. He died before his doctor reached the house." *Variety* (May 23, 1951) noted, "Death was unexpected, as he had worked that day at the Columbia studio and was apparently in good health."

Susan Granger's first-hand account differed in some aspects from the published versions. Still suffering from migraines, Simon had been receiving regular injections of a medication from a male nurse who visited the house. Eventually, the nurse left a supply of needles, so that his patient could inject himself as needed. As his daughter recalled, she was in her bedroom before school that morning, talking to her father through the adjoining bathroom door as he prepared to go to work. Unexpectedly, she heard him fall with a thud, and a frightening silence followed. The family cook, Andrew, entered the bathroom from the other side, a connecting door to the master bedroom. He had injected himself incorrectly, causing his heart to stop.

Absent from the house that day, according to Stephen Simon, was his mother, who had unwittingly chosen the wrong time to make a stand about his "growing addiction to work and also to the painkillers he was taking."[222] Harriet had left him the night before, having dinner with their friends the Starks before checking herself into a nearby hotel. "She carried a lot of guilt around about that," Stephen noted.[223]

Simon's death certificate was signed by Dr. Louis A. Motchan, whose practice was in Beverly Hills. The physician stated that he had been Simon's doctor since November 1949, and had seen him as recently as the previous day. Dr. Motchan wrote that his death was due to a pulmonary edema, with an antecedent cause being myocardial infarction. The *Los Angeles Times* (May 19, 1951) reported that Simon's funeral would take place at Temple Israel. His mother Eva and her sister, Mrs. David Berman, flew in from Pittsburgh to attend the service.

Harriet Simon flatly stated that his strenuous job, and the chaotic work environment fostered by Harry Cohn, bore the lion's share of responsibility for his death at the age of 41. "Harry was an evil man," she said.[224] Her friend Lee Annenberg, Cohn's niece, according to author Christopher Ogden, "had warned Harriet's husband, Sylvan, not to work for Harry, that her uncle would destroy him. But Harry had been a mentor to Sylvan, whose own father died when he was thirteen, and had promised the director that he would one day run Columbia."[225]

Susan Granger acknowledged that her father was indeed under stress—there was "so much anger and politics at the studio." However, in hindsight she concluded that to lay the tragedy entirely at Cohn's feet was an oversimplification. While Simon's migraines had indeed worsened during his time as a Columbia executive, they were not entirely new; he had suffered from them for some years. When she returned to school, the headmistress at Susan's school had her classmates write condolence notes to her. Her father's friend Ray Stark, she said, "took me on a long drive to the beach," trying to console the bereft girl.

Back East, too, Simon was grieved by friends and colleagues. In the *Jewish Criterion* (May 25, 1951), columnist Milton K. Susman wrote, "Plenty of water will flow under the bridge before this wanderer realizes that Sylvan Simon's chair on the Hollywood film lot is eternally empty ... it's the hurt that stems from the loss of a boy who died a boy, even though he was ... a man."

Stephen Simon was not yet five years old at the time of his father's death. Many years later, he recalled his mother's reaction: "She was in such shock that she wouldn't tell me that he was dead."[226] Instead, the little boy was given to understand that his father was away on a long business trip. He recalled that his older sister urged their mother to be honest with him. But it was Susan, finally, who sat the little boy down in their backyard, near the swimming pool, and told him the truth.

His father's death, and the explanations he was given, would have a long-term impact on Stephen, who went into young adulthood imbued with the notion that hard work could be life-threatening. In the months after his father's death, however, young Stephen felt his presence. "I had the sense that there was a 'man' in my bedroom wall," he later wrote. "It wasn't until much later that I came to realize that this presence was actually my father—checking in on me and making sure I was okay."[227]

When Cohn himself passed away several years later, Simon's dear friend Red Skelton expressed the feelings of many when he noted the large turnout at the memorial service, and commented, "It proves what Harry always said: 'Give the public what they want and they'll come out for it.'" Harriet Simon seconded the sentiment, adding that "the only sad thing about Cohn's death was that it had been painless."[228]

Simon's death had an impact on the career of his friend, Lucille Ball, and her contract with Columbia. Her biggest champion at the studio could no longer speak up on her behalf. Near the end of her tenure there, Harry Cohn decided that he longer valued her services. He concocted a scheme to get out of making the last film for which she was contracted, thereby saving the money she was to earn for that assignment.

The devious Cohn sent Lucy the script for a low-budget Arabian Nights drama, to be produced by Sam Katzman, known for his hastily-made "Jungle Jim" adventures. Horrified, she turned to her longtime friend Edward Sedgwick, who advised her, "Cohn handed you a lease breaker. He expects you to turn it down; then he's automatically free of paying you eighty-five thousand dollars. Tell him you'll do the picture. It'll break Katzman. His whole budget is less than your salary."[229] Husband Desi Arnaz echoed the advice. Lucy, already pregnant with daughter Lucie, made *The*

Magic Carpet in a few days, banked the check, and plunged wholeheartedly into television, gambling her career prospects on a weekly half-hour series. *I Love Lucy* would make her a bigger star than she'd ever been in films, and within a few years, Cohn's studio would be rereleasing her Columbia movies, cashing on its massive popularity. When she did return to movies in 1954, with *The Long, Long Trailer*, she and Desi signed with MGM.

Being widowed at the age of 35, with two children, left Harriet Simon not only bereft, but in straitened circumstances. Although her late husband's studio salary was said by various sources to be either $2,000 or $3,000 a week, her son Stephen later said, "I don't think Dad left her a lot of money."[230] Her closest friends, among them Mrs. Ray Stark, decided that what Harriet needed was to meet an eligible man who could support her and her children. Harriet's pal introduced the young widow to Armand Deutsch, heir to the Sears-Roebuck fortune. Deutsch had come to Hollywood as an apprentice to Dore Schary, and became an MGM producer in the early 1950s, where he oversaw films such as *Green Fire* (1954) and *Carbine Williams* (1952). Columnist Sheilah Graham (August 22, 1950) crassly pegged Deutsch as quite a catch—"Armand has millions. His mother is a Rosenwald, of Sears, Roebuck." However, she also noted that he was "a very charming guy."

Deutsch had been divorced the previous year from Broadway actress Benay

Venuta, with whom he had two daughters. Though Miss Venuta cited Deutsch with mental cruelty when she filed for divorce in the summer of 1950, columnist Harrison Carroll (August 9, 1950) later called their split "one of Hollywood's friendliest split-ups." During 1950 and the first half of 1951 Deutsch was involved with actress Audrey Totter. By early 1951, various columnists reported that the pair had set wedding plans for the summer. Ardie, as friends knew him, was also an occasional escort of young MGM contract player Nancy Davis, before her 1952 marriage to Ronald Reagan. The Reagans would figure largely into both his and Harriet's futures.

Portrait of Harriet Berk Simon, Sylvan's wife from 1935 until his death in 1951 (Simon Family Collection).

After meeting Harriet at the Starks' home, Deutsch

sent her flowers the next day, and a courtship soon began. Several months later, the *Los Angeles Times* (December 9, 1951) reported that Simon's widow and her new beau had taken out a marriage license. They were married on December 8, 1951, at the Beverly Hills home of her parents, the Berks. Afterwards, Harriet and the kids moved into her new husband's house on Bedford Drive in Beverly Hills, and the Simon family home on Sunset Boulevard went up for sale. A few months later, its contents were auctioned off, the sale advertised in the pages of the *Los Angeles Times* (April 20, 1952).

After Simon's death, work continued at Columbia Pictures on some of the projects he had been assigned, notably *From Here to Eternity*, which became the responsibility of producer Buddy Adler. Released in the summer of 1953, *Eternity* quickly became both a commercial and critical success, winning multiple Academy Awards including Best Picture. His longtime supporter Harold V. Cohen wrote, "What a pity Pittsburgh boy S. Sylvan Simon couldn't have lived to share in the glory of an Oscar for *From Here to Eternity*. For it was Simon ... who first saw the screen possibilities in the James Jones novel and practically blackjacked his studio into buying the movie rights."[231] Showing more class than his reputation would suggest, Cohn concurred, saying in an interview, "The man who is really the unsung hero of that film project is now deceased. It was S. Sylvan Simon who told me the story of the James Jones novel. His recital of it went on all night long and we consummated the deal with Jones early in the morning."[232]

As adults, both of Sylvan Simon's children followed in his footsteps, choosing careers in the motion picture industry. Stephen became a film producer, working on projects that included *All the Right Moves* (1983), an early lead role for Tom Cruise, and *What Dreams May Come* (1998). His sister Susan, developing her writing skills as her stepfather had suggested, established herself as a syndicated newspaper movie reviewer.

Stephen crossed paths with Red Skelton in 1968, when he was 22 years old. As a young adult, Stephen so resembled his dad that the comedian, who hadn't seen him in many years, nonetheless recognized him instantly, proclaiming, "You're Sylvan's son." Skelton said, "He was such a warm, sweet, funny man," assuring Stephen, "He really loved you kids."[233] Red told Stephen "how much he loved Dad, how much he depended on him to direct his films and, most importantly, how much he loved him as a man ... how much he loved people, how easily he laughed, and how much he loved both my sister and me."[234]

Having survived her only child for more than 20 years, Simon's mother Eva died in Pittsburgh on September 23, 1972. For much of her life, she had continued to honor the memory of her long-dead husband David, making donations to church and charitable causes in his honor. After 1951, she began doing so for her son as well. Still, the passage of years hadn't reined in her flamboyant personality. Said granddaughter Susan, "After Gorey died–Nana–as I called her—was in her 60s/70s—I forget how old—went to Paris often to 'buy.' I don't know where she stayed or what she did on these trips but, after she died, I found a beautifully wrapped package in her closet and the card said, 'For Pierre.' As it turned out, she had a lover named Pierre in Paris—and I sent the package to him."

Eva was survived by her brother, Sid Marke, her grandchildren Susan and Stephen, nieces and nephews. The family having by then sold out its interest in the Penn

Hat and Gown Shop, she was described in her *Pittsburgh Press* obituary (September 25, 1972) as its "former owner." She was buried at the Tree of Life cemetery, with a gravestone inscription describing her as "Wife & Mother."

Simon's widow Harriet entered the second chapter of her life with her marriage to Armand Deutsch (known to his friends as "Ardie"). The wealthy couple became patrons of the arts, and he served for a number of years on the board of the Los Angeles Music Center. Mr. and Mrs. Deutsch became friendly with Ronald and Nancy Reagan, and despite differing political views were supportive of his entry into politics in the 1960s. Later, when Reagan was elected president, he appointed Deutsch to the Presidential Task Force on the Arts and Humanities.

Publisher Bennett Cerf, in his syndicated newspaper column (September 11, 1965), once quoted Harriet as saying, "Look at this way: when a wife charges expensive jewelry, furs, and gowns, she is merely displaying confidence in her husband." Author Bob Colacello snidely described the latter-day Harriet as "a clotheshorse of the first rank," adding, "Perhaps more than any other woman in the Group, she fit the press image of a flighty socialite largely concerned with gowns, parties, and social status." Like Nancy, Harriet was not to the manor born, but aspired to greater things, and blossomed under the purview of social mentors like heiress Anita Keiler May. "She kind of adopted four gals," Harriet said years later. "Anne Douglas, Edie Wasserman, Nancy Reagan, and me. We were her special girls."[235]

Syndicated columnist Mike Royko (January 16, 1980) gleefully lampooned Harriet and her circle of affluent friends, who had described to the fashion-focused newspaper *Women's Wear Daily* their techniques for conserving energy and running their households economically. Mrs. Deutsch confessed to having "a marvelous chef who guides us along those lines," to which Royko retorted, "That's something for the rest of us to think about. When hiring chefs, we should think beyond the texture of his salmon mousse and ask whether he knows how to roast a quail with solar energy."

The Deutsches' marriage lasted until his death on August 13, 2005. Only a few weeks after being widowed for the second time, Harriet Berk Simon Deutsch passed away on September 7, 2005, at the Santa Monica Health Care Center, her death attributed to "complications from a stroke."

Had Sylvan Simon's life not been cut so tragically short, he almost certainly would have added to what was already an impressive list of accomplishments. Whether he would have ascended to the top post at Columbia Pictures is uncertain; Harry Cohn managed to hang onto his job until his sudden death of a heart attack in February 1958 at the age of 66. But he surely would have continued to latch onto opportunities to entertain audiences.

His daughter Susan Granger believes that he might have followed the example of his best-known comedy players, who found even greater demand for their abilities in the television industry. She says, "He would have gone where the laughter was."

PART II

Filmography

Hollywood Screen Test (1937)

Kay Hughes (*Herself*), Cesar Romero (*Himself*), Charles Brokaw (*Director*), Billy Wayne (*Bill*), Robert Dalton, Robert Spencer, Grace Goodall, Rita Gould, Lynn Gilbert

Director: S. Sylvan Simon. *Producer*: Charles E. Ford. *Screenplay*: Lionel Margolies. *Photography*: Stanley Cortez.

Universal; released August 1937. 20 minutes.

Simon's first released film was this two-reeler showing the test a Hollywood newcomer, singer-actress Kay Hughes (1914–1998), undergoes in hopes of winning a studio contract. Miss Hughes is seen rehearsing a scene, working with hair, makeup, and wardrobe professionals, and then shooting the test alongside actor Cesar Romero. Her completed test is shown in the studio projection room, and she is signed as a contract player.

A studio advertisement for the short exclaimed, "She's going into the movies! Go with her! Watch her be prepared for the screen test! Listen to the coaching of the dramatic teacher! See what happens when the make-up man applies his art!" Even more to the point, another ad mat promised, "It shows how YOU get into the movies!"

Some sources report that Simon played himself in the short. However, an item in *Boxoffice* (May 29, 1937), noting a new Screen Actors Guild ruling against non-union actors appearing onscreen stated, "Sylvan Simon, Universal test director, was the first to feel the effects of the ban when ... he was forced to withdraw [from *Hollywood Screen Test*] in favor of a Guild actor, Charles Brokaw."

Reviews: "Audiences will get a kick out of this trip behind the scenes in a movie studio to see the complicated process which a movie test involves from the time a prospect is caught by a talent scout at a local theater. Kay Hughes, a singer with a hot vocal delivery, is the gal who gets the screen test. The whole business is well staged." *Film Daily*, July 22, 1937

"By far the best treatment of the subject to be offered. Here, in an informal and lightly technical manner, the inner workings of the quest for new talent are revealed.... It is the stuff which audiences of all kinds will receive with approval and enjoyment." *Motion Picture Daily*, July 16, 1937

A Girl with Ideas (1937)

Wendy Barrie (*Mary Morton*), Walter Pidgeon (*Thomas Potter "Mickey" McGuire*), Kent Taylor (*Frank Barnes*), Dorothea Kent (*Isabelle Foster*), George Barbier (*John F. Morton*), Ted Osborne (*Pete Dailey*), Henry Hunter (*William Duncan*), Samuel S. Hinds (*Rodding Carter*), George Humbert (*Toni*), Horace MacMahon [McMahon] (*Al*), Ed Gargan (*Eddie*), Norman Willis (*Hanson*), William Lundigan (*Herman*), Kathleen Nelson (*Stenographer*), Frances Robinson (*Maggie*)

A Girl with Ideas: Mary Morton (Wendy Barrie) doesn't share the enthusiasm of Mickey McGuire (Walter Pidgeon) for the headline story in the *Morning Dispatch*.

Director: S. Sylvan Simon. *Associate Producer*: Edmund Grainger. *Screenplay*: Bruce Manning, Robert Shannon. *Story*: William Rankin. *Director of Photography*: Milton Krasner. *Art Director*: Jack Otterson. *Associate*: John Ewing. *Film Editor*: Philip Cahn. *Musical Director*: Charles Previn. *Sound*: Charles Carroll, Edwin Wetzel. [*Assistant Directors*: Vernon Keaye, Seward Webb. *Script Clerk*: Dorothy Wright.]

Universal; released November 1937. 70 minutes.

When Mickey McGuire's newspaper, the *Morning Dispatch*, loses a libel lawsuit to socialite Mary Morton, he informs her that, in lieu of the $750,000 judgment, which he cannot pay, he is turning over control of the corporation to her. Mickey and his managing editor, Frank Barnes, argue over who is to blame for the inaccurate stories that prompted the legal action, causing a rift between the two men.

Annoyed when her family smirks at the idea of her running a newspaper, Mary decides to prove them wrong. She shows up at the editorial office ready to take charge. Mickey urges Frank to stay on in Mary's employ, and produce "the worst newspaper on Earth," figuring they'll then be able to reacquire it for a bargain price. To Frank's surprise, Mary and her well-connected friends are full of inside information about big business mergers and high society gossip, making the first issue she produces quite informative.

Undaunted, Mickey tries another tack to undermine her. Putting himself deeper into debt, he has an envelope full of cash delivered to key staff members at home, telling them the new boss is giving them a week's paid vacation. Rising to the challenge, Frank puts out a "man in the street" issue, written entirely by nonprofessionals.

Without missing a beat in their efforts to outsmart each other, Mickey and Frank are both taken with Mary, whom the latter deems "a swell girl." Upping the stakes, Mickey concocts his most outrageous scheme yet, enlisting the help of his ex-girlfriend Isabelle Foster to stage a phony kidnapping of Mary's father. He doesn't anticipate that J.F. Foster is perfectly delighted to be AWOL for a few days, and the plan soon spins out of Mickey's control.

In its early stages, *A Girl with Ideas* was known as "Mightier than the Sword." That title appeared throughout Simon's copy of the script, marked August 3, 1937, with revisions dated August 12. Some of the changes were in response to an August 7, 1937, letter from Joseph I. Breen, which advised Universal executives that the script "meets the basic requirements of the Production Code," but suggested several minor alterations. The word "Cripes" was deemed unacceptable, and Breen raised a red flag considering the use of alcohol: "While some of the drinking called for in these scenes seems legitimate [*sic*] from a story standpoint, we must urge you to tone it down *as much as possible*" (emphasis in original letter).

Breen also pointed out that the name "Appennelli" for a lawbreaking character, plus "the comedy characterization of Tony will surely be considered objectionable by the Italian censors." (Mr. Appennelli was thus rechristened Slocum.) At the last minute, someone (perhaps Simon himself) decided that the damages awarded to the libeled Mary Morton were inadequate; alongside the original amount of $350,000 is a handwritten note, "Should be $750,000."

S. Sylvan Simon's feature film debut is a sprightly, energetic comedy that never lets up its pace. His flair for physical comedy gets a workout in the film's climax, when Horace McMahon and Edward Gargan, as Isabelle's dopey brothers, prove to be no match for Mary's dad, who's enjoying himself thoroughly putting them through their paces as would-be kidnappers. Trade publications noticed his work; *Hollywood Spectator* (December 4, 1937) deemed him "a new director who will bear watching." Production began on August 16, 1937, and concluded on September 4.

Wendy Barrie (1912–1978) has an air of dignity and culture that fits the role of a wealthy socialite, but she's also charming as the woman who, when the occasion calls for it, can step behind a bar in a low-class dive and serve up a few drinks. Miss Barrie, born in Hong Kong to English parents, acted in British films and theater before relocating to the United States in 1935. She was earmarked to earn $2200 per week for the role, with the expectation of three weeks on the payroll.

Walter Pidgeon (1897–1984) and Kent Taylor (1907–1987) handle the male leads more than capably. Taylor gets some snappy lines (initially deriding Mary as "a wacky dame who thinks a two-column head is something Mother Nature slapped on the Siamese twins"), but he's also believable as a man firmly attached to his chosen profession. "When printer's ink gets into your blood," he tells Mary, "you're a lost soul." Studio paperwork indicated that Taylor would be paid $2000 per week, while Pidgeon was to get $1750.

Seen only briefly in the film's first half hour, Dorothea Kent (1916–1990) figures prominently in its second half, delightful as the none-too-bright Isabelle. With a voice box that seems to have been injected with a slight dose of helium, a frequently befuddled look on her face, and a curvy figure, she makes a good foil for Barrie's Mary

Morton. The role was evidently tailor-made for her, as the script describes Isabelle as "a Dorothea Kent type." Likewise, the minor character of assistant editor Pete Dailey specifies "a Ned Sparks type," but that role went to another actor, Ted Osborne. A studio document listing cast expenses showed that Hobart Cavanaugh would play the role, but this was crossed out, and Osborne's name substituted, with a handwritten note, "Saving."

An interoffice memo from Jack Lawton to production manager Martin Murphy concerned the possibility of using the facilities of a local newspaper, the *Hollywood Citizen-News*, to give the film some authentic atmosphere. Lawton reported, "To photograph press room with presses in operation, the time to start from arrival to departure of company, is $25.00 per hour. For main title setting the type, casting same, and placing on the press, the price is $20.00 ... Mr. Koeplinger advises that the press usually turns out between 35,000 and 50,000 newspapers per hour. However, it can be slowed down so that it will turn out approximately 100 to 200 a minute."

For whatever efforts made to give it verisimilitude, author Larry Langman complained, "The farfetched world of journalism depicted in this film might make reporters and editors cringe."[1] Simon later joked, "I'd never been in a newspaper office in my life, so consequently I was able to give a very authentic picture of a newspaper office in the film."[2] He had, however, written a one-act play with a journalistic theme, "The Scoop Reporter," which appeared in his anthology *Thrillers*, published the same year that *A Girl with Ideas* was filmed.

Shortly after the film wrapped, the *Los Angeles Times*' Edwin Schallert (September 3, 1937) reported that studio bosses liked the chemistry between Miss Barrie and Kent Taylor well enough to make plans for "their second adventure as romantic opposites," which became Simon's next film, *Prescription for Romance*.

Reviews: "Bright and original comedy, briskly directed and acted, *A Girl with Ideas* is a better than average B film.... Contains plenty of laughs legitimately obtained from amusing situations.... S. Sylvan Simon has directed tersely and humorously without straining for any of his points." *Variety*, November 3, 1937

"It may be screwy, wild and a thing that could hardly happen, but it furnishes a lot of laughs and makes very enjoyable program fare.... S. Sylvan Simon's direction injects a happy-go-lucky air to the piece, the pace set is fast and furious, with the players coming through in fine style." *Film Daily*, November 5, 1937

Prescription for Romance (1937)

Wendy Barrie (*Valerie Wilson*), Kent Taylor (*Steve Macy*), Frank Jenks (*Smitty*), Mischa Auer (*Count Sandor*), Gregory Gaye (*Dr. Paul Azarny*), Dorothea Kent (*Lola Carroll*), Henry Hunter (*Kenneth Barton*), Samuel S. Hinds (*Maj. Goddard*), Frank Reicher (*Jozsef*), Ted Osborne (*Corney*), Torben Meyer (*Desk Clerk*), Hugh Sheridan (*Feodor*), Robert Fischer (*Veterinarian*), Constance Moore (*Girl*), Dorothy Granger (*Cashier*), Greta Meyer (*Marie*), Christian Rub (*Train Conductor*), Otto Fries, Bert Roach (*Police Sergeants*), William Lundigan (*Officer*), Paul Weigel (*Peasant*), Dick

Wessel (*Sailor*), Paul Newlan (*Bearded Hungarian*), William Gould (*Doorman*), Elsa Janssen (*Elsa*), George Cleveland, Sidney D'Albrook, Michael Mark (*Taxi Drivers*)

Director: S. Sylvan Simon. *Associate Producer*: Edmund Grainger. *Screenplay*: James Mulhauser, Robert T. Shannon, Albert R. Perkins. *Original Story*: John Reinhardt, Robert Neville. *Director of Photography*: Milton Krasner. *Art Director*: Jack Otterson. *Associate*: Charles H. Clarke. *Musical Director*: Charles Previn. *Film Editor*: Paul Landres. *Sound Recording*: William Hedgcock, Edwin Wetzel.

Universal; released December 1937. 70 minutes.

Private detective Steve Macy of the Bankers' Protective Association is on the trail of embezzler Kenneth Barton, who fled the country with $500,000, leaving behind his gold-digging companion Lola Carroll. Following Barton to Budapest, Hungary, Steve gets himself put in the local jail using the embezzler's name, hoping this will smoke out one or more of the fugitive's lady friends. Dr. Valerie Wilson, an American practicing medicine in Budapest, shows up at the jail after reading of Barton's arrest in the local newspaper. Also hearing of the arrest is a local living-by-his-wits type who calls himself "Count Sandov," though one skeptic remarks, "Last week he was a duke."

Valerie informs the police that the man they're holding is not Barton, and Steve is released. He takes the beautiful doctor out to dinner, and later follows her to her apartment. When the real Kenneth Barton shows up there, he insists he is innocent of the crime with which he's been charged. Valerie hides him from Steve, and later offers him the use of a remote cabin that belongs to her co-worker, Dr. Paul Azarny. When Lola arrives in Budapest in search of Kenneth, Sandov, eyeing her jewelry, cultivates her acquaintance, promising to help her find her missing beau. Having fallen for Valerie, Steve is determined not only to find Barton, but make certain that she is not incriminated as an accessory. A mad chase ensues, with Steve, Valerie, Sandov, and newspaper reporter Smitty all hurrying to reach the cabin that is serving as Kenneth's hideout.

Prescription for Romance, according to studio records, had originally been earmarked as an "A" film, only later being handed down to producer Edward Grainger to make on a "B" budget. Sylvan Simon's copy of the script, dated September 13, 1937, is marked "Final Revised." A few blue pages, dated September 22, have been inserted. Production was scheduled to begin on September 20, 1937. In a memo dated the previous Friday, studio production manager Martin F. Murphy noted, "Last week we had the budget figured at approximately $145,000 but this amount only covered the use of Robert Wilcox as leading man at a salary of $200.00 per week. Kent Taylor who fits the role much better—and whom we would be paying salary to anyway—has been cast for the part, increasing our budget to $151,840."

Simon and his company strained to finish the film in the 18 days allotted. On October 9, 1937, Murphy reported, "During the past week the company has put in exceptionally long hours, working practically day and night with not much more than twelve hours off between calls. Most of the work was exteriors and difficult night shots and expensive [on] account [of] the number of people necessary to operate what was being put before the camera." A week later, principal photography was complete, and, as Murphy noted, "A first, rough cut was quickly made in order to take advantage of the remaining time left on Miss Barrie's contract in case retakes or additional scenes were necessary." Retakes costing some $3,000 were subsequently approved and made.

Leading players (left to right) Mischa Auer, Kent Taylor, and Wendy Barrie are spotlighted in this *Prescription for Romance* lobby card.

Stars Wendy Barrie and Kent Taylor again head the cast for Simon's second feature film. But it was comic actor Mischa Auer, earning $1,000 per week to play "Count" Sandor, who attracted most of the positive notice from reviewers with his slapstick antics as an ineffectual detective. The screenwriters apparently wrote the role of Sandor to order for Auer; his name appears in a note accompanying the character's first appearance. For some other key characters, they suggested various actors who might fit the roles, or at least serve as examples—Kenneth Barton is described as a "Warren William type," while Lola is said to be "a Binnie Barnes type." They didn't have a specific performer in mind for the role of Sandor's faithful canine companion Mitzi, but wrote that she should be "an attractive but sly-looking dog."

Film Daily (September 30, 1937) reported that Universal contract player William Lundigan, who'd played a featured role in *A Girl with Ideas*, was initially cast as Dr. Paul Azarny, Steve's rival for Valerie's affection. However, on the first shooting day he was found to photograph too young for the role. "Even a hurried makeup with whiskers added no age, so Gregory Gaye was substituted in the role." Lundigan was demoted to a smaller, unbilled role. He would later become an MGM contract player, where he appeared in Simon's films *The Bugle Sounds* and *Salute to the Marines*.

Prescription for Romance frequently filled the lower half of a double bill with major films such as *Western Union* or *Wells Fargo*.

Reviews: "Whenever Mischa Auer is on the screen, this comedy drama is very entertaining.... Sylvan Simon, the director, did an excellent job in getting as much as he did from such ordinary matter as he had to work with.... The fact that the affair does make pleasing diversion can be attributed to the efforts of the players and the director." *Film Daily*, December 21, 1937

"Mild program fare. If it weren't for Mischa Auer's clowning, it would be somewhat boresome, for the action is not particularly exciting. It is difficult for one to take the far-fetched plot seriously.... Wendy Barrie and Kent Taylor make a pleasant romantic team." *Harrison's Reports*, December 18, 1937

The Crime of Doctor Hallet (1938)

Ralph Bellamy (*Dr. Paul Hallet*), Josephine Hutchinson (*Dr. Mary Reynolds*), William Gargan (*Jack Murray*), Barbara Read (*Claire Saunders*), John King (*Dr. Phillip Saunders*), Charles Stevens (*Talamu*), Honorable Wu (*Molugi*), Nella Walker (*Mrs. Carpenter*), Eleanor Hansen (*Anna*), Constance Moore (*Susan*)

Director: S. Sylvan Simon. *Associate Producer*: Edmund Grainger. *Screenplay*: Lester Cole, Brown Holmes. *Story*: Lester Cole. *Director of Photography*: Milton Krasner. *Art Director*: Jack Otterson. *Associate*: Charles H. Clarke. *Dialogue Director*: Philip Cahn. Musical *Director*: Charles Previn. *Sound*: Robert Pritchard, Edwin Wetzel.

Universal; released March 1938. 67 minutes.

In the jungles of Sumatra, researcher Dr. Paul Hallet and his assistant, Jack Murray, have been seeking a cure for a deadly disease, red fever, for the past three years. The death of their colleague, Dr. Adams, who infected himself with the virus in order to test a serum, leaves them feeling discouraged and defeated.

The Tropical Disease Foundation, which is financing Dr. Hallet's work, sends him a replacement for Dr. Adams, but he's not pleased to see that the new man is a young, relatively inexperienced doctor from New York. Dr. Phillip Saunders is enthusiastic about the chance to make life-saving discoveries, but his wife Claire, who stays behind in the city, resents being left on her own. Upon arrival in Sumatra, Saunders is frustrated that Hallet does not respect his abilities, and confines him to menial tasks around the laboratory. On his own initiative, Saunders conducts surreptitious tests of an alternate type of medication.

When he develops a serum that seems to have potential, Dr. Hallet intends to test it on himself, but Saunders, wanting to contribute something of value to the project, makes himself the guinea pig. Just as a letter from the Foundation advises that research monies are drying up, Saunders continues to get sicker, and dies. On his deathbed, he implores Dr. Hallet to review the notes he took of his own hypothesis.

Hallet realizes that, while his own serum doesn't work, Saunders' does. Finding $4,000 in travelers' checks among Saunders' effects, Hallet and Jack stay on to continue their work, hoping to use their late colleague's money to validate his hypothesis and earn him the credit he deserves. To keep the outside world at bay, Hallet spreads word of his own death, and claims that Saunders will continue the project. Sending

Ralph Bellamy looks askance at co-star John King in *The Crime of Doctor Hallet*.

for a trained field worker, Hallet is none too pleased by the arrival of Dr. Mary Reynolds, thinking the job unsuitable for a woman doctor.

Working together, Hallet and Dr. Reynolds grow closer, though she still believes him to be Dr. Saunders. But when Mrs. Saunders gets fed up with awaiting her husband's return, and arrives in Sumatra by plane, she finds Hallet posing as her husband and spending his money, and announces that she will see him prosecuted for forgery. Before she can board the plane for her return, Mrs. Saunders falls ill with red fever, and Hallet, with Dr. Reynolds' help, faces the ultimate test of their fight against disease.

Ralph Bellamy (1904–1991) delivers an effective performance as the title character, whose good motives and character are blunted by his lack of warmth and kindness; as Dr. Hallet himself says late in the film, "When it comes to dealing with human beings, I've certainly bungled things." In Bellamy's hands, the character wins audience approval and sympathy despite his flaws.

William Gargan (1905–1979) provides most of the film's lighter moments as Hallet's assistant, a Brooklyn-born chemist with a wryly cynical outlook. Gargan's Jack tells a native worker that a cooler is the most important piece of equipment in the laboratory; we soon realize that's because he keeps his beer there. At one bleak point, Gargan's Jack says, "How did I come to get into this? Must've been a band playing something very inspiring." Hallet says, dryly, "Or else you were anxious to get out of Brooklyn."

Young leading man John King (1909–1987) shows promise as idealistic Dr. Saunders, who after practicing medicine in New York City is eager to do something more than "advising debs to get more sleep, sending hard-drinking captains of industry to hot springs, [or] holding hands with neurotic wives." According to studio publicists, King had difficulty with his death scene, having never previously played one: "Director S. Sylvan Simon shot the scene 15 times before he was satisfied, since dying is one of the hardest tricks of cinema technique, even to experts."[3] In the 1940s, King enjoyed some success as the star of a series of low-budget Westerns at Monogram, but his career petered out after World War II. Josephine Hutchinson (1903–1998), who's better remembered for her role in *Son of Frankenstein* (1939) a year later, is fine as Dr. Mary Reynolds, though the role demands little of her.

While this was a modestly budgeted film, director Simon gives it his best, and makes more of it than another hurried director might have. He takes full advantage of a tight script, and plays the dramatic scenes for their full worth without exaggerating them. He succeeds in giving the soundstage jungle an air of mystery and intrigue. Simon's comic touch is evident in the scenes with Junior, a baby monkey. Junior concludes the film by pulling down a blind that reads, "The End," a piece of business that does not appear in Cole and Holmes' script.

Simon's copy of the screenplay, dated December 28, 1937, overall shows relatively few changes, and the film tracks it closely. However, several pages of carbon copies on yellow paper, undated, are inserted at the end, outlining the finale as it appears in the finished film. These pages, which may have been taken from an earlier draft, provide a more complete and satisfying resolution to the story than the ending stipulated in the main body of the script. In the yellow pages, the character of Dr. Mary Reynolds is referred to as "Irina."

Production began on Monday, January 3, 1938, with an estimated budget of $130,000. Almost from the beginning the film was slightly behind schedule. Two weeks in, studio production manager Martin Murphy reported (January 15, 1938) of the lost time, "Producer Grainger and Simon are quite aware of this and expect to make up the time during the next and last week of shooting." However, there were more delays the following week, which were, according to Murphy's January 22 update, "partially due to the difference in opinions of Barbara Read playing the role of 'Claire.'" Filming concluded on Monday, January 24, one day over schedule. After studio executives approved the shooting of some extra scenes, the four principal players worked additional days, ultimately bringing the film's cost to $138,000.

Art director Jack Otterson built the Sumatran jungle on a Universal soundstage, with a combination of real and artificial flora and fauna. As a result, according to one set visitor, "It is so warm and damp that the actors hardly need the mixture of witch hazel and glycerine, which is sprayed regularly upon their brows to make tropical perspiration." A medical advisor was employed so that the cast could "learn how to pronounce the multi-syllable words which physicians habitually use, and how to handle the shiny implements which are the equipment of germ hunters."[4]

The *Motion Picture Herald*'s Vance King (March 12, 1938) reported that audiences at the preview screening "expressed agreeable surprise at the quality of the picture."

Reviews: "Universal's *The Crime of Dr. Hallet* is not ordinary entertainment. With proper showmanship, this story ... has possibilities of climbing notches above the expected returns ... the story, direction and editing, plus competent performances ... provides good entertainment." *Motion Picture Daily*, March 12, 1938

"From the unpromising material involving the discovery of a medical serum to fight the Sumatra fever, is developed a really engrossing drama that holds the interest easily.... Directed with telling suspense by S. Sylvan Simon." *Film Daily*, March 24, 1938

Nurse from Brooklyn (1938)

Sally Eilers (*Elizabeth Thomas*), Paul Kelly (*Jim Barnes*), Larry Blake (*Larry Craine*), Maurice Murphy (*Danny Thomas*), Morgan Conway (*Insp. Francis X. Donohue*), David Oliver (*Det. Branch*), Lucile Gleason (*"Ma" Hutchins*), James Blaine (*Det. Saunders*), Hal K. Dawson (*Tommy Tucker*), Eddie Fetherston (*Ambulance Surgeon*), Joe Kenny (*Parking Attendant*), Edwin Stanley (*Bill, Ballistics Expert*), Franco Corsaro (*Headwaiter*), Peggy Bermer (*Smitty*), Ralph Brooks (*Cab Driver*), Dora Clement (*Reception Clerk*), Frances Robinson, Marilyn Stuart (*Nurses*)

Director: S. Sylvan Simon. *Associate Producer*: Edmund Grainger. *Screenplay*: Roy Chanslor, based on the *Liberty* magazine story by Steve Fisher. *Director of Photography*: Milton Krasner. *Dialogue Director*: Philip Cahn. *Art Director*: Jack Otterson. *Associate*: Charles H. Clarke. *Film Editor*: Paul Landres. *Musical Director*: Charles Previn. *Sound*: Joseph Lapis, Edwin Wetzel. [*Cutter*: Phil Cahn. *Assistant Directors*: Fred Frank, Jack Bernhard. *Script Clerk*: Myrtle Gibsone.]

Universal; released April 1938. 66 minutes.

Nineteen-year-old Danny Thomas, just released from a three-year stretch in the state reformatory, visits his sister Beth, a nurse at Brooklyn General Hospital. Larry Craine, who has known the Thomases since childhood, has been keeping watch over Beth while her brother served time, but she doesn't know that he, too, was involved in the crime for which Danny was imprisoned.

Larry offers Danny a ride, not disclosing that the car he's driving is stolen. Larry drives him down to the docks, where he wants Danny to help him pull a warehouse robbery, but Danny wants no part of it. When policeman Jim Barnes spots them lurking outside the warehouse, Larry opens fire and wounds the cop. Horrified, Danny goes to the policeman's aid, but Larry shoots him in the back and flees the scene.

Both gunshot victims are brought to the Brooklyn hospital, where Beth attends the friendly, flirtatious Jim, who sustained a bullet wound to the hip. Not until later does she learn that the second shooting victim was Danny, who died. Larry, visiting Beth surreptitiously, tells her that Jim shot her brother maliciously, and encourages her to avenge Danny's murder.

Jim is visited at the hospital by his commanding officer, Inspector Donohue, who tells him that the shooting at the waterfront offers a chance to close a cold case involving a fellow officer, Sergeant Sam Graham. The bullet extracted from Jim's hip matches the one used to kill Danny. Beth is unaware that the police have searched her apartment, and found a photograph of Larry, whom Jim identifies as the killer. Larry

Beth (Sally Eilers), the *Nurse from Brooklyn*, must decide whether Larry (Larry Blake, center) or Jim (Paul Kelly) is worthy of her loyalty.

urges Beth to cultivate Jim's attentions, waiting for an opportunity to eliminate the only witness to his crime. Jim, meanwhile, is getting better acquainted with her in the hopes that Danny's sister can help him solve the case involving Sergeant Graham.

Inspector Donohue arranges for Jim to spend a week convalescing at the boss' Long Island cottage, with Beth appointed to accompany him as nurse. While policemen stake out the cottage, Jim waits to see if Beth will convey their whereabouts to Larry. She doesn't, but Inspector Gleason tries to smoke out the criminal by having Jim's whereabouts broadcast on the radio. When Jim finds the pistol slug Beth still carries in her purse, he has it analyzed by ballistics experts. The surprising results lead to a final confrontation in which Beth must decide whether to ally herself with Larry or the policeman she still believes killed her brother.

Just over an hour long, *Nurse from Brooklyn* is an entertaining programmer that unfolds at a brisk pace under Simon's direction. The story moves from the first scene, seldom slowing down in the hour to follow. He successfully integrates the varied elements into a pleasing combination, advancing the plot without confusion while maintaining interest. Though there's little out-and-out comedy here, he elicits a few smiles with his portrayal of the bored cops at the beach house, annoyed that Jim is living it up with Beth while they're cooped up in a small room subsisting on a diet of canned pork and beans. There's also a likable dog that figures into the story.

Film Daily reported in November 1937 that Sally Eilers had been signed for the lead role. Miss Eilers was to be paid $2500 per week, while her co-star Paul Kelly was expected to earn a $1500 weekly stipend. Studio contract player Larry Blake (1914–1982) was budgeted for $800 per week.

This was Simon's first collaboration with screenwriter Roy Chanslor, who would also pen the scripts for *The Road to Reno* and *Washington Melodrama.* Chanslor's script was adapted from Steve Fisher's story "If You Break My Heart," which appeared in the November 13, 1937, issue of *Liberty* magazine. Fisher received $1500 for the rights to his story. Simon's fee as director was $2500.

Production was originally scheduled to begin on Monday, February 14, 1938. Schedule conflicts for three cast members caused a two-day delay. By the end of the week, Martin Murphy reported, "During the first days of shooting we encountered difficulties with Larry Blake, playing the role of 'Larry,' and were delayed to the extent of finishing up our first four days tonight one day behind schedule." The Assistant Director's Daily Report for the first day of shooting (February 16, 1938) noted the cause of delay as "Trouble with actor on dialogue," and a similar note appeared the following day. The log showed that scene 79-B, on Day One, had been shot 14 times, with "n.g. dialogue" the most commonly recorded reason for a spoiled take. With some relief Murphy noted in his end-of-week update that Blake was booked to work only three more days to complete his role. Another particularly difficult day, not attributed specifically to Blake, was February 22, 1938, in which the company began with a 9 a.m. call, and called it quits in the wee hours of the morning, dismissed at 4:40 a.m.

After executives saw a rough cut of the film in March, "it was decided to make a sequence of additional scenes changing the end of the story," Murphy reported (March 19, 1938). "This necessitated calling back Sally Eilers, Paul Kelly and Larry Blake—consumed a full day of shooting and cost approximately $1500.00." Despite the additional shooting, which furnished a more dramatic outcome to Larry's criminal career, the film's final cost was calculated at $125,000, only a few hundred dollars over budget.

Simon elicits uniformly strong performances from his cast. Paul Kelly (1899–1956) nicely limns Jim Barnes, who self-assuredly tells Beth, "I'm an unusual cop." In Kelly's hands, he's also a well-rounded character, slightly cynical, used to romancing women with flowery passages from the Rubaiyat of Omar Khayyam, but who finds himself responding on a deeper level to Sally Eilers' Beth. Miss Eilers (1908–1978), cast as what studio publicity described as "a girl whose caresses whispered of death to come!" capably conveys the character of Beth and her changing emotions. According to a column item, the actress "has been hopping from one picture to another," with *Nurse from Brooklyn* being "her fifth picture since her return from Europe five months ago."[5]

Lucile Gleason (1888–1947), sometimes billed as Lucille Webster Gleason, adds color in a character role as "Ma" Hutchins, the housekeeper who serves as Jim and Beth's chaperone at the beach cottage. The film offers some period flavor with reporter Tommy Tucker's gossip column item reporting Jim's first evening out with Beth, which reads, "'Strong-arm' Jim Barnes, mopping up giggle-water at the Lancaster Roof last night with his eye-filling nurse, Beth Thomas."

According to the film's pressbook, *Nurse from Brooklyn* marked the 22nd time featured actor Maurice Murphy (1913–1978) had died onscreen—he "explained that he had been blown up, shot down, and gassed to death in war pictures, beheaded, lined up against a wall, hanged and strangled in gangster pictures." Recent roles in *Romeo and Juliet* (MGM, 1936) and Warner Brothers' *Tovarich* (1937) were named as exceptions to his cinematic fatality rate.

Response to *Nurse from Brooklyn* made it clear that S. Sylvan Simon was a director to watch, and it soon became clear that decision makers at Universal and elsewhere were paying attention.

Reviews: "This offering has been given excellent direction by S. Sylvan Simon and holds the interest from the start. Sally Eilers and Paul Kelly do highly creditable work." *Film Daily*, April 13, 1938

"When members of an audience at the Pantages theatre, generally conceded to be a 'tough' place in which to preview a picture—especially a melodrama—go out audibly praising the offering, it is a good indication that the film will please virtually any type of audience ... the film offers well balanced action, suspense and romance." *Motion Picture Herald*, April 16, 1938

The Road to Reno (1938)

Randolph Scott (*Steve Fortness*), Hope Hampton (*Linda Halliday*), Helen Broderick (*Aunt Minerva Fortness*), Alan Marshal (*Walter Crawford*), Glenda Farrell (*Sylvia Shayne*), David Oliver (*Salty*), Samuel S. Hinds (*Lawyer Pierce*), Spencer Charters (*Judge*), Charles Murphy (*Mike*), Ted Osborne (*Lawyer Graves*), Dorothy [Dot] Farley (*Mrs. Brumleigh*), Mira McKinney (*Hannah*), Renie Riano (*Female Bailiff*), Lita Chevret (*Gladys*), Willie Fung (*Lame Duck*), Jack Clifford (*Trucker*), Grace Goodall (*Court Clerk*)

Director: S. Sylvan Simon. *Associate Producer*: Edmund Grainger. *Screenplay*: Roy Chanslor, Adele Comandini. *Story*: Charles Kenyon, F. Hugh Herbert. *Based on the Novel by* I.A.R. Wylie. *Director of Photography*: George Robinson. *Art Director*: Jack Otterson. *Associate*: Charles H. Clarke. *Film Editors*: Maurice Wright, Paul Landres. *Gowns*: Vera West. *Set Decorator*: R.A. Gausman. *Assistant Director*: Vernon Keays. *Songs*, "I Gave My Heart Away," "Tonight is the Night": Harold Adamson (lyrics), Jimmy McHugh (music). *Musical Director*: Charles Previn. *Sound Supervisor*: Bernard B. Brown. *Technician*: William Hedgecock.

Universal; released August 1938. 72 minutes.

Singing star Linda Halliday is on her way to Reno, seeking a divorce so that she can marry her new love Walter Crawford. On the train, she befriends Sylvia Shayne, a well-known aviatrix who's a four-time divorcee. At Reno, Linda encounters her estranged husband Steve Fortness, who operates a nearby ranch. To Linda's surprise, Steve tells her he won't give her a divorce, even though they are still unable to settle their basic disagreement—he wants her to be a rancher's wife, while she refuses to give up her musical career.

After the plane Sylvia pilots causes Steve's livestock to stampede, he drains the vehicle of its gas, and takes both ladies back to the ranch with him. He offers Linda his hospitality, but makes it clear that he expects her to share "bed and board" with him.

Instead, she serves him with divorce papers, but he informs her that they are invalid, as the ranch is on the Nevada-California border, and he is a legal resident of the latter state. At a stalemate with Steve, Linda accepts the help of his Aunt Minerva, who suggests that she aggravate him into giving her a divorce to get rid of her.

Linda promptly transforms Steve's working ranch into a dude ranch, populated with other "grass widows" awaiting their divorces. A battle of wills finds Steve and Linda doing their best to irritate and inconvenience each other. Linda refuses to admit she's jealous when Steve seems to take an interest in Sylvia, who challenges her friend to make up her mind between the two men in her life. Linda sends a telegram to her fiancé, telling him she has decided against the divorce, and it seems that she and Steve may reconcile, until a misunderstanding comes between them. Matters come to a head with Walter's unexpected arrival at the ranch.

Before production was underway, Simon and screenwriter Roy Chanslor visited Reno, Nevada, according to *Daily Variety* (March 23, 1938) "to delve into divorce court practices and other phenomena peculiar to the town." Simon was allotted a week's location shooting in and around Kernville, California, in the Sierra Nevadas, which took place in June 1938. He also sought out a suitable dude ranch location, settling on one in Ventura County, California. "All we had to do was provide the grass and the divorcees-to-be came running," joked Simon, according to the film's pressbook.

Leading lady Hope Hampton (1897–1982), making a return to the screen after an absence of several years, was for the first time being featured in a sound film. Studio publicity claimed that she had been awaiting better sound reproduction for her singing voice, and was suitably impressed by the skill of Universal technicians who made the Deanna Durbin vehicle *One Hundred Men and a Girl* (1937). The tailor-made script allows her to showcase her singing ability (in the opening scenes, she's heard performing an excerpt from "La Boheme"), but also shows her to good advantage in a lightweight romantic comedy. The screenplay lays out clearly the adulation that her character's public displays. At the concert hall where she performs, the entire front row consists of nothing but men in evening clothes, "all deeply admiring of the glamorous star." Farther back, there are couples in the audience, but, "The males, we observe, are captives to a man to the star."

Daily Variety (May 3, 1937) reported that Hampton was given "one of the most elaborate screen tests ever made," lasting 17 days, before production was given the go-ahead: "Results are said to be highly satisfactory and presage important screen singing assignments for Miss Hampton at U." The singer-actress reportedly signed a seven-year contract with the studio, and was given co-star billing under the title in her comeback vehicle. However, *The Road to Reno* proved to be her only star turn at Universal. A rash of bad publicity may have been a contributing factor. In January 1939, newspapers reported that she was "called before a grand jury Wednesday to explain how her wealthy husband, Jules Brulatour, got shot in the neck last Sunday and why it wasn't reported to the police until two days later."[6]

Randolph Scott (1898–1987), though not yet established as the Western star he will become, is well-suited to the role of down-to-earth Steve, in a comedy that has occasional echoes of his better-known (and better) *My Favorite Wife* (1940). Not surprisingly, he's quite believable as a rancher, but he also shows a flair for comedy under Simon's direction. He underplays moments such as Steve's response to being served

Steve (Randolph Scott) is flanked by the two most important women in his life, Aunt Minerva (Helen Broderick) and estranged wife Linda (Hope Hampton) in *The Road to Reno*.

a divorce summons (he feeds it to his goat), and gets laughs with his queasy reaction to a stomach-churning plane ride. The film's storyline may have cut a bit close for comfort. Syndicated columnist Jimmie Fidler (July 15, 1938) visited the set and reported, "Watched Randy Scott do a divorce court scene with Hope Hampton.... He carried himself with admirable composure—sober and masterful as only Randy can be. I couldn't help but wonder, though, whether he'd do as well if he should have to appear in the divorce action to be brought against him by his wife. It is scheduled to be brought soon." Scott and Marion DuPont divorced in 1939.

Glenda Farrell (1904–1971), always a lively addition to any cast, gives verve to the role of the heroine's pal Sylvia. Getting her first look at Steve, she obviously likes what she sees, asking Linda, "You're trading *him* in?" Another top-notch character actress, Helen Broderick (1891–1959), plays Steve's pragmatic Aunt Minerva, who takes it upon herself to make sure her nephew doesn't throw away his marriage too hastily. Simon will later produce *Born Yesterday*, with Miss Broderick's son, actor Broderick Crawford, in a starring role.

The film's pressbook offered the usual suggestions for publicity stunts to drum up business, some of them definitely products of a bygone era. Among them: "Plug the title by sending a pretty girl around the busy part of town asking people to tell her the way to *The Road to Reno*. Girl should be an attractive, conspicuous blonde type." The young lady was to thank those who responded, and "slip them" publicity material for the film. A variation on the same involved the young lady at the wheel of "a sporty looking roadster" bearing a sign: "For a laugh-laden love lark, follow me to *The Road to Reno* at ... Theater."

Minutes from a studio executive meeting on August 16, 1938, noted of *The Road to Reno*, "Ready for sneak preview Wednesday night." For reasons unspecified, normal procedure for previews was not being followed: "The purpose of this being, of course, to make this an absolute 'sneak' in the full sense of the word."[7]

Although the screenplay of *The Road to Reno* is serviceable rather than spectacular, Simon fashions an enjoyable, fast-moving musical comedy that bubbles along steadily to its predictable outcome. Louella O. Parsons (August 1, 1938) reported that Hampton celebrated the completion of the shoot "with a party such as seldom has been qualed [*sic*] on a movie set." She also noted, for "those who felt Hope should have had a more experienced director" for her comeback film that Simon had just been signed to an MGM contract.

Reviews: "This dude ranch musical ... provides Hope Hampton an entertaining vehicle [that] showcases enough talent and personality to warrant promising continuance in pictures.... Excellent is the direction by S. Sylvan Simon, capitalizing every entertainment value in the script and adding very materially to the blueprint, progressing the light narrative with appropriate pace and showing a flair for exceptionally well pointed satirical comedy." *Daily Variety*, August 26, 1938

"Under S. Sylvan Simon's direction the players perform admirably, and there is always something doing in the way of a laugh, a song or some piece of action.... This enjoyable romantic comedy ... is the sort of thing that should play to gratifying returns." *Film Daily*, August 31, 1938

Spring Madness (1938)

Maureen O'Sullivan (*Alexandra Benson*), Lew Ayres (*Sam Thatcher*), Ruth Hussey (*Kate McKim*), Burgess Meredith (*The Lippencott*), Ann Morriss (*Frances*), Joyce Compton (*Sally Prescott*), Jacqueline Wells [Julie Bishop] (*Mady Platt*), Frank Albertson (*Hat*), Truman Bradley (*Walter Beckett*), Marjorie Gateson (*Miss Ritchie*), Renee [Renie] Riano (*Mildred*), Sterling Holloway (*Buck*), Dick Baldwin (*Doc*), Edward Gargan (*Jim*), Willie Best (*Porter on Train*), Charles R. Moore (*Porter in Diner*), Thurston Hall (*Charles Platt*), Lee Phelps (*Ofcr. Ryan*), Egon Brecher (*Soviet Travel Bureau Agent*), Spencer Charters (*Police Chief*), Edgar Dearing (*Policeman*), J.M. Kerrigan (*Mr. Maloney*), Harry Tyler (*Taxi Driver*), William Bailey (*Train Conductor*), Jack Baxley (*Railroad Train Announcer*)

Director: S. Sylvan Simon. *Producer*: Edward Chodorov. *Screenplay*: Edward Chodorov, based on the play "Spring Dance" by Philip Barry, adapted from an original play by Eleanor Golden, Eloise Barrangon. *Photography*: Joseph Ruttenberg. *Musical Score*: William Axt. *Art Director*: Cedric Gibbons. *Associate*: Stan Rogers. *Set Decorator*: Edwin B. Willis. *Film Editor*: Conrad A. Nervig. *Recording Director*: Douglas Shearer. *Wardrobe*: Dolly Tree.

MGM; released November 1938. 67 minutes.

Only a few weeks away from receiving their degrees at Harvard, Sam Thatcher and his roommate, known to all as The Lippencott, have plans to see the world after graduation. They've bought tickets for a journey by boat to Russia, where they intend to live and work for the next two years. Sam has recently met Alex, a co-ed at a nearby college for women, but assures his pal that it's not a serious relationship. Alex, on the other hand, tells her friends that she's fallen in love with Sam. Her friends urge her to have Sam escort her to the Spring Dance.

Sam and Lippencott receive word that their ocean voyage has been pushed forward by two weeks. Even though this will mean missing graduation, as well as the dance, Sam tells his buddy they should go ahead with their trip as planned. He arrives at Alex's school one day prior to the occasion, and breaks the news. Seeing that their friend is brokenhearted, Alex's pals conspire to bring about a happy ending for her.

Simon's first directorial assignment at MGM was this adaptation of a lesser Philip Barry play, "Spring Dance," that lasted only a few weeks on Broadway in the late summer of 1936. The studio acquired the rights to it just as it concluded its brief run. Early publicity for the film indicated that the play's title would be retained, but shortly before release it was renamed *Spring Madness*.

Although Simon's film received largely favorable reviews, movie studios would find far greater success with adaptations of other Barry plays, notably *Holiday* (1938) and *The Philadelphia Story* (1940). Simon's youth will lead MGM to assign him multiple films dealing with college life.

Taking a break from the popular "Tarzan" series, leading lady Maureen O'Sullivan (1911–1998) gives charm and verve to the role of the romantically inclined Alex. Though there's not a lot here to suggest a commitment to academia on the part of any character, Alex does at least make reference to completing a thesis. Her increased self-assurance in the film's latter half is satisfying to see. Simon will direct her again in *Sporting Blood* (1940).

This is the first of two films Lew Ayres (1908–1996) will make under Simon's direction; both find him playing rather stodgy, arrogant college men whose appeal to the leading lady is somewhat difficult to see. His character, Sam, starts out seeming bland, and goes downhill from there as the film progresses. Like most of the principal actors here, he is a bit long in the tooth to be playing a college undergraduate. Just weeks before *Spring Madness* was released, moviegoers saw him for the first time in his most famous role, in the "Dr. Kildare" movie series. As reported by columnist Louella O. Parsons (September 30, 1938), Ayres inherited the role after Franchot Tone rejected it.

Ruth Hussey (1911–2005) is effective as the assertive, no-nonsense Kate ("The important thing about a love affair is the struggle to decide who cracks the whip"), who takes it upon herself to get Alex's head out of the clouds. According to Simon, this wasn't the first time he'd crossed paths with the actress. "She was one of my classmates at the University of Michigan. She knew all about my Hillel Players and how I had all but flunked the course in The Art of Direction. That was one time when a director was at the mercy of his leading lady."[8] Miss Hussey will attract far more attention for her performance playing another Philip Barry character in *The Philadelphia Story*.

Burgess Meredith (1907–1997), in only his second important film role (after his dramatic performance in *Winterset* two years earlier), is suitably cast as Sam's quirky,

Lew Ayres is caught between Maureen O'Sullivan and Burgess Meredith (surely not a difficult choice) in *Spring Madness*.

iconoclastic roommate (a role originated on stage by José Ferrer). Miss Hussey's character memorably (and not inaccurately) assesses him as "a first-class, A Number One striped African jackass." The two of them become incongruous dinner companions after a biting exchange:

> **KATE:** "Be real fun to have dinner with you, on the chance that you might get poisoned."
> **LIPP:** "You might stab yourself with a slippery knife."

Joyce Compton (1907–1997) is seen to good advantage as the seemingly feather-brained Sally, who may have more on the ball that is initially apparent. The scenes in which Sally cheerfully gets Sam and Lipp in hot water with the local police give the boys an overdue comeuppance. Truman Bradley (1905–1974), later the host of TV's *Science Fiction Theatre*, appears as Mr. Beckett, a literature instructor who struggles to keep the minds of his female students on their work instead of their social lives. His character comes into play late in the film, when he helps Alex's friends win her a commitment from Sam. It's a shame we don't see more of Marjorie Gateson (1891–1977) as the young ladies' house mother, who offers an apropos lament: "Why must we women waste our lives waiting for a kind word from some utterly worthless man?"

Character players seen in minor vignettes include Renie Riano (1899–1971), whose name is misspelled in the credits, as a maid at the women's dormitory, and Willie Best (1916–1962) as (what else?) a porter, who's taken aback when Sally considers occupying a berth in an otherwise all-male train car. Ironically, Best, at 22, is one of the few performers here actually in the right age range to play a college student. Among the up-and-coming young actors in minor roles as students are Clayton Moore, Phillip Terry, and Ralph Bowman, who would later take the stage name John Archer after winning radio's *Gateway to Hollywood* competition.

Reviews: "This is a very different kind of college comedy and a far livelier and funnier one than has come from the cameras in many seasons. Every member of the big cast turns in a sparkling performance.... S. Sylvan Simon's direction is a masterly lesson in the fine art of keeping a large number of evenly emphasized characters moving steadily and swiftly from a running start to a photograph finish." *Motion Picture Herald*, November 12, 1938

"Superb romance-comedy of college life done with beauty and fine dramatic feeling ... presents the girls and boys as intelligent human beings ... and not a bunch of zany nitwits.... There is great hope for bringing back a lot of customers to the theater if this type of production becomes more common in the Hollywood studios.... Direction of S. Sylvan Simon is deft and understanding, handling a delicately molded theme with fine artistry." *Film Daily*, November 15, 1938

Four Girls in White (1939)

Florence Rice (*Norma Page*), Una Merkel (*Gertie Robbins*), Ann Rutherford (*Patricia Page*), Mary Howard (*Mary Forbes*), Alan Marshal (*Dr. Stephen Melford*), Kent Taylor (*Robert Maitland*), Buddy Ebsen (*Express*), Jessie Ralph (*Miss Tobias*), Sara Haden (*Miss Bennett*), Phillip Terry (*Dr. Sidney*), Tom Neal (*Dr. Phillips*), Edward Earle (*Druggist*), Minerva Urecal (*Miss Perch*), Margaret Bert (*Miss Waring*), Shirley Coates (*Young Patient on Crutches*), Edgar Dearing (*Motorcycle Cop*), James C. Morton (*Policeman at Drugstore*), Maxine Marx (*Telephone Operator*), Bruce Sidney (*Dr. Herbert*), Mariska Aldrich (*Disturbed Patient*), J. Lewis Smith (*Ambulance Driver*), Lester Dorr (*Ambulance Orderly*), Kathryn Sheldon (*Miss Keener*), Joy Anderson (*Susan Forbes*), Jo Ann Sayers (*Drowsy Nurse*), Lee Phelps (*Foreman at Accident*)

Director: S. Sylvan Simon. *Producer*: Nat Levine. *Screenplay*: Dorothy Yost. *Original Story*: Nathalie Bucknall, Endre Bohem. *Photography*: Leonard Smith. *Film Editor*: George Boemler. *Montage Effects*: Peter Ballbusch. *Art Director*: Cedric Gibbons. *Associate*: Stan Rogers. *Set Decorator*: Edwin B. Willis. *Wardrobe*: Dolly Tree.

MGM; released January 1939. 73 minutes.

Norma Page and her younger sister Pat are among the latest class of nurse trainees at Maitland Memorial Hospital, as are Southern-accented Gertie, and Mary Forbes, a young woman who is worried about the job keeping her away from her baby. Pat is ready to devote herself to the three years' work that will be required of them, but Norma's primary interest is in finding a well-heeled husband. Under the supervision of crusty Miss Tobias, the young ladies undergo rigorous training. Norma runs afoul of the strict supervisor when she speaks up in defense of Mary, who gets woozy while observing an operation.

Assigned to extra duties as punishment, Norma becomes better acquainted with Dr. Stephen Melford, a gifted doctor using the hospital as a home base for his medical research. Norma and Steve begin dating, and are looking toward a future together, but she is irritated by his long hours, relatively modest pay, and single-minded concentration on his work.

In their third year of training, the student nurses swoon over a handsome new patient. Playboy Robert Maitland, grandson of the hospital founder, has supposedly sworn off women after being shot by a nightclub dancer. Soon, however, Bob is taken with Norma, and she with him. When she neglects her duties for a few minutes while visiting Bob, it's Mary, who tried to cover for Norma, who's blamed.

With Norma and Pat's vacation coming up, they accept Bob's invitation to serve as nurses on his yacht while he completes his recuperation. Realizing that Pat is falling in love with Bob, Norma unselfishly withdraws, returning to the hospital early. Mary, being punished with extra shifts after taking the rap for Norma, is attacked by a violent patient. Guilt-ridden, and being given the cold shoulder by Steve and the other nurses, Norma writes out her resignation. But when the hospital staff is notified of a large-scale railroad accident, she is given an unexpected opportunity to show her mettle.

Four Girls in White is, for the bulk of its running time, is an enjoyable if somewhat familiar story of hospital life, young nurses undergoing the rigors of training, and romance among patients and staff. But the climactic scenes involving rescue efforts at a train wreck give it a boost that sets it apart from other programmers. Even at MGM, B movies were made as economically as possible, but Sylvan Simon makes the rescue sequences involving and atmospheric with the limited resources available to him. He also elicits generally fine performances from his very capable cast.

Top-billed Florence Rice (1907–1974) may be most familiar to modern-day audiences as the ingénue in the Marx Brothers' comedy *At the Circus* (also 1939). She tackles the frequently unsympathetic role of self-involved, husband-hunting Norma, who bluntly explains her rationale for taking the job: "This hospital has the richest patients and the highest-paid doctors in the city." When we first meet her, she's called in a phony emergency to the hospital, for the express purpose of catching a lift in the ambulance after missing her bus. Miss Rice does a creditable job of depicting Norma's faults, and also the maturation that slowly takes place. As Pat, Ann Rutherford is wide-eyed and cute almost to excess, but her character wins audience sympathy nonetheless. One amusing moment finds her shy character startled to encounter a male patient who "isn't even dressed!" The script originally called for stern Miss Tobias to snap, "What do you want him to wear—a diving suit?" In Simon's copy, "diving suit" has been crossed out, and "raccoon coat" written in by hand, and that was the line ultimately filmed.

The supporting cast is strengthened by the presence of some fine character actresses, including Una Merkel (1903–1986) as the slightly scatterbrained—and frequently hungry—Gertie, and Jessie Ralph (1864–1944) as the nurses' tough-talking supervisor. Early on, Miss Ralph's character tells the young trainees, "If any of you graduate, it will be a miracle!" (She has, of course, a softer side that she mostly keeps under wraps). This is the first of four films in which Sylvan Simon will direct Sara Haden (1898–1981), best-known for her appearances as Aunt Milly in MGM's popular "Andy Hardy" series. Unfortunately, she has little to do here. Likewise, Minerva Urecal (1894–1966) has only one scene, cast as the replacement nurse who takes Norma's place at Bob Maitland's bedside, much to his disappointment.

The *Four Girls in White*, **pictured on bottom row, are (left to right) Florence Rice, Ann Rutherford, Mary Howard, and Una Merkel. Also pictured are Alan Marshal (back left) and Buddy Ebsen.**

Two up-and-coming young leading men, Phillip Terry (1909–1993) and Tom Neal (1914–1972), are seen in minor roles as two doctors who argue over the privilege of taking Norma on a date. (Though Terry's character is named Dr. Sydney in the screenplay, it's spelled "Sidney" in the film's closing credits.) Buddy Ebsen (1908–2003) gives one of the film's weaker performances as a goofy intern nicknamed "Express," who takes a liking to Miss Merkel's character. Express is happy to model the fancy clothes that were cut off the wealthy Bob upon intake, though he's not as impressed by the newcomer as his female co-workers are:

GERTIE: Is he as romantic as the girls say he is?
EXPRESS: Not in his underwear.

This was the only film made for MGM by producer Nat Levine (1899–1989), formerly head of production at Republic Studios. Once it was ready for release, he announced that his doctor had advised six months of rest, and vacated the studio premises. Although he lived for another 50 years, he never produced another feature film. Co-author of the film's original story was Russian-born Nathalie Bucknall (1895–1959), who was the head of MGM's research department. Simon's copy of the script was dated November 30, 1938, and still retained the original title "Women in White." Pink sheets with changes carry various dates in the month of December. They include several pages in which the scenes depicting the train wreck and its aftermath are meticulously laid out, shot by shot.

According to syndicated columnist Erskine Johnson (December 29, 1938), Simon's company spent much of one morning shooting an operating room sequence, with Alan Marshal's Dr. Melford performing surgery. An unidentified extra took his place on the table, covered in a white sheet that had a hole through which Marshal could simulate his surgical moves. When the scene was finally completed to Simon's satisfaction, the extra player stuck a hand through the hole in the sheet, saying to Marshal, "Thanks, doc. You sure saved my life."

As scripted, Norma's growing interest in Dr. Melford is telegraphed in a scene that finds him making a long and dull speech about "undulant fever," with most of the nurse probationers "listening indifferently," while Norma is "apparently fascinated." Simon noted in the margin of his script, "This speech to be longer, to cover shot of Norma watching him raptly, others not—at back. May slightly embarrass him." However, in the finished product, Marshal delivered the dialogue as written, with a two-shot of Norma and her sister, and then close-ups of Norma, intercut.

The screenplay called for a wrap-up (following the railroad rescue sequence) that tied up all the story elements in a neat bow. However, much of this was ultimately discarded, and the film works better that way, with the audience being allowed to reach some conclusions without being beaten over the head with them. Simon apparently sensed that the scenes were over the top; one stage direction calling for a leading man to "sweep Norma into his arms" has been firmly crossed out.

Four Girls in White was parodied on the April 9, 1939, episode of Jack Benny's radio show. Mary Livingstone played one of the quartet of nurses, with the other female roles assigned to Kenny Baker, Don Wilson, and Phil Harris. Benny was cast as the head of the hospital, Dr. DeSchnook. It's a fairly amusing skit, but owes little to the story told in the film.

Motion Picture Herald (April 22, 1939) reported that a theater manager in Evansville, Indiana promoted the film with the help of four pretty young ladies who greeted passersby, "distributing health certificates.... Copy on certificate entitled holder to a clean bill of health providing he saw the film."

Reviews: "Just fair program entertainment. The story is not particularly engrossing; as a matter of fact it is unpleasant in some respects, particularly in the characterization of the heroine.... The picture depends mainly on the closing scenes for its dramatic power.... These scenes have been handled realistically and with considerable excitement." *Harrison's Reports*, February 11, 1939

"That the picture does develop a fair amount of interest is due in the main to S. Sylvan Simon's direction and the splendid work of the players. The manner in which the final scenes are handled, in which doctors and nurses work at a railroad wreck during a raging storm ... is a credit to Simon's directorial ability." *Film Daily*, January 24, 1939

The Kid from Texas (1939)

Dennis O'Keefe (*William Quincy Malone*), Florence Rice (*Margo Thomas*), Anthony Allan [John Hubbard] (*Bertie Thomas*), Jessie Ralph (*Aunt Minetta Thomas*),

Buddy Ebsen ("*Snifty*" *Edwards*), Virginia Dale (*O'Kay Kinney*), Robert Wilcox ("*Duke*" *Hastings*), Jack Carson (*Stanley Brown*), Helen Lynd (*Mabel*), J.M. Kerrigan (*Farr*), Tully Marshall (*Adam Lambert*), Eddy Chandler (*Captain Babcock*), Spencer Charters (*Deputy Sheriff*), George Meeker (*Henry Smith-Harrington*), Gerald Oliver Smith (*Noel*)

Director: S. Sylvan Simon. *Producer*: Edgar Selwyn. *Screenplay*: Florence Ryerson, Edgar Allan Woolf, Albert Mannheimer. *Original Story*: Milton Merlin, Byron Morgan. *Song*, "Right in the Middle of Texas": music, Ormond Ruthven, lyrics, Milton Merlin, Albert Mannheimer, music score, William Axt. *Recording Director*: Douglas Shearer. *Art Director*: Cedric Gibbons. *Associate*: Stan Rogers. *Set Decorator*: Edwin B. Willis. *Women's Gowns*: Dolly Tree. *Men's Costumes*: Valles. *Photography*: Sidney Wagner. *Montage Effects*: Peter Ballbusch. *Film Editor*: Fredrick Y. Smith. [*Sound Mixer*: Joe Edmundson. *Unit Manager*: Charles Hunt. *Prop Man*: George Elder. *Makeup Man*: Keester Sweeney. *Hairdresser*: Betty Lee. *Wardrobe Man*: Milton S. Ehrlich. *Wardrobe Woman*: Vicki Nichols. *Script Clerk*: Russ Haverick]

MGM: released April 1939. 71 minutes.

Texas cowpuncher William Quincy Malone spends his time "playing polo with a croquet mallet and a tennis ball." When his favorite horse, Lone Star, is sold to Long Island socialite Bernie Thomas, Bill conspires to go East with Thomas and his sister Margo, talking himself into a job on their estate.

Brashly confident Bill, the only man who can ride Lone Star, longs to be allowed to play polo, but the Thomases find him useful only as a stable hand. Bill has an eye for the snobbish Margo, but their relationship has been chaotic since he inadvertently caused her to take a unexpected plunge into the river, and then mistakenly pushes her into the Long Island Sound. After an unflattering photo of a dripping-wet Margo is splashed across the front page of a newspaper (with the headline "'Wild Bill' Malone Rescues Debutante"), she does her best to get him fired. But plain-spoken Aunt Minetta, who holds the purse strings in the Thomas family, thinks Bill is just the man to curb the spending of her niece and nephew.

Allowed to fill in at the last minute for an injured player, Bill plays in his first polo match, but is thrown off the team after getting into a spat with Margo's boyfriend Duke. A despondent Bill decides to accept an offer from his old pal Snifty to join a nearby Wild West show, only to find that the troupe is in financial straits.

A lightly likable romantic comedy with action sequences, *The Kid from Texas* was the second released feature in a planned MGM series of B movies with a sports-related theme. Not for the first time in a Simon picture, a four-legged performer gets the last word when the curtain falls. Though he's no Mister Ed, Bill's horse Lone Star is depicted throughout the story as a creature with a mind of his own, one who demonstrates his displeasure when he thinks his master is in the wrong.

According to *Daily Variety* (April 17, 1939), MGM signed O'Keefe to a long-term contract shortly after *The Kid from Texas* completed shooting. O'Keefe and Rice had teamed the previous year in *Vacation from Love*. Although O'Keefe's ascension to lead roles, sparked by his appearance in *The Bad Man of Brimstone* (1937) happened quickly after he joined MGM, he had been toiling in the industry for some years before that "overnight" success. Early announcements for *The Kid from Texas* said that O'Keefe's leading lady would be Ruth Hussey, with whom he had previously teamed in *Burn 'Em Up O'Connor*.

O'Keefe succeeds in making his character appealing despite his more-than-healthy self-esteem (bordering on arrogance)—according to Margo, Bill Quincy "thinks he's a one-man Wild West show," while even Aunt Minetta, who likes him, acknowledges that he's "an awful liar."

Florence Rice, in her second film under Simon's direction, gamely takes part in the slapstick sequences, which find her taking two dives into water. (She had already received a thorough soaking in their previous collaboration, *Four Girls in White*). An item from his hometown newspaper said that Simon was pleased to learn that Rice married featured player Robert Wilcox after the film wrapped. "I guess I'm Cupid," he said, the

Dennis O'Keefe is *The Kid from Texas,* with Florence Rice as his sometimes-reluctant admirer.

columnist noting, "'It was [Simon] who introduced Miss Rice and Wilcox on their first day on the set,' and continue to bring them together during the shoot because 'they made such a nice couple.'"[9] Be that as it may, they were separated within a few months, and divorced in 1940.

Character actress Jessie Ralph, in her second role for Simon (after *Four Girls in White*) registers strongly as Aunt Minetta, described by the screenwriters as "an irascible, raucous old dame." While she's indeed a pretty tough character, she finds Bill unexpectedly appealing. She's prone to hand out frank opinions (greeting a dowager friend, she says, "Hello, Eva. Is that a hat, or a mousetrap?"), but does prove to have her niece and nephew's best interests at heart. Helen Lynd (1902–1992) steals a scene or two in her minor role as a Cockney maid; a few months later, she will turn up briefly in *Of Mice and Men*.

This is Simon's first collaboration with screenwriter Albert Mannheimer (1913–1972), who will become not just a valued colleague but also a personal friend. Filming took place during February and March 1939. The original script was dated February 2, 1939, with numerous pink-sheeted changes carrying various dates throughout the first half of the month.

Reviews: "There are enough good laughs and acting bits to bring this to top spots of many bills as action half.... S. Sylvan Simon turns in a top notch directorial effort with his snappy pacing and deft handling of the not too strong screenplay." *Showmen's Trade Review*, April 8, 1939

"Dennis O'Keefe and Florence Rice turn in some very fine work.... Director S. Sylvan Simon does the best he can with the material and every now and then gets a very interesting moment. But it all adds up to the fact that a 'B' picture is a 'B' picture, regardless of the trade mark." *Box Office Digest*, April 3, 1939

These Glamour Girls (1939)

Lew Ayres (*Philip Griswold*), Lana Turner (*Jane Thomas*), Tom Brown (*Homer Ten Eyck*), Richard Carlson (*Joe*), Jane Bryan (*Carol Christy*), Anita Louise (*Daphne Graves*), Marsha Hunt (*Betty Ainsbridge*), Ann Rutherford (*Mary Rose Wilston*), Mary Beth Hughes (*Ann*), Owen Davis, Jr. (*Greg Smith*), Ernest Truex (*Alumnus*), Sumner Getchell (*Blimpy*), Peter [Lind] Hayes (*Skel*), Don Castle (*Jack*), Tom Collins (*Tommy Torgler*), Nella Walker (*Mrs. Christy*), Henry Kolker (*Philip S. Griswold II*), Dennie Moore (*Mavis*), Frederika Brown (*Mrs. Wilston*), Robert Emmett Keane (*Mr. Wilston*), Mary Forbes (*Mrs. Van Reichton*), John Kelly (*Featherfoot*), Aldrich Bowker (*Charlie*), Tom Kennedy (*Joylane Manager*), Gladys Blake (*Joylane Cashier*), James Pierce (*Joylane Bouncer*), Jesse Graves (*Porter*), Robert Winkler (*Newsboy*), David Oliver (*Cabby*), Helena Phillips Evans (*Ann's Maid*), Lee Phelps (*Policeman*), Ernie Alexander (*Parking Attendant*), Arthur Q. Bryan (*Dance Customer*)

Director: S. Sylvan Simon. *Producer*: Sam Zimbalist. *Screenplay*: Jane Hall, Marion Parsonnet, from the *Cosmopolitan* story by Jane Hall. *Song*, "Loveliness": music, Edward Ward, lyrics, Bob Wright, Chet Forrest. *Musical Score*: Edward Ward, David Snell. *Vocal and Orchestral Arrangements*: Wally Heglin. *Recording Director*: Douglas Shearer. *Art Director*: Cedric Gibbons. *Associate*: Harry McAfee. *Set Decorations*: Edwin B. Willis. *Wardrobe*: Dolly Tree. *Director of Photography*: Alfred Gilks. *Film Editor*: Harold F. Kress.

MGM; released August 1939. 79 minutes.

The debutantes of New York are eagerly awaiting the house parties being held at upper-class Kingsford College, hoping for invitations from the young men of their choice. One of those men, Philip Griswold III, has invited his frequent date Carol Christy, a young woman he's known since childhood. On a night out at a club, a tipsy Philip meets taxi dancer Jane Thomas at a rowdy club, and impulsively invites her to the college weekend. Although her down-to-earth roommate, Mavis, discourages her, saying, "Honey, you don't belong with that crowd," Jane decides to go.

Taking the train to Kingsford, Jane is hurt to realize that Philip has completely forgotten his impromptu invitation, and brought his date Carol. Lacking an escort, she agrees to accompany Blimpy. At a dance, Jane's beauty catches the eye of all the boys, inciting jealousy from the other young ladies. Snooty Daphne, eavesdropping on a conversation in which Jane's life is discussed, maliciously arranges for everyone to hear that she grew up in modest circumstances, a farmer's daughter from

Maybe not the kind of girl you take home to Mother, but stuffy Philip (Lew Ayres) can't overlook Jane (Lana Turner) in *These Glamour Girls*.

Kansas. Blimpy, heir of an old Southern family, instantly loses interest in her. But Phil, ashamed of the spot he's put Jane in, tries to help her fit in, though she wants to leave after witnessing his friends' snobbery. As it happens, Carol, though she's grown up with Phil, really prefers working-class Joe, who earns his keep as a waiter. But Carol, who's managed to keep her family's diminished finances a secret, is not yet willing to give up her plan of marrying a well-to-do man.

Annoyed by Jane's popularity with the college boys, Daphne presses Phil and Carol to announce their engagement. Hurt, Jane decides to go home, after telling off Phil and his rich friends. But an unexpected death among their crowd, as well as headlines announcing that Phil's father has been charged with embezzlement, give Jane and her erstwhile beau a new perspective.

These Glamour Girls is the first and probably least effective of the three films in which Simon directed up-and-coming starlet Lana Turner. It has its moments, and some good performances, but it would take a stronger story and script to make a truly successful film. The film throws too many characters at us in the first 20 minutes or so, making it occasionally difficult to keep them straight. Some of them, despite some good actors' best efforts, will not be much clearer an hour later, given the limitations of the script.

The film was based on a story idea by MGM screenwriter Jane Hall, who had joined the staff in 1937. Her treatment, written with the assistance of colleague Marion Parsonnet, attracted the interest of producer Sam Zimbalist. Miss Hall's agent also sent a copy to *Cosmopolitan* magazine, whose editor offered to purchase it, if it could be adapted into a novella. She did so, and it appeared in the magazine's December 1938 issue. Miss Hall's story was based on social activities among the student body of Princeton University, which was renamed Kingsford for the purposes of the film. Sharp-eyed viewers may notice that Kingsford bears a certain resemblance to the town of Carvel, seen in the "Andy Hardy" series, as both drew on the "New England Street" of MGM's backlot.

Film censors had multiple concerns about the script as initially submitted, including the characters' free use of alcohol, an unflattering depiction of American sailors becoming involved in a brawl, and implied sexual activity. Simon's copy of the script was dated June 8, 1939, with revised pages dated June 21, 1939.

Miss Turner, still a teenager during production, generally acquits herself well. "Mother enjoyed working with him," daughter Cheryl Crane later noted, and Simon's guidance helped the inexperienced actress make the most of her abilities.[10] Clearly, Miss Turner was grateful. Some 15 years later, Simon's daughter Susan took her first job in a clothing store managed by Lana's mother. When the star herself visited the store, and realized the teenage employee was Sylvan Simon's daughter, she gave Susan "a big hug and a kiss."

Top-billed Lew Ayres, in his second Simon outing, tries to give some humanity to Phil, a character described in the screenplay as "handsome, debonair, arrogant and with a great air of authority." It wins him no audience sympathy when, realizing belatedly that he did indeed invite Jane to the dance, mutters, "I must have been tight." With censors insisting that the drinking in the script be toned down, the result is somewhat illogical, as Phil seems perfectly normal and personable when he meets Jane, only to claim later that he was so inebriated he's forgotten about her. Unfortunately for Ayres, his leading lady demonstrates more chemistry in her few scenes with Richard Carlson (1912–1977), which may explain the casting of Simon's next film with Miss Turner.

Marsha Hunt (born 1917) gives nuance and gravitas to the featured role of Betty Ainsbridge, a troubled young woman who's afraid the opportunity for love has passed her by—at the age of 23. No longer attracted to the romantic leads she'd been assigned at Paramount, Miss Hunt jumped at the chance to sink her teeth into "my first offbeat role." Her performance, under Simon's direction, would set her on the path to being labeled "Hollywood's youngest character actress." Years later, she said, "It changed my entire professional life."[11]

Tom Brown (1913–1990) is cast as Homer Ten Eyck, Phil's roommate, described by the screenwriters as "Peach Cheeked Casanova and mad zany from way back. Most girls like Homer—and Homer likes most girls." A young Peter Lind Hayes (1915–1998) is Miss Turner's dance partner in a key scene. Dennie Moore (1902–1978) makes the most of her few scenes as Jane's cynical coworker and roommate.

When he found himself in need of a singer to warble "Loveliness," Simon remembered Dale Fellows (1914–1954), whom he had discovered and brought to Hollywood for a screen test a few years earlier. Fellows went home empty-handed that time, but was deemed perfect for the musical role in *Those Glamour Girls*.

Even if they had not worked together, Simon and actress Jane Bryan (1918–2009) would have far fewer than six degrees of separation between them. Miss Bryan, loaned out from Warners' for this project, retired from the movies in 1940 upon her marriage to business executive Justin Dart. She later became a close friend of Nancy Reagan, as did Simon's wife Harriet after marrying second husband Armand Deutsch.

An MGM press release claimed that Simon elicited a promise from his lead actresses that they would forego dating while the film was in production: "Director Sylvan Simon requested the 'no date' pledge at the beginning of the picture so that none of their natural vivacity and glamour would be dimmed by the strain of social activity. Strangely enough, they all agreed."[12] Columnist Sheilah Graham (July 11, 1939) was on set for one particularly early call time, where she found the actresses slow to come to life, and Simon "fast asleep on a camp bed." Revived, he asked his cast members, "Are we now in the mood?" only to find Anita Louise had dozed off.

Longtime Pittsburgher Simon may have chuckled at the line that finds Ann's socially prominent mother declaring, "There's a certain civilization, even in Pittsburgh." He evidently didn't contribute the line, however; it's in Hall and Parsonnet's script.

The film generally received favorable reviews, with the harshest response coming from an unexpected source—screenwriter Jane Hall. After attending a preview, she wrote bitterly in a letter to a family member, "They gave it cheap production, the worst director on the lot, and a no-name cast."[13] She may have been surprised to see that more than one review made favorable mention of Simon's directorial skills.

Reviews: "Combines good production by Sam Zimbalist, excellent direction by S. Sylvan Simon, and fine acting by the entire cast, to make this picture grand entertainment for any theater and on any bill." *Film Daily*, August 22, 1939

"Seldom excites more than passing interest ... Lew Ayres ... struggles hard to overcome the silly situations and mawkish lines.... Dialog is as feeble as the story. Direction is not half bad compared to what S. Sylvan Simon had to work with." *Variety*, September 6, 1939

Dancing Co-Ed (1939)

Lana Turner (*Patty Marlow*), Richard Carlson ("*Pug" Braddock*), Artie Shaw and His Band (*Themselves*), Ann Rutherford (*Eve Greeley*), Lee Bowman (*Freddy Tobin*), Thurston Hall (*Henry W. Workman*), Leon Errol ("*Pops" Marlow*), Roscoe Karns (*Joe Drews*), Mary Field (*Miss May*), Walter Kingsford (*President Cavendish*), Mary Beth Hughes (*Toddy*), June Preisser ("*Ticky" James*), Monty Woolley (*Professor Lange*), Chester Clute (*Braddock*), Rand Brooks (*Steve*), Helen Deverell (*Babe Harkness*), Gwen Kenyon (*Jean Royce*), Edythe Elliott (*Housemother*), Benny Baker (*Chief Evans*), Celia Travers (*Carol*), Mavis Mims (*Christie Carter*), Art Miles (*Masseur*), Laura Tredwell (*Dean of Women*), Lynn Lewis (*Toots*), John Wald (*Newscaster*)

Director: S. Sylvan Simon. *Producer*: Edgar Selwyn. *Screenplay*: Albert Mannheimer. *Story*: Albert Traynor. *Music Score*: Edward Ward, David Snell. *Dance Director*: George King. *Recording Director*: Douglas Shearer. *Art Director*: Cedric Gibbons. *Associate*: Harry McAfee. *Set Decorator*: Edwin B. Willis. *Wardrobe*: Dolly Tree. *Director of Photography*: Alfred Gilks. *Film Editor*: W. Donn Hayes.

MGM; released September 1939. 84 minutes.

Dancing movie stars Freddy and Toddy Tobin are elated at the news of their impending parenthood, but Henry Workman, head of Monarch Studios, and his publicity man Joe Drews fail to share their enthusiasm. Toddy's pregnancy will disrupt production of the studio's million-dollar film, *Dancing Co-Ed*. Sensing his job is on the line, Joe suggests a solution: a nationwide talent contest to be conducted on college campuses, with first prize to be the feminine lead in *Dancing Co-Ed*. Not trusting that a sufficiently talented amateur can be found, Joe arranges a "plant" at Midwestern University—dancer Patty Marlow, who's yet to graduate beyond small-time jobs. Joe's secretary, Eve, who hasn't finished college herself, is enrolled at Midwestern alongside Patty, to help her with the coursework for which the latter's grade-school education hasn't prepared her.

Patty tries to maintain a low profile at Midwestern, but she makes the acquaintance of Pug Braddock, reporter for the college newspaper, the *Porcupine*. When Monarch's talent competition is announced on the radio, Pug is immediately suspicious, sure that such a contest must be fixed for a pre-determined winner. Pug is determined to root out the phony contest winner if she is on the Midwestern campus, and casts a suspicious eye at the numerous co-eds who excitedly enroll in Miss May's tap dancing class. Patty decides that her best option for remaining incognito is to turn on the charm for Pug, and convince him that she will help root out the phony college girl.

When Pug and Patty run afoul of the university president, who's upset about some unflattering photos they published in the *Porcupine*, both of their fathers are summoned. Pug's dad refuses to be bothered, so the young man hires an actor to play the role. Pug's phony parent, with some help from Patty's real one, only adds to the havoc, and eventually she confesses everything about the contest to the man she has grown to love. Angered by the deception, Pug nevertheless wants to marry her—provided she give up any idea of taking part in the dance contest.

Dancing Co-Ed is a sprightly comedy of college life that showcases some of MGM's brightest, most appealing up-and-coming players of the late 1930s, notably Lana Turner, Richard Carlson, and Ann Rutherford. Their youthful appeal is neatly balanced by the seasoned character players who enliven the supporting roles. Aside from Roscoe Karns, Leon Errol, and Thurston Hall, all of whom contribute solid featured performances, Monty Woolley (1888–1963) makes quirky Professor Lange likable in his few scenes. This is Simon's first time directing busy character actress Mary Field (1909–1996), seen here as Midwestern University's nervous dance instructor; she will turn up again in his later films *Salute to the Marines*, *Her Husband's Affairs*, and *The Fuller Brush Man*.

One set visitor reported that Lana Turner struggled with the line, "We'll publish a retraction," which kept coming out as "We'll publicize a reaction." Said the observer, "Six times Mr. Simon had to shoot that particular line.... Mr. Simon was very nice and patient."[14]

Simon never allows the pace to lag. He employs swish pans in the film's opening scenes—as word of Toddy Tobin's pregnancy spreads like wildfire among the various interested parties—and again later in the film, cutting back and forth between the climactic dance contest and the last-minute developments that threaten to make Patty miss out on her chance.

Simon wrote a letter to his college fraternity, Kappa Nu, about the film, which was published in the campus newspaper. "My latest picture 'Dancing Coed' is partly based upon my own experiences at Michigan," he reported. "I hope that all my friends on the campus like my picture, and if they look sharply, I'm sure that they will recognize their alma mater behind the name of Midwestern."[15]

Despite the title and subject matter, the dancing sequences in the film are not extensive, and the footage spotlighting Artie Shaw and his orchestra is limited. Nonetheless, a studio publicity release claimed that director Simon was "pleasantly surprised with Artie's adaptability and claims that he could easily put his

Lana Turner and Richard Carlson are a charismatic couple in *Dancing Co-Ed.*

clarinet on the shelf and complete quite successfully with the current crop of screen juveniles."[16] However, a column item told it differently, saying that "Shaw raised so many objections to the dialogue that first one line and then another was dropped out or assigned by Director Sylvan Simon to other players."[17] According to Lana Turner, Shaw didn't ingratiate himself with many of his co-workers: "The crew plotted to drop an arc light on his head. I hated him too, and I even told the press that I thought he was the most egotistical man I'd ever met."[18] She married him a few months later.

In trade-paper ads, MGM publicists told exhibitors, "It is important for all showmen to screen it at once to see for themselves what a smash box-office attraction it is. Not since 'Dancing Daughters' days has there been a 'sleeper' of this type and it too will make a new star—Lana Turner." Simon served as one of the judges (along with talent scout Billy Gordon) in a contest to select Southern California's "Miss Dancing Co-Ed," held at the Florentine Gardens on November 2, 1939, with the winner and her partner awarded portable radios.

Reviews: "[*Dancing Co-Ed*] is gay, amusing and musical by turns, and there's a neat little romance thrown in for good measure. The direction of S. Sylvan Simon is expert, giving the picture a zippy pace that bubbles with action from start to finish … should be a solid hit with the pop trade." *Film Daily*, October 13, 1939

"Not only does the show give another demonstration that the studio has a valuable property in Ann Rutherford, but it reveals Lana Turner as a glamorous personality who in this vehicle exhibits all the earmarks presaging future stardom. The gay, airy quality of Albert Treynor's [sic] original has been expertly preserved in Albert Mannheimer's screenplay and its lively qualities were expertly brought out in S. Sylvan Simon's direction." *Motion Picture Daily*, September 22, 1939

Two Girls on Broadway (1940)

Lana Turner (*Pat Mahoney*), Joan Blondell (*Molly Mahoney*), George Murphy (*Eddie Kerns*), Kent Taylor ("*Chat*" *Chatsworth*), Richard Lane (*Buddy Bartell*), Wallace Ford (*Jed Marlowe*), Otto Hahn (*Ito*), Lloyd Corrigan (*Judge*), Don Wilson (*Announcer*), Charles Wagonheim (*Bartell's Assistant*), Jimmy Conlin (*Poem Vendor*), Daisy Bufford (*Powder Room Attendant*), George Lollier (*Henry*), Charles R. Moore (*Bus Station Porter*), May McAvoy (*Chatsworth's Secretary*), Edward Gargan (*Policeman*), Hal K. Dawson (*License Bureau Clerk*), Adrienne D'Ambricourt (*Miss Apricots*), Joe Devlin (*Taxi Driver*)

Director: S. Sylvan Simon. *Producer*: Jack Cummings. *Screenplay*: Joseph Fields, Jerome Chodorov. *Story*: Edmund Goulding. *Director of Photography*: George Folsey. *Musical Presentation*: Merrill Pye. *Musical Director*: Georgie Stoll. *Musical Arrangements*: Walter Ruick. *Orchestration*: Leo Arnaud, George Bassman. *Dance Directors*: Bobby Connolly, Eddie Larkin. *Film Editor*: Blanche Sewell. *Recording Director*: Douglas Shearer. *Art Director*: Cedric Gibbons. *Associate*: Stan Rogers. *Set Decorations*: Edwin B. Willis. *Wardrobe*: Dolly Tree.

MGM; released April 1940. 73 minutes.

Their show business career stalled by the demise of vaudeville, dancers Eddie Kerns and his fiancée Molly Mahoney are staying afloat running a dance school in a small Nebraska town. Eddie dreams up a scheme to get a free ticket to New York, appearing on a radio talent show, "Oddities of the Air." His appearance, dancing to a musical number he wrote, pays off big, as casino owner Buddy Bartell wants the song for his fall show. Wealthy playboy "Chat" Chatsworth watches in amusement as Eddie not only scores a dancing gig in the show for himself, but persuades Buddy to give Molly and her younger sister Pat auditions as well.

Upon their arrival, the sisters audition for Buddy, who wants Pat, rather than Molly, to team with Eddie for a dance number. For Molly, he has nothing better than a job as a cigarette girl. Pat indignantly refuses, but her more pragmatic sister argues that they should all accept. Pat's beauty and charm quickly attract the attention of not only the smooth Chatsworth, but Eddie himself, who finds himself falling for her as they work together.

Molly is reunited with another ex-hoofer, Jed Marlowe, now a successful newspaper columnist. He warns her of Chat's bad reputation: "That boy keeps in shape by hot-footing between the license bureau and the divorce courts." Pat and Eddie finally acknowledge their mutual attraction with a kiss, but she will have no part of stealing her sister's man.

According to producer Jack Cummings, *Two Girls on Broadway* was assembled hurriedly when MGM needed a film to plug a hole in its release schedule. He remembered working on *The Broadway Melody* (1929), and had the idea to do a lightly disguised remake. Growing impatient with internal delays in getting the script approved, Cummings told Simon, "I know you're fast, but you've got to be plenty fast. I'm putting this picture in production right now."[19] Simon completed the film in 14 days.

This was the last of a trio of films in which Simon directed the up-and-coming Lana Turner. Turner's dancing was sufficiently impressive that *Los Angeles Times* critic Edwin Schallert expressed doubt, in reviewing the film, that she had done it without the aid of a double. He later noted (April 18, 1940) that Simon and the film's dance director Bobby Connolly "both testify that Miss Turner performed all the steps." Given the camera angles employed in the dance numbers, it's difficult to see how Schallert could have doubted this, as Miss Turner is prominent in almost every shot.

However she may have felt about being second-billed to Turner after a decade in Hollywood, Joan Blondell (1906–1979) delivers the best performance here, cast as the older sister. She effortlessly knocks off a few typical cracks as the slightly jaded Molly. Tired after a long stretch on her feet, she says, "I used to dream of having this town at my feet. Now I'd settle for a good chiropodist." But it is her dramatic moments, mostly played in silence, that are the most memorable.

George Murphy (1902–1992) practically defines chutzpah in the role of the brash Eddie. After he bulldozes his way into a job, makes a long-distance call on Bartell's phone, and talks his new friend into giving his fiancée and her sister a shot as well, the casino owner says dryly, "Haven't you got any folks from the old country you'd like to bring over here?" His character doesn't deserve much audience sympathy, deciding to trade in his loyal fiancée for her younger sister. Murphy's strongest contribution, of course, is his dancing skill; he's even balletic when he's knocked on his rear end (twice) by another man's fist.

In his autobiography, Murphy recalled, "During the first few days of shooting, there were very few people on the set. This was not one of those Metro spectaculars that drew curiosity seekers from all over the studio." However, word quickly spread about his new leading lady. "Everyone at Metro was talking about this fascinating new blonde.... You could hardly get on the set, so many people had come to see the lovely newcomer in the flesh."[20]

Kent Taylor (1907–1987) fits the role of Chatsworth, the sophisticated smoothie, like a pair of leather gloves. He embodies the well-to-do suitor whose accouterments include a pop-up bar in his car, and a line of patter that includes sallies like, "I wish I'd met you four wives ago." Wallace Ford is effective in his understated performance as Jed. According to the *Los Angeles Times'* Edwin Schallert (January 22, 1940), Ford was on his way to New York when MGM tracked him down to play the role; "they were able to pull him off the train at Pasadena."

Though Simon doesn't go in for needless directorial flourishes, he nonetheless adds interest and energy to scenes with his fluid camera that's frequently on the move. In one continuous sequence, he opens on actor Charles Wagonheim standing on the stage of Bartell's club, pans rapidly to Kent Taylor and Richard Lane on the club floor chatting, and, once they walk out of the shot, closes in on Joan Blondell seated at a table, as Wallace Ford makes his entrance from upstage.

Kent Taylor works his wiles on Lana Turner in *Two Girls on Broadway*.

Simon allows even bit players a moment or two to shine, including Charles R. Moore as the befuddled porter caught in the middle of an argument between Molly and Pat. Another scene finds Pat in the casino's powder room, employing a pair of scissors to make some impromptu alternations to her evening gown; Miss Turner walks out of frame while Simon's camera stays on the startled reaction of the attendant on duty (Daisy Bufford). Former silent film actress May McAvoy's brief appearance as Bartell's secretary supposedly won her a studio contract.

A studio publicity item claimed that Turner took ice skating lessons in preparation for the scene in which she visits a rink while on a date with Chatsworth. She purportedly mastered the sport so well that Simon complained, "But you're not supposed to know how. You're supposed to be a novice." His leading lady said, "I'll practice forgetting this week."[21]

Screenwriters Joseph A. Fields and Jerome Chodorov will hit the big time a few months after the film's release, when their play *My Sister Eileen*, also about a couple of girls making their way in New York, becomes a smash hit.

Reviews: "Although the plot is well-worn, patterned after the first 'Broadway Melody' picture, this film has plenty of entertainment, due mostly to the fine trouping of the cast ... the direction of S. Sylvan Simon lifts it above the material.... Joan Blondell turns in one of the finest performances of her career." *Showmen's Trade Review*, April 27, 1940

"What the story lacks in originality is compensated for by the high degree of entertainment value put into it by the direction of Sylvan Simon. He keeps it moving, gets good performances from its players without stressing points, and by presenting them as a batch of ordinary humans for whom he enlists our interest and maintains it throughout." *Hollywood Spectator*, May 1, 1940

Sporting Blood (1940)

Robert Young (*Myles Vanders*), Maureen O'Sullivan (*Linda Lockwood*), Lewis Stone (*Davis Lockwood*), William Gargan (*Duffy*), Lynne Carver (*Joan Lockwood*), Clarence Muse (*Jeff*), Lloyd Corrigan (*Otis Winfield*), George H. Reed (*Stonewall*), Tom Kennedy (*Grantly*), Russell Hicks ("*Sneak*" *O'Brien*), George Lessey (*Cobb*), Eugene Jackson (*Sam*), William Tannen (*Ted Milner*), Edward Hearn (*Bank Guard*), Allen Wood (*Jockey*), Alfred Hall (*Horse Owner*)

Director: S. Sylvan Simon. *Producer*: Albert E. Levoy. *Screenplay*: Lawrence Hazard, Albert Mannheimer, Dorothy Yost. *Original Story*: Grace Norton. *Director of Photography*: Sidney Wagner. *Musical Score*: Franz Waxman. *Art Director*: Cedric Gibbons. *Associate*: Stan Rogers. *Set Decorator*: Edwin B. Willis. *Film Editor*: Frank Sullivan. *Recording Director*: Douglas Shearer. *Wardrobe*: Dolly Tree. [*Assistant Director*: Gilbert Kurland. *Prop Man*: Harry Lazarre. *Sound Mixer*: Newell Sparks. *Unit Manager*: Charles Hunt. *Makeup Man*: Lyle Dawn. *Hairdresser*: Anna Delph.]

MGM; released July 1940. 82 minutes.

Stable owner Myles Vanders loses big in a horse race due to an unscrupulous rival. With his best horse Skipper injured, Myles retreats to his childhood home in Virginia after a 20-year absence. He finds the family property in a badly dilapidated condition, and the local residents none too friendly. Still, he's determined to let Skipper's leg injury heal, so that the horse can be entered in the Thomas Jefferson Handicap race in a few months.

Myles explains to his friend and trainer Duffy that his late father ran away with the wife of a powerful man, Davis Lockwood some years ago, making him and his family *persona non grata* in the community. After being refused a bank loan, Myles goes to confront Lockwood, but the older man claims he bears the Vanders family no animosity. Lockwood agrees to give Vanders a $3000 loan to cover his expenses in training Skipper.

While at the Lockwood house, Myles meets the wealthy man's two beautiful daughters, Joan and Linda. Immediately attracted to Joan, he pays less attention to Linda. On a stormy night, Myles' horse Sweetheart is ready to give birth, but there are complications. With Linda's help, the horse is saved, but Myles only has eyes for Joan. Lockwood makes it clear to his daughters that he will not tolerate a Vanders in the family.

A deadly fire breaks out in Myles' stable, started by Lockwood's loyal manservant, and Myles confronts the older man in a fury. Intending to marry Joan in defiance of her father's wishes, Myles is stunned to learn that she has eloped with another man. He proposes to Linda, who accepts, but he feels guilty about taking advantage of her love for him. With the Jefferson Handicap race imminent, Myles takes on the challenge of training Linda's horse for the race. As it turns out, not only Myles' professional future, but also his marriage, may depend on the outcome of the race.

Sporting Blood is a very competently made film that, unfortunately, isn't much fun. Racetrack fans are apt to be disappointed at how much of the film's footage is devoted to personal dramas, and horse lovers may find some of the scenes uncomfortable to watch. Simon's flair for comedy, which lightened even the likes of *The Crime of Doctor Hallet*, would be out of place here, as he undoubtedly recognized, but in its absence the proceedings are pretty grim.

The basis for the film was Grace Norton's story "One Came Home," and that title was retained while it was in production. Early reports indicated that Robert Taylor would play the lead role, but by the time cameras rolled, another Robert had taken his place.

Robert Young (1907–1998) struggles gamely with the frequently unsympathetic role of Myles, a hothead whose treatment of the woman who loves him is cavalier at best. (He somehow charms his bride-to-be with the lackluster offer, "Would you be interested in getting married?") Myles finally earns a well-deserved punch from William Gargan's Duffy, who comes across as substantially more level-headed and loyal.

William Gargan makes Duffy a more appealing character than the leading man in *Sporting Blood* (1940).

If nothing else, Myles can turn a phrase; he says Joan "happens to look like something you sip through a straw," which would seem to be a compliment. Later, in a line that provokes a sorely needed laugh, unintentional though it may be, he tells Duffy, "Did you ever try making love to a horse? They don't know what you're talking about!"

Leading lady Maureen O'Sullivan's accent and diction make her seem a bit out of place in rural Virginia. She gives her character a vulnerable quality that breathes life and depth into the role of Linda. Somewhat better-suited to the story's setting than the Irish Miss O'Sullivan is her co-star Lynne Carver (1916–1955), in the first of two films she will make in quick succession under Simon's direction. Signed to an MGM contract in 1937, the young actress, originally known in films as Virginia Reid, was renamed by the studio, which already had too many Virginias on the payroll. Never achieving top stardom, Miss Carver died young, of cancer.

Lewis Stone (1879–1953), taking a brief holiday from the Andy Hardy series, plays the role of Linda and Joan's stuffy father, hardly a model parent. Though the Hardys' town of Carvel represented the best of small-town American life, here Stone's character inhabits a place Myles decries for its "rotten small-town lies" and "smug, thin-minded citizens." Clarence Muse (1889–1979), as Lockwood's servant Jeff, gives the role as much dignity as the script allows; two of the white characters call him a "black rascal." Another servant, Stonewall, has virtually every one of his lines scripted in exaggerated dialect, as when he remarks, "Dat what yo' pappy allus usta say when sump'n went wrong.... An' yo' is jes like yo' pappy, Mistuh Miles—yo is de spit'n image of him."

The script underwent substantial revision before being captured on film; the earliest version is dated April 4, 1940, but there are numerous changes throughout, some carrying dates later in the same month, while pink pages with various May dates appear with some frequency as well. Even the latest pages, dated in mid–May, carry the title "One Came Home." In Simon's copy, there are also numerous lines of dialogue crossed out, and revisions written in by hand.

Studio publicity promised moviegoers "one of the most thrilling fire scenes ever filmed," adding, "The scenes required two nights of work on exteriors of the barn and two days inside a stage. Controlled fire was used, firemen being on hand to extinguish the blaze after each thrilling shot."[22]

Reviews: "An absorbing little race-track story that should please and prove satisfactory on any program. What it lacks in originality of theme is more than compensated for by its efficient performances, its fine photography, and the masterful direction of S. Sylvan Simon. Robert Young and Maureen O'Sullivan are splendid." *Showmen's Trade Review*, July 13, 1940

"*Sporting Blood*, while not a great picture, is still a good one of its kind.... Mr. Young, able horseman himself, is ably equipped for this role ... as a romantic lead he's hard to beat.... Maureen O'Sullivan invests her portrayal with sincerity and charm.... The film has quite a lot of suspense, relieved by some leavening laughs. You'll like it." Mae Tinée, *Chicago Tribune*, October 1, 1940

Dulcy (1940)

Ann Sothern (*Dulcy Ward*), Ian Hunter (*Gordon Daly*), Roland Young (*C. Roger Forbes*), Reginald Gardiner (*Schuyler Van Dyke* a/k/a *Horace Patterson*), Billie Burke (*Eleanor Forbes*), Lynne Carver (*Angela Forbes*), Dan Dailey, Jr. (*Bill Ward*), Donald Huie ("*Sneezy*"), Jonathan Hale (*Homer Patterson*), Guinn "Big Boy" Williams (*Henry*), Hans Conried (*Vincent Leach*), Gerald Oliver Smith (*Huggins*), Mary Treen (*Miss Twill*), Philip Van Zandt (*Taxi Driver*), Joe Yule (*Dock Attendant*), George Lessey

(*Judge*), Robert Middlemass (*Mr. Van Dyke*), May McAvoy (*Miss Murphy*), David Oliver (*Tom*), Bert Moorhouse (*Judge's Clerk*), Bobby Callahan (*Young Boy*), Ivan Miller (*Ship's Captain*), Jerry Fletcher (*Photographer*), Eddie Dunn (*Policeman*)

Director: S. Sylvan Simon. *Producer*: Edgar Selwyn. *Screenplay*: Albert Mannheimer, Jerome Chodorov, Joseph A. Fields, based on the play by George S. Kaufman and Marc Connelly. *Director of Photography*: Charles Lawton. *Musical Score*: Bronislau Kaper. *Recording Director*: Douglas Shearer. *Art Director*: Cedric Gibbons. *Associate*: Howard Campbell. *Gowns*: Adrian. *Miss Sothern's Hairstyles*: Sydney Guilaroff. *Film Editor*: Frank E. Hull.

MGM; released October 1940. 73 minutes.

Lovely, impulsive Dulcy Ward is a goodhearted young lady who unwittingly creates chaos and confusion wherever she goes. En route to the pier to meet her brother Bill's fiancée Angela and her parents, Dulcy stops by a judge's office, where she accepts responsibility for a newly paroled man, Henry, appointing him as her family's new butler. At the pier, she meets a young Chinese boy, who's being delivered to the care of his new adoptive father, Gordon Daly. When the little boy takes a shine to Dulcy, she decides to serve as his godmother. Gordon is an aspiring inventor who has developed a new airplane motor, and Dulcy plots to introduce him to the father of Bill's fiancée, whose company designs and builds aircraft.

Dulcy invites Angela and her parents to a weekend at the Wards' resort cottage, but the good impression she means to make on Bill's future in-laws goes awry. One disaster after another befalls Roger Forbes, until he's reduced to a helpless rage. Bill persuades Angela they should elope, but her letter to her father reaches him too soon, thanks to Dulcy. With her brother's romance in jeopardy, and Forbes refusing to have anything to do with Gordon's motor, Dulcy's luck seems to have run out.

Some amusing vignettes show the havoc Dulcy creates without even trying. Alerted that she is working on the boiler in the basement, her panicked servants run for the hills, just in time to avoid the explosion that rocks the house. At the resort, seeing Dulcy racing toward the shore at the helm of a speedboat, an attendant at the dock rushes to blow a loud whistle, explaining, "Dulcy Ward is coming, and I'm giving everyone on the lake on the lake an even chance!" Not only do those in sailboats scurry to get out of her path, but the nearby ducks take cover under water. Introduced to Bill's fiancée, Angela, Dulcy remarks, "Bill has always had the most dreadful taste in girls up to now. Why, if you could have seen the last one, my dear, you wouldn't have believed it!"

Ann Sothern (1909–2001) delivers a fine comedy performance, making Dulcy endearing and sympathetic despite the character's genius for pandemonium. (At one unusually self-aware juncture, when Gordon calls her "the best-hearted person I know," Dulcy ruefully replies, "Yes, only my heart's probably where my brain ought to be.") Just a few months earlier, the actress had launched her popular "Maisie" series for MGM, but here she garners plentiful laughs with a comic persona that's quite different. Before her casting was announced in February 1940, columnists had reported that the *Dulcy* remake was earmarked for Rosalind Russell. Columnist Hedda Hopper (February 13, 1940) reported that Miss Russell had refused the role, but that producer Edgar Selwyn was "delighted he's got Ann Sothern for it, 'cause he loves 'Dulcy' and has ever since Lynn Fontanne made her famous."

Miss Sothern is supported by a top-flight cast of character actors, including

Ann Sothern, as *Dulcy*, unwittingly arouses the ire of Roland Young.

Roland Young (1887–1953) and Billie Burke (1884–1970) as the wealthy parents of her brother's fiancée. Guinn "Big Boy" Williams (1899–1962) garners his share of laughs as the rough-hewn parolee turned butler, while Reginald Gardiner (1903–1980) is cast as the Wards' eccentric houseguest. Our first glimpse of Dan Dailey (1915–1978), in the film's opening moments, find him singing up a storm in the shower ("the glass door of which is frosted to a decent height," the script cautions). Hans Conried (1917–1982) has two brief appearances as an eccentric playwright who becomes yet another of Dulcy's unintentional victims. Conried would later remember gratefully that Roland Young invited the young actor into his dressing room after the wet, messy scenes were shot, offering him some whisky to get warm. Among the bit players cast as businessmen in Bill Ward's office are Ralph Byrd (later to play Dick Tracy in films and an early TV series), and Hal Le Sueur, elder brother of then–MGM star Joan Crawford.

Simon was quoted in the film's pressbook as saying, "At the present, with the demand for comedies reaching a new high point in popular favor, comedians are scarce.... We were extremely fortunate in gathering together a cast which for my money spells tops in comedy." He credited his players with embellishing what was on the written page: "When a group of comedians get together, a gag is inevitable. Many times these impromptu stunts prove funnier than the action in the original script." Another item described the jitters Roland Young experienced shooting the scene in which he's nearly attacked by Dulcy's large dog. The Great Dane cast in the latter role growled and snarled convincingly on cue. Gentlemanly as ever, Young reportedly turned to Simon and said, "I don't mean to interfere, but I do think a Peke would be more appropriate for this scene."[23] Young's responses to the various mishaps that befall him are a master class in comic timing and reactions. As his wife, Billie Burke has fewer opportunities for laughs in the script, but is charming nonetheless.

Dulcy began life as a comedy by George S. Kaufman and Marc Connelly, which ran for some 241 performances on Broadway during the 1921–22 season. Lynn Fontanne played the title role onstage. Its first film adaptation came in 1923, starring Constance Talmadge. Marion Davies took the lead in a 1930 remake, *Not So Dumb*. MGM acquired the rights to mount this version in late 1938, with early announcements indicating that Norman Z. McLeod would direct.

Simon's copy of Albert Mannheimer's screenplay is dated March 28, 1940, but contains some pages dating from February 24. Changes on inserted pink pages are plentiful, some dated as late as July 1940. Simon relished the chance to direct a film rich in physical comedy. Before the shenanigans at the lake are finished, about half the male cast has taken a dive into the water. Under his guidance, *Dulcy* offers both witty dialogue and beautifully executed slapstick, making a winning combination. Location footage was shot in and around Lake Arrowhead. A revised script page dated June 27, 1940, gave 6-year-old featured player Donald Huie, as Dulcy's ward Sneezy, the film's curtain line, when he remarks, "You're nuts!" But the finished film instead allowed Hans Conried the last word, or rather the last gesture, when he sticks out his tongue to express his opinion of our hapless heroine.

Reviews: "In this her third appearance on the screen, 'Dulcy' is still hilariously entertaining.... Ann Sothern makes her more laughingly beguiling than either of her predecessors in the role.... Director Simon does a slick job in romping the farce situations along with speedy pace, at the same time keeping a kind of credibility in the main character to sustain interest in her as a human misfit." *Daily Variety*, September 27, 1940

"A face-lifting job done expertly by M-G-M and all concerned.... The old Kaufman-Connelly comedy [is] fresh as a daisy and quite able to hold its head up high alongside the clever farces of the day.... Miss Southern [*sic*] offers further proof that she is Hollywood's most finished feminine comedian.... S. Sylvan Simon's accelerated direction keeps it from sagging even in thin spots." Wanda Hale, *New York Daily News*, November 28, 1940

Keeping Company (1940)

Frank Morgan (*Harry C. Thomas*), Ann Rutherford (*Mary Thomas*), John Shelton (*Ted Foster*), Irene Rich (*Susan Thomas*), Gene Lockhart (*Mr. Hellman*), Virginia Weidler (*Harriet Thomas*), Virginia Grey (*Anastasia Atherton*), Dan Dailey (*Jim Reynolds*), Gloria DeHaven (*Evelyn Thomas*), Sara Haden (*Mrs. Foster*), Harry Tyler (*Joe Green*), Fern Emmett (*Miss Miller*), Richard Crane (*Eddie Lane*), John Webb Dillion (*Postman*), Buddy Messinger (*Ticket Seller at Basketball Game*), Robert Winkler (*Urchin with Compact*), Sally Martin, Ann E. Todd (*Harriet's Sidekicks*)

Director: S. Sylvan Simon. *Producer*: Samuel Marx. *Screenplay*: Harry Ruskin, James H. Hill, Adrian Scott. *Original Story*: Herman J. Mankiewicz. *Director of Photography*: Karl Freund. *Musical Score*: Daniele Amfitheatrof. *Recording Director*: Douglas Shearer. *Art Director*: Cedric Gibbons. *Associate*: Wade B. Rubottom. *Set Decorator*: Edwin B. Willis. *Film Editor*: Elmo Veron.

MGM; released December 1940. 80 minutes.

Real estate agent Harry Thomas and his wife are bringing up three daughters in the small town of Thornridge. Snoopy tween Harriet, after eavesdropping on her older sister, tells her mother that Mary is planning to be married. Mary's parents aren't sure which of her steady dates, Ted Foster or Jim Reynolds, she has chosen. Harriet arranges for both contenders to come to dinner at the Thomas house, where Ted pops the question and Mary eagerly accepts. Mary's parents try to prepare their daughter and her fiancé for the ups and downs of married life, but the young people insist they'll never quarrel or disagree.

Mr. Hellman, Ted and Jim's boss at a local car dealership, is eager to retire, and plans to leave the agency in the hands of one of the two young men. Wanting to show up his rival, Ted proposes an ambitious sales effort involving a new factory soon to be constructed. Meanwhile, his old flame Anastasia Atherton returns to town, and wants him back. Ted firmly tells Anastasia he loves only Mary, but agrees to buy his ex-girlfriend's used car at a discounted price.

Mary and Ted's marriage starts off joyously, but the newlyweds have their first crisis when she opens a letter from Anastasia, who's looking for a compact she dropped in the car. Mary finds the compact, and believes that Ted is rekindling his old flame with her rival. After a heated argument, Mary runs out on him, and goes back to her family. Meanwhile, Ted's potentially lucrative deal at work falls through, imperiling not only his job but the future of the dealership.

While *Keeping Company* benefits from its ensemble of appealing performers, the standout here is 13-year-old Virginia Weidler (1927–1968), cast as the Thomases' mischievous youngest daughter, Harriet. With a passion for ice cream, a tendency to scheme, and a gift for snooping, Harriet says resignedly of herself, "Things just happen when I'm around." She's delighted when she catches the bouquet at her sister's wedding, but is pragmatic enough to hand it to a pal, saying, "Here, put this in water. I know where I can sell it."

Though her parents do their best to keep the incorrigible girl in line, they're largely unsuccessful, as she points out when she finds herself being disciplined yet again: "'The number of spankings I've had, I should think people around here would start to see it wasn't doing any good!" Not intimidated by the uppity Anastasia, Harriet evens the score in her own memorable way. Five years before a similar line found its way into *Mildred Pierce* (1945), Anastasia disdainfully says of Harriet, "Now I know why some animals eat their young!" For all her shenanigans, Miss Weidler makes Harriet an endearing character, one who sheds a few tears at the idea of Mary leaving home.

Virginia Grey (1917–2004) plays yet another slinky, sophisticated type, "a streamlined redhead" as Mr. Thomas calls her. Ann Rutherford and John Shelton (1915–1972) make an attractive couple, even when they are forced to soldier through some ill-chosen dialogue; Shelton, as Ted, has a few bones to pick about their relationship, among them, "I haven't had any buttons on my drawers since we were married!"

In *Keeping Company*, newlywed Mary (Ann Rutherford, center) thinks the compact she found in her husband's car means trouble. Her parents Susan (Irene Rich) and Harry (Frank Morgan) lend sympathetic ears.

Marriage seemed to present a few challenges for Shelton off-camera as well, though he tried it five times. His divorce from Sally Sage, who worked frequently as a double for Bette Davis in the 1930s, was finalized shortly before *Keeping Company* arrived in theaters.

Irene Rich (1891–1988), an accomplished actress whose film credits dated back to the late 1910s, is warmly appealing as the family's sensible mother, whose husband fondly calls her "Chief." Of the three Thomas sisters, it's Evelyn, played by Gloria DeHaven (1925–2016), who gets the short end of the story stick, having only a few scenes. Young Dan Dailey, still billed here as Dan Dailey, Jr., is prominent in the film's early scenes, but goes by the wayside as it progresses.

Simon supervised the construction of the film's small town setting, Thornridge, adjoining the Hardys' town of Carvel on the studio back lot. "Just like Carvel," he told a reporter, "it will have a personality all its own. That is an amazing characteristic of American towns, each is distinctive. That makes our work in pictures easier. We can build towns such as Carvel and Thornridge that will be both remembered and recognized by the public."[24]

At Louis B. Mayer's upscale studio, even a B movie wasn't just thrown together. Simon's copy of the *Keeping Company* script includes more than 40 pages of planned revisions, additions, and retakes. One page describes a change to Scene 81: "Retake

CLOSE SHOT of Mary in bed, lying in the dark. We would eliminate the tears and sobs, and she would just be very angry when she hears Ted in the hall and his voice calling, 'Mary, Mary, where are you?'"

MGM executives had high hopes that *Keeping Company* would launch a new series for the studio, which had already made a bundle on Andy Hardy and clan. Simon's copy of the screenplay contains a pink revision page that would provide a plug for further adventures of the Thomases, to be delivered by Frank Morgan in character. Addressing the audience directly, he was to say, "You know, folks, all these years the movies have been telling us that when the girl goes into the boy's embrace, it's a happy ending to all their troubles. That's not true.... Ladies and gentlemen, Metro-Goldwyn-Mayer intends to bring you some of the further adventures that happen to Ted and Mary [and other family members] ... Be seeing you."

But tepid public response to the first film led to a substantial shake-up before the studio tried a second time, with *This Time for Keeps* (1942). Once again, Miss Rutherford played the young bride, with Weidler and Rich reprising their roles as her sister and mother, but all of the characters' names were changed, and all the male roles recast. Simon played no part in the follow-up film, which put an end once and for all to MGM's plans for a series.

Reviews: "The picture as a whole is thoroughly delightful entertainment for the family trade particularly, and audiences generally will be interested and amused.... The film has been peopled with a charming and competent cast that makes the characterizations true to life.... Much credit is due Director S. Sylvan Simon for his sympathetic and smooth handling of the players and the story, with nothing to be desired on this score." *Film Daily*, January 14, 1941

"The prospect of having a series emerge from this first adventure of the Thomas family is too horrible to contemplate! The story is as old as the proverbial hills, the dialogue is noisy and tiresome, the complications are abundant and uninteresting and the whole picture smacks of 'quickie'—in short, this is an enterprise of which Metro should be ashamed." *Film Bulletin*, January 11, 1941

Meet the Stars #2: Baby Stars (1941)

Ella Bryan, Lucia Carroll, Peggy Diggins, Lorraine Elliott, Jayne Hazard, Joan Leslie, Kay Leslie, Marilyn [Lynn] Merrick, Gay Parkes, Lois Ranson, Sheila Ryan, Patricia Van Cleve, Tanya Widrin (*Contestants*), Joan Blondell, Eleanor Boardman, Evelyn Brent, Sue Carol, June Collyer, Dolores del Rio, Sally Eilers, Helen Ferguson, Janet Gaynor, Carmelita Geraghty, Evalyn Knapp, Anita Louise, Jobyna Ralston, Jacqueline Wells [Julie Bishop], Lois Wilson, Claire Windsor, Fay Wray (*Former Baby Stars*), John Brahm, Tay Garnett, Eddie [Edward] Goulding, J. Theodore Reed, S. Sylvan Simon, Paul Sloane, Raoul Walsh, Orson Welles (*Judges*)

Producer-Director: Harriet Parsons.

Republic; released January 1941. 10 minutes.

At a dinner party in Hollywood, 13 aspiring young actresses present skits showcasing their talents, and are judged by a panel of current motion picture directors, including S. Sylvan Simon. Also appearing are actresses who were winners of the original WAMPAS Baby Stars contests in the 1920s and early 1930s.

Syndicated columnist Louella O. Parsons (August 30, 1940), whose daughter Harriet would make this short film some months later, reported, "Raoul Walsh is back of a plan to revive the old Hollywood tradition of selecting the 13 baby stars who have the most promise of succeeding…. Each studio will be privileged to submit two or three girls under 21 years of age who have played not more than two speaking parts. An eligible person may submit herself." Given Simon's ongoing interest in discovering and training new talent, it wasn't surprising that he took part in the competition. The finalists were chosen in fall 1940.

As was the norm with such contests, the initial spurt of publicity benefited some contestants, while others flamed out quickly. Syndicated columnist Jimmy Fidler (February 12, 1941) pointed out that, only a few months after their initial selection, "four of them … are now working as dance instructresses for Arthur Murray!" Joan Leslie, under contract to Warners' for much of the 1940s, was the most successful alumna of this group. Simon would later direct contestant Marilyn Merrick, who would shorten her professional name to Lynn Merrick, in *I Love Trouble* (1948).

Reviews: "Judging from this film there is a vast array of talent which has yet to hit the screen in a big way … should dazzle the average fan." *Showmen's Trade Review*, February 1, 1941

"The [featured] names … and shots of directors … should attract and interest most audiences." *Motion Picture Herald*, February 1, 1941

Washington Melodrama (1941)

Frank Morgan (*Calvin Claymore*), Ann Rutherford (*Laurie Claymore*), Kent Taylor (*Hal Thorne*), Dan Dailey, Jr. (*Whitney King*), Lee Bowman (*Ronnie Colton*), Fay Holden (*Mrs. Claymore*), Virginia Grey (*Teddy Carlyle*), Anne Gwynne (*Mary Morgan*), Sara Haden (*Mrs. Harrington*), Olaf Hytten (*Parry*), Douglass Dumbrille (*Donnelly*), Cliff Clark (*Simpson*), Hal K. Dawson (*Logan*), Thurston Hall (*Senator Morton*), Joseph Crehan (*Phil Sampson*), Frederick Burton (*Dean Lawford*), Howard Hickman (*Bishop Chatterton*), Virginia Brissac (*Mrs. Curzon*), James Millican (*Police Detective*), Charles Sherlock (*Composing Room Clerk*), Bert Roach (*Taxi Driver*), William Tannen (*Airport Official*), Russell Custer (*Reporter*), Dick French (*Dick*), George Noisom (*Newsboy*)

Director: S. Sylvan Simon. *Producer*: Edgar Selwyn. *Screenplay*: Marion Parsonnet, Roy Chanslor, based on a play by L. du Rocher Macpherson. *Director of Photography*: Harold Rosson. *Art Director*: Cedric Gibbons. *Associate*: Stan Rogers. *Recording Director*: Douglas Shearer. *Film Editor*: Gene Ruggiero. *Musical Score*: David Snell. *Song*, "Fishing for Suckers": Earl Brent. *Water Ballet*: Lottie Horner. *Dances*: Sammy Lee. [*Makeup*: Karl Herlinger, Jr. *Casting*: Jasper Russell. *Unit Manager*: Charles Levin. *Assistant Director*: Bert Spurlin. *Properties*: Harry Albiez. *Wardrobe Woman*: *Hairdresser*: Beth Langston. Violet Smith. *Script Clerk*: Wally Worsley.]

MGM; released April 1941. 80 minutes.

Calvin Claymore is a wealthy business executive who operates a philanthropic foundation. He is championing a "Feed Europe" program to benefit refugee children trapped behind enemy lines, but his board members warn him there will be opposition. Among those opposed to the plan is Hal Thorne, editor and publisher of a tabloid newspaper, the *Washington Tab.* Thorne also happens to be dating Calvin's daughter Laurie.

With his wife and daughter traveling for the summer, a lonely Calvin is taken out to a nightclub by his friend, Senator Morton. The club's live entertainment includes an elaborate water ballet featuring beautiful young ladies. One of them, Mary Morgan, arranges to meet Calvin, on instructions from the show's unscrupulous emcee, Whit King. Over the next few weeks, Calvin and Mary form a platonic friendship. Appreciating the older man's kindness and decency, a remorseful Mary refuses to carry out the scheme as Whit decreed. Angry, Whit punches her, resulting in a fall that kills the young woman.

Hal's newspaper publishes a front-page story, "Mermaid Morgan Murdered," and a blind item alluding to the unidentified older man that was Mary's frequent companion. Unaware that the mysterious friend was Calvin, Hal hires his old pal, Ronnie Colton, to take an apartment in Mary's building and snoop. Meanwhile, in possession of a note that Calvin wrote to Mary, Whit proceeds to blackmail the industrialist.

Laurie tells her father that she and Hal are to be married. When Ronnie finds Calvin's missing glove in the dead woman's apartment, Hal seizes upon it to help identify the murderer. Calvin burns the glove's mate, but Laurie finds pieces of it in the fireplace. After Calvin tells his wife and daughter about his relationship with Mary, Laurie vows to stand by him, unlike her mother. Calvin confesses to Hal that the glove is his, and the newspaperman tries to cover for his soon-to-be father-in-law. As he prepares to testify before the Senate Foreign Relations Committee about his "Feed Europe" bill, Calvin faces the possibility that his friendship with the late Miss Morgan will cause lasting injury to both his philanthropy, and his private life.

Released several months prior to the Japanese attack on Pearl Harbor, and United States' entry into World War II, *Washington Melodrama* is accurately summed up by its title, though it takes a few unexpected turns. After the opening scenes depicting Claymore's business and philanthropic activities, it's a bit surprising when we're transported to the Club Marigold, and a floor show featuring an elaborately staged water ballet. Syndicated columnist Harrison Carroll (March 31, 1941) visited the set during production, where he saw Dan Dailey and Virginia Grey doing a dance routine before "the whole dance floor rolls back revealing an illuminated swimming pool. Then, at a cue from Director Sylvan Simon, a line of pretty mermaids swarms out and dives into the pool. They cut the water so cleanly that they don't even splash the gowns of the dress extras sitting at the ringside tables."

The screenplay reflects the isolationist sentiment that was still commonplace among American citizens. (Hal Thorne says that helping foreign refugees would "lighten the burden of our enemies.") The film was adapted from L. du Rocher Macpherson's unproduced play "She Takes the Wheel," which MGM had acquired in 1933. *Variety* (November 27, 1934) described it as "a newspaper yarn, probably for Joan Crawford." Simon's script, dated February 15, 1941, has numerous instances in

Anne Gwynne makes friends with Frank Morgan in *Washington Melodrama*.

which dialogue has been crossed out, trimmed, or rephrased, as well as a number of rewrites typed on pink paper.

Frank Morgan makes Calvin Claymore a kind and dignified man, one who we can accept having a strictly platonic, somewhat paternal relationship with a beautiful younger woman in his wife's absence. In his third film for Simon, Dan Dailey switches gears to play an incorrigible scoundrel, and delivers a noteworthy performance. The scene in which Whit, without warning, delivers a brutal blow to Mary is still startling. This is one of seven 1941 releases to feature young leading lady Anne Gwynne (1918–2003). She will earn lasting acclaim for her "Scream Queen" roles in some of Universal's most popular horror and monster movies of the decade.

Lee Bowman (1914–1979) has a few amusing moments as Hal Thorne's slightly disreputable buddy Ronnie, who's no fan of regular work but doesn't mind picking up a few bucks in less conventional ways. Moviegoers were accustomed to seeing Ann Rutherford and Fay Holden (1893–1973) in the Andy Hardy film series; here, they're cast as mother and daughter. Describing Miss Rutherford's character, the screenwriters say Laurie "has the superficial glitter developed by her mother, although if you scratch her deep you'll find her father's girl." Early casting announcements for *Washington Melodrama* indicated that the young actress would be reunited with her *Keeping Company* leading man John Shelton, but it was ultimately Kent Taylor who was tabbed for the assignment.

Newspaper ads for the film promised "High adventure in the world's most dramatic city!" The film's pressbook claimed that Sylvan Simon's oversight of the film extended to personally selecting its extra and bit players, saying he "is noted for the authenticity of his crowd scenes. Whether it be a courtroom, a Senate chamber, a night club, or a newspaper office, one of Simon's sets always draw[s] comment because the people in them look exactly like the people one would expect there."

Reviews: "Another of Metro's consistently good S. Sylvan Simon program pictures ... a tight little film, with few dull moments.... Ticket buyers will enjoy every minute of it." *Film Daily*, April 23, 1941

"*Washington Melodrama* rides formula story lines. Expert performances by a well-molded cast headed by Frank Morgan, and neatly paced direction by S. Sylvan Simon, lift the picture to good program status for strong support in the duals." *Variety*, April 23, 1941

Whistling in the Dark (1941)

Red Skelton (*Wally Benton*), Conrad Veidt (*Joseph Jones*), Ann Rutherford (*Carol Lambert*), Virginia Grey (*Fran Post*), "Rags" Ragland (*Sylvester Conway*), Henry O'Neill (*Philip Post*), Eve Arden ("*Buzz*" *Baker*), Paul Stanton (*Jennings*), Don Douglas (*Gordon Thomas*), Don Costello ("*Noose*" *Green*), William Tannen (*Robert Graves*), Reed Hadley ("*Beau*" *Smith*), Mariska Aldrich (*Hilda*), Lloyd Corrigan (*Harvey Upshaw*), George Carleton (*Deputy Commissioner O'Neill*), Will Lee (*Herman*), Ruth Robinson (*Mrs. Robinson*), Emmett Vogan (*Radio Show Producer*), Leon Tyler (*Gerry Farrell*), Dorothy Adams (*Mrs. Farrell*), Inez Cooper (*Stewardess*), Dora Clement (*Mrs. Upshaw*), Billy Bletcher (*Radio Effects Man*), Joe Devlin (*Taxi Driver*), Betty Fairington (*Mrs. Moriarity*), Jennie Mac (*Mrs. Kendall*), John Picorri (*Gatekeeper*), Lester Dorr (*Dispatcher*), Mel Ruick (*Studio Engineer*), Larry Steers (*Harry*), John Dilson (*Radio Actor*)

Director: S. Sylvan Simon. *Producer*: George Haight. *Screenplay*: Robert MacGunigle, Harry Clork, Albert Mannheimer. *Director of Photography*: Sidney Wagner. *Musical Score*: Bronislau Kaper. *Recording Director*: Douglas Shearer. *Art Director*: Cedric Gibbons. *Associate*: Gabriel Scognamillo. *Set Decorations*: Edwin B. Willis. *Gowns*: Kalloch. *Film Editor*: Frank E. Hull.

MGM; released August 1941. 78 minutes.

Wally Benton, known as "The Fox," is the star of a nightly radio show, *The Grapomix Crime Hour*, in which he dramatizes and then solves fictitious crimes. Joseph Jones is the leader of a bogus religious cult that specializes in separating lonely women from their worldly goods, while promising them a life of "radiant contentment." Jones is angered to learn that a wealthy member who passed away left her considerable fortune to the cult, but only after her surviving nephew, Harvey Upshaw, dies.

Jones and his henchmen kidnap Wally Benton, demanding he concoct "a unique, foolproof idea" for a real-life murder—one that will eliminate Harvey Upshaw. Also

Whistling in the Dark: **Wally (Red Skelton, left) and Fran (Virginia Grey) fail to find "radiant contentment" in the company of cult leader Joseph Jones (Conrad Veidt).**

captured are Wally's fiancée, Carol Lambert (an actress on his radio show), and his sponsor's daughter, Fran Post. Held captive at Silver Haven, the cult's gloomy headquarters, Wally devises a suitable plot so as to win freedom for himself and the two women. A poison packet is assembled from his instructions, but Wally manages to substitute a placebo that will do Mr. Upshaw no harm. But the three captives are not released, and Wally's harmless concoction is replaced by the real thing, to be administered while Upshaw is aboard an airline flight. None-too-brave Wally must devise a way to alert the authorities, prevent Mr. Upshaw's murder, and escape the Silver Haven.

This was Simon's first time directing up-and-coming young comedian Red Skelton (1913–1997), signed to a long-term MGM contract the previous year. At first, the studio seemed to see its new player as best-suited to comic-relief supporting roles. *Whistling in the Dark* presented him as a star for the first time, in a vehicle that followed on the heels of other comedies tinged with mystery, such as Paramount's *The Ghost Breakers* (1940). The enthusiastic reaction (both critically and at the box office) gave him a large boost. Simon and Skelton had an immediate rapport, and they would ultimately make five films together (plus a cameo appearance by the comedian in *The Fuller Brush Girl*).

This initial outing doesn't feature quite as much slapstick physical comedy as will figure into Skelton's later vehicles. However, as his biographer Wes D. Gehring points out, some of his best moments onscreen draw on his previous experience, such as his pained reaction to a supposed health tonic he's given by the bad guys. His facial contortions are lightly reminiscent of what Lucille Ball will do 10 years later, when Lucy Ricardo takes her first swigs of Vitameatavegamin.

Virginia Grey skillfully delivers some sharp comedy lines as Fran Post, the sponsor's daughter whom Wally's agent tries to fix up with him. Offered a bottle of her father's product, Grapomix, she demurs: "Not me. That's what killed Mama." (Her retort was apparently an eleventh-hour inspiration on someone's part; it's been written in by hand on Simon's script, and her original line, "Don't mention it," crossed out.) This was Simon's sixth time directing Ann Rutherford, who plays Wally's loyal girlfriend Carol. With the help of stunt players, both ladies' characters do more than look on during the film's climactic scenes; they're in there duking it out with the bad guys.

The always-welcome Eve Arden (1908–1990) provides laughs as well, though it's disappointing that she's absent from the story for a long stretch in the middle. Former burlesque comedian "Rags" Ragland (1905–1946), signed to an MGM contract after attracting attention in the Broadway musical *Panama Hattie*, makes the most of a stereotypical character, the dimwitted lug who is one of the bad guy's henchmen. He will appear in all three of Skelton's "Whistling" films; like their director, he will die young, shortly before turning 41. Mariska Aldrich, previously seen in Simon's *Four Girls in White*, registers effectively as the dour, forbidding housekeeper who seems to be part and parcel of such stories; at one point, Skelton's Wally says to her, "Aren't you wrestling somewhere tonight?" She and Skelton share an impromptu kiss that shocks them both.

Whistling in the Dark was a remake of an MGM comedy of the same title, released in 1933, which starred Ernest Truex as Wally. That film, in turn, was an adaptation of Laurence Gross and Edward Childs Carpenter's Broadway comedy of the same name, which had also starred Truex, and ran for more than a year in 1932–33. Tucked into Simon's copy of the screenplay was an interoffice studio memorandum dated June 19, 1941, which noted, "The name of *Mecca* has been changed to *Sylvester*, at suggestion of Production Code Administration." The director also kept a copy of a mock proclamation signed by some 30 cast and crew members, which read, "Let it be known that we the unersigned [*sic*] have no objection to parting in radiant contentment at promptly 6:00 p.m. to-nite—July 3, 1941." Skelton and his two leading ladies were among those campaigning to wrap a bit early on the eve of Independence Day.

The film was released only a few years after Orson Welles and his troupe threw radio listeners into a panic with his dramatization of H.G. Wells' *The War of the Worlds*. That incident is referenced here, when Wally and his companions manage to broadcast live a plea for rescue from inside the Silver Haven. The local police chief hears them, but says with a cynical snort, "It's a fake, like the other time."

A set visitor noticed that Simon, observing a scene being shot, silently mouthed the actors' dialogue. "I thought I'd cured myself of that," he admitted when asked about it. "When I was directing on the stage, the actors wouldn't let me stand in the wings. Said it made them forget their lines to see me standing there saying every word with them."[25]

The success of *Whistling in the Dark* would lead to two sequels, one in 1942 and a third in the following year.

Reviews: "MGM has given Red Skelton a chance to show his stuff. The result is a bang-up comedy that should do a swell business.... Skelton romps in a manner that should create a tremendous following for him among comedy seekers.... Together with the fun, Director Simon has maintained a steady stream of suspense adding to the perfect entertainment.... Play up Skelton, for he will build quite a following from this." *Showmen's Trade Review*, August 2, 1941

"Enhanced by good old down-to-earth hokum and comedy situations that lend themselves well to Skelton's ability and personality.... To Director S. Sylvan Simon goes full acclaim for his deft handling of what might otherwise have proved itself to be a mediocre slap-stick opus, but under his understanding guidance becomes comedy deluxe, as noted by audience reaction." *Film Daily*, August 4, 1941

The Bugle Sounds (1942)

Wallace Beery (*Sgt. Patrick Aloysius "Hap" Doan*), Marjorie Main (*Susie*), Lewis Stone (*Col. Jack Lawton*), George Bancroft (*"Russ" Russell*), Henry O'Neill (*Lt. Col Harry Seton*), Donna Reed (*Sally Hanson*), Chill Wills (*Sgt. Larry Dillon*), William Lundigan (*Joey Hanson*), Tom Dugan (*Sgt. Strong*), Guinn ["Big Boy"] Williams (*Sgt. Krims*), Ernest Whitman (*Cartaret*), Roman Bohnen (*Mr. Leech*), Jerome Cowan (*Mr. Nichols*), Arthur Space (*Hank*), Jonathan Hale (*Brigadier-General*), Dick Wessel (*Jerry*), Reed Hadley (*Court-Martial Judge*), Donald Douglas (*Mr. Clyde*), Stanley Andrews (*Veterinarian*), Walter Sande (*Headquarters Sergeant*), Lee Phelps (*Sergeant at Guard House*), Dorothy Granger (*Visitor with Cake*), Mahlon Hamilton (*Train Engineer*), Jack Luden (*First Adjutant*), Bradley Page (*Second Adjutant*)

Director: S. Sylvan Simon. *Producer*: J. Walter Ruben. *Screenplay*: Cyril Hume. *Story*: Lawrence Kimble, Cyril Hume. *Director of Photography*: Clyde De Vinna. *Musical Score*: Lennie Hayton. *Recording Director*: Douglas Shearer. *Art Director*: Cedric Gibbons. *Associate*: Leonid Vasian. *Film Editor*: Ben Lewis. *Special Effects*: Arnold Gillespie. *Gowns*: Kalloch. *Men's Wardrobe*: Gile Steele. *Technical Advisor*: Capt. Arthur W. Field.

MGM; released January 1942. 102 minutes.

After nearly 30 years of military service, Sgt. "Hap" Doan is having trouble adjusting to modern methods of warfare. He's upset when told that his Army regiment will be phasing out horses in favor of tanks, and that he'll be tasked with training a batch of new recruits. Among them is Joey Hanson, who doesn't know that his wife Sally is pregnant.

After a weekend bender, Hap wakes up at the home of his longtime lady friend Susie. For 18 years, she has operated a hotel and restaurant that moved from one Army base to the next so as to be close to the gruff sergeant. She's frustrated that Hap seems to take her for granted, but he reacts with jealousy when another suitor, Russ, pays her a visit. When Sally comes in looking for a job, softhearted Susie hires her.

Unbeknownst to Hap and his men, the tanks they were sent have been sabotaged by the enemy. One of them catches fire, and the resulting explosion results in a deadly injury to Hap's beloved horse Cantigny. Heartbroken, Hap goes AWOL. Though his boss and friend, Col. Jack Lawton, tries to cover for him, Hap returns to the base in such a rage that he is court-martialed and recommended for a dishonorable discharge. Susie, though she still loves him, will have nothing more to do with him, saying, "I don't put up no traitors in my hotel."

Seemingly at loose ends after returning to civilian life, Hap is offered friendship from an unexpected source, Susie's other beau. Russ is working with enemy agents to bomb an upcoming transport of Army equipment and men. Hap wins the trust of the traitors with inside information from Army sources, but they are

Susie (Marjorie Main) pleads her man's case to his superior officer (Lewis Stone) in *The Bugle Sounds* (1942).

unaware that, reporting to Col. Lawton, he is actually a double agent whose loyalty to his country remains unchanged.

The film was shot in the fall of 1941 under the title "Steel Cavalry," with several scenes shot on location at Fort Knox in Kentucky. Cast and crew members also "went along with maneuvers in Louisiana and worked under regular military regulations to make pictures of tanks, airplanes and infantry in action." The War Department assigned Army Captain Arthur W. Field to serve as the film's technical advisor. His main task was to insure that military scenes and costumes were as authentic as possible. He also enforced a departmental directive that servicemen not be shown frolicking with pretty young ladies, as this was considered to be bad for morale back home (upsetting soldiers' wives and girlfriends awaiting their return). Another edict: "Leading lady Donna Reed must never be photographed with her legs crossed."[26]

Of his experiences making the film, Simon said, "Until you've directed over a loud-speaker through a mask, while you stand on a sixty-foot platform that shakes when a flock of tanks roll by, you can't understand what it was like. But strangely, it was fun. It's definitely a fact that however much a soldier may grouse—and they say the best ones do it regularly—he also laughs. I learned that among other things from the soldiers themselves."[27]

Simon's copy of the script contains notes for assembling the montage that shows the training that recruits receive under Hap's command. The brief vignettes were to be cobbled together from scenes Simon had shot, as well as some done by the company's second unit. Some of the latter did not meet with his approval, and a note about the mess hall sequence says, "Note for Mr. Ruben [producer J. Walter Ruben]: As this scene is rather badly handled by the second unit, I would like to shoot it over with Hanson and a couple of recruits..."

Another bit that appears in the montage finds the soldiers getting a little relaxation with a movie, featuring "a hot kissing flash of 'Honky-Tonk' or any other good kissing scene from an M.G.M. picture." Several suggested lines to be heard in voice-over are included: "come up for air, baby—she doesn't like it, does she? Not much! etc." In the final cut, we hear instead this exchange between two recruits as Gable and Turner smooch:

> "Don't forget you're a married man!"
> "What're you bringing up that now for?"

Simon elicits fine performances from his cast, making the emotional scenes as memorable, if not more so, than the action elements. Any animal lover will be moved by Wallace Beery's final scene with his beloved mount. Though Beery and Marjorie Main are always a memorable team, good for boisterous laughs (after Hap's drunken night out, Susie tells him, "You looked like a package of homework for the medical students"), here the two show they can be touching as well. Miss Main, playing with more subtlety than many directors got from her, makes the most of a scene with Lewis Stone, in which an unusually subdued and dignified Susie pleads the case of her far-from-perfect man. The film's various elements are skillfully blended, leading into an exciting and suspenseful finale.

Featured actor Arthur Space (1908–1983) credited Simon with giving him his break in films. A few years after Space and Simon worked together in a stock company, the young actor noticed that his old acquaintance had made it to the ranks of Hollywood director. After some back-and-forth correspondence, Simon sent Space, then living in New Jersey, a telegram saying, "I have a part for you ... if you can get here in 10 days."[28] Space leapt at the chance, delivered a fine performance, and went on to have a Hollywood career that lasted nearly 40 years. After The Bugle Sounds, Space won roles in other Simon pictures, including Tish, Rio Rita, and The Fuller Brush Girl.

Donna Reed (1921–1986), only 20 years old at the time of filming, is strikingly lovely and up to the demands of her role, which were not strenuous. She and Miss Main make an interesting duo onscreen, their characters providing a contrast in terms of age, demeanor, and pretty much everything else.

A "gala world premiere" of The Bugle Sounds was held at the Loew's Theater of Louisville, Kentucky in January 1942. Aside from star Wallace Beery, the event, which included a parade, was attended by Governor Keen Johnson and the city's mayor. As MGM's in-house publication described it, "The colorful procession from the City Hall to the theatre included a military band, soldiers, army tanks and 'jeeps' and 'peeps' from nearby Fort Knox ... [Beery] also took part in Red Cross and Infantile Paralysis Drive activities during the two-day period preceding the opening."[29]

Beery reprised his role when "The Bugle Sounds" was dramatized as an episode of *Lux Radio Theater*, broadcast on January 4, 1943; Marjorie Rambeau stepped into the role of Susie.

Reviews: "Good mass entertainment.... Although the plot is not novel, it has been handled well, combining melodrama with comedy, and the performances are good.... Should prove interesting to audiences in general." *Harrison's Reports*, December 20, 1941

"Mr. Beery may not be the critics' best-loved and admired Hollywood actor, but *The Bugle Sounds* is timely, exciting drama, directed ingeniously and forthrightly by S. Sylvan Simon, and ending with a bang-up bridge wreck that leaves you clutching your seat." *Boston Globe*, April 17, 1942

Rio Rita (1942)

Bud Abbott (*Doc*), Lou Costello ("*Wishy*" *Dunne*), Kathryn Grayson (*Rita Winslow*), John Carroll (*Ricardo Montera*), Patricia Dane (*Lucette Brunswick*), Tom Conway (*Maurice Craindall*), Peter Whitney (*Jake*), Eros Volusia (*Herself*), Barry Nelson (*Harry Gantley*), Arthur Space (*Trask*), Dick Rich (*Gus*), Eva Puig (*Marianna*), Joan Valerie (*Dotty*), Mitchell Lewis (*Julio*), Joe Kirk (*Pet Shop Owner*), Dorothy Morris (*Gas Station Attendant*), Inez Cooper (*Pulque*), Johnny Mitchell (*Control Man*), Norman Abbott (*Hotel Laundry Boy*), Jennie Mac (*Club Woman*), David Oliver (*Golfer*), May McAvoy (*Hotel Guest*)

Director: S. Sylvan Simon. *Producer*: Pandro S. Berman. *Screenplay*: Richard Connell, Gladys Lehman. *Special Material*: John Grant. *Director of Photography*: George Folsey. *Art Director*: Cedric Gibbons. *Associate*: Eddie Imazu. *Set Decorator*: Edwin B. Willis. *Recording Director*: Douglas Shearer. *Film Editor*: Ben Lewis. *Musical Director*: Herbert Stothart. *Songs*, "Rio," "The Ranger's Song": Harry Tierney, Joseph McCarthy. *Song*, "Long Before You Came Along": Harold Arlen, E.Y. Harburg. *Vocals and Orchestrations*: Murray Cutter, Leo Arnaud, Paul Marquardt. *Special Effects*: Warren Newcombe. *Gowns*: Kalloch. *Men's Wardrobe*: Gile Steele.

MGM; released April 1942. 91 minutes.

Fired from their most recent job in a pet shop, buddies Doc and Wishy stow away in the trunk of a car, and find themselves in Vista Del Rio, Texas, where radio singer Ricardo Montera has been booked to perform at a three-day fiesta. Maurice Craindall, the hotel manager, is in reality the leader of a group of Nazi spies. Craindall and his cronies have a plan to distribute secret messages through radio transmitters built to look like apples. Starving Doc and Wishy steal the phony apples, but throw them away in disgust when they realize they're inedible. The transmitters are then swallowed by dogs, goats, and other animals in the vicinity.

At the hotel, Montera is reunited with lovely Rita Winslow, who has been in love with him since they grew up together in Vista Del Rio. Feeling sorry for unemployed Doc and Wishy, Rita gives them jobs as hotel detectives. Sensing that Rita has a rival for Montera's affections in beautiful Lucette, Doc urges Wishy to romance the interloper, but she firmly rebuffs him.

Just before he is shot and killed, a Secret Service agent entrusts Doc and Wishy with a code book that they are to keep out of Nazi hands. Craindall demands that Lucette retrieve the book, causing her to display a change in attitude toward a startled Wishy.

Abbott and Costello became huge moneymakers for Universal Pictures in the early 1940s, resulting in hard feelings between the executives of that studio and MGM. Louis B. Mayer and his associates believed that Universal had "stolen" the comedians just as they were on the verge of signing with Metro. To settle the tiff, Universal agreed to a deal allowing its rival studio to borrow the red-hot comedians for one picture per year.

Chosen for their first MGM vehicle was a remake of *Rio Rita*, which began life in the 1920s as a highly successful stage musical by Florenz Ziegfeld. It had already been adapted to film in 1929, with the comic team of Wheeler and Woolsey in featured roles. MGM's remake tossed out much of the plot and the music from the original show, though the title song was retained. While the resulting film was more lavish than anything Abbott and Costello had made for Universal, it was a less-than-optimal vehicle for their talents. Too often the finished product resembles two unrelated films spliced together, cutting incongruously from broad slapstick sequences to elaborately staged musical numbers for singing stars Kathryn Grayson and John Carroll.

Nonetheless, Abbott and Costello have some very funny set pieces here. Raucous physical comedy includes Lou's wild ride atop a convertible hoisted high above the ground on a rack, and a frenetic sequence that finds him dumped into the hotel's industrial washing machine, and soaked in suds. His reactions to what seems to be a talking dog (one that has swallowed a radio transmitter, and is now giving updates on a Brooklyn Dodgers game) are another high point. An early scene that finds the two of them as the incompetent staff of a pet shop is amusing, though it has absolutely nothing to do with the rest of the film.

Louella Parsons (October 27, 1941) reported Simon's assignment to the director slot, "which discounts the rumor that Arthur Lubin would move with the boys to M-G-M." However, they did have access to their favored comedy writer, John Grant, who punched up the script, not always with the freshest material.

Simon's directorial style worked to their advantage. He told a reporter, "We shoot a scene, and it runs 100 feet of film. Then we make a second take and Lou and Bud have thought of something funny and the scene builds to 250 feet."[30] Wanting to catch their best moments, Simon employed three cameras when shooting scenes, explaining to columnist Harrison Carroll (January 4, 1942), "That's for spontaneity.... The boys ad-lib a lot and this way, when they get hot on a take, we are completely covered. Lou and Bud don't have to worry about going back and recapturing a piece of an ad-libbed scene. It enables them to work nice and easy."

Another column item described the shooting of a complicated scene involving the star comedians and two canine cast members. When Simon called for a break, a grateful Abbott, short on breath, said, "Thanks for the rest, Sylvan," to which the jovial director replied, "Oh, it isn't for you. The dogs are tired."[31] On the other hand, he immediately vetoed Costello's plan to jump from a high window in another scene. The comedian told him he had done far riskier falls on the MGM lot in years past, when he was earning $45 a week as a stuntman for such films as *The Crowd* (1928). "That was twelve years ago," Simon retorted, "and you were just one of 'The Crowd.'"[32]

Bud Abbott gets a grip on Lou Costello in *Rio Rita*.

Tom Conway (1904–1967), not having yet begun his popular B movie series as the Falcon, provides suave villainy here. This is the first of two films in rapid succession that find Simon directing actress Patricia Dane (1919–1995), who had become an MGM contract player the previous year. In both, she demonstrates her skill at playing beautiful but somewhat sinister women; little wonder that Costello's character reacts to her with a heartfelt, "She scares me!"

Simon gives a quick nod to his previous year's comedy hit *Whistling in the Dark*, when a radio is heard playing an advertisement for Grapomix, sponsor of Wally Benton's program in that film. His aunt, Jennie Mac, is seen briefly as one of the matrons whose meal is disrupted when Costello's character, on the run, dives under their long table.

Simon's copy of the script is dated November 21, 1941, but most of the pages devoted to Abbott and Costello's scenes are pink "Chgs" [changes] sheets, with various dates during November and December. Still, not all the scenes play out onscreen as they did on the page. After the lights go out and Harry is shot, the script called for Wishy to hide under the office desk. When he finds himself stuck there, Doc pulls him loose, but in doing so Wishy's pants come down. Instead, in the final version, Doc turns the light back on to find Wishy cowering between the top of the window and the ceiling. The pet shop sequence that opens the film does not appear in the original script at all, but has been added at the end, in a section marked "Retakes/Changes," dated February 10, 1942.

A list of necessary retakes and insert shots was dated February 5, 1942. Most were fairly straightforward, such as "Make a scene of [Kathryn] Grayson putting on a record on phonograph. INSERT Ricardo Montera's name on record." While on that set, the second unit was instructed, "Also protect bad lines of dialogue from John Carroll in same sequence in CLOSEUPS."

Production Code concerns led to other revisions. The film's setting was changed from Mexico to Texas, to avoid offending Latin American audiences with the implication that Nazis were prevalent south of the border. Another sticking point was the scene in which drinking from a bottle of "pulque" had Wishy hallucinating a mirage in the form of a beautiful young woman who, according to him, is "taking off her clothes." In the finished film, the scene comes to a halt after Doc demands, "Gimme a drink of that stuff!" However, the routine runs longer in the script, and contains lines such as Doc's comment, "That's the little red head [sic] I used to play around with in Williamsburg." On the typed page, "play around with" has been crossed out, and "know" written in by hand. In Wishy's vision, she's a blonde rather than a redhead, and after she disrobes he cautions her, "Blondie, you can't go out like that. You'll get pinched. Put on your clothes. I won't look."

Reviews: "A bright, expansive musical with its comedy content developed to take advantage of the talents of Bud Abbott and Lou Costello.... Their familiar antics will give audiences their money's worth of laughs.... The film has smart, fast direction by S. Sylvan Simon." *Film Daily,* March 11, 1942

"Here they are again, folks ... in the brand of comedy to which they have accustomed the theatre-going public at large in a degree profitable to all concerned ... [MGM] offers more in the way of production values and supporting talent, but this drops out of notice when the boys turn on the gags and let the laughs pop where they may.... Direction by S. Sylvan Simon is commonsense enough to sidetrack story and such at frequent intervals to give the comedians elbow room for their gag sequences, which are many and potent." *Motion Picture Daily,* March 12, 1942

Grand Central Murder (1942)

Van Heflin (*"Rocky" Custer*), Patricia Dane (*Mida King*), Cecilia Parker (*Constance Furness*), Virginia Grey (*Sue Custer*), Samuel S. Hinds (*Roger Furness*), Sam Levene (*Insp. Gunther*), Connie Gilchrist (*Pearl Delroy*), Mark Daniels (*David V. Henderson*), Horace [Stephen] McNally (*Turk*), Tom Conway (*Frankie Ciro*), Betty Wells (*"Baby" Delroy*), George Lynn (*Paul Rinehart*), Roman Bohnen (*Ramon*), Millard Mitchell (*Arthur Doolin*), Frank Ferguson (*Det. Mike McAdams*), Tom Dugan (*Eric "Schnelly" Schneller*), Sam McDaniel (*Night Watchman*), Frank Moran (*Louie Scarpi*), Norman Abbott (*Whistling Messenger*), Christina Teague (*Morgue Nurse*), Joe Yule (*Stagehand*), Arthur Space (*Police Detective*), Walter Soderling (*Autopsy Surgeon*), Bert Roach (*Tubby*), Arthur Q. Bryan (*Medical Examiner*), John Maxwell (*Det. Strom*), Aileen Haley (*Doll*), Evalene Bankston (*Blonde*)

Director: S. Sylvan Simon. *Producer*: B.F. Zeidman. *Screenplay*: Peter Ruric

From left: Inspector Gunther (Sam Levene) didn't ask for the help of private eye Rocky Custer (Van Heflin) in investigating the *Grand Central Murder*, but he's getting it nonetheless. Cast as either suspect or victim are Cecilia Parker, Virginia Grey, Horace [Stephen] McNally, Patricia Dane, and Mark Daniels (Simon Family Collection).

(based on the novel by Sue MacVeigh). *Director of Photography*: George Folsey. *Music Score*: David Snell. *Recording Director*: Douglas Shearer. *Art Director*: Cedric Gibbons. *Associate*: Eddie Imazu. *Set Decorator*: Edwin B. Willis. *Gowns*: Shoup. *Hair Styles for Miss Dane*: Sydney Guilaroff. *Film Editor*: Conrad A. Nervig.

MGM; released May 1942. 73 minutes.

On opening night of her new show, "Take It Broadway," actress Mida King receives a threatening phone call from escaped prisoner Turk, who tells her, "Death and me are just around the corner, waiting for you. Don't keep us waiting, Mida." Terrified, she abandons the theater after the first act for the safety of her private train car at Grand Central Station. But her accommodations prove no safe harbor, as she is found murdered there soon afterwards.

Although Turk comes under immediate suspicion, Inspector Gunther of the New York police has a wide array of other suspects from which to choose, including Mida's wealthy fiancé David Henderson, stepfather Ramon, ex-husband Paul Rinehart, understudy Babe Delroy, and producer Frankie Ciro. Also on hand are Mida's cynical maid Pearl, and lovely Constance Furness, whom David ditched in favor of the glamorous star. Found running from the scene of the crime were private investigator

Rocky Custer and his wife Sue, whose connection with the case is not immediately clear. Custer takes it upon himself to critique Gunther's handling of the case, which he terms "the dumbest murder investigation on record." The police inspector's frustration builds as the private eye continues to horn his way in on the proceedings.

Adding to the already plentiful motives is the revelation that Miss King was in possession of a substantial wad of cash, which subsequently turns up missing. After Gunther identifies the suspect he believes is the guilty party, he enters into a wager with Rocky, who says he can solve the case if he's permitted to ask three pertinent questions.

Simon's copy of the script is dated January 13, 1942, with several pages of changes from January 28 interspersed. Also enclosed is producer B.F. Zeidman's interoffice memorandum of February 18, 1942, listing several changes to be made, mostly in the names given to characters. Among them are:

KILGOUR has been changed to GUNTHER.
MIKE REILLY has been changed to MIKE McADAMS.
OTTO SCHULZ has been changed to ERIC SCHNELLER.

The most minor renaming was the assignment to the character of David Henderson a middle initial, specified to be "V." The memo also stipulates that Mida's performance venue, the Century Theatre, be dubbed the Harmony Theatre.

More changes follow the main text, the latest being 13 pink-hued pages issued during the month of March, marked "Retakes." Other additions include a carefully outlined "Rise to Fame Montage," of which the new script pages note, "To establish that Mida's rise to fame is closely connected with men searching [sic] her favors, we start this Montage with a few quick flashes of Mida first with one, then between two, then with a whole table full of eager males, just waiting to be sheared." On the same sheet, "to give the 'Show Sequence' more production value, we use flashes out of 'The Great Ziegfeld,' etc. as PROCESS PLATES in front of which we place Mida in a corresponding stock costume."

This film, along with *Kid Glove Killer*, released a few weeks earlier, represented MGM's earliest attempts to let up-and-comer Van Heflin take the leading role. Heflin spars enjoyably with Sam Levene's Inspector Gunther. The private eye is no sentimentalist (remarking of the murdered woman, "Whoever knocked that witch off ought to be a cinch for a Nobel Prize"), but he more than holds his own in a battle of wits with the beleaguered cop. As Heflin's biographer Derek Sculthorpe observes, *Grand Central Murder* was "a bright and breezy whodunit" that showed "what a generous and capable ensemble player he was."[33]

Patricia Dane embraces the nastier aspects of her character, who when her veneer of sophistication is tested by anger, is prone to describe others around her as "you cheap tinhorn fortuneteller" or "you blackmailing rat." Although the murder takes place early in the film, Miss Dane continues to be seen in the flashbacks that are used to recount the various suspects' movements, and relationship with the victim. She even creates a bit of sympathy for the hardboiled character whose overarching interest in life is money (hence her stage name, adapted from the legend of King Midas).

Structured much like a Golden Age detective novel, the film presents an engrossing murder mystery enhanced by sharp dialogue and some witty character byplay.

Among the strong character performances are Connie Gilchrist as Mida's cigar-smoking, plainspoken maid, who may be the only one still around who knows her boss' given name (Beulah). Virginia Grey gives snap to the role of Custer's wife, who doesn't always appreciate how his investigations seem to bring him into contact with other attractive women, while Betty Wells has some amusing moments as Mida's understudy, who gives her educational background as "Minsky's, class of '36."

The novel *Grand Central Murder* was published by Houghton Mifflin in 1939. Following the example of the well-known Ellery Queen, Sue Mac-Veigh is both the name of one of the lead characters, and (supposedly) the author. It was the pseud-

Grand Central Murder: Mida King (Patricia Dane, left) seems to have it all, but danger lurks at close hand. Her maid Pearl (Connie Gilchrist) may know more than she's letting on (Simon Family Collection).

onym of journalist Elizabeth Custer Nearing (1898–1960), who published four mysteries featuring the detective team of Andy MacVeigh and his wife. *Grand Central Murder* "was based on material gleaned from the experience of Mr. [Max] Neering, a railroad construction engineer," as well as that of her father, Edgar Alan Custer, an executive in that industry.[34] According to *Motion Picture Herald* (January 17, 1942), MGM purchased the movie rights in late 1941, with the idea of starring Barry Nelson and Laraine Day. Early trade paper announcements indicated that Donna Reed would have a role in this film, probably the one ultimately assumed by Cecilia Parker.

A syndicated news article talked about studios' wartime efforts to conserve materials in short supply, ranging from nails to raw film stock: "Director Sylvan Simon, on 'The Grand Central Murder,' which has a lot of New York actors like Sam Levene and Van Heflin who can remember long stretches of dialog, has been shooting scenes as long as three minutes, taking in five pages of dialog against the usual movie 'take' of only about 30 seconds covering only one page of dialog."[35]

Though much of the film's story plays out on a handful of interior sets, notably Gunther's office and the stage of a Broadway theater, director Simon gives it a sense of momentum and action nonetheless. He draws fine performances from an ensemble cast rich in experienced players. While Simon still has an eye for comedy, he demonstrates here that he can capably helm films in a variety of genres.

Reviews: "An engaging, if conventional, murder mystery has been lifted into a superior detective yarn by outstanding performances of Van Heflin and Sam Levene. With a good, sound plot ... the picture develops along logical lines and has a number of running gags which should draw laughs.... S. Sylvan Simon directed with skill." *Motion Picture Daily*, April 22, 1942

"Here's a rare opportunity to invite the amateur detectives to exercise their sleuthing talents. Four people sitting on either side of your correspondent, all of whom have been looking at these bafflers for years, guessed wrong.... While there's a good supply of melodrama, there's nothing about the show that would prove a strain on weak hearts. Yarn moves speedily." *Showmen's Trade Review*, April 25, 1942

Tish (1942)

Marjorie Main (*Letitia "Tish" Carberry*), ZaSu Pitts (*Aggie Pilkington*), Aline MacMahon (*Lizzie Wilkins*), Susan Peters (*Cora Edwards Bowzer*), Lee Bowman (*Charlie Sands*), Guy Kibbee (*Judge Horace Bowser*), Virginia Grey (*Kit Bowser Sands*), Richard Quine (*Ted Bowser*), Ruby Dandridge (*Violet*), Robert Emmett O'Connor (*Game Warden*), Al Shean (*Rev. Ostermaier*), Arthur Space (*Court Clerk*), Gerald Oliver Smith (*Parkins*), Rudy Wissler (*Newsboy*), Byron Shores (*Dr. McRegan*), George Humbert (*Tony*), Alice Ward (*Nurse*), George Noisom (*Special Delivery Boy*), Howard Hickman (*Fielding Kelbridge*), Paul Scardon (*Postal Clerk*), George Ovey (*Man with Cushion*), Nora Cecil, Gertrude W. Hoffmann, Jennie Mac, Kathryn Sheldon (*Spinsters*), Sam Ash, King Baggot (*Men on Street*)

Director: S. Sylvan Simon. *Producer*: Orville O. Dull. *Screenplay*: Harry Ruskin. *Adaptation*: Annalee Whitmore Jacoby, Thomas Seller. *Director of Photography*: Paul Vogel. *Musical Score*: David Snell. *Recording Director*: Douglas Shearer. *Art Director*: Cedric Gibbons. *Associate*: Eddie Imazu. *Set Decorations*: Edwin B. Willis. *Associate*: Edward J. Boyle. *Gowns*: Shoup. *Film Editor*: Robert J. Kern.

MGM; released November 1942. 84 minutes.

Letitia Carberry, known to all as Tish, is a middle-aged spinster who lives in the town of Sunville with her nephew Charlie, editor of the local newspaper. Strong-willed Tish has two longtime friends, Aggie and Lizzie, who live at a nearby boardinghouse, as does lovely young Cora Edwards, an orphan. Eighteen-year-old Cora pines for Charlie, but he is in love with worldly Kit Bowser. Meanwhile, Kit's kid brother, awkward teenager Ted, tries to win the heart of Cora.

Tish, unaware Charlie plans to marry Kit, decides a camping trip will be the perfect opportunity to bring him and Cora together, but everything goes awry as the three older ladies try their hands at hunting and fishing. By the end of the trip, however, Cora realizes she cares for Ted more than she thought, and her relationship with Charlie becomes brotherly. Eager to support a wife, Ted accepts a job in Canada, learning to fly bombers, which will keep him away for six months. Before he leaves, he and Cora are secretly married.

After Charlie and Kit wed, Tish begins to feel like a third wheel in their home, and moves into the boardinghouse with her friends. Unable to bear the long separation from Ted, Cora heads for Canada, using $150 of the money Tish raised to buy the church a new organ. But shortly after her arrival, a telegram gives Cora devastating news, which causes her to collapse. Rushing into action, Tish comes home to Sunville with a baby, and throws the town into an uproar when she declares that she's the mother.

Tish was adapted from the popular stories of Mary Roberts Rinehart (1876–1958), which became a staple of the *Saturday Evening Post*. Under Simon's direction, the film is a warm-hearted tale of small-town life that begins with skillfully executed comedy, but takes a more serious turn in the final half-hour. Though it is somewhat episodic, initially seeming to be a rather loosely connected set of vignettes, the various characters' stories gradually coalesce. The seemingly discursive screenplay in fact allows ample time for viewers to know the characters, adding to the impact of the later, more dramatic scenes.

Popular as a co-star for leading men like Wallace Beery, Marjorie Main steps into the starring role. It's a rich part for her, playing a woman who's stubborn, opinionated, outspoken (she calls her nephew's fiancée "a headstrong viper who'll henpeck him for the rest of his life"), and yet capable of great love and sacrifice. Her loving nephew tries (largely in vain) to rein in her excesses:

> **CHARLIE:** Aunt Tish, didn't we shake hands on letting other people run their own lives?
> **TISH:** And a fine mess everybody's been making of it ever since!

The role gives Miss Main an opportunity to shine on her own, and she rises to the occasion, giving us a character who can be both maddeningly meddlesome yet surprisingly touching, as when she realizes it is time for her to move out of her nephew's house. She displays a gift for physical comedy that predates her "Ma Kettle" series; her antics in the camping trip sequence are hilarious. Surprisingly, Miss Main herself, in retrospect, seemed to have little appreciation of *Tish*, telling interviewer W. Franklyn Moshier that she "did not believe in her role, nor does she regard this film as typical of her best work for the screen."[36]

Studio publicity asserted that her on-screen demeanor, and the voice that helped define it, did not reflect her own personality. It was actually a fictitious persona she had honed through playing roles in films such as *Dead End* (1937) and *Susan and God* (1940). She explained, "In 'Tish' I'm supposed to be domineering, pretend to be hard-boiled, but am really a sentimental woman underneath. So the voice fits the scenes where I'm pretending, and disappears in scenes where Tish drops her pose."[37]

Two other fine character actresses enact the roles of Tish's sometimes-reluctant sidekicks. The part of Aggie seemed to be made to order for ZaSu Pitts (1894–1963), though early publicity from MGM indicated that Spring Byington would play the role. ZaSu Pitts told an interviewer, "I was scheduled to play the role of 'Aggie' three different times. First was with Marie Dressler, some ten years ago. She died, however, before we could start. A few years later the Tish picture was scheduled again, but another death prevented it. Finally the picture was made with Marjorie Main and I got to play Aggie at last."[38]

Tish gave Sylvan Simon the chance to direct his cousin, Aline MacMahon, in an important role. Her character, Lizzie, who served as the narrator of Rinehart's stories, is the most practical and down-to-earth of the three women, with a dry wit. As she says resignedly, "We just blindly follow Tish to one bad idea after another." Writing to her husband back in New York during production, Miss MacMahon noted, "Yesterday we worked in the open all day, with a stiff wind blowing—it's the sequence where we are chased by a bear. But doubles will do all the bear work—even climb trees for us." Of the picture as a whole, she wrote hesitantly, "It may be funny—I enjoy so much of it."[39] Miss MacMahon's mother, Jennie Mac, is seen briefly as well, as one of the residents of the boardinghouse.

Though the film was not a major success, it provided a needed career boost to young Susan Peters (1921–1952), recently signed to an MGM contract after an unsatisfying, relatively unproductive stint at Warners. Her girl-next-door character has a fresh loveliness that is endearing, while her later scenes are poignant and moving. ("That was my first good role," the actress later recalled).[40] She is radiantly beautiful throughout, with Virginia Grey's less-likable character impeccably groomed but out-shined nonetheless. Richard Quine (1920–1989) capably portrays Ted's transition from clumsy boy to responsible young man.

Tish (Marjorie Main, seated, center) is surrounded by friends and family. Also pictured (left to right): Lizzie (Aline MacMahon), Charlie (Lee Bowman), and Aggie (ZaSu Pitts).

Tish would prove to be a milestone in the lives of the two younger players. An article that appeared in a fan magazine under Quine's byline claimed that he met Susan Peters "in the office of S. Sylvan Simon, well-known director and connoisseur of bow ties."[41] The romantic relationship that they portrayed in the script of *Tish* extended off-camera, and the two were married in 1943. Tragically, Miss Peters was seriously injured in a 1945 hunting accident, and would have to use a wheelchair from that point forward. She died in 1952, at only 31 years old.

Arthur Space recalled that Simon initially saw no role in *Tish* that the young actor could play. But when the two men next met, the director offered him one day's work as a court clerk. As bad luck would have it, Space was ill the day of the shoot, with what was later diagnosed as intestinal flu. He reported for work nonetheless, trying to give a touch of distinctiveness to the role. "I did give him a little character by pulling my mustache down over my lip and putting on that old tweed suit of mine." Still, he denigrated his own performance, writing, "I know that I didn't do a good job and that I was far from outstanding."[42]

Ruby Dandridge (1900–1987) is unbilled for her few appearances as the Sands' maid Violet, rudely described in Ruskin's script as a "fat, colored, blowsy 'hired girl.'" Gerald Oliver Smith (1892–1974) plays a haughty butler, of whom Miss MacMahon's character remarks, "Some people you have to know well to dislike. Others you can hate on very short acquaintance."

The film's opening titles described it as "founded in part on stories by Mary Roberts Rinehart." Harry Ruskin's screenplay, dated April 15, 1942, even has stage directions describing the behavior and facial expressions of a wild rabbit encountered by the three ladies on their camping trip. In his first close-up, he's "sitting up on its haunches, looking as amused as a rabbit can." Tish suggests that Aggie try her bow and arrow on the four-legged visitor, but he's "not moving ... altogether unconcerned." One page of minor dialogue changes (for the two-legged cast) bound into Simon's copy of the screenplay bears the name of screenwriter J.K. McGuinness (1893–1950).

According to the *Los Angeles Times*' Edwin Schallert (October 20, 1942), MGM expected strong results from *Tish*, and envisioned it as the opener to a film series. Only a few weeks after it opened, Schallert reported, the studio was making preparations for a second feature. That fall, studio publicity termed *Tish* one of MGM's "Terrific Twelve" to be released during the 1942–43 season, alongside features such as Judy Garland's *For Me and My Gal*, and *Somewhere I'll Find You*, with Clark Gable and Lana Turner. Trade ads described *Tish* as "one of those rare word-of-mouth shows that starts Big and finishes Big." However, response from critics and ticket buyers was less than anticipated, and plans for a follow-up film were quietly abandoned.

Reviews: "This mild program comedy is hardly worthy of an MGM label. As entertainment it might appeal to the family trade in the smaller houses.... The story, which deals with the scrapes of three middle-aged spinsters, is somewhat dragged out and too talky. Consequently, the action is slowed down." *Harrison's Reports*, July 25, 1942

"Generally satisfying family entertainment. It deals heavily in straightforward, easily understandable humor, human interest, the simple everyday things that come readily within the grasp of the average picture fan.... The Misses Main, Pitts, and MacMahon are good for plenty of laughs.... They keep the film lively at all times.... Action is the keynote of S. Sylvan Simon's direction." *Film Daily*, July 22, 1942

Whistling in Dixie (1942)

Red Skelton (*Wally "The Fox" Lambert*), Ann Rutherford (*Carol Lambert*), George Bancroft (*Sheriff Claude Stagg*), Guy Kibbee (*Judge George Lee*), Diana Lewis (*Ellamae Downs*), Peter Whitney (*Frank V. Bailie*), "Rags" Ragland (*Chester Conway/*

Sylvester Conway), Celia Travers (*Hattie Lee*), Lucien Littlefield (*Corporal Lucken*), Louis Mason (*Lem*), Mark Daniels (*Martin Gordon*), Pierre Watkin (*Doctor*), Emmett Vogan (*Radio Producer*), Hobart Cavanaugh (*Panky*), Joseph Crehan (*Deputy Police Commissioner*), Billie "Buckwheat" Thomas (*Boy at Train Depot*), Hal Le Sueur (*Sound Effects Man*), John Wald (*Radio Announcer*), Charles Lung (*Brunner*), Norman Abbott (*Attendant*)

Director: S. Sylvan Simon. *Producer*: George Haight. *Screenplay*: Nat Perrin. *Additional Dialogue*: Wilkie Mahoney. *Director of Photography*: Clyde DeVina. *Musical Score*: Lennie Hayton. *Recording Director*: Douglas Shearer. *Art Director*: Cedric Gibbons. *Associate*: Gabriel Scognavillo. *Set Decorator*: Edwin B. Willis. *Associate*: Keogh Gleason. *Gowns*: Shoup. *Film Editor*: Frank Sullivan.

MGM; released December 1942. 74 minutes.

Wally Benton and his fiancée Carol are ready to be married, but she insists upon a two-week honeymoon, which means a vacation from his nightly radio performances as "The Fox" on *The Grapomix Crime Hour*. His doctor testifies that he is suffering from a nervous condition, and needs a break from "guns, shootings, and crime problems." When Carol receives a Japanese beetle pin from her sorority sister Ellamae in Georgia, which she recognizes as the "sorority signal of distress," Wally's girl suggests that they get married there.

On arrival in Dixon, Georgia, Wally soon hears that a murder has taken place at Fort Dixon, although no one can find the body of Martin Gordon, who was researching the fort's history. Several characters proceed to act suspiciously, including Ellamae's uncle, the local judge, and his chauffeur, who bears a startling resemblance to bad guy Sylvester Conway, sentenced to prison after Wally's last adventure. Martin Gordon's notes, which were left behind at the fort, offer a clue that Wally deciphers, involving a sonnet by Longfellow.

Searching the fort, Wally, Carol, and Ellamae unearth a buried treasure, left behind by the judge's grandfather, who was the governor during the Civil War. Little do they realize that some of the people surrounding them can't be trusted, including two public officials whom they wrongly assume are on their side. Trapped in a fortified room deep underground, Wally and his friends try to make their escape, threatened by a stream of incoming water that's rapidly filling the confined space.

Nearly a year and a half after the box office success of *Whistling in the Dark*, Red Skelton and his leading lady Ann Rutherford re-team for this funny, fast-paced follow-up. Under the guidance of his favorite director, S. Sylvan Simon, Skelton has a field day in his second turn as the clumsy, cowardly, none-too-bright radio detective. His pratfalls and the contortions of his rubber face keep the audience laughing throughout the film's running time. Miss Rutherford believably plays a woman who loves Skelton's wacky character, but keeps him in check when needed. The film's other leading lady, lovely Diana Lewis (1919–1997), had married William Powell in 1940; she will retire from the screen after one more film, *Cry "Havoc"* (1943).

Also along for the ride again is funnyman "Rags" Ragland, whose supporting role in the first *Whistling* picture had considerably brightened it; here, we learn that his bad guy Sylvester has a twin brother, Chester. (Chester volunteers that his nickname is "Lester," to which Skelton retorts, "I'll bet you've got a sister named Esther.") Ragland's dual role leads to some very funny set pieces after Sylvester turns up, notably a fight scene late in the film that finds Wally unaware that one brother's on his side, and

***Whistling in Dixie*: Carol (Ann Rutherford) just received the "sorority signal of distress," and explains to Wally (Red Skelton) that their help is needed.**

the other keeps trying to punch him out. He and Skelton play off one another effectively, and the featured player garners his share of the film's laughs without upstaging the star.

Nat Perrin's screenplay has been punched up with gags from radio comedy writer Wilkie Mahoney, who had been signed to an MGM contract based on acclaim for his work with Bob Hope in Paramount's *Some Like It Hot* (1939). The result was a script with some sharp wisecracks—when the sheriff offers to hoist a mint julep with Wally, the latter retorts, "Yeah, we'll get Southern fried together." One gag was more prescient than perhaps anyone knew, when Skelton reacts to the late-night chimes of a clock with, "Don't those Good Humor men ever sleep?" *The Good Humor Man* (1950), a comedy vehicle for which Simon hoped to cast Skelton, was still several years in the future.

The final script contained pages dated between May 30 and June 6, 1942. Among the film's running gags are Wally's repeated encounters with a radio station usher determined to collect a tip for delivering a package, and his disgusted reaction to Carol and Ellamae running up a long distance telephone bill. The script's closing gag, which finds Wally's "Fox" howl attracting the attention of "two startled-eyed little foxes," did not make it into the finished film.

Once again, Simon demonstrates his ability to guide Skelton to a performance that offers him free rein, but isn't marred by the excesses sometimes found in the comedian's later television performances. The director might have considered a dialect coach, as several of the cast members deliver pseudo-Southern accents that, if a viewer is intended to be charitable, can be taken as parodic.

Visiting the set, syndicated columnist Hugh Dixon (July 31, 1942) watched as Simon laid out a fight scene between his star and actor Peter Whitney step by step: "Peter, you go for Red with a gun. Red pumps on the anvil bellows, throwing a sheet of flame in your face and you drop the pistol. Then you grab that big sickle..." Finally, Skelton broke in to say, "What are you doing directing comedies? You ought to be training Commandos."

An exhibitor in small-town New York, writing to *Motion Picture Herald*'s "What the Picture Did for Me" column (May 1, 1943), reported "smash business" for the film, adding, "Red Skelton is getting stronger at our box office and we hope Leo [i.e., MGM] keeps his pictures as good as this one." Before *Whistling in Dixie* even hit theaters, *Variety* (September 9, 1942) was reporting that a third entry in the series would be getting underway shortly, again under Simon's direction.

Reviews: "Even funnier than *Whistling in the Dark*.... Both the dialogue writer and the casting director have done right by Metro-Goldwyn-Mayer's fair-haired comedian.... S. Sylvan Simon directed this Skelton comedy and he has done a good job, by making it as spooky as it is funny and keeping [it] moving speedily along to an hilarious climax." *New York Daily News*, Wanda Hale, December 31, 1942

"While there is nothing robust about the humorous content of the film, the production does manage to entertain generously at all times, with the comedy antics fast and furious most of the way. The cast has entered whole-heartedly into the spirit of this bundle of nonsense.... Skelton's antics will keep his fans in stitches.... S. Sylvan Simon's direction keeps the action moving swiftly." *Film Daily*, October 29, 1942

Salute to the Marines (1943)

Wallace Beery (*Sgt. Maj. William Bailey*), Fay Bainter (*Jennie Bailey*), Reginald Owen (*Henry Caspar*), Keye Luke ("*Flashy*" *Logaz*), Ray Collins (*Col. John Mason*), Marilyn Maxwell (*Helen Bailey*), William Lundigan (*Rufus Cleveland*), Donald Curtis (*Randall James*), Noah Beery, Sr. (*Adjutant*), Dick Curtis (*Cpl. Mosley*), Russell Gleason (*Pvt. Hanks*), Rose Hobart (*Mrs. Carson*), William Bishop (*Cpl. Anderson*), Arthur Space (*Cpl. Swenson*), Robert Blake (*Junior Carson*), Frank Ferguson (*Pvt. Williams*), Harry Hayden (*Dr. Craig*), Jim Davis (*Pvt. Saunders*), Charles Trowbridge (*Mr. Selkirk*), Don Taylor (*Brooks*), Mary Field (*Mrs. Riggs*), Edward Fielding (*Preacher*), Hugh Beaumont (*Sergeant*), William Haade (*M.P. Sergeant*), Mark Daniels (*Myers*), Jim Davis (*Pvt. Saunders*), Robert Blake (*Junior Carson*), Dick Winslow (*Young Marine*), Jennie Mac (*Mrs. Craig*), Carl Saxe (*Orderly*), Leonard Strong (*Mr. Karitu*), Harold De Becker (*Mr. Hobbs*), William Tannen (*Adjutant Reading Commendation Letter*), Fritz Leiber (*Mr. Agno*), Tom Yuen (*Filipino Interpreter*), Myron Healey (*Gunner*), Susan Simon (*Little Girl in Window*)

Director: S. Sylvan Simon. *Producer*: John W. Considine, Jr. *Screenplay*: George Bruce. *Adaptation*: Wells Root. *Story*: Robert D. Andrews. *Directors of Photography*: Charles Schoenbaum, W. Howard Greene. *Art Director*: Cedric Gibbons. *Associates*:

Stan Rogers, Lynden Sparkhawk. *Set Decorator*: Edwin B. Willis. *Associate*: Glen Barner. *Technical Color Director*: Natalie Kalmus. *Associate*: Henri Jaffa. *Musical Score*: Lennie Hayton. *Recording Director*: Douglas Shearer. *Film Editor*: Fredrick Y. Smith. *Special Effects*: Arnold Gillespie, Warren Newcombe. *Costume Supervisor*: Irene. *Associate*: Shoup. *Makeup*: Jack Dawn. *Technical Advisor*: Lt. Col. G. McGuire Pierce, U.S.M.C. [*Unit Manager*: Jay Marchant. *Assistant Directors*: Horace Hough, Norman Elzer. *Script Clerk*: Earl McEvoy. *Set Dresser*: Glenn Barner. *Hair Dresser*: Yvette Bernier. *Wardrobe Man*: Bill Beattie. *Wardrobe Woman*: Evelyn Cornwall.]

MGM; released September 1943. 101 minutes.

Sergeant-Major Bill Bailey, a veteran Marine nearing retirement, is renowned for his skill at training new recruits. Stationed in the Philippines, he's unhappy when his commanding officer, Colonel Mason, assigns him to a new project—teaching civilians to defend their country after U.S. troops withdraw. Initially he's frustrated as he struggles to instill military discipline and skills in the Filipino men, but eventually he turns them into viable soldiers.

Bailey, who's never seen active combat, is devastated when Mason tells him he won't be going along with the last unit of American soldiers he trained, which is being deployed to China. Heartbroken, he goes on a drunken bender that lands him in the brig, but thanks to his sympathetic commanding officer he's allowed to retire with an unblemished record. Bailey's wife Jennie and adult daughter Helen welcome him home to what is supposed to be a relaxing retirement, but he has trouble adjusting to civilian life. The Baileys' neighbors in the village of Balanga are mostly avowed pacifists who have little respect for his military service. Like Mrs. Bailey, many of them are naively complacent about the prospect of attack by the Japanese, an attitude encouraged and cultivated by at least one resident who is actually on the side of the enemy.

During a Sunday morning church service, Balanga is bombed by the Japanese. Bailey knows he doesn't have enough men to fight off the coming enemy invasion, but organizes the local men he trained earlier to keep the enemy at bay until reinforcements arrive. As Bailey puts it, "None of you folks wanted a war, but you're getting it just the same. War's like a sickness. Nobody wants it, but millions of people get it. When you get sick, you send for a doctor. When you get a war, you get a soldier!"

Filmed only months after the Japanese attack on Pearl Harbor, *Salute to the Marines* is cut from largely the same pattern as the previous year's Beery-Simon collaboration, *The Bugle Sounds*. Once again, Wallace Beery is cast as an aging military man near retirement, whose skills prove to be unexpectedly valuable in a time of crisis. Like the earlier film, this one begins on a lighter note, allowing for comedic moments with the star's curmudgeonly character, then shifts into action in the last half-hour. William Lundigan, the clean-cut young soldier from the earlier picture, plays a similar role here.

A reporter visiting the set during production found the company shooting a scene in which Beery's character tries hurriedly to hide the chewing tobacco in his mouth when his wife comes home. Accidentally swallowing the tobacco, he's "brushing tears from his eyes" as he walks in. With the shot completed, Simon complimented his star, saying, "That was very realistic, Wally." Beery replied grumpily, "Should be. I really swallowed the stuff by mistake!"[43] The idea of a noted screen slob like Beery as the man teaching younger Marines the finer details of deportment and discipline is slightly far-fetched, but he pulls it off.

Bailey (Wallace Beery) chooses the wrong way to hide his chewing tobacco from wife Jennie (Fay Bainter) in *Salute to the Marines*.

Beery introduced Simon to a visiting journalist, saying, "Why this fellow was a young punk running around in knee pants when I was directing and acting in pictures. But here I got to take orders from him and do as he says."[44] According to columnist Louella O. Parsons (August 1, 1942), when Simon first advised his star that the film would be shot in Technicolor, Beery joked, "Guess I'm so pretty in black and white everybody wants to see me in my natural colors." To persuade the star to have his hair cut short, like the other actors, Simon reportedly resorted to reverse psychology, telling the star there was no need to do so. "The hell I shouldn't," Beery replied. "I'll wear a Marine haircut like everybody else."[45]

Fay Bainter (1893–1968) is cast as Bailey's long-suffering wife, a prim and dignified lady who longs for him to leave the Marine Corps, and then has second thoughts about his comportment as a retiree. Though she and Beery don't make the world's most believable screen couple, she could at least draw on real-life experience to play a military wife. At the time of the film's release, the actress had been married for some 25 years to Commander Reginald Venable of the U.S. Navy. Luminously beautiful Marilyn Maxwell (1920–1972) plays Daddy's-girl Helen, Bailey's daughter who has two handsome military men vying for her hand. She was, according to the film's pressbook, Miss Bainter's 36th screen child.

Actress Rose Hobart (1906–2000) said in her memoirs that the director of *Salute* to the Marines, whom she did not identify by name, gave her some much-needed employment. "I worked on it for six weeks because the director had a crush on me so he kept me around on salary, for which I was very grateful."[46] She would be seen the following year in Simon's *Song of the Open Road*. Ray Collins (1889–1965), perhaps most recognizable as Lt. Arthur Tragg on TV's *Perry Mason*, played featured roles in two Simon pictures in 1943, turning up here along with *Whistling in Brooklyn* a few months later. Possibly to offset any criticism of the film's racial overtones, Keye Luke has a substantial supporting role as Flashy, an ex-prize fighter who's a loyal American, and Bailey's pal. Simon's daughter Susan is seen briefly as the little girl who peeks into a window, and tattles that Bailey is teaching the neighbors' little boys to fight; most prominent among those boys is a nine-year-old Robert Blake (born 1933), already a veteran of the "Our Gang" series.

Syndicated columnist Harrison Carroll (September 17, 1942) reported "plenty of headaches" for Simon and studio bosses who needed "a beach location that resembles the Philippine Islands and where they can stage a bombardment by 24 planes, supposedly Japanese. The U.S. coastline is out because the government won't allow it to be photographed from the air."

Simon wrote that he picked up some Marine lore and lingo while making the film. "The Army always tucks its ties in the shirt. But not the Marines. 'Field scarfs,' as they are called, always hang straight. 'Battle bars' are tie pins, 'Go-to-hell' caps are overseas caps, and 'geranium pots' are steel helmets."[47]

A column item reported, "For three years Director S. Sylvan Simon tried to lose that waistline bulge that comes to men in middle age." (Simon was 32 during production.) Though diet, exercise, and medication failed to do the trick, directing this film did. Guiding the film's action scenes with Marines, "he followed them on maneuvers and he chased them over hills and across beaches in mock battles." By the time the film wrapped, he had shed 16 pounds.[48]

Reviews: "For all its routine quality, *Salute to the Marines* will draw heavily at the box office.... The film has a generous quantity of simple, direct and easily-assimilated comedy [as well as] action without stint, fine Technicolor photography ... and a climax packed with excitement.... The direction of S. Sylvan Simon possesses vitality." *Film Daily*, August 2, 1943

"The particular virtue of the picture from the novelty standpoint is that the photography is in color and the spectacular shots during the Japanese raids on the Philippines are emphasized through this medium. Beery contributes rousingly to the fun of the film whenever he has a chance.... The writing by George Bruce [and] direction by S. Sylvan Simon are both worthy of commendation." Edwin Schallert, *Los Angeles Times*, September 24, 1943

Whistling in Brooklyn (1943)

Red Skelton (*Wally "The Fox" Benton*), Ann Rutherford (*Carol Lambert*), Jean Rogers (*Jean Pringle*), "Rags" Ragland (*Chester Conway*), Ray Collins (*Grover*

Kendall), Henry O'Neill (*Insp. Holcomb*), William Frawley (*Det. Ramsey*), Sam Levene (*Creeper*), Arthur Space (*Det. MacKenzie*), Robert Emmet[t] O'Connor (*Det. Finnigan*), Steve Geray (*Whitey*), Howard Freeman (*Steve Conlon*), Tom Dillon (*Beavers Team Manager*), Morris Ankrum (*Mr. Blake*), Anthony Caruso (*Fingers*), Oscar "Dutch" Hendrian (*Joey*), Dewey Robinson (*Beavers Trainer*), Emmett Vogan (*Radio Producer*), Lillian Yarbo (*Maid*), Lee Phelps (*Police Dispatcher*), William Bishop (*Psychiatrist*), Clancy Cooper (*Ofcr. Slocum*), Harry Strang (*Gumbats*), Mike Mazurki (*Henchman on Ship*), Kay Medford (*Telephone Operator*), Harry Tyler (*Gateman*), Billy Engle (*Balloon Vendor*), Happy Felton (*Radio Announcer*), James Warren (*Sound Man*), Charles Dorety (*Drunk*), Hilda Chester (*Dodgers Fan*), Sue Moore (*Tough Girl*), Edgar Dearing (*Desk Sergeant*), Eddie Dunn (*Policeman Serving Coffee*), Gil Perkins (*Police Sergeant*), Harvey Parry (*Workman*), Kay Williams (*Office Girl*)

Director: S. Sylvan Simon. *Producer*: George Haight. *Story and Screenplay*: Nat Perrin. *Additional Dialogue*: Wilkie Mahoney. *Director of Photography*: Lester White. *Music Score*: George Bassman. *Recording Director*: Douglas Shearer. *Art Director*: Cedric Gibbons. *Associate*: Jack Martin Smith. *Set Decorator*: Edwin B. Willis. *Associate*: Mildred Griffiths. *Special Effects*: Warren Newcombe. *Properties*: Harry Edwards. *Costume Supervisor*: Irene. *Film Editor*: Ben Lewis.

MGM; released December 1943. 87 minutes.

There's a killer on the loose in Brooklyn, and an anonymous letter writer who calls himself "Constant Reader," giving the police clues to finding the latest dead body while taunting them for their incompetence. Police Inspector Holcomb believes "Constant Reader" is not just an informant, but the murderer himself. When he hears a broadcast of Wally "The Fox" Benton's radio crime show, the inspector suspects that Benton may be the know-it-all "Constant Reader."

Meanwhile, Wally and his fiancée Carol Lambert are once again on their way to get married and take their honeymoon. His loyal if dimwitted chauffeur Chester Conway has appointed himself Wally's press agent, and his first brainstorm was to claim that Benton is "Constant Reader." Subjected to various pranks by their co-workers, Wally assumes it's more of the same when policemen barge into his dressing room. He flees the scene, unaware that pushy reporter Jean Pringle has stowed away in the trunk of his car.

When Chester recognizes one of the killer's prior victims, Wally begins to piece together the connection among these seemingly unrelated people. Catching on to the motive behind the murders, Wally tries to warn the next logical victim, only to realize too late that he's just tipped off the killer. Wally struggles to escape in time to come to the rescue of the police inspector, who's being targeted for murder at a charity baseball game featuring the Brooklyn Dodgers.

Skelton's third and final go-round as "The Fox" is another winning comedy, with skillfully executed physical comedy, and gags flying everywhere. His battle with an overstuffed suitcase is very funny, as is the moment when he remarks to Carol, "I like to get to the bottom of things"—right before the floor gives way beneath him. He can also drop a sharper line occasionally, as when he remarks that a bratty kid is "smart as a whip.... I wish I had one handy."

Jean Rogers (1913–1991), best-remembered as the leading lady of popular 1930s serials like *Flash Gordon*, plays the Lois-Lane-wannabe Jean Pringle, reporter for the *New York Chronicle*. She horns in on Wally's adventures, showing a fondness for him

Red Skelton (center) is surrounded by feminine pulchritude in *Whistling in Brooklyn*. Also pictured are Ann Rutherford (left) and Jean Rogers.

that arouses Carol's ire. Loyal to the woman he loves, Wally never gives the newcomer the response she wants, reassuring Carol, "There's standing room only in this ticker of mine. Everything's reserved for you." In fact, tagalong Jean gets no respect from anyone; asked to put Wally's bag in the car, Chester says, "You can't talk about Miss Pringle like that!" Later, Wally borrows Jean's press badge in order to infiltrate the police station. "You can't impersonate me!" she protests. "Oh, yes, I can," he replies. "I can act very stupid." A good sport off-screen, Miss Rogers would later cite *Whistling in Brooklyn* as one of her favorite MGM roles.

As he has throughout the series, "Rags" Ragland contributes some of the best laughs, whether Chester's reminiscing about his Uncle Sally—"he's a bearded lady in the circus"—or cheerfully acknowledging his less-than-stellar past. Hunting for clues in the police station, Wally chides his sidekick for trying to rifle through an evidence cabinet, saying, "Don't touch things. Don't leave your fingerprints." Chester responds, "I'm not. I'm gonna take 'em with me." Seeing Jean pretend to have fainted, in order to escape from a bad guy, Chester notes, "I ain't seen a dame pass out like this since the last time I played Post Office."

The baseball sequence that takes up much of the film's last half hour is a treat for fans of the sport. Simon and his company traveled to New York to shoot on location, and cast several members of the Brooklyn Dodgers in small roles. Manager

Leo Durocher appears as himself, while several of the team's players of the period do likewise, or hide behind beards as members of the opposing team. According to one columnist, Durocher razzed both the star and director Simon, saying, "The thing you movie guys do best is waste time." Seeing Simon arrange and shoot scenes with his usual care and attention, the Dodgers manager cracked, "Don't strain yourself hurryin."[49]

April 15, 1943, was declared "Red Skelton Day" at Ebbets Field, as noted in *The Exhibitor* (April 21, 1943): "The Metro production unit ... was grinding cameras throughout the game between the Dodgers and the Battling Beavers, Skelton's team in the film, which preceded the regularly scheduled exhibition game between Brooklyn and Montreal. Borough President John Cashmore presented plaques of appreciation to Skelton and S. Sylvan Simon, director, before the game." Unusually cold springtime weather in Brooklyn, where Simon and company were shooting location footage at Ebbets Field, required a mild modification to the script. The extras, who were supposed to be sitting in the grandstand and bleachers in summer attire, rebelled and huddled together with up-turned collars. A newspaper column item noted, "A mid-summer baseball scene had to be re-written as a spring ... training exhibition game."[50]

An article in MGM's in-house newspaper outlined the odd assortment of items prop man Harry Edwards was expected to assemble for *Whistling in Brooklyn*, which included "a phonograph record which can be chewed up and swallowed" and "an explosive suitcase." Edwards recited others on his shopping list: "One celluloid baseball to be caught in beard; one wedding cake which will squirt water; one exploding brick; one box of twelve-inch matches; one jar of imitation mustard; one dog trained to stick out his tongue; one fountain pen which can change into a knife. You think those can be picked up on street corners?"[51]

Reviews: "By far the funniest of the Red Skelton 'Whistling' films and among the funniest comedies of this or any past season ... [Skelton] is a comedian of top rank, perhaps of topmost rank. He has the gift of personalizing and improving his material as he goes along.... He has been 'going places,' as they say, for a long time, and now he is there.... [The film] is a tribute to the skill and talent of everyone involved, and it's a whale of an entertainment." *Motion Picture Daily*, September 29, 1943

"The picture is one of Red Skelton's most hilarious exhibitions of his talent, being extraordinarily fast and furious entertainment that doesn't ease its breathless pace for a moment. Its comedy hits the mark solidly, convulsing the audience time and again.... S. Sylvan Simon's direction is to be commended." *Film Daily*, September 29, 1943

Song of the Open Road (1944)

Jane Powell (*Jane Powell*), Edgar Bergen (*Himself*), Bonita Granville (*Bonnie*), W.C. Fields (*Himself*), Sammy Kaye and His Orchestra (*Themselves*), Peggy O'Neill (*Peggy*), Jackie Moran (*Jack Moran*), Bill Christy (*Bill*), Reginald Denny (*Mr. Curtis*), Regis

Toomey (*Mr. Connors*), Rose Hobart (*Mrs. Powell*), The Condos Brothers, The Lipham Four, Catron and Popp, The Hollywood Canteen Kids (*Specialties*), Hugh Beaumont (*John Moran*), Sig Arno (*Spolo*), Edward Gargan (*Poultry Truck Driver*), Virginia Brissac (*Mrs. Cleat*), Irene Tedrow (*Miss Casper*), Irving Bacon (*Volunteer Picker*), Sid Tomack (*Makeup Man*), Cliff Clark (*Mr. Evans*), Ronald R. Rondell (*Waiter*)

Director: S. Sylvan Simon. *Producer*: Charles R. Rogers. *Screenplay*: Albert Mannheimer. *Story*: Irving Phillips. *Director of Photography*: John W. Boyle. *Production Manager*: Val Paul. *Film Editor*: Truman K. Wood. *Art Director*: Bernard Herzbrun. *Set Dressing*: Earl Wooden. *Sound Engineer*: John R. Carter. *Makeup*: [Bud] Westmore. *Assistant to Producer*: William J. Fender.

United Artists; released June 1944. 93 minutes.

Fourteen-year-old movie star Jane Powell has a busy and demanding life as an actress. Cast to appear in a short about the American Youth Hostels, she enjoys meeting the many young people who work as fruit pickers. When the shoot is finished, she is disappointed that she is unable to spend more time with them.

Jane's mother, who manages her career, tells her she will begin another film right away. Tired of the grind, Jane begs for a vacation, but Mrs. Powell insists she go on working. Rebelling, Jane dyes and cuts her hair to go incognito as a fruit picker. The teenagers she meets are initially welcoming of newcomer "Jane Price," and she volunteers for any task, including fixing the group's bicycles. But when she inadvertently causes a falling-out between Jack Moran and his girl Peggy, and the bikes she supposedly repaired fall apart, Jane realizes that she does not fit into the group.

Calling her mother to pick her up, she reveals her true identity to the kids at the youth hostel. Given another chance to prove herself, she tries to hide when her mother comes looking for her. But when the fruit pickers are faced with a large crop threatened by an upcoming storm, Jane uses her celebrity connections to insure dozens of volunteer helpers.

Signed to an MGM

Still photographer Spolo (Sig Arno) prepares to capture another image of starlet Jane Powell in *Song of the Open Road*.

contract under her real name, Suzanne Burce (born 1929), the film's young star, became Jane Powell both on-screen and off after she completed *Song of the Open Road* on loan-out to United Artists. Studio executives apparently liked the name of her character, and thought it was more suitable for their new player than the real one. In her memoir, Miss Powell wrote, "I *loved* making that movie; it was all new and exciting. They kept me so busy I didn't know if the film was good or bad; the question never even occurred to me."[52]

Already known for his ability to direct young performers, Simon was a natural choice to oversee a cast in which they play most of the principal roles, headed by an untrained 14-year-old girl making her film debut. "I hadn't been in front of a camera at all," she pointed out, having not even been given a screen test. As a director, she said, "I wasn't afraid of him at all. He was so gentle."[53] According to syndicated columnist Erskine Johnson (December 30, 1943), the concept of "precision chorus routines on bicycles," such as the one that opened the film, originated with Simon.

A memo to exhibitors from studio boss Charles R. Rogers (1892–1957), reproduced in the film's pressbook, compared Miss Powell to singer-actress Deanna Durbin, predicting that the newcomer would likewise "blaze a brilliant path into the hearts of every youth and adult who comes into your theatre" with her "lovely voice, vivid individuality and enchanting gayety."

The supporting cast includes actress Bonita Granville (1923–1988), herself a former child star, with dozens of movie roles to her credit. (Learning that Miss Granville was in her early 20s, older than the other youthful players in the film, Simon, according to Hedda Hopper's January 17, 1944, column, nicknamed her "Mother.") The dancing Condos Brothers are among the musical acts featured; brother Nick would marry comedienne Martha Raye shortly after filming wrapped.

Actor Reginald Denny (1891–1967) was assigned what one studio publicity blurb termed "the hardest job in Hollywood—he must portray his own director in a motion picture." Though the item claimed the gig "entails a study of S. Sylvan Simon, one of filmland's most capable directors of young people,"[54] there's nothing much about Denny's performance that suggests an effort to mimic his boss. Simon was said to be too "camera shy" to perform the role himself.

Near the end of his career, the great W.C. Fields (1880–1946) made a cameo appearance in the film's last 10 minutes. Though Simon had gained a reputation for bringing out the best in actors through kindness and patience, he had other tricks at his disposal. Columnist Erskine Johnson (April 5, 1944) reported that the director took pride in getting eight pages of script featuring Fields shot in a single day. Said Johnson, "If you know about Bill's lackadaisical working methods, this is indeed quite an achievement." The key to Fields' productivity, Simon admitted, was building a set atop a platform reachable only by ladder. "It was too much trouble for Fields to be climbing up and down the ladder after every shot, so he was always on hand when we needed him."

Seen alongside Fields is ventriloquist and radio comedian Edgar Bergen. A trade-paper item reported "Simon giving Charlie McCarthy heck on the set for blowing his lines while Edgar Bergen sits back and laughs and feeds words to Charlie which makes Simon even madder."[55]

A sad postscript to *Song of the Open Road* came with the death of featured actress Peggy O'Neill (1924–1945), several months after it opened. Romantically involved with the film's screenwriter Albert Mannheimer, Miss O'Neill was found dead in his Beverly Hills apartment. Police said she "died from an overdose of sleeping tablets, a suicide following a lovers' quarrel."[56]

Reviews: "The film presents a wide range of entertainment all expertly geared to the popular taste, panning out as a light and gay affair with a tear thrown in.... Wholesome and refreshing, [Jane] Powell plays with surprising self-assurance.... The girl has an unusually beautiful voice that will gain her immediate favor with film audiences ... fluent and lively direction by S. Sylvan Simon." *Film Daily*, May 3, 1944

"A semi-musical that throbs with the exuberance of youth, contains a catchy score, and serves to introduce an engaging youngster, Jane Powell, who ... displays a singing and acting ability that would do credit to a seasoned player ... [will] evoke a merry melody for theatre cash registers." *Motion Picture Daily*, April 28, 1944

Son of Lassie (1945)

Peter Lawford (*Joe Carraclough*), Donald Crisp (*Sam Carraclough*), June Lockhart (*Priscilla*), Nigel Bruce (*Duke of Radling*), William "Billy" Severn (*Henrik*), Leon Ames (*Anton*), Donald Curtis (*Sgt. Eddie Brown*), Nils Asther (*Olav*), Robert Lewis (*Sgt. Schmidt*), Pal (*Lassie/Laddie*), Fay Helm (*Joanna*), Peter Helmers (*Willi*), Otto Reichow (*Karl*), Patricia Prest (*Hedda*), Helen Koford [Terry Moore] (*Thea*), Leon Tyler (*Arne*), Lotta Palfi (*Old Woman*), Eily Malyon (*Washerwoman*), Charles Irwin (*Captain Grey*), Fritz Lieber (*Village Padre*), Arthur Space (*Warrant Officer*), Morton Lowry (*Blind Corporal P.O.W.*), Nelson Leigh (*Flight Coordinator*), Will Stanton (*Dog Trainer*), Lester Matthews (*Maj. Elliston*), William Tannen (*German Soldier with Grenade*), Mary Donovan (*WAC Driver*), Louis V. Arco (*Sentry*), Hans Schumm (*German Commander*), Barry Bernard (*British Sergeant*), Wally Cassell (*P.O.W.*), Marta Mitrovich (*Norwegian Woman*), Ralph Brooke (*Corporal*), Leyland Hodgson (*Sergeant*), Leslie Vincent (*Prisoner*)

Director: S. Sylvan Simon. *Producer*: Samuel Marx. *Story and Screenplay*: Jeanne Bartlett (based on some characters from the book "Lassie Come Home" by Eric Knight). *Director of Photography*: Charles Schoenbaum. *Technical Color Director*: Natalie Kalmus. *Associate*: Henri Jaffa. *Musical Score*: Herbert Stothart. *Recording Director*: Douglas Shearer. *Art Directors*: Cedric Gibbons, Hubert B. Hobson. *Set Decorator*: Edwin B. Willis. *Associate*: Paul Huldschinsky. *Special Effects*: A. Arnold Gillespie, Warren Newcombe, Danny Hall. *Costume Supervisor*: Irene. *Makeup*: Jack Dawn. *Film Editor*: Ben Lewis. [*Dog Trainer*: Rudd Weatherwax. *Unit Manager*: Jack Gertsman. *Assistant Director*: Herman Webber. *Second Assistant Director*: Rudy Camerson. *Camera Operator*: David Ragin. *Technical Advisor*: Ulf Greeber. *Prop Men*: Johnny Miller, Joe M. Peters.]

MGM; released April 1945. 100 minutes.

In Yorkshire, teenaged Joe Carraclough is delighted by the companionship of Lassie's rambunctious puppy, Laddie, who seems to be more important to him than the attentions of young Priscilla, daughter of the Duke of Radling. Though seemingly

On location in British Columbia for *Son of Lassie*, director Simon (left) and his four-legged star are greeted by Lieutenant Governor William Culham Woodward (Simon Family Collection).

not as intelligent as his mother, Laddie is given training for wartime service, but found to be an unsuitable candidate. Nonetheless, when Joe reports for active duty, Laddie follows him to a camp some 40 miles away.

Laddie comes along for the ride when Joe and his friend, Sgt. Eddie Brown, are sent on a reconnaissance flight over Norway. Their plane shot down by German soldiers, Joe and Laddie land by parachute in occupied enemy territory. The young man and his dog are separated, and Laddie is wounded by a shot from one of the Germans. A little Norwegian boy, Henrik, finds the injured dog, and with the help of his siblings Laddie is nursed back to health.

Despite the loving care he's received, Laddie runs away in pursuit of his still-missing master. Just as Laddie finds Joe in a church where a kindly clergyman is giving him shelter from the Nazis, an air raid throws the village into chaos. Once again separated, Joe and his dog meet up under circumstances that find their lives in danger, as they struggle to escape from the Nazis.

Shot in rich Technicolor, *Son of Lassie* is an unabashedly sentimental film aimed straight at the hearts of dog lovers. It was a sequel to *Lassie Come Home*, based on Eric Knight's bestseller, a box office hit two years earlier, but without original young players Elizabeth Taylor and Roddy McDowall. The story moves forward several years from the original, with Joe and Priscilla now young adults. According to Simon's copy of the script, the original screenplay was completed on March 29, 1944. He wisely takes the story at face value, deriving full measure from the warmth and heart-tugging appeal of the story. Simon skillfully stages the slapstick sequence in which Laddie runs amok in the Carraclough household, pulling their washerwoman off her feet and knocking her about with his boundless energy and enthusiasm.

Donald Crisp (1882–1974) and Nigel Bruce (1895–1953) reprise their roles from *Lassie Come Home* (1943) as, respectively, Joe's father and the Duke of Radling (or Rudling, as it appears in the script). June Lockhart (born 1925), replacing Elizabeth Taylor as Priscilla, has a somewhat thankless role as the love interest who takes a distinct back seat to the hero's affection for his dog. It's not she but Laddie who gets the first noteworthy close-up in the film's opening moments. (As the script puts it, an "extremely close shot" shows "the adorable golden head of Laddie.... The sun glints from the gold of his head to the flowers which he is tigerishly gnawing.") Miss Lockhart would spend another six years working alongside Lassie in the television series, joining the cast in 1958. Peter Lawford (1923–1984), signed to an MGM contract in 1943, would see a substantial boost in his popularity, especially among young women, thanks to his leading role in *Son of Lassie*. Teenaged Terry Moore (born 1929), still billed here under her birth name, Helen Koford, is seen briefly as one of the young Norwegian children who come to Laddie's rescue.

The hardest-working cast member is, of course, Pal (1940–1958), who plays the starring role of Laddie, as well as appearing as Lassie in early scenes. First seen in *Lassie Come Home,* Pal had won the unbridled admiration of author Eric Knight, who said, "The dog is the most magnificent collie I've ever seen.... Oh, gladly do I call him a movie star. I coveted him more than I ever did [Joan] Fontaine, [Dorothy] Lamour and all the other pretty stars."[57] Tragically, Knight, then a major in the U.S. Army, was killed in a January 1943 plane crash.

Pal, according to trade paper reports, alternated between working on this film and "Hold High the Torch" (later retitled *Courage of Lassie*) under the guidance of trainer Rudd Weatherwax. Location filming for the film began in Jackson Hole, Wyoming, with later sequences shot in Canada (standing in for a wintry Norway) during August and September 1944. Present on the Canadian location, a journalist later recalled the filming of a sequence that required both Pal and his human co-star Lawford to be submerged in the chilly water off Vancouver Island. Once Simon had obtained the footage he needed, the two emerged from the dunking; "Lassie shook vigorously while Peter shivered. Weatherwax and an assistant rushed forward with big beach towels to dry the dog. Lawford was left, teeth chattering, for several minutes before he was finally handed a towel and a hot drink."[58] Though he welcomed the chance to be top-billed in an MGM film for the first time, Lawford later grumbled, "As an actor you haven't a dog's chance when you act with a dog. You can be acting for all you're worth.... Then the dog wags its tail, or tosses a soulful glance, and the spectators whoop and coo. The human actor might as well not be there."[59] Norwegian diplomat Ulf Greeber acted as a technical advisor for the sequences depicting his native country.

A Canadian newspaperwoman observed as Simon supervised the shooting of a complicated aerial sequence, delayed for much of the morning by inclement weather. "When the sun finally did come out for a short time about 2 o'clock, Sylvan Simon got right on the job and in a very few minutes they had the plane up in the air." The scene was peppered with simulated artillery fire, recreating the moment in which Joe and Laddie escape via parachute. "It took six or seven tries over the cameras before director Simon was satisfied with the results…. Later in the afternoon they went up and tossed the dummy overboard to simulate Lawford and Lassie making the parachute jump."[60] Knowing how to win the hearts of the local population, Simon not only hired a hometown pilot for the airplane sequences, but also made a point of telling reporters that British Columbia was the most beautiful location he'd ever shot in his years as a director.

Following the box office success of *Son of Lassie*, which cleared a reported $1.5 million profit for the studio, MGM released a third entry the following year, *Courage of Lassie*, which featured a new set of characters.

Reviews: "Once again Metro has crashed through with a picture of vast universal appeal…. Those who took the earlier film to their hearts will accept this one with equal fervor … directed with understanding by S. Sylvan Simon." *Film Daily*, April 20, 1945

"The story drags in the early part and its entertainment value could be enhanced by clipping 15 or 20 minutes from the running time—mostly from the front end. Once the yarn gets underway it is a breathtaking succession of typical cliff-hanger suspense sequences." *Daily Variety*, April 20, 1945

Bud Abbott and Lou Costello in Hollywood (1945)

Bud Abbott (*Buzz Kurtis*), Lou Costello (*Abercrombie*), Frances Rafferty (*Claire Warren*), Robert Stanton [Bob Haymes] (*Jeff Parker*), Jean Porter (*Ruthie*), Warner Anderson (*Norman Royce*), "Rags" Ragland (*Himself*), Mike Mazurki (*Klondike Pete*), Lucille Ball, Preston Foster, Robert Z. Leonard (*Themselves*), Jackie "Butch" Jenkins, Sharon McManus (*Studio Classroom Students*), Carleton G. Young (*Gregory LeMaise*), Donald MacBride (*Dennis Kavanaugh*), Edgar Dearing (*Al, Studio Policeman*), Marion Martin (*Miss Milbane*), Arthur Space (*Director*), William "Bill" Phillips (*Kavanaugh's Assistant*), The Lyttle Sisters (*Vocalists*), Robert Emmett O'Connor (*Second Studio Policeman*), William Tannen (*Casting Director/Voice of Dr. Snide*), Skeets Noyes (*Wardrobe Man*), Dean Stockwell (*Dean*), Hank Worden (*Joe*), Richard Alexander (*Eddie*), Marie Blake (*Royce's Secretary*), Chester Clute (*Mr. Burvis*), Charles McNally (*Barker*), Betty Blythe (*Mrs. Murdock*), Frank Penny (*Night Clerk*), Henry Hall (*Tenant*), Nick Stewart (*Houseboy*), Karin Booth (*Louise*), Peter Miles (*Little Boy with Horn*), Joe Bacon (*Nubian Slave*), Joe Devlin (*Kelly, the Bartender*), Milton Kibbee (*Counterman*), Fred Aldrich (*Mr. Leonard's Assistant*), Wheaton Chambers (*Pedestrian*), George Calliga (*Maître D'*), George Magrill (*Actor*), Harold DeGarro (*Stilt Walker*), Mary Donovan, Beverly Haney, Zaz Vorka (*Manicurists*), Jane Hale, Nita Mathews (*Cigarette Girls*), Arno Frey, William Hawley, Frank J. Scannell (*Waiters*)

Director: S. Sylvan Simon. *Producer*: Martin A. Gosch. *Screenplay*: Nat Perrin, Lou Breslow. *Original Story*: Nat Perrin, Martin A. Gosch. *Director of Photography*: Charles Schoenbaum. *Songs*: Ralph Blane, Hugh Martin. *Dance Director*: Charles Walters. *Musical Director*: George Bassman. *Orchestrations*: Ted Duncan. *Film Editor*: Ben Lewis. *Recording Director*: Douglas Shearer. *Art Directors*: Cedric Gibbons, Wade B. Rubottom. *Set Decorator*: Edwin B. Willis. *Costume Supervisor*: Irene. *Associate*: Kay Carter. *Men's Costumes*: Valles. *Makeup*: Jack Dawn.

MGM; released October 1945. 83 minutes.

Employed by a Hollywood barber shop, Buzz Kurtis and his pal Abercrombie are in the office of agent Norman Royce, where they are impressed by the money he earns negotiating deals for his clients. Royce recognizes the potential of a young newcomer, singer Jeff Parker, but brushes him off when a lucrative client, Gregory LeMaise, objects to the competition. Buzz and Abercrombie rebrand themselves as Hollywood agents, and convince Jeff to let them represent him.

On the lot at Mammoth Studios, the two would-be agents get off to a bad start when they crash into the car of studio head Dennis Kavanaugh. Infiltrating the premises nonetheless, they raise havoc on various film sets while trying to avoid two studio policemen who witnessed the accident. Meanwhile, Buzz and Abercrombie's friend Claire Warren, a former manicurist turned movie ingénue, recommends that Kavanaugh cast Jeff as the leading man in her next film, a role that Gregory LeMaise has refused. Impressed by Jeff, who says he must consult his agents before accepting the job, Kavanaugh sends the studio cops to find the two nincompoops.

Once the deal is closed, Jeff and his friends celebrate with a night out at Ciro's, the Hollywood club, where he and Claire begin to explore their mutual attraction. But the fun comes to an abrupt halt when LeMaise tells Kavanaugh he will play the part after all, leaving Jeff out in the cold. The young singer tells Claire he's going back home, giving up on Hollywood.

With the film about to go into production, Buzz and Abercrombie take on the task of ousting Jeff's rival. On LeMaise's boat, trying to stage a photograph of the star hitting Abercrombie, the clumsy agent goes overboard. Before Buzz has much time to mourn his pal, Abercrombie turns up none the worse for wear, and the two concoct a scheme to have LeMaire arrested for murder.

Like their previous film for MGM, *Bud Abbott and Lou Costello in Hollywood* (its official title onscreen) is overproduced, surrounding the boys with musical numbers, lavish sets, and a sizable supporting cast. Some 10 years after Groucho, Chico, and Harpo had reigned supreme as the comedians of MGM, *Abbott and Costello in Hollywood* has something of the structure of the Marx Brothers' films for that studio.

But Costello, in particular, dominates the action nonetheless. One of the film's funniest sequences finds his character hiding out on the set of a Western. Pretending to be one of the inanimate dummies earmarked for fight scenes, Abercrombie finds himself unexpectedly pressed into service, where he's dragged up a flight of stairs, tossed over a balcony, and punched by burly bad guy Klondike Pete. Looking on is the fussy director (played by Sylvan Simon's pal Arthur Space), who keeps demanding retakes. Simon's daughter Susan, sporting a red-and-white checked dress, with bows in her hair, appears in the scene set in the studio classroom. She listens (along with up-and-coming child actors "Butch" Jenkins and Sharon McManus) as Costello's character tells his version of the Little Red Riding Hood story. According to the

"Rags" Ragland (center), appearing as himself, foolishly trusts Abercrombie (Lou Costello) to spruce him up at a barber shop in *Bud Abbott and Lou Costello in Hollywood*. At left is Costello's leading lady Jean Porter (Simon Family Collection).

film's pressbook, the comedian struggled to recite the tale without deviating from the script, throwing off the young performers who needed to hear specific cues. "Director S. Sylvan Simon," said the item, "brought a huge blackboard onto the set, placed it out of camera range, wrote the lines on it, and Lou read his lines from the board as the cameras rolled."

Lucille Ball and Preston Foster make cameo appearances as actors rehearsing a scene under the guidance of MGM director Robert Z. Leonard (appearing as himself). This sequence was outlined in script pages marked "Chgs" [changes] and dated May 4, 1945. Although Foster and Miss Ball are named in the typed pages, Leonard is not, the scenario calling for "an important director." One of Foster's lines of dialogue, in fact, is rendered on the page as, "How about that, Mr. [important director]?" According to the *Los Angeles Times'* Edwin Schallert (May 9, 1945), the cameo role marked Leonard's return to film acting after a hiatus of nearly 30 years.

The film finishes on a strong note with a sequence taking place on a carnival set at Mammoth Studios, where Abercrombie is on the run from an angry LeMaise. Costello's physical dexterity is fully to the fore here, with a skillfully-directed roller coaster sequence that elicits not just laughs but an occasional gasp.

"Rags" Ragland, in his final film for Simon, plays himself as the unlucky recipient of Costello's barber shop antics. The young leading man billed as "Robert Stanton" was in fact singer Bob Haymes (1923–1989), Dick's younger brother. Haymes had already had a few shots at movie success under his real name, appearing with Joan Davis in two of her B comedies at Columbia, *Two Senoritas from Chicago* and *Beautiful but Broke*. His leading lady here, Frances Rafferty (1922–2004), is pertly pretty, but the role gives her little to do. She would fare better in her next assignment for Simon, *Bad Bascomb*, and would go on to be a regular on TV's *December Bride*.

Production began in April 1945. Syndicated columnist Harrison Carroll (April 26, 1945), during a set visit, wondered why the setting used to represent Ciro's Restaurant looked nothing like the real thing. "Oh, it's quite simple," Simon responded. "We call the place Ciro's but we borrow a feature or two from the Mocambo and paint the room a little like the Crillon, then nobody can get sore."

As always, it was Simon's job to let his star comedians improvise freely, but reel them in when needed. Columnist Sheilah Graham (April 20, 1945) was present during the scene at Ciro's, and observed the bit where Abercrombie finds himself unexpectedly dancing with an older woman, instead of Ruthie. During one take, Graham reported, "When he discovers his mistake, he kicks the lady in a place you do not usually kick a lady." Simon disapproved of the improvised bit, which was surely out of character for dimwitted nice guy Abercrombie, but Costello argued for including it. "Who wins?" the columnist wrote. "I'll give you a clue. The initials of the victor are S.S."

Reviews: "A completely nonsensical film that will have [Abbott and Costello's] admirers in stitches, although much of the material has a familiar ring. The picture, directed at a mad pace by S. Sylvan Simon ... makes no pretense of telling a coordinated story. ... Those whose tastes in comedy are of a low order will relish the latest of the Abbott-Costello funfests very much." *Film Daily*, August 22, 1945

"Leo the Lion has given Abbott and Costello a new lease on screen life ... in a production that gives the widest latitude to their tomfoolery without becoming too diffuse or dull. The routines have punch and sparkle with some beautifully timed sequences.... A and C fans who have been bewailing their vehicles can take joy in the effervescent pace of this one, for which credit director S. Sylvan Simon. Simon also points up the satirical touches on the Hollywood scene." *Hollywood Reporter*, August 22, 1945

Bad Bascomb (1946)

Wallace Beery (*Zeb Bascomb*), Margaret O'Brien (*Emmy*), Marjorie Main (*Abbey Hanks*), J. Carrol Naish (*Bart Yancy*), Frances Rafferty (*Dora McCabe*), Marshall Thompson (*Jimmy Holden*), Russell Simpson (*Elijah Walker*), Warner Anderson (*Dr. Luther Mason*), Donald Curtis (*John Fulton*), Connie Gilchrist (*Annie Fremont*), Sara Haden (*Tillie Lovejoy*), Renie Riano (*Lucy Lovejoy*), Jane Green (*Hannah McCabe*), Henry O'Neill (*Gov. Winton*), Frank Darien (*Elder Moab McCabe*), John Gallaudet (*Selkirk*), Stanley Andrews (*Col. Cartright*), Eddie Acuff (*Cpl. Finch*), Arthur Space (*Timber City Sheriff*), Wally Cassell (*Curly*), Susan Simon (*Pioneer Girl*)

Director: S. Sylvan Simon. *Producer*: Orville O. Dull. *Screenplay*: William Lipman, Grant Garrett. *Original Story*: D.A. Loxley. *Director of Photography*: Charles Schoenbaum. *Film Editor*: Ben Lewis. *Musical Score*: David Snell. *Orchestration*: Wally Heglin. *Recording Director*: Douglas Shearer. *Art Directors*: Cedric Gibbons, Paul Youngblood. *Set Decorator*: Edwin B. Willis. *Associate*: Jack Ahern. *Special Effects*: Warren Newcombe. *Costume Supervisor*: Irene. *Men's Costumer*: Valles.

MGM; released May 1946. 112 minutes.

The post–Civil War American West is still plagued by lawlessness, and at the request of three state governors, Federal Agent John Fulton and nine other men under his command are sent to help. A top priority is tracking down outlaw Zeb Bascomb and his gang, whose members include his sidekick Bart and a reluctant young recruit, Jimmy. When the crooks encounter a man who tells them he's an elder in a Mormon caravan on its way to Utah, a suspicious Bart shoots him. The hoodlums' attempted robbery of the Timber City Bank goes awry when they are met with gunfire from the federal men. After making a narrow escape, Zeb and Bart, spot the Mormon travelers, and decide that joining their caravan will serve as a perfect hideout. The Mormons accept the newcomers as members of the flock; Zeb calls himself "Ezekiel Smith."

While making a late-night raid on the food larder, Zeb meets Emmy Hanks, a precocious young girl who doesn't report his pilfering, but holds the secret in abeyance. The next day, when the outlaws learn that they are expected to help the unmarried women of the caravan with chores, Emmy sees to it that Zeb is assigned to her cantankerous grandmother, Abbey. Bart, now going by the name Jonathan, chooses the spinster Lovejoy sisters, who pamper him, but Abbey puts Zeb right to work.

Zeb and Bart fear their cover has been blown when Jimmy is brought into camp, after being shot during the robbery. He's attended by beautiful nurse Dora McCabe, and there's an immediate attraction between the two. Bart is itching to get away, but Zeb is hesitant, and Jimmy tells them he's on his own now. Learning that the wagon train is carrying a substantial amount of gold, earmarked for the construction of a hospital, Zeb concocts a plan to rob the Mormons.

When the wagon train is forced to cross a raging river, Abbey and Emmy's wagon is overturned, throwing them both into the water. Zeb rescues Emmy from drowning, although he continues to insist that she is nothing but a nuisance to him. But when Emmy falls ill, and wants Zeb by her side while she recuperates, he's forced to make a choice between helping Jonathan carry off the gold, or showing himself to be a better person than even he may believe that he is.

Though some moviegoers (and critics) found *Bad Bascomb* too long, nearing the two-hour mark, there was plenty of story to be told, and the film neatly balances action sequences with personal dramas. Simon's staging of a climactic battle scene is particularly inventive and effective, delivering rousing action that has the viewer emotionally engaged as well. The majority of the film was shot on location near Jackson Hole, Wyoming, over a two-month period in the summer of 1945. Beery, who had previously shot his film *Wyoming* (1940) in the area, was also the owner of a nearby ranch, where he hosted a gathering for members of the company.

Teamed for the second time in a Simon film, Wallace Beery and Marjorie Main continue to play off each other beautifully, though their relationship off-screen was as contentious as ever. On short acquaintance, her character, telling Zeb to wrangle one of the animals, says, "She's ornery, and won't like you, but I guess you're used to that."

Abbey (Marjorie Main) and her granddaughter Emmy (Margaret O'Brien) may need divine intervention to handle the crooked Zeb (Wallace Beery) in *Bad Bascomb* (Simon Family Collection).

Later, when he claims he has work to do, she responds, "Work? Did I hear right? First time I ever heard work and you mentioned in the same breath. When'd you two get acquainted?"

But the most important relationship in the film is, of course, between Beery and his young co-star Margaret O'Brien, in their first and only pairing on film. More than a year before *Bad Bascomb* went into production, columnist Louella O. Parsons (February 26, 1944) wrote, "For months it has been whispered on the Metro-Goldwyn-Mayer lot that an effort would be made to team Margaret O'Brien and Wallace Beery in the type of picture he and Jackie Cooper made in the heyday of Jackie's childhood popularity." The need for a suitable screenplay put the idea on the back burner for a while, but when D.A. Loxley's story came along, plans shifted into high gear. It was Cooper, according to Miss O'Brien, who gave her a heads-up on what she might be in for.

The youthful star makes her first entrance as Emmy about 20 minutes into the film, while Zeb is raiding the caravan's food supply. Unexpectedly, she drops into frame from above, announcing, "Thou shalt not steal!" She finds the newcomer appealing, despite his gruff manner.

> **EMMY:** Maybe I'll like you.
> **ZEB:** Don't put yourself out any.

As John L. Scott of the *Los Angeles Times* commented, "Mr. Beery, who is no mean scene-stealer, puts on quite a show to stay even with little Margaret, who can tug at an audience's heartstrings with a laugh or a tear."[61] Indeed, for all Beery's best—and worst—efforts, the child actress more than holds her own, and once the story turns sentimental in the final half hour, even he probably knew he was fighting an uphill battle. Prior to the film's release, a Hollywood columnist had reported that her character's name would be changed to Maggie, and the film retitled "Maggie's Outlaw."[62] Though that didn't pan out, one can well imagine Beery's reaction to the idea.

As Miss O'Brien pointed out, Simon had much with which to contend in making *Bad Bascomb*. "It was not an easy movie to make. There were many obstacles." She considered him an ideal choice as director. "He had such an easy temper, and would just go with the flow. He never got overly excited."[63]

One of the film's show-stopping scenes was the caravan's trek across a rushing river. The complicated setup called for the use of multiple actors and extras, horses, and covered wagons, with precision timing needed, and safety measures for the players. For the sake of realism, Simon wanted to limit the use of doubles, and most of the cast ended up in the drink before the scene was committed to film. Miss Main, well-known for her fear of germs, was apprehensive. "She was afraid of the dirty water," said her young co-star. Not Miss O'Brien, who recalled, "I was a really good swimmer.... I loved falling into the rapids."

Aside from the usual directorial chores, Simon also had to keep Beery reined in. The fact that his co-star was an eight-year-old girl did little to dissuade him from his usual tactics to upstage other actors, or throw them off balance. "Mr. Simon had to make sure that I was treated correctly," said Miss O'Brien, whom Beery turned away from the camera whenever possible, and would pinch if he wanted her to do something differently. "Mr. Simon would say, 'Now, now...'"

Not every child actress would be pleased to take part in a location shoot with heat, wild animals, and few modern conveniences, but Miss O'Brien found it great fun, loved her costumes, and called *Bad Bascomb* "one of my favorite movies." Though she never again had the opportunity to work with Sylvan Simon, she did go on to make a picture called *Her First Romance*, produced at Columbia during his time as head of production.

J. Carrol Naish (1896–1973), who plays Zeb's more malevolent sidekick, was a Best Supporting Actor nominee for his performance in *A Medal for Benny* (Paramount, 1945). This was an early role for 19-year-old Marshall Thompson (1925–1992), who with Frances Rafferty comprises the young couple. He would be directed again by Simon in *The Cockeyed Miracle*. According to Hedda Hopper (April 17, 1945), Wallace Beery had hoped that his nephew, Noah Beery, Jr., could be borrowed from Universal to play the role Thompson ultimately won.

Character actress Renie Riano, playing one of the spinster Lovejoy sisters in her third Simon film, told a reporter that her role in *Bad Bascomb* helped her prepare for a trip she was planning. "I plan to make my trip 100 years behind the times," she said. "I'm going by 'covered wagon' instead of auto or train." She had obtained an old-fashioned buckboard, and chosen her horse. On location during the Bascomb shoot, she said, "I stuck close to the cowboys and learned how to shoe a horse and splice a harness and do all the pioneer jobs."[64] On screen, her character even takes out an Indian attacker with a flaming torch.

Reviews: "Not only does this one have all the customary action thrills, but it has, additionally, splendid characterizations.... Production values are excellent.... Little Miss O'Brien ... is utterly enchanting in this role.... S. Sylvan Simon's direction counteracts the excessive length of the picture." *Motion Picture Daily*, February 5, 1946

"*Bad Bascomb* will be a hit because it shows a pair of sure-fire performers at their best.... A down-and-out writer of dime-novel Western tales who hadn't sold a story in 10 years would repudiate the plot. But the picture provides good entertainment because it co-stars for the first time Wallace Beery and Margaret O'Brien. Together they provide hearty humor and moving tenderness." Julian T. Sullivan, *Indianapolis Star*, April 19, 1946

The Thrill of Brazil (1946)

Evelyn Keyes (*Vicki Dean*), Keenan Wynn (*Steve Farraugh*), Ann Miller (*Linda Lorens*), Allyn Joslyn (*John Harbour*), Tito Guízar (*Tito Guizar*), Veloz and Yolanda (*Themselves*), Felix Bressart (*Ludwig Kriegspiel*), Sid Tomack (*Irkie Bowers*), Pat Lane (*Stage Manager*), Antonio Filauri (*Café Manager*), Frank Yaconelli (*Photographer*), Robert Conte (*Waiter*), George J. Lewis (*Bartender*), John Laurenz (*Hotel Clerk*), Paul Monte (*Ticket Taker*), Enric Madriguera and His Orchestra

Director: S. Sylvan Simon. *Producer*: Sidney Biddell. *Screenplay*: Allen Rivkin, Harry Clork, Devery Freeman. *Director of Photography*: Charles Lawton, Jr. *Camera Operator*: Victor Scheurich. *Film Editor*: Charles Nelson. *Art Directors*: Stephen Goossón, Van Nest Polglase, A. Leslie Thomas. *Set Decorators*: James M. Crowe, Robert Priestley. *Assistant Director*: James Nicholson. *Makeup*: Clay Campbell. *Hair Stylist*: Helen Hunt. *Sound Engineer*: Jack Haynes. *Musical Recording*: Philip Faulkner. *Gowns*: Jean Louis. [*Property Master*: Charles Granucci.]

Columbia; released September 1946. 91 minutes.

Steve Farraugh, a producer of musical revues, is still in love with his ex-wife Vicki, who used to be his business partner and collaborator. While Steve's newest show is being tried out in Rio de Janeiro, Vicki turns up and tells him she's planning to get married again. Since Steve signed a previous set of divorce papers with disappearing ink, Vicki has to press him to complete a fresh batch. Claiming he needs her help with his current show, Steve stalls on signing the papers.

Starring in Steve's show is singer-dancer Linda Lorens, whose own interest in Steve goes unrequited. Vicki refuses to alter her plans to marry dull, good-hearted businessman John Harbour, saying she is retiring from show business. But when Steve finally does inscribe the necessary papers, he hires a larcenous cab driver to steal them and John's wallet, forcing the engaged couple to delay their departure.

Despite herself, Vicki can't help but be drawn into the problem of creating a new finale for Steve's show. But when a nightclub brawl over the stolen wallet lands her, her fiancé, and Linda in jail, she is infuriated. The resulting newspaper publicity puts John's job in jeopardy. Knowing he is in the doghouse with Vicki, Steve finally decides a dose of honesty might set things right.

Vicki (Evelyn Keyes) gets some bad news from her stodgy fiancé (Allyn Joslyn, of course) in *The Thrill of Brazil*.

A minor entry in Simon's filmography, *The Thrill of Brazil* shows relatively little of his personal stamp. Still, there are at least a few Simon touches, including some nice physical comedy bits—Steve's ungainly tumble backwards in his office chair, as well as the nightclub melee in which a much-sought-after wallet lands unexpectedly in another diner's plate (who gamely applies his knife and fork to it). *The Thrill of Brazil* neatly splits its running time down the middle, interspersing well-staged musical numbers into the unfolding story of Vicki and Steve's relationship.

The singing and dancing of Ann Miller (1923–2004) is nicely showcased here, with her character seen mostly onstage while Evelyn Keyes carries the bulk of the acting load. Director Simon told columnist Sheilah Graham (June 13, 1946), "This picture will make Ann a big star. For the first time in pictures she's allowed to be sexy." Her dance routine, accompanying her singing of the song "A Man is Brother to a Mule," underwent the scrutiny of a censor. "They brought on a Johnston office man this morning," Miss Miller told Graham, "to make sure I wasn't wiggling out of my dress."

For the singer-actress, making *The Thrill of Brazil* was a stressful experience, due mostly to the difficulties she was having with new husband Reese Milner. She had recently learned she was pregnant, and was under pressure from Milner to retire from performing. By her account, she had married a man prone to physical violence. After one argument, she wrote, "It was two weeks before I could report for work. My nose was still swollen, my eye was cut, and I was all black and blue."[65] After her baby was born prematurely, living only a few hours, she filed for divorce.

Miller's leading man, Keenan Wynn (1916–1986), was an eleventh-hour replacement for Lee Bowman, who bowed out of the film after contracting pneumonia. Wynn, borrowed from MGM for the role as Simon had been, would go on to co-star in Simon's *The Cockeyed Miracle*.

Talented character actor Allyn Joslyn (1901–1981) is well-cast as Vicki's stodgy fiancé, vice-president of the Pearlydent Toothpaste Company. A nice guy who lives in a small Iowa town with his mother, he's a solid if unexciting marital prospect. It was a role not unlike others Joslyn had already essayed in films like *Bedtime Story* (Columbia, 1941). Sid Tomack (1907–1962) has a few amusing moments as Irkie, the unscrupulous taxi driver whose slightly unsavory associates include an accomplished pickpocket, of whom Irkie says, "Used to work the subways in New York. Got so good he could snatch a man's suspenders at Times Square, and his pants wouldn't fall down till he hit Brooklyn."

This is the first credited collaboration of Simon with comedy writer Devery Freeman (1913–2005), who will be a strong contributor to the laughs of *The Fuller Brush Man* and *Miss Grant Takes Richmond*.

Columbia executives seemed uncertain as to the best title for the picture; in teletypes between Hollywood and the New York office during the summer prior to its release, they considered other titles, including "You Were Made for Me" and "Serenade in Rio." Simon's copy of the screenplay, dated April 15, 1946, carries the title "Rendezvous in Rio." For a seemingly uncomplicated story, the film underwent numerous rewrites; the number of revised pages in his script far outnumber those that were retained as originally written.

Box office results varied. One California exhibitor reported, in *Motion Picture Herald*'s "What the Picture Did for Me" column (May 17, 1947), "This was an all-time low [in ticket sales], even for midweek. Some of the few who came walked out."

Simon retained a memento of the shoot, a gag bill sent to him by propmaster Charles Granucci for services rendered. Among the entries on the itemized bill:

"Making coffee out of Mrs. Charles Granucci's own percolator during the entire picture ... ($0.75)"

"Having to run several times for each prop when you should have made up your mind in the first place ... $1.10."

"Carrying that 2-ton chair of yours for you to put your fanny on ... $25.25."

"For getting chair when Mrs. Simon visits you on set—this I liked, no charge ... $0.00."

Granucci concluded with instructions that his invoice be paid with "un-bounceable check," adding, "If check not received within 30 days, I will contact my earthly father, Harry Cohn."

Reviews: "Plotwise, there is nothing new in Columbia's *The Thrill of Brazil*, but theatre patrons who like their musicals lavish and filled with eye-catching production numbers will find the film packed with 91 minutes of solid entertainment.... Director S. Sylvan Simon succeeds in maintaining a proper balance between comedy and music." *Motion Picture Daily*, September 9, 1946

"S. Sylvan Simon has directed *The Thrill of Brazil* with a fine eye for visual appeal which is evident all the way in production numbers. Music, dancing and kindred angles are done with a fine, tasteful flair which suitably drape about the framework of comic plot." *Film Daily*, September 11, 1946

The Cockeyed Miracle (1946)

Frank Morgan (*Sam Griggs*), Keenan Wynn (*Ben Griggs*), Cecil Kellaway (*Tom Carter*), Audrey Totter (*Jennifer Griggs*), Richard Quine (*Howard Bankson*), Gladys Cooper (*Amy Griggs*), Marshall Thompson (*Jim Griggs*), Leon Ames (*Ralph Humphrey*), Jane Green (*Mrs. Lynne*), Morris Ankrum (*Dr. Wilson*), Arthur Space (*Amos Spellman*), Billy Chapin (*Boy*)

Director: S. Sylvan Simon. *Producer*: Irving Starr. *Screenplay*: Karen De Wolf, based on a play by George Seaton. *Director of Photography*: Ray June. *Film Editor*: Ben Lewis. *Musical Score*: David Snell. *Recording Director*: Douglas Shearer. *Art Directors*: Cedric Gibbons, Richard Duce. *Set Decorator*: Edwin B. Willis. *Associate*: Mildred Griffiths. *Costume Supervisor*: Irene. *Costumes Created by*: Valles. *Make-up*: Jack Dawn.

MGM; released October 1946. 81 minutes.

Sixtyish Sam Griggs has been sidelined from his life's work of shipbuilding by a heart condition that requires rest and freedom from worry. His loyal wife Amy doesn't know that Sam invested their savings with his lifelong buddy Tom Carter in a speculative real estate deal that isn't paying off. When son Jim has a chance to pursue a career in England, Sam can't bring himself to admit there isn't enough money to pay for the ticket. Meanwhile, daughter Jen is in love with their boarder, young professor Howard Bankson, who is too preoccupied with his work to notice.

The doctor warns Mrs. Griggs that Sam's health is precarious, and that evening he passes away. When Sam comes downstairs, he can't get his family to hear or see him, and finds his own long-dead father Ben waiting to escort him to Heaven. Before he can leave, however, Sam implores Ben to help him set things right on Earth for the family he must leave behind.

Making Sam's task more difficult is the adjustment to the new form he has taken in the afterlife. As Ben demonstrates, ghosts can walk effortlessly through walls, but are unable to grasp or hold anything in the real world. The only special power Ben has developed is the ability to influence weather, and produce rainstorms.

Going through his late father's bankbook, Jim realizes that the family has been left penniless. He and Jen agree that their own plans must be put on hold, so as to take care of their widowed mother. When there's a profitable sale of the property that Sam and Tom own jointly, the late Mr. Griggs is relieved. But as soon as Tom finds out that Sam died that evening, he has second thoughts about sharing his $10,000 windfall with the Griggs family.

The Cockeyed Miracle was adapted from George Seaton's play "But Not Goodbye," which had only a brief Broadway run, opening and closing in April 1944. The New York production was headlined by Harry Carey, and featured Elizabeth Patterson as Mrs. Griggs, Wendell Corey as Howard, and J. Pat O'Malley as the late Ben Griggs. MGM acquired the film rights for a modest $20,000. Seaton's story has an element of whimsy not dissimilar to another "miraculous" film that would be far more successful; *Miracle on 34th Street,* with a screenplay by Seaton, would be released the following year. The script still has a somewhat stagebound quality, as most scenes take place in the Griggs' modest home.

In *The Cockeyed Miracle*, **young lovers Howard (Richard Quine) and Jennifer (Audrey Totter) are surrounded by ghostly observers Ben (Keenan Wynn, left) and Sam (Frank Morgan).**

As in his previous film *Tish* (1942), Simon directs an ensemble cast in a story of small-town family life, one that mixes humor and sentiment. Simon wisely chooses special effects that are serviceable but not showy. His copy of the film script, which still carries the title "But Not Goodbye," is dated June 1945, with changes inserted as much as six months later.

Frank Morgan has a wonderful showcase here in the role of Sam, and he makes the most of it. Adding a bit of poignancy in retrospect is the knowledge that Morgan himself would in fact succumb to heart failure, in September 1949. Dame Gladys Cooper (1888–1971), who had become an MGM contract player the previous year, goes somewhat against her established movie type here, playing a woman who's neither wealthy nor snobbish. A simple woman with a loving heart, she demurs when told she's "nice," saying, "Wanting your loved ones to be happy isn't being nice, it's just habit." She's beautifully touching in the moment when she emerges from the bedroom, her stricken face telling us she's just seen that her husband is dead.

Keenan Wynn gives a playful quality to the role of Ben Griggs, who died decades earlier and wears the muttonchops and formal clothing of an earlier era, but takes puckish enjoyment of his ghostly powers. Because Ben died young, he looks far more youthful than his recently deceased son, adding to the fun. Audrey Totter (1917–2013) gives a tart delivery to Jen's more pointed remarks, as when, frustrated with the undemonstrative scientist she loves, she retorts, "I can't imagine there's anything you wouldn't know about icebergs, Howard." Richard Quine ably portrays Howard's diffidence and unworldliness, without making the character pitiable, and Cecil Kellaway (1890–1973) is always a good choice to play a character who's just enough of a rogue to bear watching. Morris Ankrum (1897–1964), who would spend much of the 1950s playing military figures in monster movies, and a judge on TV's *Perry Mason*, gets a moment in the spotlight when his doctor character shares some hard-earned wisdom on life and death.

Reporter Ann Lewis, in her *Showmen's Trade Review* column (February 16, 1946), was on the set when the scenes set in a barn were being shot. She found leading lady Audrey Totter adorned "in a blanket which reveals part of a petticoat on one side," for the sequence in which Jen is wrapped in an auto robe after being drenched by rainfall. Lewis noted, "It turns out to be a very difficult, though funny, sequence and everyone is greatly amused, except perhaps the director [Simon], who calls for many rehearsals before he gets everything to click." Another column item described the shooting of a love scene between Miss Totter and Quine, not made easier by the presence of a kibitzing Morgan and Wynn. Their joking asides finally led an irritated Simon to remark, "I wish the East Hoboken stock company in the rear would cease production."[66]

For British release, the film was titled *Mr. Griggs Returns*.

Reviews: "Here is a farce comedy that will have average audiences, in practically any situation, in an almost constant state of laughter. It is predicated on the spirit-versus-flesh theme and as such is a delightful and enjoyable bit of entertainment…. Director S. Sylvan Simon has skillfully guided his cast through proceedings that move at a pace that maintains audience interest throughout…." *Showmen's Trade Review*, July 20, 1946

"S. Sylvan Simon performed a 'cockeyed miracle' by cementing an incredible hocus pocus story and an amiable cast with 'spirited' whimsical direction…. High spots [include] Gladys Cooper's superb warmth and sincerity in her role as the devoted wife [and] the comedy teamwork of Frank Morgan and Keenan Wynn, who 'milk' their roles to the film's advantage—thanks again to Sylvan Simon." *Film Daily*, July 18, 1946

Her Husband's Affairs (1947)

Lucille Ball (*Margaret Weldon*), Franchot Tone (*William Weldon*), Edward Everett Horton (*J.B. Cruikshank*), Mikhail Rasumny (*Prof. Emil Glinka*), Gene Lockhart (*Peter Winterbottom*), Nana Bryant (*Mrs. Winterbottom*), Jonathan Hale (*Gov. Fox*), Paul Stanton (*Dr. Frazee*), Mabel Paige (*Mrs. Josper*), Larry Parks (*Himself*), Selmer Jackson (*Judge*), Frank Mayo (*Starrett*), Pierre Watkin (*Beitler*), Clancy Cooper (*Window Washer*), Frank Wilcox (*Floorwalker*), Douglas Wood (*Tappel*), Emmett Vogan (*Mr. Miller*), Harry Cheshire (*Mayor Jim Dandy Harker*), Gerald Oliver Smith (*Harold*), Arthur Space (*District Attorney*), Jack Rice (*Slocum*), Charles Trowbridge

(*Brewster*), Victor Travis (*Jury Foreman*), Charles Williams (*Cruise Line Clerk*), Carl M. Leviness (*Vice-President Brady*), Susan Simon (*Girl in Toy Store*), Eric Wilton (*Governor's Butler*), Virginia Hunter (*Miss Hunter*), Mary Field (*Hortense*), Dan Stowell (*Willowcombe*), Douglas D. Coppin (*Milkman*), Dick Gordon (*Nicholson*), Franklyn Farnum (*Juror*), Fred Howard (*Bailiff*), Stanley Blystone (*Ike*), Cliff Clark (*Gus*), H.W. Gim, Tommy Lee, Owen Song (*Acrobats*), Wanda Cantlon, Edythe Elliott, Nancy Saunders (*Nurses*), Charles Bates, Buz Buckley, Dwayne Hickman, Teddy Infuhr (*Boys*)

Director: S. Sylvan Simon. *Producer*: Raphael Hakim. *Screenplay*: Ben Hecht, Charles Lederer. *Film Editor*: Al Clark. *Art Directors*: Stephen Goosson, Carl Anderson. *Set Decorators*: Wilbur Menefee, Louis Diage. *Assistant Director*: Earl McEvoy. *Gowns*: Jean Louis. *Makeup*: Clay Campbell. *Hair Styles*: Helen Hunt. *Sound Recording*: Frank Goodwin. *Music Score*: George Duning. *Musical Director*: M.W. Stoloff. [*Property Master*: Charles Granucci. *Makeup Artist*: Bob Meiding. *Dialogue Director*: Jackson Halliday. *Script Supervisor*: Rose Loewinger.]

Columbia Pictures / Cornell Pictures; released November 1947. 84 minutes.

Margaret Weldon has been waiting more than a year for a honeymoon trip to Bermuda, but her husband Bill, an advertising executive, keeps postponing their plans. He's been promised a $5,000 bonus by his boss, J.B. Cruikshank, if he can land the account of a client who manufactures men's hats. Bill dreams up a slogan that emphasizes how lightweight Tappel's straw hats are, but the client isn't satisfied. Tappel wants a celebrity endorsement, and Bill tracks down the mayor at a ball game to obtain his. When the elected official brushes him off, Margaret steps in, slipping the hat on the mayor's head during the National Anthem. His admission that he didn't even know he was wearing a hat provides the key to a successful ad campaign, but Bill is annoyed that his boss gives Margaret credit for clinching the deal.

Eccentric inventor Emil Glinka, who's been getting money for his research from Bill, brings in his latest invention, an embalming fluid that transforms people into glass. As a byproduct, he's also stumbled upon a cream that effortlessly removes hair from men's faces without shaving. Bill and his boss quickly make a sale to industrialist Peter Winterbottom, and the product is dubbed "Off Again." At a triumphant gala, "Off Again" is demonstrated for a VIP audience that includes the governor, as well as actor Larry Parks. Bill and Margaret go home fully expecting to become millionaires. Their excitement lasts only until morning, when it develops that every man who used the product is now sprouting a massive beard. Thinking quickly, Margaret saves the day by suggesting that it be re-branded "On Again," and marketed as a hair restorer.

Once again, Bill is aggrieved that his wife has stolen his thunder. When Professor Glinka's product proves to have yet another unanticipated side effect as a hair restorer, Bill insists that his wife stop trying to help him. Even as it strains their marital bond, Margaret finds it difficult to step aside and let Bill solve his own problems, warning him that he and Glinka are about to be arrested on the governor's orders. At Glinka's lab, the professor shows Bill the latest iteration of his invention, and the "Forever Flower" seems to be the answer to all of their problems. But an explosion in the laboratory, an unreliable eyewitness, and the professor's disappearance result in Bill going on trial for murder. Knowing it may cost her her marriage, Margaret is unable to keep quiet as her beloved husband seems to be gleefully making his way to the electric chair.

The underappreciated *Her Husband's Affairs* is a marvelously inventive and zany comedy. Ben Hecht and Charles Lederer's script wastes no time shooting for believability; Professor Glinka's fevered experiments almost qualify the film as science fiction. But from the director's chair, S. Sylvan Simon embraces the spirit of nonsensical fun with abandon, and most viewers will be happy to go along for the ride. A few satirical pokes at the world of advertising only add to the fun.

Though she had certainly shown her flair for comedy in earlier films such as *The Affairs of Annabel* (1938), Lucille Ball's work under Simon's direction will set her on the path to finding her finest gifts as a performer. Here, she mostly leaves the physical comedy to others, but her fast-talking wife, who keeps trying to get her husband out of trouble, certainly brings Lucy Ricardo to mind at times. She was later quoted as saying that the key to playing outrageous comedy was to believe it yourself, and she does that here. She's also quite touching in the scenes where she proves her loyalty to Bill, even at her own expense.

Franchot Tone throws himself fully into the wild role of eccentric Bill Weldon, who's prone to answering his home phone with his impersonation of a whinnying horse. Tone's character, who regularly espouses the value of women staying in their place, can be unlikable at times, as when he snaps at Margaret, "From now on, you're staying home washing dishes—with a muzzle on!" or asks her sardonically, "Is it really torture to mind your own business?" He and Simon teamed for the purposes of making this film and one that followed a year later, the detective story *I Love Trouble.* For all Tone's efforts, author Jeffrey Brown Martin later reported, "Hecht said [the] best jokes were written for Tone but that Ball got all the laughs."[67]

Aside from his stars, Simon takes full advantage of a cast brimming with experienced character actors, including Edward Everett Horton (1886–1970) as Bill's boss, Jonathan Hale (1891–1966) as the unfortunate governor whose head is turned glassy, and Nana Bryant (1888–1955) as Mrs. Winterbottom, who unwisely dabs a little "Off Again" on her upper lip. Mary Field,

Franchot Tone (center) is all ears for director Sylvan Simon and co-star Lucille Ball in *Her Husband's Affairs.*

unbilled for her brief bit as Mrs. Winterbottom's maid, doesn't even need dialogue to get laughs, her horrified expression at seeing her mistress' new mustache saying it all. Horton reportedly balked at a scripted line that found Bill Weldon financing his honeymoon with a $1,000 bonus from his employer. "You can't take a first-class trip these days on a sum like that," Horton told the director. Simon concurred and upped the bounty accordingly.

Up-and-coming Columbia player Larry Parks appears briefly as himself; a studio press release reported that Simon talked "his old friend Larry" into the cameo role, which threatened to make Parks "Hollywood's highest-priced bit player." As with the appearance of director Robert Z. Leonard in Simon's earlier film *Abbott and Costello in Hollywood*, the guest bit was not written specifically for Parks. The script simply calls for an unspecified "Movie Star" to utter a couple of lines at the VIP gala; on Simon's copy, "Movie Star" has been crossed out, and "Larry Parks" penciled in.

Appearing in a minor role as a nurse is Lucille Ball's stand-in, Wanda Cantlon. According to studio publicity, "Unbeknownst to her, Director Sylvan Simon has had his eye on her for quite some time and suddenly decided to give her a speaking role."[68] She would turn up again in *Miss Grant Takes Richmond*.

Though he didn't take a producer credit onscreen, the film was the maiden effort of Tone's own company, Cornell Pictures. The star admitted it was an eye-opening experience. "I had to go into production," Tone said. "Otherwise I could not have picked the parts I wanted to play or the pictures I wanted to do. But until you've tried your hand at it, you can't imagine all of the hundreds of details that go into the making of a motion picture."[69]

Her Husband's Affairs went by various tentative titles during the preproduction stage. Early trade-paper announcements gave the film's title as "The Mating Call," "My Awful Wife," "The Lady Knew How," or "The Yes Woman." Lucille Ball's casting in the female lead was announced in early 1947. Hecht and Lederer's "Final Draft" script, dated January 31, 1947, still carries the name "The Mating Call."

Simon retained with his script a copy of a gag legal complaint given to him by the film's property master, Charles Granucci. Among his grievances were his erudite boss's "use of words such as equanimity in production, result[ing] in embarrassment to me, who couldn't even graduate from barber college" (a reference to *Abbott and Costello in Hollywood*). In addition, the jokester crew member complains, "The mental strain and anguish which I am confronted with, in endeavoring to keep your Goddam chair in back of the camera, between two broads, is more than I can stand...." Granucci claimed that the prop men at Simon's home studio, MGM, looked askance at the "luxurious office" he enjoyed while shooting *Her Husband's Affairs*, saying, "You are spoiling the lad—out here, all he rated was a lean-to!"

The opening scene, taking place in the Weldons' bedroom, caused censorship problems when the film was being prepared for British release. As reported in *Daily Variety* (April 28, 1947), the British Board of Film Censors' J. Broke [*sic*] Wilkinson complained that, though the actors were occupying twin beds, "The beds are in juxtaposition and during the cuddling scene the occupants might as well be in a single bed." Studio boss Harry Cohn had to arrange for an alternate version of the scene to be used in England. Simon directed Ball and Tone in two days of reshoots, beginning in late April 1947, to shoot slightly milder takes of the bedroom scenes. Some time later, a reporter told Tone that whenever he visited

Franchot Tone and Lucille Ball were sometimes too close for censors' comfort in *Her Husband's Affairs* **(Simon Family Collection).**

the set, "You were always in bed." Tone replied, "I loved that picture. That's the way I enjoy working—in bed."[70]

Columnist Hedda Hopper (July 22, 1947) claimed that Simon had a brainstorm as to how the film should be publicized: "Before HHA is shown in a town, he'll first preview it there a month in advance and invite only newspaper people, beauty-parlor operators and barbers to the showing. He figures that by the time the film opens, everybody in town will have heard about it."

Lucy reprised her role in the May 22, 1949, episode of radio's *Screen Directors' Playhouse*, with Simon directing, and Elliott Lewis taking the role of Bill. Heard in the broadcast, Sylvan Simon said that even comedy directors don't laugh at nothing, "Except maybe the night before his picture is previewed. Nobody minds then, because it might be his last laugh in a long while."

Reviews: "This is one of the wildest, merriest farces to come to the screen in many moons. In addition to its laugh-provoking zany capers, it has a love story, with one or two near-censorable situations. In all, it adds up to an attraction that deserves plugging by wise exhibitors. Director S. Sylvan Simon guided the fun with a skilled hand, getting a full measure of laughs from every situation." *Film Daily*, July 22, 1947

"A merry farce built of love, laughter and fantastic situations.... The laughter ranges from open-faced grins through the various shades of chuckles to the ultimate belly-shakers ... show is sure of hearty box office response wherever the customers are looking for an evening's frolic without problems or messages.... S. Sylvan Simon's direction brings Ben Hecht's merrily zany script into full bloom." *Daily Variety*, July 18, 1947

I Love Trouble (1948)

Franchot Tone (*Stuart Bailey*), Janet Blair (*Norma Shannon*), Janis Carter (*Ligia Caprillo*), Adele Jergens (*Boots Nestor*), Glenda Farrell (*Hazel Bixby*), Steven Geray (*Keller*), Tom Powers (*Ralph Johnston*), Lynn Merrick (*Mrs. Johnston*), John Ireland (*Reno*), Donald Curtis (*Martin*), Eduardo Ciannelli (*John Vega Caprillo*), Robert H. Barrat (*Lt. Quinn*), Raymond Burr (*Herb*), Sid Tomack (*Buster Buffin*), Eddie Marr (*Sharpy*), Roseanne Murray (*Miss Phipps*), Claire Carleton (*Irene Feston*), Louise Franklin (*Maid*), Karen X. Gaylord (*Betty*), Isabel Withers (*Gracie*), William Stubbs (*Dealer*), Harry Tyler (*Warehouse Foreman*), Vesey O'Davoren (*Butler*), Lane Chandler (*Recording Detective*), Garry Owen (*Gus*)

Producer-Director: S. Sylvan Simon. *Screenplay*: Roy Huggins, from his novel "The Double Take." *Director of Photography*: Charles Lawton, Jr. *Film Editor*: Al Clark. *Art Directors*: Stephen Goosson, Leslie Thomas. *Set Decorators*: Wilbur Menefee, Louis Diage. *Sound Recording*: Frank Goodwin. *Gowns*: Jean Louis. *Musical Score*: George Duning. *Musical Director*: M.W. Stoloff. *Assistant to Producer*: Earl McEvoy.

Columbia Pictures / Cornell Pictures; released January 1948. 93 minutes.

Private detective Stuart Bailey is investigating a series of threatening and insinuating notes sent to Jane Breeger, the beautiful young wife of Ralph Johnston, a prominent local official. The latest, sent to the lady herself, reads: "Do you want your husband to know about your past? How much is it worth to keep me quiet? I will contact you later." Though she shrugs off the message, and Johnston believes his wife has led a blameless life, he agrees that Bailey should follow the trail to Portland, where she previously lived. There he learns she worked as a dancer at a now-defunct nightclub, Keller's Carousel. Tracking down Keller at the gambling joint he now operates, Bailey receives a less-than-friendly welcome, making it clear that his pursuit of the story is not welcomed.

Learning that Jane left Portland several years earlier with a comedian, Buster Buffin, Bailey traces him to the oceanside beanery he now operates. Buffin has information available—for a price. Stymied at every turn, Bailey is surprised when a beautiful woman turns up at his office, claiming to be Jane's long-lost sister. His suspicions are aroused when he realizes that she now goes by a different name, and doesn't seem to recognize a photograph of her own sister.

Before Buffin can part with more information, he turns up murdered, leaving Bailey as the prime suspect. When the body of Johnston's wife is found at the Malibu pier, Bailey's monogrammed pen isn't far away, and it's only with the help of his loyal secretary Bix that he escapes from police custody long enough to make a last-ditch effort to solve the mystery and clear his name.

Adele Jergens is the center of attention when *I Love Trouble* goes on a location shoot—to Sylvan Simon's backyard.

Unrelated to the 1994 romantic comedy starring Nick Nolte and Julia Roberts, this *I Love Trouble* is a fast-moving, darkly cynical entry in the burgeoning genre that would later be labeled as *film noir*. After their successful collaboration on *Her Husband's Affairs,* Simon and actor Franchot Tone teamed up again for this murder mystery that offers both the opportunity to demonstrate their versatility. Tone, producing his own films in order to obtain a wider variety of roles, plays a tougher, more cynical character than he had done in many of his early films, while Simon demonstrates that he can make a film completely unlike earlier efforts such as *Son of Lassie* and *Her Husband's Affairs.* Without showy flourishes, Simon frames scenes in such a way as to heighten their effectiveness, and makes good use of some outdoor locations, particularly in a well-done chase scene.

Tone told syndicated columnist Aline Mosby (June 17, 1947) that the film aimed to present a different type of movie detective. "I go about solving this murder in a strictly mental way. Just like the detectives do in real life." Even the finale, he promised, lacked "rough stuff…. I use my wits instead."

I Love Trouble was the first produced screenplay of Roy Huggins (1914–2002), who would go on to become one of television's most successful and acclaimed creators and producers of action-adventure shows, including *Maverick* and *The Rockford Files.* He adapted his own novel, "The Double Take," published by Morrow in 1946. In his unpublished memoir, Huggins expressed himself disillusioned by the low regard in which Hollywood held unproven screenwriters, and admitted he was frustrated that Simon seemed little interested in Huggins' input on the picture he wrote. Nor was the writer pleased by the flip title studio executives gave the finished film, which was originally expected to retain the title of the book. Huggins' Stuart Bailey character was later adapted to the television series *77 Sunset Strip*, where he was considerably more refined than the rough-and-tumble version depicted here. Huggins did, however, get a screenwriting job at Columbia for $1,000 a week, but was subsequently fired by Harry Cohn, who found his output unsatisfactory.[71]

Production began in May 1947. According to *Daily Variety* (April 15, 1947), screenwriter Martin Goldsmith was engaged to "polish" the script before cameras rolled a few weeks later. Aline Mosby (June 28, 1947) reported that Simon anticipated a comfortable day working from home when he arranged for poolside scenes featuring Tone and Adele Jergens to be shot in his own backyard. After a brief commute from the bedroom, the director settled in a deck chair to oversee the shoot, saying contentedly, "This is the life." Unfortunately, noise from the Simons' young son Stephen, the family cook rattling dishes in the kitchen, and traffic on Sunset Boulevard spoiled a few takes, as did ringing chimes from UCLA and drop-in visits from starstruck neighbors. When the scene was finally in the can, Simon's crew promptly commandeered his new lawn furniture, explaining that it would be needed for matching shots back at the studio. "Simon sadly watched his furniture disappear," Mosby wrote, "and eyed what was left—his trampled lawn."

With enough assumed identities for at least three movies, *I Love Trouble* has a convoluted plot that likely left some moviegoers bewildered, but the story never fails to be engaging, and the action never lets up. Strong performances from the featured actresses add to the picture's appeal. Janet Blair, who gets the last word as the curtain falls, keeps viewers guessing as the woman who Bailey would like to trust, but is afraid he shouldn't. Adele Jergens (1917–2002) is a swimsuit-clad beauty who pulls a gun unexpectedly on Bailey and remarks, "This was for when I got bored with you." Glenda

Franchot Tone finds Glenda Farrell a help around the office in *I Love Trouble*.

Farrell brightens every scene she's in as Bailey's girl Friday, Bix. An employee with a widely varied skill set, Bix can not only take phone messages, but tail a suspect, and wield a gun when the occasion calls for it. According to *Daily Variety* (August 20, 1947), Simon liked actress Janis Carter's work well enough to consider casting her as the leading lady of his next film, *The Fuller Brush Man.*

On the distaff side, Sid Tomack, previously directed by Simon in *The Thrill of Brazil,* is well-cast as the washed-up comedian who offers a surface geniality, but has his eye on the payoff. (As the sign on his restaurant door tellingly says, "Open. We Need the Money.") John Ireland exudes menace as Keller's sinister sidekick (tabbed by Bailey as "a gorilla named Reno") who isn't reluctant to use his fists. Bringing up the rear of the cast billed in the opening credits is future television star Raymond Burr (1917–1993), seen briefly as another Keller thug.

Reviews: "A topnotch murder-mystery, blessed with an excellent scenario and smooth performances. Roy Huggins has translated his own novel into a thrill-packed script that could hardly miss ... it emerges as one of the season's real winners.... S. Sylvan Simon surely merits applause for not only producing but directing the film as well." *Showmen's Trade Review*, January 10, 1948

"*I Love Trouble* follows popular pattern for private detective heroes and spins its involved melodramatics at a good pace. Production polish is excellent.... S. Sylvan Simon produced and directed ... his handling of more or less standard ingredients of the whodunit gives it a lightness and fast pace that pleases, and wherever called for suspense is punched over." *Variety*, December 24, 1947

The Fuller Brush Man (1948)

Red Skelton (*Red Jones*), Janet Blair (*Ann Elliot*), Don McGuire (*Keenan Wallick*), Hillary Brooke (*Mildred Trist*), Adele Jergens (*Miss Sharmley*), Ross Ford (*Freddie Trist*), Trudy Marshall (*Sara Franzen*), Nicholas Joy (*Commissioner Gordon Trist*), Donald Curtis (*Gregory Cruckston*), Arthur Space (*Lt. Quint*), Verna Felton (*Junior's Grandmother*), Jimmy Hunt (*Junior*), Selmer Jackson (*Henry Seward*), Stanley Andrews (*Det. Ferguson*), Roger Moore (*Det. Foster*), Rod O'Connor (*District Attorney*), Emmett Vogan (*Police Doctor*), Charles Jordan (*Police Photographer*), Lee Phelps (*Fire Captain*), Dick Wessel (*Police Sergeant*), Cliff Clark (*Cop in Park*), Garry Owen (*Creamy*), James Logan (*Billings*), Billy Jones (*Herman*), Ann Staunton (*Trist's Maid*), Harry Tyler (*Gardener*), William Newell (*Police Announcer*), Bud Wolfe (*Jiggers*), Alex Melesh (*Bald Man*), Mary Field (*Beaver Patrol Leader*), Mary Adams Hayes (*Woman with Baby Buggy*), Jimmy Lloyd (*Chauffeur*), Donald Kerr (*Limping Fuller Brush Man*), Nan Holliday, Michael Towne (*Couple in Parked Car*), Allen Ray, Nita Mathews (*Card-Playing Couple*), Paul Kruger, Jack Perrin (*Policemen*), Susan Simon (*Beaver Patrol Member*)

Director-Producer: S. Sylvan Simon. *Executive Producer*: Edward Small. *Screenplay*: Frank Tashlin, Devery Freeman, based upon a *Saturday Evening Post* story by Roy Huggins. *Director of Photography*: Lester White. *Art Directors*: Stephen Goosson,

Carl Anderson. *Film Editor*: Al Clark. *Set Decorators*: Wilbur Menefee, Louis Diage. *Gowns*: Jean Louis. *Hair Stylist*: Helen Hunt. *Assistant Director*: Wilbur McGaugh. *Sound Engineer*: Lambert Day. *Musical Score*: Heinz Roemheld. [*Double for Red Skelton*: Gil Perkins. *Properties*: Charles Granucci. *Hair Dresser*: Ida Forgette.]

Columbia; released June 1948. 93 minutes.

Sanitation worker Red Jones buys a ring and proposes to his girlfriend Ann Elliot, but she refuses him, saying he isn't ready to take on the responsibility of a wife and family. Red has a history of changing jobs frequently, and is fired from his current one after crashing into the car of Sanitation Commissioner Gordon Trist. Ann, who works at the Fuller Brush Company, suggests that Red get a job there. He tries out his salesmanship at several houses, but his rival for Ann's affection, successful salesman Keenan Wallick, sabotages Red's efforts. To deliver the coup de grace, Wallick sends Red to the Bel Air estate of Commissioner Trist, where he's thrown out on his ear. Mrs. Trist apologizes to Red, and offers to buy 10 brushes. Triumphant, Red returns to the office, only to realize he failed to collect the money. Returning to the Trist estate, Red is just in time to witness the murder of the commissioner, who's stabbed when the lights go out in his drawing room.

The police believe Red is the guilty party, but are forced to release him when they are unable to locate a murder weapon. His every move under surveillance, Red finds all the other suspects in the case—Trist's widow, butler, business partner, nephew and possible mistress—converging on his apartment, where an unexpected object hidden in his coffeepot helps solve the mystery. Now that Red knows too much, he and Ann are lured to a supposedly vacant warehouse, where they expect to meet policeman Quint but instead find they have been set up.

The Fuller Brush Man is an energetic, fast-paced comedy that kept moviegoers laughing from start to finish, becoming a big box-office hit for Columbia. Though the gags come fast and furious, there's also a serviceable plot on which to hang them, helping to make the film more cohesive. The film's final 15 minutes are devoted to a frantic chase-and-fight sequence that takes place in a war surplus supply warehouse, where Red and Ann take on the bad guys. Teaming once again with Red Skelton after a five-year hiatus, Simon delivers another crowd-pleasing comedy. Though the star enjoyed the experience, Skelton was reportedly angry that MGM (according to the Associated Press' Bob Thomas [February 9, 1948]), charged the other studio $150,000 for his services, of which he received only $17,500. For the British market, where moviegoers were not expected to be familiar with the Fuller Brush Company, the film was retitled *That Mad Mr. Jones*.

As syndicated columnist Erskine Johnson (November 26, 1947) told it, Simon persuaded Columbia studio head Harry Cohn to make *The Fuller Brush Man* if a suitable big-name comedian would accept the lead role. Simon approached producer Edward Small, who was owed a commitment by MGM to borrow one of that studio's players. Said Johnson, "Small agreed to borrow a star, Red Skelton, from MGM if Simon would agree to cut him into the profits of the picture…. So the picture is now an Eddie Small production, produced and directed by S. Sylvan Simon for Columbia release, starring an MGM player."

Hedda Hopper (January 15, 1947) reported that the Fuller Brush people took some convincing before allowing their brand name to be used in the film: "When they finally agreed they came up with a contract of fifteen pages of do's and don'ts which must be adhered to or else." Simon later wrote that the legal paperwork eventually grew to 36 pages.

One of the company's stipulations was to make it clear that Skelton's bungling character was not typical of the firm's actual sales force. Simon explained, "If you closely inspect the plot of *The Fuller Brush Man* you'll discover that Skelton, actually, is never presented as a Fuller Brush representative. This gave us an out for the more riotous comedy situations."[72] As an item in the film's pressbook put it, any resemblance to the real thing was "absolutely accidental," adding that "Fuller dealers who have seen the picture all agree that it's funny as everything but they shudder at what would happen to Red if he had to make his living as a dealer." Hopper noted that, aside from Skelton, Milton Berle had expressed interest in the starring role.

A studio press release said that it was Simon's idea to send out a questionnaire to the company's sales force, inviting them to describe their funniest experiences on the job. Six of the best responses were incorporated into the screenplay. Speeding up shooting was the squeezing of 11 separate sets onto a single soundstage, which Simon told *Daily Variety* (November 19, 1947) saved three days' shooting: "Sets represent three private homes, a mansion, a warehouse, two cocktail bars, a section of a street, two sorority houses, and the Union League Club."

Commenting on her strenuous stint as Skelton's co-star, Miss Blair complained good-naturedly, "They didn't want an actress; they wanted an acrobat!" As Ann, she explained, "I hung from wires, jumped off prefabricated houses, ran miles, slid down chutes, pushed people around and vice versa."[73] Another scene found her keeping the bad guys at bay with the help of a lighted blowtorch, which she confessed made her "a nervous wreck."

Verna Felton (1890–1966), heard regularly as the grandmother of the Mean Widdle Kid on Skelton's radio show, plays a similar role here. Child actor Jimmy Hunt (born 1939) plays her bratty grandson, who drops Red's shoe in an aquarium, and slams the hapless salesman's head in the door. (This sequence, a late addition to the screenplay, is dated October 20, 1947, in Simon's script.) Arthur Space has one of his bigger roles for Simon as the police lieutenant investigating Triss' murder. His careful, solid performance strikes just the right note to make Quint believable without detracting from the comedy.

Adele Jergens has an amusing vignette as Miss Sharmley, an actress who's just been told by her agent that she was rejected for a role because she wasn't sufficiently alluring. Offended, she says indignantly, "I've brushed off more men than the porter at the Waldorf!" Her need to prove her sex appeal results in salesman Red being found in her shower, partially clad. Miss Jergens was one of several Columbia contract players filling supporting roles in the cast, including Don McGuire and Ross Ford.

Columbia's biggest box-office star doesn't appear in the film, but is referenced when Wallick intentionally takes Red to a neighborhood where he has never been able to make sales. In his notebook, Wallick comments alongside one potential buyer, "Would say 'no' to Rita Hayworth!" Later, the film's producer-director gets a shout-out with a radio commercial for "Simon Sausage," although a listener remarks of the product, "They always give me heartburn!" An interoffice teletype at Columbia, in September 1947, indicated that the studio wanted to sign Rudy Vallee for a role in the film: "NY DEFINITELY FEELS RUDY VALLEE AT $15,000 GOOD ADDN TO FULLER BRUSH MAN." However, this did not pan out.

This was Simon's first film collaboration with screenwriter Frank Tashlin, who would become well-known for scripting (and, later, directing) live-action comedies that had something of the flavor of cartoons. They would make three more films together before Simon's death in 1951. The screenplay, marked "Final Draft," was dated October 7, 1947, and the finished film tracks it with minimal changes. One comic insult, heard when Kennan Wallick maliciously impersonates Red, was apparently deemed unacceptable. The original line had Wallick calling Triss "maggot brain"; this was replaced with "bubble-headed dunce."

Following on the heels of *I Love Trouble*, this film

It's either a product demonstration or a new hairstyle for *The Fuller Brush Man* (Red Skelton, left, with co-star Janet Blair).

again gives a story credit to magazine writer Roy Huggins. In this case, the main thing lifted from Huggins' story was the gimmick of the disappearing murder weapon, and the scientific explanation for such a phenomenon. Huggins' contract stipulated that he would receive screen credit for the film being "based upon, adapted from, or suggested by a story written by the Seller, or words to that effect." Ultimately, "based upon" was the chosen phrase.

During rehearsal, said columnist Erskine Johnson (November 15, 1947), Simon read the lines of every other character opposite Skelton. "This picture is simple," Skelton joked. "I just keep an eye on Simon and then underplay him." Simon's inventive and lively direction of the Tashlin-Freeman screenplay makes the most of every situation. There are elaborate slapstick scenes that evoke belly laughs, but also subtler humor, as when the camera pans up the figure of glamorous Miss Sharmley, but reverses itself to go back down and take a second gander at her legs.

The screenplay called for an introductory dedication, printed out on a business card: "To those unsung heroes of this great land—those tireless individuals that neither wind, rain nor snow can keep from the swift completion of their appointed rounds. To those valiant individuals with the flashing smiles and flat feet—The Fuller Brush Men." However, this was not used in the finished film.

Skelton and leading lady Janet Blair reprised their roles for a radio adaptation of

Red Jones (Red Skelton, right) finds Junior (Jimmy Hunt) a tough customer indeed in *The Fuller Brush Man*. Also pictured is Verna Felton, playing Junior's Grandma as she did on Skelton's radio show.

the film, heard on *The Screen Guild Theater*. He also promoted the film on his own radio show, where Sylvan Simon was his guest on a February 1948 broadcast. Making a January guest appearance on Eddie Cantor's NBC radio show, Skelton brought along Howard Fuller, president of the Fuller Brush Company. The screenplay of *The Fuller Brush Man* originally called for a cameo appearance by Cantor, playing himself as one of Red's potential customers. When the newly appointed salesman asks to see the lady of the house, Cantor, whose five daughters were a well-established part of his public persona, was to respond, "Which one? This is a home for girls." He goes on to take Red's brushes without paying for them, causing Skelton to say, "That's funny. He looks like Eddie Cantor and acts like Jack Benny."

The Fuller Brush Company's actual sales force was enlisted to help carry out a publicity campaign. A letter from company president A. Howard Fuller, reproduced in the film's pressbook, explained, "In cooperation with the Brown and Williamson Tobacco Company, sponsors of Red Skelton on the air, we are asking our dealers to distribute more than 3,000,000 cartoon booklets showing a funny adventure of Red's and telling readers not to miss seeing the film. Also, more than 1,000,000 match books advertising the picture will be given out." Even those customers not at home when the salesman called wouldn't be overlooked: "We are having over 3,000,000 door hangers printed urging everyone to see the film." Theater managers were also promised "numerous picture plugs on the popular Red Skelton radio show!"

Columbia took out ads in trade journals such as *Film Daily* (June 21, 1948) to proclaim *The Fuller Brush Man* "the surprise picture of the year," adding that it was "doing sensational business in all engagements—large and small—holding over everywhere." MGM's Louis B. Mayer noted its success, according to producer Small: "To Mayer's chagrin…. Fuller Brush Man, which he had refused to make, grossed three times more at the world's boxoffices than did any other prior Skelton vehicle."[74] Its success was a key factor in Simon being offered the opportunity to produce and direct films at Columbia.

Reviews: "'The Fuller Brush Man' is a field day for Red Skelton fans. Slapstick first to last, comedy will do boffo biz…. Scripters haven't missed a bet in plugging Red into a maze of complications—including murder—in his trying to make good as a brush salesman…. S. Sylvan Simon handled dual duties of producer-director in thoroughly showmanship [*sic*] style." *Daily Variety*, May 7, 1948

"Red Skelton puts slapstick back on the screen right where it used to be…. No Mack Sennett finish was ever wilder and probably few were ever funnier than the windup of this picture…. S. Sylvan Simon, producer-director, manipulates the action with amazing efficiency, performances being kept at a furious tempo … [The film's] personnel must have worked very hard to make it. Comedies of this type don't happen easily." Edwin Schallert, *Los Angeles Times*, June 18, 1948

A Southern Yankee (1948)

Red Skelton (*Aubrey Filmore*), Brian Donlevy (*Kurt Devlynn*), Arlene Dahl (*Sally-ann Weatherby*), George Coulouris (*Maj. Jack Drumman*), Lloyd Gough (*Capt. Steve Lorford*), John Ireland (*Capt. Jed Calbern*), Minor Watson (*Gen. Watkins*), Charles Dingle (*Col. Weatherby*), Art Baker (*Col. Baker*), Reed Hadley (*Fred Munsey*), Arthur Space (*Mark Haskins*), Joyce Compton (*Hortense Dobson*), Louise Beavers (*Laundress*), Paul Harvey *(Hotel Manager)*, Bill Kennedy (*Lt. Sheve*), Ralph Sanford (*Carriage Driver*), John Hart (*Orderly*), Rod O'Connor (*Maj. Grigsby*), Harry Cording (*Guerrilla Horseman*), Cliff Clark (*Confederate Doctor*), Paul Newlan (*Man with Saber*), Shelby Bacon (*Boy*), Lane Chandler, David Newell (*Sentries*)

Directors: S. Sylvan Simon (uncredited), Edward Sedgwick. *Producer*: Paul Jones. *Screenplay*: Harry Tugend. *Original Story*: Melvin Frank, Norman Panama. *Director of Photography*: Ray June. *Art Directors*: Cedric Gibbons, Randall Duell. *Film Editor*: Ben Lewis. *Musical Score*: David Snell. *Recording Director*: Douglas Shearer. *Set Decorator*: Edwin B. Willis. *Associate*: Arthur Krams. *Special Effects*: Warren Newcombe. *Costume Designer*: Valles. *Hair Styles*: Sydney Guilaroff. *Makeup*: Jack Dawn. *Assistant Director*: Earl McEvoy.

MGM; released August 1948. 90 minutes.

As the Civil War rages, Aubrey Filmore is a bumbling bellboy at the Palmer Hotel in St. Louis, where one of the guests is Colonel Baker of the Union Army. Aubrey pleads to be allowed to join the Army's Secret Service unit, but Baker brushes him off.

Baker and his men are hunting for a Confederate spy known as "The Grey Spider." Aubrey finds a coded message belonging to a hotel guest, Maj. Jack Drumman, which identifies him as the man in question. At gunpoint, Drumman demands that Aubrey switch uniforms with him, so that the bellboy will be branded as the guilty party. By blind luck, Drumman is knocked out cold, allowing Aubrey to keep his scheduled rendezvous with another Confederate spy, beautiful Sallyann Weatherby.

With Sallyann's help, Aubrey infiltrates a meeting of Confederate spies, where he's given a map showing Union battle plans, and told to deliver it to a Southern general. Against his better judgment, Col. Baker allows Aubrey to continue the mission, altering the map to make it useless and also entrusting him with information to carry to a Union spy across the border. At the North-South border, Aubrey's plan to pose as a soldier for both sides simultaneously backfires, and he is shot. Waking up in a bed at the hospital, he's wearing a gown and realizes his uniform and boots (which contain the smuggled papers) are missing.

His mental capacity sorely taxed by the responsibilities of being a double agent, Aubrey struggles to do his duty for the Union cause, and win the hand of the lovely Sallyann. Kurt Devlynn, her fiancé, grows increasingly suspicious of the newcomer, and a series of events at his plantation, Twelve Oaks, put Aubrey in danger not only of losing at love but facing a violent conclusion to his heroics.

A Southern Yankee was designed to appease Red Skelton, who had become increasingly unhappy with his MGM assignments, most recently *Merton of the Movies*. The studio provided him with the services of producer Paul Jones, as well as scenarists Melvin Frank and Norman Panama, widely acclaimed for their work with comedian Bob Hope. In the summer of 1947, Frank and Panama submitted a 70-page treatment called "The Spy," which outlined the story in great detail. Their synopsis included a tongue-twister designed to help Aubrey keep his surveillance paperwork straight: "The paper's in the pocket of the boot with the buckle. The map's in the packet in the pocket of the jacket." It was a precursor to Frank and Panama's "pestle" routine for Danny Kaye in *The Court Jester* (1956). They also suggested a potential gag ending for the film that involved a cameo appearance by Clark Gable as Rhett Butler, after his divorce from Scarlett.

Although Edward Sedgwick is named as director in the film's credits, multiple sources confirm that S. Sylvan Simon actually directed the bulk of the film. Susan Granger, who played a small role, confirmed that her father made the film. According to an item in *Variety* (March 3, 1948), "S. Sylvan Simon completed Metro's 'A Southern Yankee' in 28 days, seven days ahead of schedule, fastest time ever made by a Red Skelton starrer." An ad in the same publication (March 31, 1948) promoting forthcoming MGM releases credited Simon as the director. Screenwriter Harry Tugend complained to Skelton's biographer, Arthur Marx, that the star made no more than a token effort to play his scenes, in hopes of encouraging MGM to terminate his contract. "But the odd thing was," Tugend said, "even when he was dogging it he was brilliant, and nobody even noticed it."[75]

Among the film's funnier sequences (not contained in Frank and Panama's treatment) is a wild encounter between a scaredy-cat Aubrey, and a Confederate dentist who pulls teeth with pliers. Perhaps because new sequences were cut into a finished film, the final product has a bit of a disjointed feel. There are many strong comedy routines, but a certain lack of cohesion. Some viewers may also find it difficult to laugh at scenes in which soldiers are shot to death, or the visit to a military hospital with wounded men on stretchers.

Arlene Dahl and Red Skelton see eye to eye in *A Southern Yankee*.

This was the last film on which Simon worked under his MGM contract, the shoot taking place in January and February 1948. According to syndicated columnist Harrison Carroll (January 30, 1948), production got off to an inauspicious start. "During the first scene.... Red Skelton jumped out of a buggy and twisted his ankle." Once his ankle had been taped up, the star carried on nonetheless. With motion picture profits on the decline, however, moviemakers were being pressed to cut costs by working faster. According to journalist Harold Heffernan, "M.G.M fastened a brief 28-day time limit on the comedy." However, he added, the haste "barely missed finishing the star, Red Skelton, who suffered a nervous collapse. Red worked 18 hours a day in some stretches, and as soon as possible the redhead will go to the Mayo Clinic ... for a thorough going-over."[76]

In April, Simon left MGM, beginning his new post as a producer at Columbia. According to Buster Keaton, preview showings of the film received a disappointing response, and he was brought on board to suggest improvements. Keaton later recalled that he found fault with the original film, which he thought made Skelton's character so blatantly stupid that audience sympathy was lost. No longer on the MGM payroll, Simon was not consulted before director Edward Sedgwick supervised several days' worth of retakes. According to *Showmen's Trade Review* (May 15, 1948), "Sedgwick took over the direction from S. Sylvan Simon for two weeks' additional shooting." (Other sources placed it at one week.) Learning that his film had been altered, Simon asked to have his name removed from the credits. If Sedgwick made changes for the better, it wasn't readily apparent to film critic Wanda Hale, who grumbled in the *New*

York Daily News (November 25, 1948) that laughs were in short supply, saying the film "runs a good half hour before the first guffaw is produced." The film's pressbook offers the usual behind-the-scenes anecdotes, but notably none that involve the director.

Columnist Bob Thomas reported (May 20, 1948) that the film would be retitled *My Hero,* supposedly after the original title was coldly received by Southerners. That title was adopted for the British market. Originally announced to be Skelton's leading lady was Ava Gardner; he also expressed interest in working again with Janet Blair.

Newly signed to an MGM contract, Arlene Dahl (born 1925) played one of her first important roles in *A Southern Yankee,* as a leading lady who, according to studio advertisements, "has more curves than the Mason-Dixon Line!" Asked to play a character who believes Aubrey to be a war hero, she gives Sallyann just the right combination of believability and absurdity. Seemingly singing his praises to her father, she says brightly, "Sometimes, believe it or not, he acts positively stupid!" When Aubrey is told that an intruder has just been shot as a Yankee spy, he asks worriedly, "Do you shoot all of them?" Nonchalantly, she replies, "No, we hang some of them." Miss Dahl would work with Skelton twice more, in *Three Little Words* and *Watch the Birdie* (both 1950).

Though he's billed above the title, along with Skelton, Brian Donlevy (1901–1972) is little seen until the film is halfway over. His biographer Derek Sculthorpe thought he functioned as "little more than a stooge" for Skelton, but decreed him nonetheless "the strongest member of the supporting cast."[77] Donlevy's cohorts in villainy are John Ireland (1914–1992) and George Coulouris (1903–1989), the latter of whom said, according to the film's pressbook, "I would slink into a scene in my most menacing manner, and this Skelton would cut loose with one of his gags. Now, I could prepare myself for the jokes in the script, but when he would pull one out of thin air, it was too much."

Joyce Compton, previously featured in Simon's *Spring Madness*, appears as Hortense, a guest at the Twelve Oaks ball, who's delighted to win a kiss from the man she believes is a war hero. Complications from crossed wires ensue when Hortense tries to collect her buss, while Aubrey believes she's engaged in espionage. Character actress Louise Beavers (1902–1962) has a funny bit near the end of the film as a laundress who's startled to find Skelton's character tangled up in her clothesline.

Reviews: "This comedy of errors should go over pretty well with the Red Skelton fans.... There is little rhyme or reason to the story, and much of the comedy is of the slapstick variety, but it is fast-moving and effective. Some of the situations are hilariously funny." *Harrison's Reports*, August 7, 1948

"Skelton fans will love this, and for the others it should pack plenty of laughs. While it isn't A-1 Skelton material, it does have several hilarious gag sequences, which audiences should eat up.... Skelton, as usual, is an ace comedian, and while the presence of several capable character actors seems out of place, they go through their parts with ability." *The Exhibitor*, September 1, 1948

Shockproof (1949)

Cornel Wilde (*Griff Marat*), Patricia Knight (*Jenny Marsh*), John Baragrey (*Harry Wesson*), Esther Minciotti (*Mrs. Marat*), Howard St. John (*Sam Brooks*), Russell

Collins (*Frederick Bauer*), Charles Bates (*Tommy Marat*), Argentina Brunetti (*Stella*), Claire Carleton (*Florrie Kobiski*), Al Eben (*Joe Kobiski*), Ann Shoemaker (*Dr. Daniels*), Frank Jaquet (*Monte*), John Butler (*Sam Green*), Gilbert Barnett (*Barry*), King Donovan (*Joe Wilson*), Virginia Farmer (*Mrs. Terrence*), Frank Ferguson (*Logan*), Arthur Space (*Police Inspector*), James Flavin (*Policeman in Park*), Earle Hodgins (*Race Caller*), Crane Whitley (*Foreman*), George J. Lewis (*Border Patrolman*), Robert R. Stephenson (*Drunk*), Isabel Withers (*Switchboard Operator*), Charles Jordan (*Man at Hamburger Stand*), Harry Tenbrook (*Job Applicant*), Buddy Swan (*Teenage Boy*), Frank O'Connor (*Policeman at Hospital*), Paul Bradley (*Airline Clerk*), Nita Mathews (*Nurse*), Eddie Foster (*Newspaper Buyer*)

Director: Douglas Sirk. *Producers*: S. Sylvan Simon, Helen Deutsch (uncredited). *Associate Producer*: Earl McEvoy. *Screenplay*: Helen Deutsch, Samuel Fuller. *Director of Photography*: Charles Lawton. *Art Director*: Carl Anderson. *Film Editor*: Gene Havlick. *Set Decorator*: Louis Diage. *Assistant Director*: Earl Bellamy. *Gowns*: Jean Louis. *Makeup*: Clay Campbell. *Hair Stylist*: Helen Hunt. *Sound Engineer*: Lodge Cunningham. *Musical Score*: George Duning. *Musical Director*: M.W. Stoloff.

Columbia; released January 1949. 79 minutes.

Released from prison after five years, Jenny Marsh is assigned to parole officer Griff Marat, who advises her to "change your brand of men." Jenny is still in contact with Harry Wesson, a smoothie for whose benefit she killed a man. Having grown up disadvantaged, Jenny defensively insists Harry is "the only man who's ever been kind to me." When she's picked up in a raid of a gambling den, where she and Harry are planning a getaway, Griff threatens to send her back to prison. A psychiatrist advises him that, with help, she can be rehabilitated, and Griff takes a personal interest in her case.

Trying to keep Jenny away from Harry, Griff takes her to dinner at his house, where she meets his mother, who is blind, and his little brother Tommy. When potential employers refuse to employ Jenny because of her criminal record, Griff hires her to be his mother's caregiver and companion. Living in the same house, Griff and Jenny's mutual attraction grows, but she's still seeing Harry behind Griff's back.

When Jenny tells Harry that Griff is falling for her, he suggests that she marry him to gain leverage over the principled parole officer. Feeling trapped, and unwilling to betray Griff, Jenny decides to leave town, but he intercepts her at the airport. They marry, keeping it secret because it violates her parole, but Harry is not willing to give Jenny up. Arguing with Harry at his apartment, Jenny shoots him. With Harry not expected to live, Griff chooses his new wife over his career and family, and they go on the run.

Filmed under the title "The Lovers," *Shockproof* is an absorbing, fast-paced *noir* thriller, smartly directed by Douglas Sirk. It was shot in a semi-documentary style, as was trendy in films of the late 1940s, allowing the modest budget to be less obvious. The film teamed Simon with two men who would go on to greater success in Hollywood, director Sirk and Samuel Fuller, on whose original screenplay *Shockproof* was based.

The film provided Cornel Wilde, popular with audiences after roles in films such as *Leave Her to Heaven* (1945) and *Road House* (1948), the chance to co-star with his wife, Patricia Knight. Miss Knight (1915–2004), whom Wilde had married in 1937, had played a few minor roles on Broadway and in film, but was not yet a known entity.

Cornel Wilde and Patricia Knight make a sexy couple in *Shockproof,* not a difficult task for the real-life husband and wife.

The Wildes had undergone a brief separation in 1947, amidst rumors that she was frustrated by her inability to have an acting career as successful as his. Reunited, they sought a vehicle for her.

A gushy article in *Modern Screen* had Simon supervising Miss Knight's screen test, then embracing her, saying, "You were great! Cornel, better make up your mind that you're just going to support her in this one."[78] Director Douglas Sirk later recalled of his leading lady, "She was not enormously talented as an actress, but I decided to use this very lack of experience—and she was most flexible and willing and kind of understood what I was after—the sparse freedom of human existence."[79]

Though Simon produced *Shockproof*, with the assistance of screenwriter Helen Deutsch (who, according to Sirk, "turned herself into the co-producer, I think, presumably to institutionalize her control"[80]), he took no screen credit. He may have been disturbed by the studio's insistence on making changes to the film, bringing in Deutsch to fashion a less downbeat ending than the one in Fuller's original screenplay. The revamped climax was, to put it mildly, implausible—film historian David J. Hogan later wrote, "To say that the conclusion of *Shockproof* is ridiculous is like saying that things get drafty during a hurricane."[81] The revamped *Shockproof* is at best a second-tier *noir* film.

Nonetheless, according to columnist Sheilah Graham (September 2, 1948), Simon was sufficiently impressed with Miss Knight's performance to consider casting her in *Lust for Gold*. She opted for a vacation with her husband instead. She would acquire only a few film credits thereafter, and the Wildes were divorced in 1951.

Co-star John Baragrey (1918–1975), who would find career success primarily on television, neatly plays slimy Harry, allowing viewers to understand his appeal to Jenny, despite his less-than-honorable behavior. Among the effective supporting performances are character actress Claire Carleton (1913–1979) as a busybody neighbor, and Esther Minciotti (1888–1962) as Griff's mother. A 1949 profile of Mrs. Minciotti noted, "After her long years in comparative obscurity in the Italian theater in America, she has also become a highly-prized Hollywood personality this year,"[82] with her role in *House of Strangers* as well as *Shockproof*. She went on to appear as Ernest Borgnine's mother in *Marty* (1955). King Donovan (1918–1987) is unbilled for his brief but showy role as one of Jenny's fellow parolees, who reacts with blind panic at the idea of being incarcerated again.

Reviews: "Good entertainment for adult audiences, who will find in it plenty of heart appeal and interest. It is a well-produced, capably directed offering that should satisfy in any situation. Cornel Wilde, as the parole officer, and Patricia Knight as the parolee, seem completely at home in their roles, playing their parts with conviction and ability." *Showmen's Trade Review*, January 29, 1949

"This melodrama should appeal to the action fans, for it keeps moving all the time and turns into a 'hunted' action in the last few reels. But the story is not pleasant [and] the motivation for her crime remains obscure.... Despite the film's shortcomings, though, it should satisfy those who do not stop to analyze a story as long as the action keeps them interested.... The direction and acting are good, and so is the photography." *Harrison's Reports*, January 29, 1949

Lust for Gold (1949)

Glenn Ford (*Jacob "Dutch" Walz*), Ida Lupino (*Julia Thomas*), Gig Young (*Pete Thomas*), William Prince (*Barry Storm*), Edgar Buchanan (*Wiser*), Will Geer (*Deputy Ray Covin*), Paul Ford (*Sheriff Lynn Early*), Myrna Dell (*Lucille*), Hayden Rorke (*Floyd Buckley*), Will Wright (*Parsons*), Antonio Moreno (*Ramon Peralta*), Anne O'Neal (*Mrs. Butler*), Virginia Mullen (*Pioneer Home Matron*), Jay Silverheels (*Deputy Walter*), Arthur Space (*Old Man*), Tom Tyler (*Luke*), Maudie Prickett (*Wife*), Elspeth Dudgeon (*Martha Bannister*), Karolyn Grimes (*Young Martha*), Percy Helton (*Barber*), Paul E. Burns (*Bill Bates*), Eddy Waller (*Coroner*), Harry Cording (*Joe*), Arthur Hunnicutt (*Ludi*), Virginia Farmer (*County Clerk*), Billy Gray (*Boy*), Suzanne Ridgway (*Saloon Girl*), Kermit Maynard (*Man in Lobby*), Alvin Hammer (*Husband*), John Doucette (*Man in Barber Shop*), Si Jenks (*Man at Assayer's Window*), David O. McCall (*Mexican Man*), William Tannen (*Eager Man*), Robert Malcolm (*Luke's Bartender*), Tiny Jones (*Nursing Home Resident*), Frank Matts, Jack Tornek (*Barflies*)

Producer-Director: S. Sylvan Simon. *Screenplay*: Ted Sherdeman, Richard English, based upon the book *Thunder Gods' Gold* by Barry Storm. *Associate Producer*: Earl McEvoy. *Director of Photography*: Archie Stout. *Art Director*: Carl Anderson. *Film Editor*: Gene Havlick. *Set Decorator*: Sidney Clifford. *Assistant Director*: James Nicholson. *Miss Lupino's Wardrobe*: Jean Louis. *Makeup*: Clay Campbell. *Hair*

Styles: Helen Hunt. *Sound Engineer*: Lodge Cunningham. *Musical Score*: George Duning. *Musical Director*: M.W. Stoloff.

Columbia; released June 1949. 90 minutes.

Modern-day gold prospector Barry Storm hears a shot and finds the dead body of Floyd Buckley. He reports the murder to the sheriff of Florence, Arizona. He explains that he is the grandson of Jacob Walz, owner of the Lost Dutchman Gold Mine, and hopes to find what his grandfather left behind.

Deputy Ray Covin shows Storm the markers that are believed to give clues to the location of the lost mine. He relates the legend of how three Spanish brothers supposedly found gold in the mountains some 100 years earlier. One of them, Pedro Peralta, hid the fortune worth some $20 million, but his expedition was attacked by Apache Indians. The Indians believed Peralta and his men had defiled a sacred space, and after killing the Spaniards, closed off access to the mine.

An elderly woman at a nursing home tells Barry the story of how Jacob Walz discovered the mine, by following Ramon Peralta when he returned to town years after his brother was killed. After killing Peralta and his companion, Jake returns to town laden with gold. A gold rush starts among the townspeople, but Jake shares his secret with no one.

Julia Thomas, who runs the local bakery, sees an opportunity when Jake collapses in a drunken stupor outside her store. She takes him in, telling her husband Pete to make himself scarce. Jake, who's attracted to Julia, believes her when she claims she has no interest in the mine. They grow closer, and no one in town dares tell the truculent stranger she's a married woman. When she finally confesses to him, he gives her money with which to bribe Pete into divorcing her. Pete, however, has no intention of doing so, setting up a potentially deadly confrontation between Julia, her husband, and her lover.

The framing sequence, spotlighting Barry Storm's attempt to follow in his grandfather's footsteps, leads into the main story, set in the 1880s. Just after the opening titles fade, the camera focuses on a letter signed by then-Arizona Governor Dan Garvey, saying, "The picture which you are about to see represents, to the best of our knowledge, the true facts concerning this unusual situation, as substantiated by historical records and legends of the State of Arizona." Storm's narration, establishing the premise, says of Superstition Mountain, "It's like Satan's private art gallery," and adds that the story to follow is "the biography of a death trap."

Lust for Gold had its genesis when Simon picked up Barry Storm's book *Thunder Gods' Gold*, and became intrigued with the legend of the Lost Dutchman Mine. He negotiated successfully with Storm for the rights to his book, taking a six-month option on it until he could convince his colleagues at Columbia that it could be the basis of an exciting film. Since the real-life mine had yet to be found, the screenplay shapes the story as an intriguing mystery with a participatory element, studio publicity telling moviegoers that the clues presented in the film might lead them to discover it. ("If YOU are interested in picking up $20,000,000 in gold," read one frequently used tagline, "this picture will give you authentic clues based on historical records of the State of Arizona.") Columnist Louella Parsons (April 21, 1948), given an outline of the story by the enthusiastic producer, joked, "I was so fascinated when Sylvan Simon was telling me all this I thought I might give up 'columning' for a while and get me a pick and shovel."

Jake (Glenn Ford) and Julia (Ida Lupino) discover their mutual dislike of poverty in *Lust for Gold*.

It proved to be something of a troubled production that tested Simon's mettle as a producer and an executive, even before the location shoot in Arizona began. An interoffice teletype between the studio's West and East Coast offices suggested that Gordon Douglas was considered to direct: "IF U THINK GORDON DOUGLAS CAN DO COMPETENT JOB WE WOULD PREF HIM TO MARSHALL AT EXTRA COST." However, veteran filmmaker George Marshall (1891–1975) ultimately got the job, which resulted in an unhappy collaboration.

Shooting began in October 1948, with interiors being filmed in Hollywood, but difficulties soon arose. Marshall, as per *Variety* (October 29, 1948), "walked out of Columbia yesterday afternoon, following several days of conflict with S. Sylvan Simon, producer.... Simon had been advising Marshall how to direct several sequences. One was a drunk scene involving Glenn Ford, for which there was a large number of takes. Another, a scene with Gig Young, required 25 rehearsals and 35 takes." When Marshall left the project, Simon took over the directorial chores, delivering an exciting product that makes it hard to regret the directorial switch.

As reported in *Daily Variety* (December 3, 1948), Simon was injured in Arizona when he was thrown from a horse, resulting in "a badly wrenched knee ... [He] continued on through day without taking any time off except for bandaging of knee." Daughter Susan Granger, who came along on the location shoot, didn't remember that episode, but noted, "We did a lot of horseback riding when we were staying at the Arizona Biltmore Hotel during the filming."[83]

Most Arizona residents were quite enthusiastic about the location shoot, and its effects on the local economy. A few months prior to filming, Simon told a Phoenix newspaper, "I do want to make the picture right in the Superstition Mountains and use in the cast, in addition to the all-star troupe from Columbia's roster, as many local Arizonans as I can."[84] Per another source, "Producer-director S. Sylvan Simon estimates from $50,000 to $125,000 will be spent during the two weeks the company of 73 from Columbia Studios is working here."[85] Governor Garvey, who supplied the letter seen in the film, was present for the first day of the shoot, on November 29, 1948, and called "Action!" to get things going.

In its earliest incarnations, the film was known as either "Bonanza" or "Greed." It was still called the former when staff of the Production Code office critiqued an early version of the script. The changes requested were not substantial—two foreign-language terms employed as curses ("Madre de Dios" and "Verdamptes" [sic])—were to be cut. As for Lucille and her co-workers, the censors cautioned, "There must be nothing suggestive of prostitutes about the girls who work in the saloon." In an interoffice memo, Simon reassured screenwriter Ted Sherdeman as to the changes required, "These are very unimportant, and we will discuss them at a later date."[86]

After the censors had approved the title *Lust for Gold*, some executives in Columbia's New York office suggested that "Lust" alone might be even better: "We felt if could get the one word cleared was a much stronger title." However, they reported that this title, more open to various interpretations, was rejected. The Los Angeles contingent, possibly Cohn himself, thought *Lust for Gold* was an effective title.

As discussed in the Biography section, the real-life Barry Storm saw red (so to speak) when he watched the finished film, and filed a lawsuit against Columbia. He later wrote, "I am neither the Dutchman's grandson, nor the half-witted dope, without prospecting or historical knowledge, displayed by an actor in my name, and without my previous knowledge."[87] He asserted that the film defamed him, and hurt his professional reputation as a miner and prospector. Though he's depicted as a bit callow, and perhaps foolhardy, the fictional Barry is actually the closest thing to a sympathetic character in a film where they are in short supply. It's difficult to see how, having been present during much of the Arizona shoot, he can have been unaware of the film's basic story, or the fact that much of the action centered on fictionalized characters such as Julia Thomas.

Nor, in his complaints, did Storm mention that the filmmakers gave his book a substantial amount of free publicity. The film's pressbook contains a section called, "Use the Book to Sell the Film!" Included are several suggestions for tie-ins with local bookstores and libraries, distributing free copies to media outlets, and other public relations efforts that would have helped line Storm's pockets.

Making no effort to claim sympathy for her character is second-billed Ida Lupino, cast as the duplicitous Julia. She makes her first entrance nearly 30 minutes into the film, going on to give an impressive performance as a thoroughly unscrupulous woman who knows what she wants, and pursues it relentlessly. According to her biographer, Miss Lupino accepted the role in *Lust for Gold* primarily so that she could spend time with her then-husband, Columbia executive Collier Young. "I thought I could at least have lunch with Collie," she recalled; they had been married only a few months.[88] In that she was destined for disappointment, as many of her scenes were shot on location in Arizona.

The film's assistant director James Nicholson later recalled that Lupino spent much of her time on set observing director Simon, his cinematographer, and crew, as she was already planning to take up film production herself. Susan Simon Granger concurred, noting that not only was her father encouraging to Miss Lupino, but that he liked having his daughter see that such career aspirations were possible for women. According to the film's pressbook, the physical demands of Miss Lupino's role were intense; she purportedly "cracked two ribs, pulled a ligament in her leg, caught a bad cold on the desert location … and amassed an unprecedented amount of contusions and abrasions! All for the sake of her art." Another column item said that, during one take, she narrowly escaped being hit by a rolling boulder, causing Simon to break the tension by cracking, "Hey, don't kill Ida! We need her for another month."

Leading man Glenn Ford is effective as Jacob Walz, mostly a bad guy but showing possible flickers of regret that his good fortune has put him at odds with most of the townspeople. According to Ford's son Peter, Sylvan Simon wanted the actor to play the modern-day Barry Storm as well, but Ford refused. Gig Young's biographer George Eells reported that the actor accepted his third-billed role as Miss Lupino's cuckolded husband primarily because studio head Harry Cohn had tied the job to the promise of a long-term Columbia contract. It's anything but a career-enhancing role for a leading man, though Young plays it well.

William Prince (1913–1996) has a certain quality of vulnerability, if not weakness, that is well-suited to the role of Barry. Prince had a modestly successful movie career in the 1940s, followed by steadier work on television, where his appearances ranged over some 45 years, until shortly before his death. Will Geer (1902–1978), playing a talkative sheriff's deputy, tries to take the curse off some necessary exposition, relating the legend of the mine at some length. "You know, I generally charge tourists ten bucks for telling that yarn," he says when he's done, favoring Storm with a wink and a grin.

Also representing local law enforcement is Jay Silverheels (1912–1980), several months before making his debut as Tonto on TV's *The Lone Ranger*, cast as a sheriff's deputy who is an Apache Indian. Hayden Rorke (1910–1987), best-known as the hapless Dr. Bellows on TV's *I Dream of Jeannie*, plays the supercilious author and explorer who learns the hard way about the dangers of Superstition Mountain. According to a blurb in the *Arizona Republic* (December 11, 1948), stuntmen Dave Sharpe and Gil Perkins were put to work doubling for two of the principal actors in a raucous fight scene set high atop the mountain.

Character actress Elspeth Dudgeon (1871–1955), perhaps best-known for her unusual cross-dressing role in *The Old Dark House* (1932), appears as the ornery old lady who tells Barry Storm about meeting Jacob Walz in her childhood. Maudie Prickett (1914–1976) has a brief scene as a townswoman in the flashback sequences, who, like Julia Thomas, isn't impressed with her man's abilities as a provider. Learning of the fortune Jacob Walz has just found, Miss Prickett tells her spouse disgustedly, "And you get $11 a week clerking in a hardware store. You and your high school diploma. Ha!"

For all the difficulties encountered in its making, *Lust for Gold* was well-received. Syndicated columnist Edith Gwynn (February 20, 1949) reported that the film might be the sleeper of the season: "Sylvan Simon had the unique story developed from his research about the ill-famed Superstition Mountain in Arizona where so many have died trying to mine its gold.... The fight scenes were photographed on the edge of a cliff over a thousand feet up. Gave the whole troupe heart failure!"

Reviews: "Highly suspenseful screen fare.... *Lust for Gold*, for all that it is somewhat reminiscent in theme and treatment of *Treasure of the Sierra Madre*, is an unusual and brilliantly directed and enacted film. Glenn Ford is outstanding as the taciturn and ruthless young German, a role considerably at variance from any he has essayed before, and Ida Lupino turns in a great performance as the ambitious girl who is trapped by her own avarice." *Hartford Courant*, June 16, 1949

"A pretty good outdoor melodrama, but the story is not very pleasant.... There is no human interest and none of the characters arouse any sympathy, but the picture has been produced well and the acting is good. Moreover, it has plenty of rough melodramatic action and keeps the spectator in suspense. There are a number of outstanding tense sequences." *Harrison's Reports*, May 28, 1949

Miss Grant Takes Richmond (1949)

Lucille Ball (*Ellen Grant*), William Holden (*Dick Richmond*), Janis Carter (*Peggy Donato*), James Gleason (*Timothy P. Gleason*), Gloria Henry (*Helen White*), Frank McHugh (*Mr. Kilcoyne*), George Cleveland (*Judge Ben Grant*), Stephen Dunne (*Ralph Winton*), Charles Lane (*Mr. Woodruff*), Wanda Cantlon (*Peggy's Maid*), Arthur Space (*Willacombe*), Claire Meade (*Mae Grant*), Don Hayden (*Prospective Homeowner*), Jimmy Lloyd (*Homer White*), Ola Lorraine (*Jennie Meyers*), Loren Tindall (*Charles Meyers*), Roy Roberts (*Foreman Roberts*), Harry Cheshire (*Leo Hopkins*), Stanley Waxman (*Sig Davis*), Harry Harvey (*Councilman Reed*), Eddie Acuff (*Bus Driver*), Will Wright (*Roscoe Johnson*), Charles Marsh (*Court Clerk*), Cosmo Sardo (*Maître D'*), Peter Brocco (*Father of Triplets*), Jerry Jerome, Ted Jordan, Paul Newlan, Michael Ross (*Hoods*)

An S. Sylvan Simon Production. *Director*: Lloyd Bacon. *Screenplay*: Nat Perrin, Devery Freeman, Frank Tashlin. *Story*: Everett Freeman. *Art Director*: Walter Holscher. *Film Editor*: Jerome Thoms. *Set Decorator*: James Crowe. *Assistant Director*: Carl Hiacke. *Gowns*: Jean Louis. *Makeup*: Clay Campbell. *Hair Styles*: Helen Hunt. *Sound Engineer*: Lambert Day. *Musical Score*: Heinz Roemheld. *Musical Director*: Morris Stoloff.

Columbia; released September 1949. 87 minutes.

Ellen Grant, the Woodruff Secretarial School's least promising student, is not a skilled typist and struggles to take down letters by shorthand. Dick Richmond visits the school to meet its students, and select a secretary for his real estate agency. To the shock of the school's principal, Mr. Woodruff, Dick chooses Ellen.

Unbeknownst to Ellen, Dick and his associates Gleason and Kilcoyne are using the realty company as a front for an illegal gambling operation. Dick thinks that hiring "the dumbest one in the whole school" to staff the front office will give their business an air of authenticity, and save them the trouble of dealing with the many potential clients looking to find a home amidst the post-war housing shortage.

Ellen Grant (Lucille Ball) has a *very* friendly boss (William Holden) in *Miss Grant Takes Richmond*.

Since Ellen knows several young couples who need housing, she suggests to Dick that he build a low-cost development. She urges him to buy property at Vincent Knolls, and even negotiates a reasonable price on his behalf. Dick's cronies urge him to fire her immediately. However, having learned that Ellen's suitor is a local assistant district attorney, and her uncle is a judge, Dick deems it inadvisable to take any rash action.

Unable to explain why he doesn't *want* to generate real estate business, Dick decides to make Ellen quit, first by loading her down with work, and then with inappropriate attentions in the office. Intending to resign, Ellen hesitates when she learns how excited her friends are about the construction of affordable homes. She decides to see the project through, while Dick and his cronies are forced to maintain the appearance of working on it while simultaneously running a bookie joint.

Their back-room business is seriously imperiled when Ellen's tardy delivery of a phone message puts Dick $50,000 in debt to glamorous but shady Peggy Donato, who wants him to manage her criminal syndicate. With money coming in from homebuyers, Dick tries to pay off Peggy, while Ellen blithely goes ahead with construction of the development, unaware the financing is about to dry up.

Miss Grant Takes Richmond is a fun, lightweight comedy that makes good use of leading lady Lucille Ball. The film's humor is primarily situational, as the goings-on at

Richmond Realty become increasingly complex, and finally spin out of control. But Lucy does get a few opportunities to showcase her talent for physical comedy as well. A strong early scene finds her hopelessly mangling her work as a typist, highlighted by a shot in which she energetically slings back the machine's carriage, sending it flying. Later, on a construction site, she runs afoul of the heavy equipment, getting a load of dirt dumped on her, and struggling with a jackhammer that seems to be getting away from her.

A set visitor watched as the company shot what Simon told her was "the trickiest scene," in which Lucy receives a telephone call at the office that makes her realize the man she loves is involved is involved in a front for gambling. "The producer was assisting Director Lloyd Bacon in interpreting the denouement, an unusual procedure," according to the publicist who accompanied her. "Simon, Bacon, Ball and Holden went into a huddle to decide just how a gal would react when she finds out that the guy she loves is up to no good."[89] Multiple takes ensued.

The moment in which Dick points into the roomful of prospective secretaries, and indicates to Mr. Woodruff that he wants "that girl," may remind viewers of the prologues that later became a standard feature of TV's *That Girl*. George Cleveland (1885–1957), as Ellen's uncle, gets an amusing bit when she tells him she must either graduate from business school, or get married; aware of her secretarial skills, he says nothing, but walks away whistling "The Wedding March."

Lucille Ball and William Holden are nicely teamed; he manages to keep the character of Dick from being too unlikable, despite his criminal activities, and dialogue like his description of Ellen: "nice eyes, nice hat, nothing under it." As all Lucy fans know, he later made a guest appearance as himself on one of *I Love Lucy*'s most famous episodes.

Those same fans will enjoy seeing her interactions with character actor Charles Lane (1905–2007), playing one of his typical grouchy roles as the head of the secretarial school. He will later turn up in guest roles on *I Love Lucy*, and play her banker Mr. Barnsdahl on *The Lucy Show*. Another of her future TV bankers, actor Roy Roberts (1906–1975), plays the frustrated foreman on the construction site. Don Hayden (1926–1998), best-known as nitwit boyfriend Freddie on TV's *My Little Margie*, appears briefly as one of the young clients looking to buy a house. Character actor James Gleason (1882–1959), strongly featured here as one of Dick's cronies, would later be considered for the role of Fred Mertz on *I Love Lucy*, but his asking price was too high. His deese-dem-and-doze speech causes Peggy to say snidely to him, "Still carry a grudge against the English language, don't you?"

Columbia did well with *Miss Grant Takes Richmond*, and raked in additional coin with its mid–50s re-release, capitalizing on the popularity of *I Love Lucy*.

Reviews: "Delightfully amusing entertainment.... Lucille Ball is the star, and that's not merely from a billing standpoint. She is the screen's only feminine performer who is lovely to look at and able to tickle an audience's risibilities at the same time.... Lloyd Bacon's direction succeeds admirably for comedy's sake, and S. Sylvan Simon's production values are of a high standard." *Showmen's Trade Review*, September 24, 1949

"A good romantic comedy.... The story is nonsensical and far-fetched, but it should go over well with most audiences, for it has many comical gags and situations, some of which will provoke uproarious laughter. Lucille Ball is very good as the secretary, playing the part in broad style ... will cause the audience to laugh so heartily that many of the gags will be drowned out." *Harrison's Reports*, September 24, 1949

Father Is a Bachelor (1950)

William Holden (*Johnny Rutledge*), Coleen Gray (*Prudence Millett*), Mary Jane Saunders (*May Chalotte*), Charles Winninger (*Prof. Mordecai Ford*), Stuart Erwin (*Constable Pudge Barnham*), Clinton Sundberg (*Plato Cassin*), Gary Gray (*Jan Chalotte*), Sig Ruman (*Jericho Schlosser*), Billy Gray (*Feb Chalotte*), Lloyd Corrigan (*Judge Millett*), Frederic Tozere (*Jeffrey Gilland, Sr.*), Peggy Converse (*Genevieve Cassin*), Lillian Bronson (*Adelaide Cassin*), Arthur Space (*Lucius Staley*), Ruby Dandridge (*Lily*), Warren Farlow (*March Chalotte*), Wayne A. Farlow (*April Chalotte*), Tommy Ivo (*Jeffrey Gilland, Jr.*), William Tannen (*George Willis*), Hank Worden (*Finnegan*), Al Thompson (*Court Clerk*), Cosmo Sardo (*Otto*), Dooley Wilson (*Blue*)

An S. Sylvan Simon Production. *Directors*: Norman Foster, Abby Berlin. *Screenplay*: Aleen Leslie, James Edward Grant. *Story*: James Edward Grant. *Director of Photography*: Burnett Guffey. *Art Director*: Carl Anderson. *Gowns*: Jean Louis. *Makeup*: Clay Campbell. *Hair Styles*: Helen Hunt. *Sound Engineer*: George Cooper. *Musical Score*: Arthur Morton. *Musical Director*: Morris Stoloff.

Columbia; released February 1950. 83 minutes.

Johnny Rutledge is a drifter who goes through life as effortlessly as possible, avoiding commitments and relationships. When his employer of the moment, snake oil salesman Professor Mordecai Ford, is jailed in a small town, Johnny decides to stick around and wait out his boss' 30-day sentence.

Planning nothing much during his time off—"I fish and I roam"—he finds himself reconsidering when he meets a little girl, May Chalotte, and her four brothers, named January, February, March, and April. May tells him her parents are traveling, but her older siblings have kept secret the fact that the kids are actually orphaned and on their own. Visiting with the kids, Johnny takes a liking to them, especially May, but resists getting involved. When he accidentally burns May's only dress, Johnny tries and fails to make a replacement, then sells his watch fob to buy her a new one.

A young woman, Prudence Millett, visits the Chalotte home to ask why the children have not been attending school. Rather than expose the fact that they are orphaned, Johnny claims to be their uncle, and sees to it that they resume their schooling. More attached to the children than he cares to admit, Johnny takes offense when wealthy, influential Jeffrey Gilland insults them as "riverbottom trash," and the two men get into a fistfight. Though Johnny defends the Chalotte children's honor, he soon finds himself charged with assault. When his trial is postponed, and Prudence pays his bail, Johnny extends his stay, but runs afoul of unscrupulous lawyer Plato Cassin. Aware that the Chalotte children's parents are dead, and that Johnny is no relation to them, Cassin uses that knowledge to blackmail Johnny into marrying one of his spinster sisters. Doing so will insure that May and her brothers live in comfort

Although *Father Is a Bachelor,* his family circle is about to grow. Pictured (left to right) are William Holden, Mary Jane Saunders, and Coleen Gray.

and security, but will cost him his relationship with Prudence, whom he has realized he loves. Released from jail, Professor Ford urges Johnny to leave the town behind and go back on the road with him.

Boxoffice (January 6, 1945) noted that Columbia had purchased the rights to James Edward Grant's original story, and was assigning him to produce the film and write the screenplay, with Bing Crosby expected to star. Grant had previously written the screenplay for *The Great John L.* (1945). Later, *Showmen's Trade Review* (January 18, 1947) reported that "A Mother for May" would be produced by Maurice [Buddy] Adler, and directed by Alexander Hall.

In 1949, columnists revealed that Simon had pulled "A Mother for May" from the Columbia files, and assigned Aleen Leslie to pen a new screenplay based on the material. Grant's original story "deal[t] with a young man who sets out to find a mother for his orphaned little sister."[90] Screenwriter Leslie (1908–2010), whose credits included several films in Paramount's "Henry Aldrich" B series, had more recently written another "Father" movie, *Father Was a Fullback.*

In the summer of 1949, Barbara Hale was said to be set for the female lead. A few weeks later, Gail Russell was assigned the part, but went on suspension rather than play it, at which point Coleen Gray was borrowed from 20th Century–Fox. Miss Gray later recalled that there were some melancholy moments relating to the film's musical sequences, for which Holden was dubbed by popular vocalist Buddy Clark. "We were all in tears during the filming because Buddy Clark had been killed in a plane crash several months before. He was a great singer."[91]

Publicly, at least, Holden proclaimed himself pleased to be offered a variety of roles. Columnist Hedda Hopper (February 12, 1950) told him, "You're getting typed as untyped," to which he responded, "That's what I want." About six months after the release of *Father Is a Bachelor*, Holden returned to movie screens for one of his most highly acclaimed performances, in *Sunset Blvd.*

Child actress Mary Jane Saunders (born 1943) was playing her second major film role in *Father Is a Bachelor*, after being acclaimed for her work in the Bob Hope comedy *Sorrowful Jones,* which led Paramount publicists to dub her "another Shirley Temple in the offing." However, while she continued to act throughout the 1950s, primarily in television, she received few substantial roles in later years.

Strong character actors enrich the film as well. The full-out performance of Charles Winninger (1884–1969) as a snake oil salesman is nicely balanced by Stuart Erwin's subtle underplaying as the constable. The studio was a bit stingy with billing; among those who don't get an onscreen credit are the twin boys who play March and April.

A preview showing of *Father Is a Bachelor* on November 22, 1949, elicited a mostly positive response from attendees, with 148 of the 171 viewers who filled out comment cards rated it "excellent" or "good." Response to William Holden's performance in an atypical role was largely positive; one audience member wrote, "Pleasantly surprised by voice, if it is his voice, he should be case [*sic*] in musicals." However, another respondent said, "Waste of Holden who deserves better." Billy Gray (born 1938), as Feb, received a few accolades; one viewer wrote, "Harmonica player has star possibilities."

Studio executives in attendance at the preview made several notes for suggested cuts or changes, including:

"Am dissatisfied with the OPENING—it doesn't get us anything."

"Little girl says to Holden 'A dress as good as the judge's daughter'—THE AUDIENCE ASKS WHO THE JUDGE'S DAUGHTER IS."

They also noted that the orchestral accompaniment in scenes with Feb playing his harmonica drowned out the sound of the smaller instrument, and suggesting cutting back the piped-in music.

An earlier version of the script, dated February 17, 1949, had included a scene which was either cut or never filmed. It shows Professor Ford, Johnny, and helper Blue before they arrive in town, and introduced the idea that Holden's character is, as his boss describes him, "A born evader of effort." Blue, for his part, says of Johnny, "Never did see a man what had so little truck with effort of any kind. Especially work."[92]

Further cuts were likely made after the preview, resulting in some minor continuity problems. Coleen Gray's first scene finds her upbraiding Holden's character for the children's absence in school, without letting us know why she's making it her business (later, we learn she's a member of the school board).

Studio suggestions for publicizing *Father Is a Bachelor* included the posting in theater lobbies of "a business directory listing 'Bachelor Services,' to include 'local tailors' who repair socks and buttons, laundries, restaurants with 'home cooking,' etc. Merchants listed should, in turn, give window space to your picture and playdate."

Reviews: "A heart-warming comedy-drama, with considerable human interest ...

the story is rather thin, but its human appeal and brand of comedy should entertain family audiences in small-town theatres. The more sophisticated big-city audiences, however, will probably find it too draggy and 'sticky.'" *Harrison's Reports*, February 11, 1950

"Based on a plot that is as thin as tissue paper and with most of its characters slightly overdrawn, this film still manages to provide some amiable, if not remarkable, entertainment. Bill Holden is responsible for most of its best moments, [performing] with an easy humor and a likable nonchalance.... It's a fine film for youngsters." Mae Tinée, *Chicago Tribune*, February 21, 1950

The Good Humor Man (1950)

Jack Carson (*Biff Jones*), Lola Albright (*Margie Bellew*), Jean Wallace (*Bonnie Conroy*), George Reeves (*Stuart Nagle*), Peter Miles (*Johnny Bellew*), Frank Ferguson (*Insp. Quint*), David Sharpe (*Slick*), Chick Collins (*Fats*), Pat Flaherty (*Officer Rhodes*), Richard Egan (*Officer Daley*), Arthur Space (*Steven*), Victoria Horne (*Bride*), Jack Overman (*Shirtless Stoker*), Paul E. Burns (*Mr. Watkins*), Edgar Dearing (*Desk Sergeant*), Jack Rice (*Roger*), Robert B. Williams (*Factory* Guard), Billy Gray (*Junior*), Leslie Bennett (*Ambrose*), Chester Clute (*Meek Man*), Maxine Gates (*Customer*), Teddy Infuhr (*Young Football Player*), Babe London (*Inmate*), Susan Simon (*Susan*), Joel Colin (*Dennis*), Bill McKenzie (*Rollie*), George Magrill, Jeffrey Sayre (*Police Detectives*)

An S. Sylvan Simon Production. *Director*: Lloyd Bacon. *Screenplay*: Frank Tashlin, from the *Saturday Evening Post* story "Appointment with Fear" by Roy Huggins. *Director of Photography*: Lester White. *Art Director*: Walter Holscher. *Film Editor*: Jerome Thoms. *Set Decorator*: James Crowe. *Assistant Director*: Paul Donnelly. *Gowns*: Jean Louis. *Makeup*: Clay Campbell. *Sound Recording*: George Cooper. *Voice Effects*: Sonovox. *Musical Score*: Heinz Roemheld. *Musical Director*: Morris Stoloff.

Columbia; released June 1950. 80 minutes.

Ice-cream salesman Biff Jones wants to marry pretty Margie Bellew, but she's hesitant, aware she has to provide for her little brother, Johnny. Meanwhile, Margie has also caught the eye of her boss, insurance investigator Stuart Nagle. Johnny, who's rooting for Biff, warns him that his sister is impressed by Nagle, who sells himself as "a big important detective."

While at work, Biff comes to the rescue of a beautiful stranger, who's being chased by three sinister-looking men. He helps her escape, but isn't so lucky himself, being locked into the freezer compartment of his truck. The ensuing melee, along with Stuart's complaints about his romantic rival, cause Biff's job to be endangered. Doing his best to drum up sales, and possibly avoid being fired, Biff is summoned to a strange house by a woman who proves to be Bonnie, the blonde he helped earlier. She tells him she's in great danger, and promises him a huge sale if he will stay at the house overnight and guard her.

Boarding up the house as his hero, Captain Marvel, would do, Biff is shocked

Jack Carson learns that being an ice cream salesman should rate hazard pay in *The Good Humor Man.*

to wake up and find Bonnie's lifeless body. He's still clad in the frilly nightgown she loaned him when Margie arrives on the scene, and concludes that her man has been unfaithful to her. Inspector Quint of the police finds Biff's whole story ridiculous, especially when they check the house where he stayed overnight, and find no body. Quint suspects Biff of being involved in a robbery at a manufacturing plant the previous night, as a Good Humor salesman signed the night watchman's log.

Suspected of killing the watchman, Biff tries to figure out what became of Bonnie. A laundry mark from her nightgown leads him and Margie to a hotel room, where he once again finds her lifeless body, followed by the arrival of the same three men who were after her earlier. They're in for several surprises, including the sudden appearance of Bonnie back on her feet, brandishing a gun, as well as the true identity of the gang's leader. Biff and Margie escape, but when they arrive at their designated hiding place—the clubhouse belonging to Johnny and his friends—they realize they've been betrayed. On the run from the bad guys, Biff and his lady take refuge in the nearby elementary school. Their efforts to evade capture are helped significantly when Johnny rallies dozens of boys his own age to come to his sister's rescue.

The box-office success of Simon's *The Fuller Brush Man* led to no less than three follow-up efforts that landed in theaters in 1950. Skelton's home studio capitalized on the initial film's popularity with its own slapstick comedy for him, *The Yellow Cab Man*, released that spring. Simon and his colleagues had hoped to cast Skelton in *The*

Good Humor Man, but had to regroup when MGM declined to loan their star comedian a second time. They ultimately borrowed Warners' contract player Jack Carson (1910–1963), who'd played a featured role in Simon's *The Kid from Texas* some 10 years earlier, for the starring role.

Billed above the title, Carson had more screen time than he sometimes did as a supporting player in Warner films, but the attention came at a price. As one reporter noted, "He is plastered with soot, flour, ice cream in assorted flavors, pies and glue. He is frozen solid, set afire, used as a human basketball, and beaten on the head by all sorts of blunt instruments ... pitched head first into a grand piano, thrown through a bass drum..."[93] He also found himself playing various scenes in a negligee, or in his boxer shorts. Though not Skelton's equal as a physical comedian, Carson goes through the comedy routines with energy, and creates sympathy for his desire to win Margie's hand. The script gives him some endearing qualities, such as the way he plays the song "Margie" on the chimes of his truck as a tribute to his lady. Carson gets a few funny lines alongside the broad physical routines, as when he reacts to his firing with, "Through? You mean I have to turn in my chimes?"

Lola Albright (1924–2017) was signed to a Columbia contract in 1949, with this film to be her first assignment. Evidently the chemistry between Miss Albright and her leading man extended to real life; she and Carson were married in 1952, but divorced a few years later. Jean Wallace (1923–1990) was borrowed from Fox for the sultry role of Bonnie. Character actress Victoria Horne (1911–2003) has some funny moments as a nearsighted bride who mistakes Biff for her husband and plants a kiss on him. Given the film's silent-comedy flavor, it's appropriate that actors like Chester Conklin and Vernon Dent turn up in minor roles.

Once again, Simon combined the slapstick comedy with a mystery element borrowed from one of author Roy Huggins' published short stories, in this case "Appointment with Fear," which had appeared in the September 28, 1946, issue of the *Saturday Evening Post.* Huggins took the $5,000 and ran, wanting no part of creating another slapstick screen comedy.

As several reviewers remarked, the film is at its liveliest in the final 20 minutes, when Biff and Margie have a showdown with the villains, and a brigade of boys pitches in. The result is comic pandemonium that scarcely lets up for a moment. The strenuous physical comedy employs not only the expected slapstick elements, like pies in the face, but every form of torture little boys (and screenwriter Frank Tashlin) can dish out. The result is something like the much later comedy *Home Alone* (1990), but with dozens of little boys instead of just one.

Veteran Hollywood stuntman Gil Perkins once explained, "The staples of the stuntman are slapstick and Westerns. Without them, you wouldn't need stuntmen." He got quite a workout while working on *The Good Humor Man.* "We threw 6,000 pies in one week on the stage at Columbia Studios. The L.S. Pie Company trucks came in every day with 1,000 pies. We'd throw them all day long."[94]

The authentic Good Humor trucks seen in the film were provided by the company. Since trucks used on the East Coast were different from the ones close at hand in Los Angeles, the company sent two of them cross-country. The first one was shipped, but "the freight bill gave Simon the shivers," causing him to ask if the second one could be driven out. Clarence Wellersdieck, of the company's Brooklyn office, got it there in six days, but his trip was fraught with mishaps. In Indianapolis, he was suspected of stealing the truck because it was empty, and had to show the local police a letter verifying his mission. In St. Louis, Missouri, the vehicle's chimes became stuck, and wouldn't stop ringing, again attracting the attention of the authorities. A flat tire slowed him down near Gallup, New Mexico. In yet another indignity, "the truck's radiator boiled over between Needles and Los Angeles, and Wellersdieck got laughed at by a lot of passing motorists who seemed to think that an ice cream truck stranded on the Mojave Desert was just about the funniest thing they ever saw." The weary driver ultimately arrived in Los Angeles with only two hours to spare, and fortunately was sent home by airplane.[95]

According to *Daily Variety* (May 7, 1949), a location shoot at Griffith Park went awry when nearby kids heard the chimes of the Good Humor truck Carson was driving. For the purposes of the scene, it was unnecessary to stock the truck with ice cream, but filming was interrupted when disappointed potential customers "started giving Carson some good old fashioned booing which even police were unsuccessful in breaking up." Only after the Good Humor Company came to the rescue, sending two loaded trucks to the scene, was the company able to resume shooting, having lost some two hours. Production was completed in July 1949.

It took a substantial amount of ingenuity to carry out some of the gags devised by screenwriter Frank Tashlin. One scene found Biff selling an ice cream bar to a man working alongside an industrial furnace. The heat from the equipment repeatedly melts the ice cream within seconds, while still in Biff's hand. The secret? "Wires from an electrical source led down Carson's sleeve to a resistance coil inside the bar. At the crucial moment a prop man turned on the juice. The bar melted in a second and a half. 'That's a lot quicker than it took the writer fellow to put it down on paper,'" said the triumphant crew member. Budget breakdowns for the film gave a hint of what items were needed for various scenes: "Two rubber baseball bats, $39. Breakaway pulls for filing cabinet drawers, $10. Gag tuba with rubber bell and extended mouthpiece, $12...."

The priciest item on the list, at $205, was the dummy suit donned by Carson to simulate his being a frozen block of ice. The budget-conscious crew wrote, "Note! Dummy will be rental! Please do not ruin!"[96] Further complicating that scene was Carson's inability to hear director Lloyd Bacon while encased in the suit. The problem was ultimately resolved with a short-wave radio issued to Bacon, and a small amplifier placed in the actor's ear.

Though *The Good Humor Man* had a different star comedian, publicity for the film took pains to connect it in moviegoers' minds with Simon's hit comedy of two years earlier. Tag lines included "Following in the hilarious footsteps of..." or "Screamingly funny adventures in the tradition of..." *The Fuller Brush Man.*

Reviews: "Nifty slapstick in the same broad style of the very successful *Fuller Brush Man....* The laugh payoff is hearty and Columbia would seem to have a winner ... [Carson] gives the character just the right amount of bumbling sincerity to pull the laughs from the broad situations." *Daily Variety*, May 29, 1950

"The picture gets off to a hilarious start.... In the middle it begins to sag under the weight of a 'murder' plot even sloppier than usual for this sort of thing.... The real uproar, though, is reserved for the chase finish, which is what everyone is marking time for anyway.... Some of the gags are inventive and funny, and some aren't." Philip K. Scheuer, *Los Angeles Times*, June 9, 1950

The Fuller Brush Girl (1950)

Lucille Ball (*Sally Elliott*), Eddie Albert (*Humphrey Briggs*), Carl Benton Reid (*Christy*), Gale Robbins (*Ruby Rawlings*), Jeff Donnell (*Jane Bixby*), Jerome Cowan (*Harvey Simpson*), John Litel (*Mr. Watkins*), Fred Graham (*Rocky Mitchell*), Lee Patrick (*Claire Simpson*), Arthur Space (*Insp. Rogers*), Isabel Randolph (*Mrs. South*), Lelah Tyler (*Mrs. North*), Sarah Edwards (*Mrs. East*), Lois Austin (*Mrs. West*), Roger Moore (*Salesman*), Syd Saylor (*Wardrobe Man*), Jean Willes (*Mary*), Isabel Withers (*Mrs. Finley*), Sid Tomack (*Bangs*), Gail Bonney (*Babysitter*), Bobby Hyatt (*Henry*), Gregory Marshall (*Alvin/Albert Finley*), Mary Treen (*Magazine Saleswoman*), Lorin Raker (*Mr. Deval*), Frank Wilcox (*Mr. Roberts*), Barbara Pepper (*Wife Watching TV*), Paul Bryar (*Husband*), Raoul Freeman (*Detective*), Charles Sullivan (*Bus Driver*), Sam Lufkin (*Man on Bus*), Emil Sitka (*Man on Sidewalk*), Sumner Getchell (*Magazine Salesman*), Bert Stevens (*Man in Office Corridor*), Jean Willes (*Mary*), Jay Barney (*Fingerprint Man*), Joet Robinson, Amzie Strickland, Shirley Whitney (*Dancers*), Ed Haskett (*Burlesque Club Patron*), James L. Kelly, Jack Little (*Comics*), George Lloyd, Bud Osborne (*Old Sailors*)

An S. Sylvan Simon Production. *Director*: Lloyd Bacon. *Screenplay*: Frank Tashlin. *Director of Photography*: Charles Lawton, Jr. *Art Director*: Robert Peterson. *Film Editor*: William Lyon. *Set Decorator*: James Crowe. *Assistant Director*: Earl Bellamy. *Gowns*: Jean Louis. *Makeup*: Clay Campbell. *Hair Stylist*: Helen Hunt. *Sound Engineer*: Lambert Day. *Musical Score*: Heinz Roemheld. *Musical Director*: Morris Stoloff. Columbia; released September 1950. 85 minutes.

Sally Elliott and Humphrey Briggs are a young couple ready to get married, but they lack the money to buy the starter home they want. After her clumsy handling of the office switchboard wreaks havoc, boss Harvey Simpson fires Sally from the Maritime Steamship Company. Her pal Jane suggests that she try working as a Fuller Brush girl, selling cosmetics. Meanwhile, Humphrey, still in the employ of the steamship company, gets a promotion, unaware that the dishonest Simpson chose him as someone gullible enough to serve as a patsy for his criminal operation.

Sally borrows Jane's case for a stint selling cosmetics door-to-door, but only encounters one difficulty after another. Also having trouble is her ex-boss, whose wife Claire smelled scented powder on his clothes, a remnant of Sally's office mishap. Simpson tells Humphrey to have his fiancée go to his house and verify his story. Before she can get there, a mysterious woman posing as Sally gains admittance, and shortly afterwards Claire Simpson is dead on the living room floor. When Humphrey arrives on the scene, he finds Sally groggy after being knocked out and the killer's gun beside her, leading him to fear his fiancée committed the murder.

Humphrey and Sally go to Simpson's office, where they find he's been shot and killed. Across the street is a burlesque theater, where Sally spots a large poster of featured dancer Ruby Rawlings. Recognizing her as the woman who attacked her at the Simpson house, she and Humphrey seek her out. Backstage, Sally is mistaken for the substitute dancer expected to take the place of Ruby, who's about to go on the lam. When they finally escape from the theater, Sally and Humphrey accept a ride from the wrong person, and find themselves aboard the *Claire S*, a ship headed out to sea with

Sally (Lucille Ball) and her co-worker Humphrey (Eddie Albert) are in love, but her losing battle with the office switchboard leads her into a new career as *The Fuller Brush Girl*.

smuggled diamonds in the cargo hold. With Inspector Rogers and his men following in a police vessel, the bad guys chase Sally and her fiancé over and around the *Claire S.*, where they encounter talking parrots, dozens of slippery bananas, and a leaky wine barrel that renders Miss Elliott drunk as a skunk.

Director Lloyd Bacon (1889–1955) was well-suited to the film, being a veteran of physical comedy going back to the days of Mack Sennett. He issued a call to some old-time comedians, casting them in minor roles, and set about putting Lucille Ball and Eddie Albert through their paces. As a set visitor reported, "Hank Mann, veteran dean of pie throwers, watched Lucille Ball with a paternal eye as she ran the gamut of comedy misfortunes." Seeing her cheerfully endure pies in the face and a succession of pratfalls, Mann said admiringly to a buddy, "Now there's an *actress* for you!"[97] Bacon concurred, saying, "Rough-house comedy may look easy, but it isn't. Believe me, a Mabel Normand, a Rosalind Russell or a Lucille Ball is as great an histrionic technician when she does a fall as Bernhardt was when she played the death scene in 'Camille.'"[98]

An early announcement in Edwin Schallert's *Los Angeles Times* column (August 2, 1949) indicated that writers Robert Lees and Fred Rinaldo would pen the screenplay. However, Frank Tashlin received sole screenplay credit on the finished film. Red Skelton, the star of Simon's previous hit *The Fuller Brush Man*, reprises that role in a cameo appearance.

Studio publicity claimed that real-life Fuller Brush saleswoman Grace Johnson, engaged to serve as a technical advisor on the film, attracted the interest of Simon and other studio executives who thought she might have promise as an actress. But the 29-year-old Miss Johnson reportedly nixed the offer, saying, "If they'd asked me a few days earlier I might have considered it. But I'd already seen how hard Lucille works, how she has to be on the set at 6 a.m., and how many times she has to say the same lines over and over and over. I should think she'd get bored to death."[99]

In one of her last films before launching a hugely successful television career, Lucille Ball finally gets the chance to show Hollywood, and moviegoers, what she does best. *The Fuller Brush Girl* is a prime showcase for her slapstick abilities, often anticipating the types of comic routines that will make *I Love Lucy* a nationwide phenomenon. She is strenuously funny as she impersonates a burlesque dancer, copes with an exploding switchboard, and gets drunk.

Miss Ball reported that, to play such an active role, "You have to get in condition for it. You can't just suddenly hang by your hands from netting, or a steamship stack, for take after take without preparing for it. Three weeks before I started the picture, I went into regular training. I took exercises. I rode a bicycle. I strengthened my muscles and developed them gradually."[100] Still, given the rigors of her assignment, it was no surprise that her vitality began to give out, and shortly after filming concluded, she went into the hospital for treatment of pneumonia. She had already been injured shooting the switchboard scene, when a blast of talcum powder went straight into her eye. She later recalled, "I sprained both wrists and displaced six vertebrae, then irritated my sciatic nerve by walking on the outside of my ankles for hours doing a drunk scene.... A three-day dunking in a wine vat gave me a severe cold, and I also was bruised by several tons of coffee beans."[101]

Her leading man, Eddie Albert, took a vacation from Broadway's *Miss Liberty* to appear in the film. "Of course I like the salary that I get paid in Hollywood much better," he admitted. "I never want to get too far away from the films. That is why I left the show to make *The Fuller Brush Girl* at Columbia."[102] The supporting cast was populated with talented character actors, several of whom were veterans of previous Simon films.

As with *The Fuller Brush Man*, the company's sales force was urged to send in their funniest on-the-job anecdotes. According to the film's pressbook, "C.A. Peterson, West Coast agency head of the Fuller Brush Co., walked into S. Sylvan Simon's office and casually dumped about 14,000 jokes in the surprised Columbia producer's lap." Once again, the Fuller Brush people clearly didn't want the lead character playing a legitimately employed salesperson for the firm.

The sequence in which Sally, mistaken for a babysitter, is nearly burned at the stake by her rambunctious charges, may have inspired a similar predicament in the *I Love Lucy* episode "The Amateur Hour" (January 14, 1952). Screenwriter Tashlin reprises a gag he used in *The Fuller Brush Man*, in which home viewers are baffled when a fight causes broadcasting equipment to go haywire, madly scrambling various shows. Done with radio programs in the first film, it's updated here, with TV viewers bewildered by what appears.

Columbia executives attended the film's first preview in Santa Barbara on June 2, 1950. The secretary or assistant transcribing the notes during the drive back wrote, "On next preview Mr. Simon wants to mimeograph on all cards 'Did you see The Fuller Brush Man'?"

Sally (Lucille Ball) is floored when she stumbles onto a murder in *The Fuller Brush Girl*. Fiancé Humphrey (Eddie Albert) comes to her aid.

Many of the executives' comments pertained to tightening the picture. Among them were:

"TRIM reactions when phone switchboard blows up.... TRIM second insert— BALL trying to pick up plugs at switchboard."

"TRIM leaking barrel scene—not so much with hands—cut to where she starts to drink from barrel."

Similar concerns were expressed when the film was previewed at the Picwood Theatre in Los Angeles on June 20, 1950. One executive said, "There are always too many shots in every gag sequence—cut them down—all the scenes are overplayed and you're just milking them beyond funniness." Another commented, "Cut down the scene where Ball tries to stop the flowing barrel—drinking from barrel, etc. This is not funny and she looks so dirty."

Preview audiences enjoyed it nonetheless. Of the 73 viewers in attendance at the Picwood, 61 of them rated it "excellent" or "good," though they too indicated in several instances that the film was too long.

An exhibitor from Wisconsin reported, in the *Motion Picture Herald*'s "What the Picture Did for Me" column (December 29, 1951), "What a comedy for small towns! Good old villain and chases hero and heroine, with all the slapstick of a Mack Sennett epic! ... Columbia makes some very good small town shows."

Reviews: "Lucille Ball ... proves to be an expert slapstick comedienne in The Fuller Brush Girl.... Miss Ball dominates the farce, appearing in almost every scene, and it's a good thing she does ... some hilarious situations and gags.... Miss Ball carries the ball for a comedy touchdown in this one." John L. Scott, *Los Angeles Times*, September 29, 1950

"Should give ample satisfaction to those who enjoy this type of comedy ... many comical gags and situations, some highly inventive, that are reminiscent of the Mack Sennett Keystone comedies. The pace is fast and furious from start to finish." *Harrison's Reports*, September 16, 1950

Born Yesterday (1950)

Judy Holliday (*Billie Dawn*), Broderick Crawford (*Harry Brock*), William Holden (*Paul Verrall*), Howard St. John (*Jim Devery*), Frank Otto (*Eddie*), Larry Oliver (*Congressman Norval Hedges*), Barbara Brown (*Anna Hedges*), Grandon Rhodes (*Sanborn*), Claire Carleton (*Helen*), Helen Eby-Rock (*Manicurist*), Mike Mahoney (*Elevator Operator*), Paul Marion (*Interpreter*), Charles Cane (*Policeman*), Smoki Whitfield (*Bootblack*), David Pardoll (*Barber*), Bhogwan Singh (*Native*), William Mays (*Bellboy*)

Producer: S. Sylvan Simon. *Director*: George Cukor. *Screenplay*: Albert Mannheimer, from the play by Garson Kanin. *Director of Photography*: Joseph Walker. *Film Editor*: Charles Nelson. *Production Designer*: Harry Horner. *Set Decorator*: William Kiernan. *Dialogue Supervisor*: David Pardoll. *Assistant Director*: Earl Bellamy. *Gowns*: Jean Louis. *Musical Director*: Morris Stoloff. *Musical Score*: Frederick Hollander. *Makeup Artist*: Clay Campbell. *Hair Stylist*: Helen Hunt. *Sound Engineer*: Jack Goodrich.

Columbia; released December 1950. 103 minutes.

Crude, loudmouthed Harry Brock, a junk dealer who's a self-made millionaire, comes to Washington, D.C., where he intends to bribe a congressman to further his business interests. He's accompanied by his flashy, younger fiancée of seven years, Billie Dawn, a retired chorus girl who's no more proficient in social graces, or erudition, than Harry himself. After an awkward first meeting with the congressman and his wife, Harry decides that Billie, who's never heard of the Supreme Court, is a "dumb broad" who will be an obstacle to accomplishing his goals among the Washington elite. He hires journalist Paul Verrall for $200 a week to smarten Billie up, and smooth down her rough edges.

Billie agrees to the plan, and Paul begins expanding her knowledge of American history, current affairs, and culture. She is clearly attracted to him, and impulsively bestows a kiss on her teacher, but Paul gently rebuffs her. His tutelage of Billie has an effect Harry didn't anticipate, as the broadening of her horizons causes her to take a harder look at her life choices, and at her relationship with the rough-hewn millionaire.

Garson Kanin's *Born Yesterday* was a smash hit on Broadway from the time of its opening in February 1946. It ran for some 3½ years, racking up more than 1,600 performances. The show's leading lady was Judy Holliday (1921–1965), who stepped into the starring role as an eleventh-hour replacement for the better-known Jean

Billie Dawn (Judy Holliday) takes on longtime fiancé Harry Brock (Broderick Crawford) at gin rummy in *Born Yesterday*.

Arthur. *Film Daily* (September 15, 1947) reported that Columbia had closed the deal for screen rights to Kanin's play while it was still running on Broadway. According to early announcements, it was earmarked as a vehicle for Columbia contract player Rita Hayworth.

Having paid a record high fee (10 yearly payments in the amount of $100,000 each) to acquire the screen rights to Kanin's play, Harry Cohn was angered when the playwright refused to help shape the screenplay without additional compensation. Instead, Simon's longtime collaborator Albert Mannheimer was assigned the task of adapting Kanin's play to the screen, but his work satisfied neither Cohn nor director Cukor. Cukor implored Kanin to rework the draft screenplay, urging him "to protect the play's integrity at all costs," and he finally agreed to give some surreptitious assistance.[103] Despite Kanin's contribution, only Mannheimer received screenplay credit, which left the playwright out in the cold at Oscar time.

Born Yesterday languished in studio limbo for nearly two years before Columbia began preparations for the film, which Simon would produce. Despite Judy Holliday's widespread acclaim and popularity as star of the Broadway show, Harry Cohn was not interested in hiring her to reprise her role on-screen. When his contract difficulties with Rita Hayworth prevented her from taking the assignment, the studio boss considered Lucille Ball, who had recently signed a multi-picture deal with Columbia. Nor was Cohn interested in casting Miss Holliday's stage co-star Paul Douglas, despite that actor's growing popularity as a film player. Cohn insisted that Broderick Crawford, already a Columbia employee, was just as well-suited to the role.

Further casting complications arose when William Holden, who'd made *Father Is a Bachelor* for Simon just a few months earlier, balked at playing Paul. Holden thought it a thankless part that paled in comparison to the two leads. In fact, once on board, he made a strong contribution to the film, depicting Paul as a kind, intelligent man who is quite different from his peroxided pupil. Paul encourages Billie to read the daily newspaper, and circle anything she doesn't understand. Later, alluding to the vast gulf of life experience between the two, Billie says, ""I ought to take this pencil, and make a circle around you."

By most accounts, it was only after George Cukor and Garson Kanin gave Miss Holliday a show-stopping featured role in *Adam's Rib* (1949) that Cohn was persuaded she should play his Billie Dawn. But the actress claimed otherwise, telling columnist Hedda Hopper (March 5, 1950), "On the contrary, [Cohn] felt that he wanted to be the first to make a successful picture with me, and after *Adam's Rib* I thought *Born Yesterday* was gone and forgotten." When Miss Holliday arrives in Hollywood for filming, she had a distinctly inauspicious first meeting with Cohn, who reportedly gave her the once-over, and remarked, "Well, I've worked with fat asses before."[104]

Recently named Vice-President in Charge of Production at Columbia, Sylvan Simon was assigned to produce *Born Yesterday*. As with most film adaptations of stage plays, the makers of *Born Yesterday* sought to "open up" the script, including scenes that took place outside the four walls of the hotel suite that had been the only set of the Broadway production. Simon arranged to take a contingent of actors, crew, and director George Cukor for a location shoot in Washington, D.C. The resulting footage allowed the film to depict rather than discuss (as in the play) how Billie is affected by the city's landmarks, awakening her interest in American history.

Simon, according to the film's pressbook, learned that "Washington is probably America's toughest city in which to film background shots because of the red tape involved." After much difficulty, he obtained clearance for scenes shot at the National Museum of Art, the Library of Congress, and on the steps of the Capitol. Aside from obtaining the needed permissions, he had to insure that caution was used in shooting the scene in which Billie visits the Library of Congress, awed by the Bill of Rights and the Declaration of Independence. "These documents are so fragile that library representatives permitted only lights of a certain intensity to be focused on them."[105]

Not surprisingly, the screenplay caused censorship arguments for studio executives, as the Hays Office balked at some of the dialogue and situations from Kanin's play. The Columbia contingent successfully argued for the retention of key lines depicting Billie's flirtation with Paul, notably "If you don't act friendly, I don't act friendly. If you know what I mean."[106] Still, as author Gerald Gardner remarked, "With or without the occasional ripe remark, *Born Yesterday* was a thoroughly moral and ethical story."[107] Some changes could not be avoided. In the play, it's implicit that Billie is Harry's mistress; the screen version labels her a "fiancée," and the elaborate, multi-roomed set depicting their hotel suite makes it clear that she has her own room. The character of Norval Hedges, in Kanin's original script, is said to be a U.S. Senator, but the screenplay leaves it at "Congressman."

Though it would be an exaggeration to call *Born Yesterday* a one-woman show, it inevitably rises or falls on the performance of the actress who plays Billie. Mostly silent during her first scene, Holliday's first spoken line shatters any appearance of gentility, when she screeches "Whaa—aat?" at Harry from a distance. From there, she goes on to create a marvelously detailed portrait of Kanin's multilayered character, who reveals much more than the seemingly dumb blonde we originally assume her to be. As her biographer later wrote of her stage portrayal, the actress "gave Billie a naïve charm and child's ingenuousness that contrasted with the outward brassiness. Her attention to detail led to a rare blend of simplicity and density, a sort of unformed integrity which lent credibility to the show's more transparent plot turns."[108]

Miss Holliday gives spot-on deliveries of the many comic lines in the script, but doesn't stop at that. When Harry yells at Billie, embarrassing her in front of Paul and others, one can sense the tears welling in her eyes. The actress gives Billie a beautiful smile, all the more dazzling because it's kept under wraps until some 40 minutes into the film, when she bestows it unexpectedly on Holden's character.

She was not the only veteran of the Broadway cast to be given the opportunity to reprise her role on film; Columbia also signed featured players Howard St. John, Frank Otto, and Larry Oliver. David Pardoll (1908–1988) was an experienced Broadway stage manager who had performed that function for the Broadway production of *Born Yesterday*. He was engaged to assist in the making of the film, overseeing dialogue, and also appeared briefly on-camera as Harry's barber. Character actress Barbara Brown (1901–1975) provides a stark contrast to the character of Billie, playing the senator's very proper spouse. Miss Brown enjoyed recurring roles in two movie series—as wife to Raymond Walburn in Monogram's "Father" series, and as snobbish kinfolk Elizabeth Parker in Universal's Ma and Pa Kettle pictures.

At a studio preview in Santa Barbara on August 31, 1950, overall reaction indicated that casting Miss Holliday had been the right choice. Comments on her performance included:

"Let's see more of the female star—she is very rare."

"Stole the picture—her versatile personality kept the audience in an uproar—she's terrific."

"Finest comedienne ever—should win the Oscar."

"Almost had me believing there are people that dumb."

Simon was delighted when, against stiff competition, Miss Holliday won the Academy Award for Best Actress on March 29, 1951.

Reviews: "An excellent adult comedy.... What really puts the picture over is the brilliant performance of Judy Holliday.... What she says and does is so uproariously funny that many a line of the witty dialogue is drowned out by the audience's hearty laughter." *Harrison's Reports*, November 25, 1950

"The bright, biting comedy of the Garson Kanin legit piece adapts easily to film.... The dumb, sexy character [Holliday] plays is one the public will take to its heart.... George Cukor's direction, always with emphasis on the chorine character, belts many laughs as he sends the players through their paces.... The S. Sylvan Simon production dress has a costly look in the hotel setting as photographed by Joseph Walker." *Variety*, November 22, 1950

Appendix: Books Written or Edited by S. Sylvan Simon

- *Camp Theatricals: Making Your Camp Entertainments More Effective.* New York: Samuel French, 1934.

Simon's first published book drew largely on his experiences at the Schroon Lake Camp, explaining why and how to incorporate dramatics into the summer camp experience. Topics include set design, choosing appropriate plays, rehearsing and training inexperienced actors, and the introduction of music into shows. A bibliography of recommended plays is included.

Review: "In *Camp Theatricals*, Mr. Sylvan Simons [*sic*] offers an invaluable handbook for the director of camps, and indeed the book offers suggestive help for directors of amateur groups in any environment. With directions and suggestions very clearly presented, fully illustrated with drawings and plans ... the practical value of Mr. Simon's manual can scarcely be overstated." *Hartford Courant*, June 24, 1934

- *Easily Staged Plays for Boys: Nine New Non-Royalty Plays*, compiled by S. Sylvan Simon. New York: Samuel French, 1936.

This is the first of Simon's four published volumes of plays and skits that can be performed by amateur groups without payment of royalties, and with modest requirements for sets and technical skills. In his Foreword, Simon explains, "Many of the plays contained herein were written especially for this volume at my request.... A few of the plays have already been successfully produced in preparatory schools and drama league contests." A note preceding his play "The Knothole" indicates that it was "originally presented at Schroon Lake Camp for Boys, Schroon Lake, N.Y., August, 1935."

The anthology contains two plays written by Simon:

"The Knothole," a detective play for high schools. Gang leader Joe, a "gentleman crook," plots to eliminate his rival, Red Hennessey. A fan of S.S. Van Dine's detective stories, Joe makes plans for Hennessey's murder, deliberately incriminating himself, but his scheme includes a twist that he feels sure will torpedo the police's case against him. The authorities are initially stymied when Hennessey is fatally shot, as Joe challenges them to produce the missing murder weapon. Marlowe, a new young detective, finds his experience working in his father's pet shop unexpectedly helpful in cracking the case.

"Two True," a comedy of camp life. At a summer camp in the Adirondacks, four boys who are bunkmates try to solve the mystery of who subjected them to a series of pranks, including sheets tied in knots, and a bucket of water set to soak one unlucky camper.

Also included are the following plays by other authors:

"The Scary Ape," a farce for all ages, by Albert Mannheimer.
"Away from the Road," a serious drama for older boys, by Hugh MacMullan.
"Alas, Poor Yorick," a comedy for young boys, by Ray E. Hurd.
"The Interrupted Flight," a prep school adventure, by Marion Holbrook.
"The Devil Waits," a melodrama for older boys, by Hugh MacMullan.

"Zebra Dun," a comedy for Dude Ranchers, by Iris Vinton.
"Chief Standum Bull," a black-out sketch for young boys, by E.P. Conkle.

- *Thrillers! Seven New No-Royalty Plays for Men and Boys*, compiled by S. Sylvan Simon. New York: Samuel French, 1937.

This anthology contains the following plays written by Simon:

"Trouble in Tunnel Nine," a melodrama. Coal miner Jan Novak is foreman over a three-man crew that includes his two sons, burly Dave and younger, bookish Pete. Jan, who thinks Pete looks down on him for his lack of education, discourages his son's efforts to better himself. But when a cave-in puts the lives of all four men in jeopardy, it's Pete who proves his mettle with a plan derived from his book learning.

"Everything's Just Dandy," a comedy. Teenage Duke Warren and his pals begin a two-week camping trip by settling the question of who will take on the unwanted role of camp cook. Chubby "Lardpail" draws the short straw, but the others agree that the first one who complains about his cooking will have to take his place. Frustrated by his friends' determinedly positive attitudes, even as various mishaps befall them, Lardpail serves them a meal they'll never forget.

"The Scoop Reporter," a melodrama. Chris, proprietor of a nondescript beanery that caters to newspapermen, is none too happy to have racketeers Zeiger and Pappas demand the use of his back room. Jerry Shaw, an unsuccessful cub reporter for the *Chronicle* whose job is hanging by a thread, sees a chance to redeem himself when he's tipped off to the presence of the gangsters. But the scoop he's dreamed of landing comes at a heavy price.

"Nothing Up His Sleeve," a farce. Young Tom earns $3 a week clerking at Hardwick's General Store, but he yearns to become a famous magician. His efforts to complete his correspondence course in prestidigitation irritate his boss, but finally pay off when the store becomes the scene of an attempted robbery.

Also included are the following plays by other authors:

"Remember Death!" a drama, by Charles Grayson.
"Black Male," a comedy, by Ray E. Hurd.
"Signal at Dawn," a drama, by Iris Vinton.

The H.W. Wilson Company's *Standard Catalog for Public Libraries*, a well-established book selection source for librarians, recommended purchase of *Thrillers!* "Short plays without literary value but pleasant and entertaining and suitable for high school or amateur production."

"Trouble in Tunnel Nine" was reprinted in *Adventures in Reading*, an anthology of recommended readings for Catholic high school students, with follow-up questions and notes for discussion, such as "Find speeches of Pete's which show that he is somewhat scornful and intolerant. Find others which prove him sympathetic and ambitious." Another excerpt is used to introduce the concept of foreshadowing.

- *Easily Staged Plays for Girls: Nine New Non-Royalty Plays*, compiled by S. Sylvan Simon. New York: Samuel French, 1937.

A counterpart to Simon's previous volume of plays for boy actors. In the introduction, Simon explains, "I made a survey of the present catalogues of the leading publishers and have tried to include in this book the types of plays hardest to find ... the majority of the plays can be produced simply and inexpensively."

The volume includes the following plays by Simon:

"Murder at Mrs. Loring's," a melodrama. Young nurse Jane Peterson is assigned to care for wealthy Mrs. Loring, whose psychiatrist says she suffers from a persecution complex. Jane soon realizes that one of the inhabitants of the Loring household does in fact have malevolent intentions. But when a fatal shot is fired in the dining room, the victim is not Mrs. Loring but her husband. Revealing herself as a detective, Jane deduces the method and the motive behind his murder.

"Merry Wives of Boredom," a farce. Suburban wife Mary leads her friends and neighbors in a revolution against their husbands. Among the demands in their "New Code for Domestic

Happiness" manifesto are more social outings, new clothes, and spending money. After holing up at Mary's house while chores are neglected and meals fail to appear as scheduled, cracks begin to appear in their united front. One of Simon's most frequently staged one-acts, produced by amateur groups from the 1930s into the 1970s.

"American Beauty," a comedy for adolescents. Several teenage students at the Fairdale School for Girls are excited by the upcoming visit of Lady Gilda, an alumna seeking a fresh face to model her cosmetics line. Snobbish, rich Joan feels confident she'll be chosen, while Ellen, who can't afford a suitable dress, decides it's useless for her to compete. A Cinderella story.

Along with Simon's contributions, this volume also contains the following pieces attributed to his wife Harriet Lee Berk.

"When Love Is Very, Very Young," a comedy for youngsters. Seven-year-old tomboy Katherine "Kit" Carson and eight-year-old vamp "Bobby" Jones, both attending a camp for girls in the Adirondacks, discuss the boy that has caught their attention, in this "little episode of life's first love."

"Information Please!" a vaudeville sketch. A series of brief blackouts depicts the confusion that results when stenographer Maizie temporarily fills in for a friend at the information desk of a large metropolitan depot, answering in her own fashion the inquiries of an old maid, a miser, and a nudist, among others.

The following plays by other authors are also included.

"Silver Lining," a drama, by Dmitri Komonosov.

"Fur A-Flyin'," a comedy, by John Allen.

"Just Another Saturday," a drama, by John Wiley.

"Storm Bound," a drama for one, by Dmitri Komonosov.

- *Melodramas for Madame: Nine New Non-Royalty Plays for Women.* New York: Samuel French, 1938.

This anthology provides material for use by women's clubs and other groups with exclusively female casts. All but one of the plays were written by Simon. "I have tried to include in this volume many plays off the beaten track; so that the experimental theatres might find some expression for their work." His introduction thanks Mannheimer, "one of Hollywood's leading scenarists, for permission to use his play."

The contents include:

"Women's Ward," a prison drama. Young mother Mary was convicted of manslaughter after killing the abusive husband who mistreated their child. Sharing a cell with hardened prisoner Sadie and her more sympathetic sidekick Goldie, Mary becomes caught up in their plot to escape. A guard suspicious that a breakout is imminent reassigns Mary to a cell with stool pigeon May, who resorts to a cruel hoax to get the information that will earn her a parole.

"Girls in White," a drama of a metropolitan hospital. Good-hearted nurse Margaret applauds the efforts of young Dr. Bonner to treat a critically ill child. But when the patient receives a deadly overdose, Dr. Bonner accepts the blame. Margaret, who knows there's more to the story, is determined to make her colleague, another nurse, confess the truth.

"The Road to Glory," a tragedy of Hollywood. Hollywood hopeful Rose, an aspiring singer, resents newcomer Jane, who's been booked to perform at the nightclub where Rose earns her keep as a waitress. Unbeknownst to either of them, Rose's co-worker, an elderly scrubwoman, had dreams of her own that are showcased in a tragic denouement. A cautionary tale.

"Domestic Tie-Up," a matrimonial adventure. Housewife Mary argues with her husband over a new dress she wants. Following the example of workers at a nearby mill, Mary declares a sit-down strike, refusing to do any housework until her demands are met.

"Entre Act," a backstage drama. Stage star Judith Gregory sets her sights on the younger boyfriend of her understudy Lucy. After firing Lucy, Judith collapses in her dressing room. But the doctor who's summoned to treat her proves to be a surprise in more ways than one.

"Wish You Were," a summer camp adventure. Christine is one of several disadvantaged young women spending two weeks at a municipal summer camp. Despising her impoverished existence, she sneaks out at night to see bank robber Joe Willson. Conspiring to aid his get-away after his latest heist, she has second thoughts when one of her fellow campers unknow-ingly walks into danger.

"Sanitarium," a drama of an insane asylum. It's difficult to tell the staff from the patients at Dr. Miller's sanitarium, where young Miss Dickson just arrived to apply for a nursing job.

"Blonde Brigade," a drama which is almost a comedy. Ruth and her friends have formed the Tuesday Afternoon Improvement Club, dedicated to solving the problems of the modern world. Deciding to tackle the issue of warfare, the ladies brainstorm "a battalion of blondes" that no soldier would dare attack. Their idea is put to the test when noises from the next room suggest the presence of an intruder.

The only play not by Simon is "Two Against the Odds," a melodrama, by Albert Mann-heimer, Jr.

Review: "There is reason to believe that if these plays are so alluring and enjoyable when read, their success on the stage would not be uncertain.... There are touching scenes of mater-nal devotion, hard boiled maneuvers characteristic of prison hussies, reflections of tender regard and thwarted ambitions, and there is a good deal more." Streeter Stuart, *The Daily Oklahoman*, October 16, 1938.

• *Laughingly Yours*, by Milton Berle; edited by S. Sylvan Simon. New York: Samuel French, 1939.

Simon compiled this collection of jokes and skits for comedian Milton Berle, a personal friend. In his introduction, Simon explains, "When this book was first contemplated it was our desire to provide the amateur thespians of the country with material for use in their vaude-ville sketches and short programs. However.... I felt that numerous letters and word-by-word stenographic descriptions of Milton Berle's acts might provide interesting reading ... and so it is that this book consists of both anecdotes to be read and sketches to be acted." The contents are as follows:

"My philosophy of life."
"Berle plays Loew's State."
"My experiences in Hollywood."
"Some letters stolen from the mailman."
"Seven vaudeville sketches: Berle meets a heckler—One drink. One drunk—Berle meets a girl in Central Park—Nuts for two—John X. Dope meets Milton Berle—Sally is silly in the spring—Berle, the bookmaker."
"A radio play adaptable for the stage: You can't try an insane man."
"A complete one-act play: Hotel hokum."

Review: "It's as laugh provoking as Berle often can be." *Brooklyn Daily Eagle*, November 28, 1939

• *Let's Make Movies*. New York: Samuel French, 1940.

Published a few years after he had begun his Hollywood directing career, this book is aimed primarily at the amateur learning to effectively use his motion picture camera. Simon, himself a camera buff, offers tips for better photography and in-camera visual effects.

Reviews: "Contains everything the amateur motion picture cameraman should know. Pro-fusely illustrated, [it] also provides many inexpensive means of achieving startling effects with the camera." *Pittsburgh Sun-Telegraph*, July 3, 1940

"Gives concise, readable and helpful hints on getting the proper equipment, photograph-ing indoors, film editing, trick photography and filming weddings and parties." *Leader-Post* (Regina, Saskatchewan, Canada), August 11, 1951

A report in the *Oakland Tribune* (December 20, 1942) indicated, "Simon is now gather-ing material for another book on the motion picture industry ... a treatise on motion pictures and the part they're playing in the war effort." However, such a volume was never published.

Notes

Part I

1. Richard Simon, personal interview. All other quotes from Richard Simon in this section are from this interview.
2. Cindy De La Hoz, *Lucy at the Movies* (Philadelphia: Running Press, 2007). p. 293.
3. *Ibid.*, p. 305.
4. Susan Granger, personal interview. All other quotes from Susan Granger in this section are from this interview.
5. Charles Higham, *Lucy: The Life of Lucille Ball* (New York: St. Martin's Press, 1986), p. 100.
6. "100 Proof Stimulant," *Lion's Roar*, November 1945.
7. Margaret O'Brien, personal interview. All other quotes from Margaret O'Brien in this section are from this interview.
8. Maxine Garrison, "Hollywood Pattern Changes While You Watch It," *Pittsburgh Press*, September 15, 1941.
9. https://popularpittsburgh.com/pittsburgh-jewish-heritage, accessed December 2, 2019.
10. www.jewishfamilieshistory.org/entry/-simon-family, accessed November 12, 2019.
11. Eleanor M. Sickels, *Twelve Daughters of Democracy: True Stories of American Women, 1865–1930* (Freeport, NY: Books for Libraries Press, 1968), p. 211.
12. "Driven to His Death," *San Francisco Chronicle*, February 10, 1892.
13. "Local Brevities," *Hanford* (CA) *Semi-Weekly Journal*, February 23, 1892.
14. Sickels, *Twelve Daughters*, p. 211.
15. Sophie Irene Loeb, *Everyman's Child* (New York: Century, 1920), unpaged.
16. Marie M'Swigan, "East End Woman, Mother, Is Graduated at Pitt Exercises," *Pittsburgh Press*, June 11, 1929.
17. Sophie Irene Loeb, "Hasty Weddings Often Cause Repentance," *Oakland Tribune*, April 23, 1910.
18. Mrs. Walter Ferguson, "Sophie Irene Loeb," *Pittsburgh Press*, February 11, 1929.
19. "Sophie Irene Loeb Honored as Public Benefactress; New York Mayor Lauds Her Welfare Work," *Shamokin News-Dispatch*, December 28, 1926.
20. Ishbel Ross, *Ladies of the Press: The Story of Women in Journalism by an Insider* (New York: Harper, 1936), p. 118.
21. Ferguson, "Sophie Irene Loeb."
22. Maxine Schwartz Seller, ed., *Immigrant Women* (Philadelphia: Temple University Press, 1981), p. 246.
23. www.jewishfamilieshistory.org/entry/-markowitz-family, accessed November 12, 2019.
24. "Overnight Burlesque Circuit," *Variety*, September 24, 1910.
25. "Burlesque Coming," *San Francisco Dramatic Review*, October 8, 1910.
26. "Pantages Opens His New Theatre in Los Angeles," *San Francisco Dramatic Review*, October 1, 1910.
27. Advertisement, *Lawton* (OK) *News*, August 10, 1915.
28. *Morning News* (Wilmington, DE), February 17, 1916.
29. "David Simon Opens Branches," *Moving Picture World*, January 1, 1916.
30. "In the Courts," *Wid's Daily*, June 13, 1919.
31. Barbara Burstin, "Squirrel Hill's Jewish History." In Helen Wilson, ed., *Squirrel Hill: A Neighborhood History* (Charleston, SC: History Press, 2017), p. 76.
32. Patricia Lowry, "A Push to Preserve Urban Villages," *Pittsburgh Post-Gazette*, March 6, 2000.
33. "Big Booze Profits Asked for in Suit," *Pittsburgh Press*, September 17, 1922.
34. Advertisement, *Pittsburgh Press*, September 16, 1928.
35. Stephen Simon, personal interview.
36. Legal notice, *Pittsburgh Press*, October 28, 1929.
37. Lewis Mumford, *Sketches from Life: The Autobiography of Lewis Mumford, the Early Years* (New York: Dial Press, 1982), p. 348.
38. *Ibid.*
39. Quoted in Kristen Larsen, *Community Architect: The Life and Vision of Clarence S. Stein* (Ithaca, NY: Cornell University Press, 2017), p. 1.
40. Larsen, *Community Architect*, p. 68–69.
41. Kermit Carlyle Parsons, *The Writings of Clarence S. Stein: Architect of the Planned Community* (Baltimore: Johns Hopkins University Press, 1998), p. 183n1.

42. Mumford, *Sketches from Life*, p. 348.

43. Garrison, "Hollywood Pattern."

44. Lynne Conner, *Pittsburgh in Stages: Two Hundred Years of Theater* (Pittsburgh: University of Pittsburgh Press, 2007), p. 104.

45. *Ibid.*

46. "Will Repeat Tolstoy Play in 'Y' Tomorrow," *Pittsburgh Press*, November 7, 1927.

47. "Schenley High School to Open with Fall Term," *Pittsburgh Daily Post*, September 17, 1916.

48. "Sid Marke," *Pittsburgh Press*, June 1, 1985.

49. Andrei S. Markovits and Kenneth Garner, *Hillel at Michigan, 1926/27–1945: Struggles of Jewish Identity in a Pivotal Era* (Ann Arbor, MI: Maize Books, 2016), p. 28.

50. *Ibid.*

51. "Local Freshman Wins Michigan Honors," *Pittsburgh Press*, May 5, 1929.

52. "Sophie Irene Loeb Bequeathes [*sic*] All $100,000 to Family," *American Israelite*, February 8, 1929.

53. www.centralparknyc.org/attractions/-sophie-loeb-fountain, accessed December 12, 2019.

53. "Hillel Players to Appear Soon," *Michigan Daily*, March 5, 1930.

54. "Play Group Plans Series of Dramas," *Michigan Daily*, October 10, 1930.

55. Jerry E. Rosenthal, "Music and Drama," *Michigan Daily*, April 30, 1932.

56. "Buzzers, Lights, Telephones, and Five Alert Men Make Broadcasting Possible," *Michigan Daily*, November 3, 1929.

57. "Bates Will Speak on Radio Tonight," *Michigan Daily*, December 7, 1929.

58. "Detroit Station to Radio J-Hop," *Lansing State Journal*, February 13, 1930.

59. "Is Your Darling a Broadcaster?" *The Michigan Alumnus*, v. 37 (1930–1931), p. 407.

60. S. Sylvan Simon, supplementary alumni file, April 1940. Bentley Historical Library, University of Michigan, Ann Arbor, Michigan.

61. Marianne R. Sanua, *Going Greek: Jewish College Fraternities in the United States, 1895–1945* (Detroit: Wayne State University Press, 2003), p. 78.

62. Bill Treadwell, *50 Years of American Comedy* (New York: Exposition Press, 1951), p. 140.

63. "Simon Asserts One-Sex Opera Is Valueless," *Michigan Daily*, February 24, 1940.

64. A. Ellis Bell, "Spooks, Cemeteries, To Bring Shivers to 'Dybbuk' Audience," *Michigan Daily*, March 26, 1933.

65. Donald B. Hirsch, "Local Youth Directs Play," *Pittsburgh Press*, April 16, 1933.

66. "Biography of S. Sylvan Simon," *Nanaimo* (British Columbia) *Daily News*, November 21, 1939.

67. Milton K. Sussman, "As I See It," *Jewish Criterion*, May 25, 1951.

68. "Abbott and Costello Are Unpredictable But Director's Sense of Humor Saves Him," *Havre Daily News*, January 4, 1946.

69. Lois Hollander, "A Tour Through Our Junior Hall of Fame," *Jewish Criterion*, September 7, 1934.

70. Nadine Brozan, "Renewing Ties Years After Camp," *New York Times*, September 20, 1982.

71. Bide Dudley, "Theatrical Advertising Capitulates to Radio," *Broadcasting*, September 15, 1932.

72. Naomi Bentan, "Youthful Director Says He Owes All to 'Breaks,'" *Honolulu Advertiser*, September 1, 1940.

73. *Ibid.*

74. Arthur Space, unpublished writings, courtesy Susan Swan and Sondra Thiederman. Hereafter cited as "Space Papers."

75. "Plays and Players," *Pittsburgh Sun-Telegraph*, December 3, 1934.

76. Chester Klevins, "They're Back Again: Amateur Dramatics Are Being Restored to the Eminent Position They Held in the Not Too Distant Past," *Brooklyn Daily Eagle*, December 2, 1934.

77. "Arthur Space on Broadway Stage," *Sunday Times* (New Brunswick, NJ), March 24, 1935.

78. Kate Taylor, "Everything Old Is New Again," *New York Sun*, October 10, 2006.

79. Don Finkelhor, "Interviewing Sylvan Simon," *Jewish Criterion*, April 5, 1935.

80. "Brown Swan Club Popular Resort," *Post-Star* [Glens Fall, NY], July 6, 1920.

81. Quoted in Janet Loughrey, *Gardens Adirondack Style* (Lanham, MD: Down East Books, 2005), p. 21.

82. "Schroon Lake Features," *Philadelphia Inquirer*, June 23, 1935.

83. Don Finkelhor, "Players Group, Inc.," *Jewish Criterion*, August 30, 1935.

84. *Ibid.*

85. "Review Lauds Play Held at Schroon Lake," *Post-Star* [Glens Falls, NY], August 7, 1935.

86. "'Madame Bovary' to Be Given Thursday," *Post-Star* (Glens Falls, NY), August 27, 1935.

87. Bentan, "Youthful Director."

88. "Hollywood," *The Daily Notes* (Canonsburg, PA), July 21, 1947.

89. Harold W. Cohen, "The Drama Desk," *Pittsburgh Post-Gazette*, May 15, 1936.

90. Paul Harrison, "The Blind Test for Movie Talent," *Laredo Times*, February 14, 1937.

91. "Many Are Called," *Motion Picture Studio Insider*, April 1937.

92. S. Sylvan Simon, interoffice memorandum, Universal Studios Collection, USC.

93. Ralph Wilk, "A 'Little' from Hollywood 'Lots,'" *Film Daily*, July 16, 1937.

94. Milton K. Susman, "As I See it," *Jewish Criterion*, August 13, 1937.

95. Martin Murphy, interoffice memorandum, September 4, 1937. Universal Studios Collection, USC.

96. Robbin Coons, "Hollywood Speaks," Mansfield (OH) *News-Journal*, September 1, 1937.

97. Read Kendall, "Around and About in Hollywood," *Los Angeles Times*, October 14, 1937.

98. Milton Harker, "In Hollywood," *Hammond* (IN) *Times*, May 16, 1938.

99. Martin Murphy, interoffice memorandum, July 16, 1938. Universal Studios Collection, USC.

100. "Baby Born on Film Director's Schedule," *Los Angeles Times*, July 23, 1938.

101. Harold W. Cohen, "The Drama Desk," *Pittsburgh Post-Gazette*, November 16, 1938.

102. "He's Youngest Film Director: S. Sylvan Simon is Only 28." *Philadelphia Inquirer*, December 4, 1938.

103. Edwin Schallert, "Picture Career Slated for Sheila O'Sullivan," *Los Angeles Times*, February 17, 1939.

104. Read Kendall, "Around and About in Hollywood," *Los Angeles Times*, March 3, 1939.

105. "Directing Glamour Girls Comes Very Easy to Him!" *Vidette-Messenger* of Porter County, November 13, 1939.

106. "Hollywood's Undeclared War," *Modern Screen*, October 1941.

107. Whitney Bolton, "Lana Turner In Line for Jean Harlow's Mantle," *Philadelphia Inquirer*, September 3, 1939.

108. "Anonymous Gift," *Austin Daily Texan*, June 13, 1940.

109. J.D. Spiro, "On the Lots with the Candid Reporter," *Detroit Free Press*, January 21, 1940.

110. S. Sylvan Simon, "Give the Kids a Break," *Hollywood Reporter*, October 8, 1940.

111. "She Doesn't Want to Be Glamour Girl," *Boston Globe*, March 7, 1940.

112. Harold W. Cohen, "The Drama Desk," *Pittsburgh Post-Gazette*, September 7, 1939.

113. Brecher, Irving, as told to Hank Rosenfeld. *The Wicked Wit of the West*....Teaneck, NJ: Ben Yehuda Press, 2008.

114. Groucho Marx, *The Groucho Letters* (New York: Simon and Schuster, 1967), p. 22.

115. "There's No Joke Like Old Joke," *Oakland Tribune*, January 7, 1940.

116. Dusty Burke, personal interview.

117. Hugh Dixon, "The Monday Wash," *Pittsburgh Post-Gazette*, June 2, 1941.

118. Lynn Thomas, "Dead Man's Leap Beginning of Simon's Stage Career," *Honolulu Star-Bulletin*, September 5, 194

119. Karl Krug, "Simon Pens Tome on Movies," *Pittsburgh Sun-Telegraph*, July 3, 1940.

120. Aline MacMahon, letter to Clarence Stein, March 10, 1941. Clarence Stein papers #3600, Division of Rare and Manuscript Collections, Cornell University Library. Hereafter cited as "Stein Papers."

121. Arthur Marx, *Red Skelton* (New York: Dutton, 1979), p. 139.

122. Maxine Garrison, "Hollywood Pattern Changes While You Watch It," *Pittsburgh Press*, September 15, 1941.

123. Treadwell, *50 Years*, p. 86.

124. MacMahon, Stein Papers.

125. S. Sylvan Simon, "Off the Cuff—On the Cob," *Hollywood Reporter*, November 2, 1943.

126. Todd Livingston, "Scarlett's Sister Ann Rutherford," *Scarlet Street*, #48, 2003.

127. "Comedy on the Cuff," *Lion's Roar*, April 1943.

128. Wes D. Gehring, personal interview.

129. S. Sylvan Simon, letter to Arthur Space, January 29, 1941. Space Papers.

130. Aline MacMahon, letter to Clarence Stein, April 21, 1942. Stein Papers.

131. MacMahon to Stein, May 31, 1942. Stein Papers.

132. Andrew Marton, and Joanne D'Antonio. *Andrew Marton* (Metuchen, NJ: Scarecrow, 1991), p. 131–132.

133. "Simon Meets Red Skelton, His Star, in New York Today," *Pittsburgh Post-Gazette*, March 29, 1943.

134. Helen Tooth, "Victoria Proves Beautiful Location, Says Movie Director," *Times-Colonist* (Victoria, BC), August 28, 1944.

135. Harold V. Cohen, "New Film: Wallace Beery Star of 'Salute to the Marines' at Penn," *Pittsburgh Post-Gazette*, August 27, 1943.

136. Lawrence Perry, "Notables Brunching at Sardi's Talk Films, Dress and Baseball," *Miami News*, May 16, 1943.

137. Erskine Johnson, "Sonja Performs a Tarzan Act," *Kenosha* (WI) *News*, June 17, 1943.

138. *The Cockeyed Miracle* pressbook, Universal collection, USC.

139. Hugh Dixon, "Hollywood," *Pittsburgh Post-Gazette*, February 24, 1944.

140. Harold V. Cohen, "Drama Desk," *Pittsburgh Post-Gazette*, March 14, 1945.

141. Terry Moore, personal interview. All other quotes from Terry Moore are from this interview.

142. Bob Furmanek, and Ron Palumbo, *Abbott and Costello in Hollywood* (New York: Perigee, 1991), p. 130.

143. "Abbott and Costello Are Unpredictable but Director's Sense of Humor Saves Him," *Havre* (MT) *Daily News*, January 4, 1946.

144. *Bud Abbott and Lou Costello in Hollywood*, pressbook.

145. Stephen Simon and Gay Hendricks, *Spiritual Cinema: A Guide to Movies That Inspire, Heal, and Empower Your Life* (Hay House, 2005), p. 9.

146. *The Cockeyed Miracle*, pressbook. Universal Studios Collection, USC.

147. Jerry Ross, "Director Hits Hollywood by Way of Ann Arbor," *Detroit Free Press*, June 28, 1947.

148. Melissa Greene, personal interview. All other quotes from Melissa Greene are from this interview.

149. "Hollywood Film Shop," *Montana Standard*, September 19, 1946.

150. Irving Bennett, "Movies in Homes (Via Phone) Seen," *Pittsburgh Sun-Telegraph*, September 14, 1947.

151. "Movies in Your Parlor Promised," *Austin-American Statesman*, September 18, 1947.

152. "Dial Operator for Latest Movie," *Pittsburgh Sun-Telegraph*, September 13, 1947.

153. Virginia McPherson, "Home Movies by Telephone Advanced to Patent Stage," *Berkshire Eagle* (Pittsfield, MA), September 17, 1947.

154. Edwin Schallert, "'Scarlet Lily' to Italy, with Valli Likely Star," *Los Angeles Times*, February 16, 1948.

155. S. Sylvan Simon, "Sometimes It Doesn't Make Sense," *Hollywood Reporter*, October 11, 1948.

156. *Ibid.*

157. Edward Small, as told to Robert E. Kent. "You Don't Have to Be Crazy to Be in Show Business But It Helps! Autobiography of Edward Small," unpublished memoir. Edward Small Papers, Cinematic Arts Library, University of Southern California, Los Angeles, California. Hereafter cited as "Small Papers."

158. Paul Green, *Roy Huggins: Creator of Maverick, 77 Sunset Strip, The Fugitive, and* The Rockford Files (Jefferson, NC: McFarland, 2014), p. 27.

159. Simon, "Sometimes It."

160. S. Sylvan Simon, letter to Edward Small, September 9, 1947. Small Papers, USC.

161. Small, "You Don't," p. 340.

162. John Todd, "Hollywood Chatter," *Daily Times* (New Philadelphia, Ohio), February 14, 1948.

163. Treadwell, *50 Years*, p. 141.

164. Pat White, "Hollywood Stars Discover Charm of Square Dance," *Courier-Post*, August 11, 1948.

165. "In Hollywood," *The Herald* (Jasper, IN), October 25, 1947.

166. Paul Manning, letter to Edward Small, May 6, 1948. Small papers, USC.

167. "Program Cut Here," *Film Bulletin*, January 5, 1948.

168. Arlene Dahl, personal interview.

169. "Movieland Briefs," *Los Angeles Times*, April 1, 1948.

170. "Cohn Careful Not to Spoil Columbia Customers," *Film Bulletin*, May 10, 1948.

171. S. Sylvan Simon, "Sometimes It Doesn't Make Sense," *Hollywood Reporter*, October 11, 1948.

172. "Thomas Savage, 88, Novelist Drawn to the American West," New York Times, August 25, 2003.

173. Myrna Oliver, "Thomas Savage, 88; Writer Best-Known for Western Novels Set in Montana," *Los Angeles Times*, August 30, 2003.

174. Bernard F. Dick, *Forever Mame: The Life of Rosalind Russell* (Jackson: University Press of Mississippi, 2011), p. 70.

175. Rochelle Larkin, *Hail, Columbia* (New Rochelle, NY: Arlington House, 1975), p. 23.

176. Betty Garrett, with Ron Rapoport. *Betty Garrett and Other Songs: A Life on Stage and Screen* (Lanham, MD: Madison Books, 1997), p. 89.

177. "Motion Picture Units Returning to Arizona," *Arizona Daily Star*, November 29, 1948.

178. Peter Ford, *Glenn Ford: A Life* (Madison: University of Wisconsin Press, 2011), p. 99.

179. C. Courtney Joyner, *The Westerners: Interviews with Actors, Directors, Writers and Producers* (Jefferson, NC: McFarland, 2009), p. 14.

180. Ford, *Glenn Ford*, p. 99.

181. Les Hegele, "Short Take Requires Half Day to Shoot on Columbia Set in Arizona," *Arizona Republic* (Phoenix), December 5, 1948.

182. "Studio in Error, Rita Hayworth Says," *San Francisco Examiner*, December 6, 1948.

183. Barbara Leaming, *If This Was Happiness: A Biography of Rita Hayworth* (New York: Viking, 1989), p. 164.

184. Bernard F. Dick, *The Merchant Prince of Poverty Row: Harry Cohn of Columbia Pictures* (Lexington: University of Kentucky Press, 2015), p. 69.

185. Leon Gutterman, "Our Film Folk," *Wisconsin Jewish Chronicle*, July 22, 1949.

186. Stephen Simon, personal interview.

187. Will Holtzman, *Judy Holliday* (New York: Putnam, 1982), p. 137.

188. Stephen Simon, personal interview.

189. Erskine Johnson, "Johnson's Hollywood," *News-Herald* (Franklin, PA), July 28, 1949.

190. Barry Storm, *I Was Swindled by Red Movie Makers* (Quincy, IL: Storm-Mollet Publishing, 1954), p. 15.

191. Storm, *I Was Swindled*, p. 10.

192. S. Sylvan Simon, letter to Barry Storm, July 13, 1949. www.lost-dutchman.com/dutchman/entries/strtwel.html, accessed November 12, 2019.

193. Doug Stewart, "Tale of the Lost Dutchman: Bibliography, Notes and Chronology," www.-lost-dutchman.com/dutchman/entries/strtwel.html, accessed November 12, 2019.

194. Barry Storm, *Thunder Gods Gold: The Amazing Story of America's Most Famed Lost Gold Mines* (Quincy, IL: Storm-Mollet Publishing, 1954), p. 22.

195. Edwin Schallert, "Clarence Darrow Role Looms for Gary Cooper," *Los Angeles Times*, October 16, 1945.

196. Anthony Slide, *Actors on Red Alert: Career Interviews with Five Actors and Actresses Affected by the Blacklist* (Lanham, MD: Scarecrow, 1999).

197. Slide, *Actors on Red Alert*, p. 29.

198. "Phoenix Author Arranges Row Over Film Portrayal," *Arizona Republic* (Phoenix, AZ), April 16, 1950.

199. Bob Thomas, "Arthur Godfrey Is Waiting for Right Offer from Movies," *Alton* (IL) *Evening Telegraph*, December 3, 1948.

200. Leon Gutterman, "Our Film Folk," *Wisconsin Jewish Chronicle*, July 22, 1949.

201. Garson Kanin, *Hollywood: Stars and Starlets, Tycoons and Flesh-peddlers, Moviemakers and Moneymakers, Frauds and Geniuses, Hopefuls and Has-Beens, Great Lovers and Sex Symbols.* (New York: Viking, 1974), p. 375.

202. "'Born Yesterday' Sample of Waste, Poor Judgment," *Film Bulletin*, August 30, 1948.

203. Harold V. Cohen, "The Drama Desk," *Pittsburgh Post-Gazette*, May 9, 1950.

204. Kanin, *Hollywood*, p. 376.

205. James Sheridan and Barry Monush, *Lucille Ball FAQ: Everything Left to Know About America's Favorite Redhead.* (Milwaukee, WI: Applause, 2011), p. 318.

206. Patricia Clary, "Star Doubts She's Type for Role," *Journal-Herald* (Dayton, OH), June 25, 1949.

207. Ruth Prigozy, "Judy Holliday: The Star and the Studio." In Bernard F. Dick, ed., Columbia Pictures: Portrait of a Studio (Lexington: University Press of Kentucky, 1992), p. 135.

208. "Ten High-Budgeters Gives [*sic*] Studio Busiest Three Weeks," *Film Bulletin*, June 19, 1950.

209. "Step-Up in Profits Gives Col Shot-in-Arm," *Film Bulletin*, November 20, 1950.

210. "Reissues, Remakers, Oaters and Quickies Cohn's Formula," *Film Bulletin*, September 23, 1950.

211. Bob Thomas, *King Cohn: The Life and Times of Harry Cohn* (New York: McGraw-Hill, 1990), p. 204.

212. Stephen Simon, *Bringing Back the Old Hollywood: Wild Times and Life Lessons with Sinatra, Cruise, Reeve, Madonna and More* (Portland, OR: Mystical Movies, 2011), p. 23.

213. Karl Krug, "Weedes Will Write Grand Opera History in 'Rigoletto' Here," *Pittsburgh Sun-Telegraph*, March 14, 1951.

214. Gary Carey, *Judy Holliday: An Intimate Life Story.* (New York: Seaview Books, 1982), p. 117.

215. Harold V. Cohen, "The Drama Desk," *Pittsburgh Post-Gazette*, April 5, 1951.

216. "Fort Myers Author Signs with Movies," *Fort Myers* (FL) *News-Press*, April 2, 1951.

217. Frank MacShane, *Into Eternity: The Life of James Jones, American Writer.* (Boston: Houghton Mifflin, 1985), p. 129.

218. Vincent Sherman, *Studio Affairs: My Life as a Film Director.* (Lexington: University Press of Kentucky, 1996), p. 227.

219. Simon, *Bringing Back*, p. 31.

220. *Ibid.*

221. *Ibid.*, p. 24.

222. *Ibid.*, p. 23.

223. Stephen Simon, personal interview.

224. Christopher Ogden, *Legacy: A Biography of Moses and Walter Annenberg.* (Boston: Little, Brown, 1999), p. 309.

225. *Ibid.*

226. Stephen Simon, personal interview.

227. Stephen Simon and Gay Hendricks, *Spiritual Cinema: A Guide to Movies That Inspire, Heal, and Empower Your Life* (Carlsbad, CA: Hay House, 2006), p. 42.

228. Simon, *Bringing Back*, p. 51.

229. Thomas, *King Cohn*, p. 267.

230. Stephen Simon, personal interview.

231. Harold V. Cohen, "The Drama Desk," *Pittsburgh Post-Gazette*, March 29, 1954.

232. Edwin Schallert, "Guild Pays Honor to Colleges; Cohn Hails Miscasting," *Los Angeles Times*, August 30, 1953.

233. Stephen Simon, personal interview.

234. Simon, *Bringing Back*, p. 47.

235. Bob Colacello, *Ronnie and Nancy: Their Path to the White House, 1911 to 1980* (New York: Warner Books, 2004), p. 286.

Part II

1. Larry Langman, *The Media in the Movies: A Catalog of American Journalism Films, 1900–1996* (Jefferson, NC: McFarland, 1998), p. 107.

2. Naomi Bentan, "Youthful Director Says He Owes All to 'Breaks,'" *Honolulu Advertiser*, September 1, 1940.

3. "'Tropic Holiday' Opens at Stanley; 'I'll Give a Million' Seen at Savar," *Courier-Post* (Camden, NJ), August 6, 1938.

4. Frederick C. Othman, "Hollywood Roundup," *Delta Democrat-Times* (Greenville, MS), January 8, 1938.

5. "Schedule of Actress Filled," *Los Angeles Times*, February 24, 1938.

6. "Hope Hampton Questioned in Mate Shooting," *Nevada State Journal*, January 26, 1939.

7. Universal Studios Collection, Cinematic Arts Library, University of Southern California, Los Angeles, California. Hereafter cited as USC.

8. Treadwell, Bill, *50 Years of American Comedy* (New York: Exposition Press, 1951), p. 141.

9. "29-Year-Old Pittsburgher Movies' Youngest Director," *Pittsburgh Post-Gazette*, April 3, 1939.

10. Cheryl Crane, with Cindy De La Hoz, *Lana: The Memories, the Myths, the Movies* (Philadelphia: Running Press, 2008), p. 254.

11. *Marsha Hunt's Sweet Adversity.*

12. "Seen…Heard…At the Ritz." *Boonville* (IN) *Enquirer*, December 29, 1939.

13. Robin R. Cutler, *Such Mad Fun: Ambition and Glamour in Hollywood's Golden Age.* (Palm Beach, FL: View Tree Press, 2016), p. 169.

14. Harold W. Cohen, "Hollywood," *Pittsburgh Post-Gazette*, August 9, 1939.

15. "College Film Series Is Directed by Grad," *Michigan Daily*, October 24, 1939.

16. "Artie Shaw Has Become 'Double Threat' Man," *Detroit Free Press*, August 13, 1939.

17. Harrison Carroll, "Behind the Scenes in Hollywood," *Morning Herald*, August 10, 1939.

18. Lana Turner, *Lana: The Lady, the Legend, the Truth* (New York: Dutton, 1982), p. 48.

19. Sylvia Shorris, and Marion Abbott Bundy, *Talking Pictures: With the People Who Made Them* (New York: New Press, 1994), p. 53.

20. George Murphy, with Victor Lasky, *"Say ... Didn't You Used to Be George Murphy?"* (New York: Bartholomew House, 1970), p. 225.

21. "Starlet's Plan Proves Love's Labor Lost," *Lansing State Journal*, March 4, 1940.

22. "Young and Gargan Stage Thrilling Rescues in Flames," *MGM Studio News*, May 21, 1940.

23. "Actor Wants Peke If Dog Must Bite," *Pittsburgh Press*, August 4, 1940.

24. "New Town: City of 'Thornridge' Is Built for Movies," *Pittsburgh Press*, December 18, 1940.

25. Maxine Garrison, "Hollywood Pattern Changes While You Watch It," *Pittsburgh Press*, September 15, 1941.

26. Harold Lamb, "Hollywood," *Pensacola News-Journal*, October 8, 1941.

27. "Director Gets Action When He Asks Army..." *Lion's Roar*, issue #5, undated.

28. Will Baltin, "I Saw Stars," *Central New Jersey Home News*, August 9, 1942.

29. "The Bugle Sounds at Louisville," *Lion's Roar*, issue #6, ca. 1942.

30. John Chapman, "Looking at Hollywood," *Chicago Tribune*, December 15, 1941.

31. "Hollywood Notebook," *El Paso Times*, February 1, 1942.

32. "What's Playing at the Theaters," *News-Leader* (Staunton, VA), May 23, 1944.

33. Derek Sculthorpe, *Van Heflin: A Life in Film* (Jefferson, NC: McFarland, 2016), p. 48.

34. Harry R. Warfel, *American Novelists of Today* (New York: American Book Company, 1951), p. 318.

35. Gladwin Hill, "Economy of Materials Turns Paper Into Lumber," *Pittsburgh Sun-Telegraph*, March 21, 1942.

36. W. Franklyn Moshier, "Marjorie Main," *Films in Review*, February 1966, p. 106.

37. "The Other Main," *Lion's Roar*, September/October 1942.

38. Frank F. Gill, "Death Takes a Holiday at Last for ZaSu Pitts," *Detroit Free Press*, December 25, 1942.

39. Aline MacMahon, letter to Clarence Stein, May 12, 1942, Clarence Stein Papers, #3600, Division of Rare and Manuscript Collections, Cornell University Library.

40. Virginia MacPherson, "Susan Goes Musical," *Des Moines Register*, December 7, 1944.

41. Richard Quine, "The Bravest Girl in Town," *Photoplay*, April 1948.

42. Arthur Space, unpublished writings, courtesy of Susan Swan and Sondra Thiederman. Hereafter cited as "Space Papers."

43. "Actor Wally Beery Swallows 'Chaw' of Tobacco for Art," *Baltimore Evening Sun*, November 13, 1942.

44. May Mann, "Wallace Beery Becomes New Taxpayer in Utah," *Ogden Standard-Examiner*, January 17, 1943.

45. "Inside Hollywood," *Long Beach* (CA) *Independent*, June 20, 1943.

46. Rose Hobart, *A Steady Digression to a Fixed Point* (Metuchen, NJ: Scarecrow, 1994), p. 117–118.

47. S. Sylvan Simon, "Film Comment," *Pittsburgh Sun-Telegraph*, August 29, 1943.

48. "Hot Flashes About Actors," *Oakland Tribune*, February 7, 1943.

49. Harold Parrott, "Both Sides," *Brooklyn Daily Eagle*, April 22, 1943.

50. Bruce Peacock, "Stage and Screen," May 4, 1943, *The Leader-Post* (Regina, Saskatchewan, Canada), May 4, 1943.

51. "He Does the Impossible," *Lion's Roar*, April 1943.

52. Jane Powell, *The Girl Next Door ... and How She Grew* (New York: Morrow, 1988), p. 53.

53. Jane Powell, personal interview.

54. "Reginald Denny Gets Role of Director," *Rochester* (NY) *Democrat and Chronicle*, December 10, 1943.

55. John Truesdell, "In Hollywood," *Des Moines Register*, December 6, 1943.

56. "Film Beauty Kills Self After Lovers' Scrap," *New York Daily News*, April 14, 1945.

57. Peter Haining, ed., *Lassie: The Extraordinary Story of Eric Knight and the World's Favourite Dog* (London: Peter Owen, 2006), p. 72–73.

58. Bob Willett, "Lassie Made a Lasting Impression," *Times-Colonist* [Victoria, BC], August 15, 1993.

59. James Spada, *Peter Lawford: The Man Who Kept the Secrets* (New York: Bantam, 1992), p. 114.

60. Helen Tooth, "Governor Sees Shooting of 'Son of Lassie,'" *Times-Colonist* (Victoria, BC), August 16, 1944.

61. John L. Scott, "Covered Wagons Roll Again on Four Screens," *Los Angeles Times*, August 17, 1946.

62. Harold Heffernan, "War Movies Running into Fans' Disfavor; 'Robe' Shelved Too," *Ottawa Citizen*, July 14, 1945.

63. Margaret O'Brien, personal interview. All other quotations from Margaret O'Brien in this section are from this interview.

64. "Hollywood Roundup," *Belvidere* (IL) *Daily Republican*, December 3, 1945.

65. Ann Miller, *Miller's High Life* (Garden City, NY: Doubleday, 1972), p. 142.

66. "Ghosts in Barn Upset 'Lovers,'" *South Bend Tribune*, January 20, 1946.

67. Jeffrey Brown Martin, *The Screenplays of Ben Hecht* (Ann Arbor, MI: University Microfilms, 1980), p. 307.

68. "Stand-In Stars with a Star," *Oakland Tribune*, April 27, 1947.

69. "Being Actor, Executive Quick Way to Breakdown, Says Tone," *Syracuse Post-Standard*, December 22, 1947.

70. John Todd, "Fairbanks Says Catnaps Secret of His Vitality," *Tampa Bay Times*, June 2, 1947.

71. Paul Green, *Roy Huggins: Creator of* Maverick, 77 Sunset Strip, The Fugitive, *and* The Rockford Files (Jefferson, NC: McFarland, 2014).

72. S. Sylvan Simon, "Sometimes It Doesn't Make Sense," *Hollywood Reporter*, October 11, 1948.

73. John L. Scott, "Glamorous Girl Learns She Should Have Been Acrobat for Role in Skelton Film," *Los Angeles Times*, December 28, 1947.

74. Edward Small as told to Robert E. Kent. "You Don't Have to Be Crazy to Be in Show Business But It Helps! Autobiography of Edward Small." Unpublished memoir. Edward Small Papers, Cinematic Arts Library, University of Southern California, Los Angeles, California.

75. Arthur Marx, *Red Skelton* (New York: Dutton, 1979), p. 140.

76. Harold Heffernan, "Speedup of Film Making Threat to Health of Actors," *Boston Globe*, March 9, 1948.

77. Derek Sculthorpe, *Brian Donlevy, the Good Bad Guy: A Bio-Filmography* (Jefferson, NC: McFarland, 2017), p. 111.

78. Ida Zeitlin, "'It's Not a Dream, Darling,'" *Modern Screen*, October 1948.

79. Halliday, Jon, *Sirk on Sirk: Conversations with Jon Halliday* (London: Secker & Warburg, 1971), p. 79.

80. *Ibid.*, p. 77.

81. David J. Hogan, *Film Noir FAQ: All That's Left to Know About Hollywood's Golden Age of Dames, Detectives and Danger* (Milwaukee, WI: Applause, 2013), p. 46.

82. "Wiseman Repays Stage Debt; Mrs. Minciotti Reaps Reward," *Brooklyn Daily Eagle*, November 20, 1949.

83. Susan Granger, personal interview.

84. "Superstition Mountain Location of New Picture," *Arizona Times*, May 27, 1948.

85. Bill Hines, "Start of 'Greed' Film Signaled by Governor," *Phoenix Gazette*, unpaged.

86. S. Sylvan Simon, memo to Ted Sherdeman. Ted Sherdeman papers, Box 12, American Heritage Center, University of Wyoming, Laramie, Wyoming.

87. Storm, *Thunder Gods' Gold: The Amazing Story of America's Most Famed Lost Gold Mines* (Quincy, IL: Storm-Mollet Publishing, 1954), p. 166.

88. William Donato, *Ida Lupino: A Biography* (Lexington: University Press of Kentucky, 2001), p. 145.

89. Peg O'Brien, "Movies Strive for Perfection in Every Scene—and Get It by Endless Retakes," *Janesville* (WI) *Daily Gazette*, April 14, 1949.

90. Thomas F. Brady, "Columbia Revives 'Mother for May,'" *New York Times*, June 16, 1949.

91. Boyd Magers and Michael Fitzgerald, *Westerns Women: Interviews with 50 Leading Ladies of Movie and Television Westerns from the 1930s to the 1960s.* (Jefferson, NC: McFarland, 1999), p. 98).

92. James Edward Grant, "A Mother for May," first draft, February 17, 1949. Aleen Leslie Papers, American Heritage Center, University of Wyoming, Laramie, Wyoming.

93. Donald Kirkley, "Superior Slapstick," *Baltimore Sun*, June 16, 1950.

94. Bernard Rosenberg and Harry Silverstein, *The Real Tinsel* (New York: Macmillan, 1970), p. 285.

95. Howard C. Heyn, "Good Humor Man Takes Record Trip for Movie," *Newport News* (VA) *Daily Express*, June 26, 1949.

96. Howard C. Meyn, "Those Movie Gag Shots Strain Picture Budgets," *Pensacola News-Journal*, November 27, 1949.

97. Buddy Mason, "Behind the Movie Sets," *The Messenger* (Paterson, NJ), May 25, 1950.

98. "Call Pie Hurling a Very Rare Art," *Lansing State Journal*, April 7, 1950.

99. "Fuller Brush Girl Spurns Film Role," *Austin American* (Austin, TX), February 28, 1950.

100. "100 Star Secrets of Hollywood Glamour," *Photoplay*, January 1951.

101. Lucille Ball with Betty Hannah Hoffman, *Love, Lucy* (New York: Putnam, 1996), p. 193.

102. Marjory Adams, "Eddie Albert, Wife Margo Are Looking for a Play," *Boston Globe*, April 23, 1950.

103. Emanuel Levy, *George Cukor, Master of Elegance: Hollywood's Legendary Director and His Stars* (New York: Morrow, 1994), p. 191.

104. Bob Thomas, *King Cohn: The Life and Times of Harry Cohn* (New York: McGraw-Hill, 1990), p. 290.

105. "Film Version of 'Born Yesterday' Opening at the Palace on Friday," *Montreal Gazette*, April 10, 1951.

106. Gerald Gardner, *The Censorship Papers: Movie Censorship Letters from the Hays Office, 1934 to 1968* (New York: Dodd, Mead, 1987), p. 150.

107. *Ibid.*, p. 149.

108. Will Holtzman, *Judy Holliday* (New York: Putnam, 1982), p. 117.

Bibliography

Books

Anna Mercedes, Leo F. Halpin, Marie Theresa, and Basilian Richard, eds. *Adventures in Reading*. Cardinal Newman ed. New York: Harcourt, Brace, 1954.

Ball, Lucille, with Betty Hannah Hoffman. *Love, Lucy*. New York: Putnam, 1996.

Bingen, Stephen, Stephen X. Sylvester, and Michael Troyan. *M-G-M: Hollywood's Greatest Backlot*. Solana Beach, CA: Santa Monica Press, 2011.

Brecher, Irving, as told to Hank Rosenfeld. *The Wicked Wit of the West: The Last Great Golden-Age Screenwriter Shares the Hilarity and Heartaches of Working with Groucho, Garland, Gleason, Berle, Burns, Benny, and Many More*. Teaneck, NJ: Ben Yehuda Press, 2008.

Carey, Gary. *Judy Holliday: An Intimate Life Story*. New York: Seaview Books, 1982.

Colacello, Bob. *Ronnie and Nancy: Their Path to the White House, 1911 to 1980*. New York: Warner Books, 2004.

Conner, Lynne. *Pittsburgh in Stages: Two Hundred Years of Theater*. Pittsburgh: University of Pittsburgh Press, 2007.

Crane, Cheryl, with Cindy De La Hoz. *Lana: The Memories, the Myths, the Movies*. Philadelphia: Running Press, 2008.

Cutler, Robin R. *Such Mad Fun: Ambition and Glamour in Hollywood's Golden Age*. Palm Beach, FL: View Tree Press, 2016.

De La Hoz, Cindy. *Lucy at the Movies*. Philadelphia: Running Press, 2007.

Dick, Bernard F. *Forever Mame: The Life of Rosalind Russell*. Jackson: University Press of Mississippi, 2011.

_____. *The Merchant Prince of Poverty Row: Harry Cohn of Columbia Pictures*. Lexington: University Press of Kentucky, 2015.

_____, ed. *Columbia Pictures: Portrait of a Studio*. Lexington: University Press of Kentucky, 1992.

Donati, William. *Ida Lupino: A Biography*. Lexington: University Press of Kentucky, 2001.

Ebsen, Buddy. *The Other Side of Oz*. Newport Beach, CA: Donovan Publishing, 1993.

Eells, George. *Final Gig: The Man Behind the Murder*. San Diego: Harcourt Brace Jovanovich, 1991.

Ellenberger, Allan. *Margaret O'Brien: A Career Chronicle and Biography*. Jefferson, NC: McFarland, 2000.

Ford, Peter. *Glenn Ford: A Life*. Madison: University of Wisconsin Press, 2011.

Furmanek, Bob, and Ron Palumbo. *Abbott and Costello in Hollywood*. New York: Perigee, 1991.

Fury, David. *Maureen O'Sullivan: No Average Jane*. Minneapolis, MN: Artist's Press, 2006.

Gardner, Gerald. *The Censorship Papers: Movie Censorship Letters from the Hays Office, 1934 to 1968*. New York: Dodd, Mead, 1987.

Gargiulo, Suzanne. *Hans Conried: A Biography, With a Filmography and a Listing of Radio, Television, Stage, and Voice Work*. Jefferson, NC: McFarland, 2002.

Garrett, Betty, with Ron Rapoport. *Betty Garrett and Other Songs: A Life on Stage and Screen*. Lanham, MD: Madison Books, 1997.

Gehring, Wes D. *Forties Film Funnymen: The Decade's Great Comedians at Work in the Shadow of War*. Jefferson, NC: McFarland, 2010.

_____. *Red Skelton: The Mask behind the Mask*. Indianapolis: Indiana Historical Society Press, 2013.

Granger, Susan. *150 Timeless Movies*. Stamford, CT: Hannacroix Creek, 2017.

Green, Paul. *Roy Huggins: Creator of Maverick, 77 Sunset Strip, The Fugitive, and The Rockford Files*. Jefferson, NC: McFarland, 2014.

Grimes, Karolyn. *Zuzu's Wonderful Life in the Movies: The Story of Karolyn Grimes*. Seattle, WA: Artful Dragon, 2000.

Haining, Peter, ed. *Lassie: The Extraordinary Story of Eric Knight and the World's Favourite Dog*. London: Peter Owen, 2006.

Halliday, Jon. *Sirk on Sirk: Conversations with Jon Halliday*. London: Secker & Warburg, 1971.

Higham, Charles. *Lucy: The Life of Lucille Ball*. New York: St. Martin's Press, 1986.

Hobart, Rose. *A Steady Digression to a Fixed Point*. Metuchen, NJ: Scarecrow, 1994.

Hogan, David J. *Film Noir FAQ: All That's Left to Know about Hollywood's Golden Age of Dames, Detectives and Danger*. Milwaukee, WI: Applause, 2013.

Holtzman, Will. *Judy Holliday*. New York: Putnam, 1982.

Huggins, Roy. *The Double Take.* New York: Pocket Books, 1948.

Joyner, C. Courtney. *The Westerners: Interviews with Actors, Directors, Writers and Producers.* Jefferson, NC: McFarland, 2009.

Kanin, Garson. *Hollywood: Stars and Starlets, Tycoons and Flesh-peddlers, Moviemakers and Moneymakers, Frauds and Geniuses, Hopefuls and Has-Beens, Great Lovers and Sex Symbols.* New York: Viking, 1974.

Keyes, Evelyn. *Scarlett O'Hara's Younger Sister: My Lively Life In and Out of Hollywood.* Secaucus, NJ: Lyle Stuart, 1977.

Langman, Larry. *The Media in the Movies: A Catalog of American Journalism Films, 1900–1996.* Jefferson, NC: McFarland, 1998.

Larkin, Rochelle. *Hail, Columbia.* New Rochelle, NY: Arlington House, 1975.

Larsen, Kristin E. *Community Architect: The Life and Vision of Clarence S. Stein.* Ithaca, NY: Cornell University Press, 2017.

Leaming, Barbara. *If This Was Happiness: A Biography of Rita Hayworth.* New York: Viking, 1989.

Levy, Emanuel. *George Cukor, Master of Elegance: Hollywood's Legendary Director and His Stars.* New York: Morrow, 1994.

Loeb, Sophie Irene. *Everyman's Child.* New York: Century, 1920.

Loughrey, Janet. *Gardens Adirondack Style.* Lanham, MD: Down East Books, 2005.

MacShane, Frank. *Into Eternity: The Life of James Jones, American Writer.* Boston: Houghton Mifflin, 1985.

Magers, Boyd, and Michael Fitzgerald. *Westerns Women: Interviews with 50 Leading Ladies of Movie and Television Westerns from the 1930s to the 1960s.* Jefferson, NC: McFarland, 1999.

Markovits, Andrei S., and Kenneth Garner. *Hillel at Michigan, 1926/27–1945: Struggles of Jewish Identity in a Pivotal Era.* Ann Arbor, MI: Maize Books, 2016.

Martin, Jeffrey Brown. *The Screenplays of Ben Hecht.* Ann Arbor, MI: University Microfilms, 1980.

Marton, Andrew, and Joanne D'Antonio. *Andrew Marton.* Metuchen, NJ: Scarecrow, 1991.

Marx, Arthur. *Red Skelton.* New York: Dutton, 1979.

Marx, Groucho. *The Groucho Letters: Letters to and from Groucho Marx.* New York: Simon & Schuster, 1967.

Miller, Ann, with Norma Lee Browning. *Miller's High Life.* Garden City, N.Y.: Doubleday, 1972.

Mumford, Lewis. *Sketches from Life: The Autobiography of Lewis Mumford, the Early Years.* New York: Dial Press, 1982.

Murphy, George, with Victor Lasky. *"Say ... Didn't You Used to Be George Murphy?"* New York: Bartholomew House, 1970.

Nollen, Scott Allen. *Abbott and Costello on the War Front: A Critical Study of the Wartime Films.* Jefferson, NC: McFarland, 2009.

Ogden, Christopher. *Legacy: A Biography of Moses and Walter Annenberg.* Boston: Little, Brown, 1999.

Parsons, Kermit Carlyle. *The Writings of Clarence S. Stein: Architect of the Planned Community.* Baltimore: Johns Hopkins University Press, 1998.

Powell, Jane. *The Girl Next Door ... and How She Grew.* New York: Morrow, 1988.

Rosenberg, Bernard, and Harry Silverstein. *The Real Tinsel.* New York: Macmillan, 1970.

Ross, Ishbel. *Ladies of the Press: The Story of Women in Journalism by an Insider.* New York: Harper, 1936.

Sanua, Marianne R. *Going Greek: Jewish College Fraternities in the United States, 1895–1945.* Detroit: Wayne State University Press, 2003.

Sculthorpe, Derek. *Brian Donlevy, the Good Bad Guy: A Bio-Filmography.* Jefferson, NC: McFarland, 2017.

_____. *Van Heflin: A Life in Film.* Jefferson, NC: McFarland, 2016.

Seller, Maxine Schwartz, ed. *Immigrant Women.* 2d ed. Albany: State University Press of New York, 1994.

Sheridan, James, and Barry Monush. *Lucille Ball FAQ: Everything Left to Know About America's Favorite Redhead.* Milwaukee, WI: Applause, 2011.

Sherman, Vincent. *Studio Affairs: My Life as a Film Director.* Lexington: University Press of Kentucky, 1996.

Shorris, Sylvia, and Marion Abbott Bundy. *Talking Pictures: With the People Who Made Them.* New York: New Press, 1994.

Sickels, Eleanor M. *Twelve Daughters of Democracy: True Stories of American Women, 1865–1930.* Freeport, NY: Books for Libraries Press, 1968.

Simon, Stephen. *Bringing Back the Old Hollywood: Wild Times and Life Lessons with Sinatra, Cruise, Reeve, Madonna and More.* Portland, OR: Mystical Movies, 2011.

Simon, Stephen, and Gay Hendricks. *Spiritual Cinema: A Guide to Movies That Inspire, Heal, and Empower Your Life.* Carlsbad, CA: Hay House, 2006.

Slide, Anthony. *Actors on Red Alert: Career Interviews with Five Actors and Actresses Affected by the Blacklist.* Lanham, MD: Scarecrow, 1999.

Spada, James. *Peter Lawford: The Man Who Kept the Secrets.* New York: Bantam, 1992.

Standard Catalog for Public Libraries: 1934 Edition, Fourth Supplement. New York: H.W. Wilson, 1938.

Storm, Barry. *I Was Swindled by Red Movie Makers.* Quincy, IL: Storm-Mollet Publishing, 1954.

_____. *Thunder Gods Gold: The Amazing Story of America's Most Famed Lost Gold Mines.* Quincy, IL: Storm-Mollet Publishing, 1954.

Thomas, Bob. *Bud and Lou: The Abbott and Costello Story.* Philadelphia: Lippincott, 1977.

_____. *King Cohn: The Life and Times of Harry Cohn.* New York: McGraw-Hill, 1990.

Treadwell, Bill. *50 Years of American Comedy.* New York: Exposition Press, 1951.

Turner, Lana. *Lana: The Lady, the Legend, the Truth*. New York: Dutton, 1982.

Warfel, Harry R. *American Novelists of Today*. New York: American Book Company, 1951.

Wilson, Helen, ed. *Squirrel Hill: A Neighborhood History*. Charleston, SC: History Press, 2017.

Zierold, Norman. *The Moguls: Hollywood's Merchants of Myth*. Los Angeles: Silman-James, 1991.

Documentaries

Finding Lucy. Directed by Pamela Mason Wagner. Hollywood, CA: Paramount, 2000.

Marsha Hunt's Sweet Adversity. Directed by Roger C. Memos. Los Angeles, CA: Zelda Can Dance Productions, 2015.

Interviews

Burke, Dusty. Telephone and email, September 2019.

Dahl, Arlene. Email, November 5, 2019.

Gehring, Wes D. Email, January 8, 2020.

Granger, Susan. Telephone and email, January 2019–February 2020.

Greene, Melissa. Telephone, November 12, 2019.

Moore, Terry. Telephone, January 29, 2020.

O'Brien, Margaret. Telephone, May 6, 2019.

Powell, Jane. Telephone, April 26, 2019.

Simon, Stephen. Telephone, February 2019–January 2020.

Weltzien, Alan. Email, March–April 2019.

Archival Materials

California Un-American Activities Committees Records, 1935–1971. California State Archives, Sacramento, California.

The Chronicle, 1930–1941. Schroon Lake Camp, Schroon Lake, New York. Private collection.

Columbia Pictures Records, 1929–1974. American Heritage Center, University of Wyoming, Laramie, Wyoming.

The Hillel News, 1927–1950. Bentley Historical Library, University of Michigan, Ann Arbor, Michigan.

Leslie, Aleen. Papers, 1930–1966. American Heritage Center, University of Wyoming, Laramie, Wyoming.

MGM Collection, Cinematic Arts Library, University of Southern California, Los Angeles, California.

Sherdeman, Ted. Papers, 1930–1987. American Heritage Center, University of Wyoming, Laramie, Wyoming.

Small, Edward, as told to Robert E. Kent. "You Don't Have to Be Crazy to Be in Show Business But It Helps! Autobiography of Edward Small." Typescript of unpublished memoir. Cinematic Arts Library, University of Southern California, Los Angeles, California.

Stein, Clarence. Papers, #3600, 1905–1983. Division of Rare and Manuscript Collections, Cornell University Library, Ithaca, New York.

Universal Studios Collection, Cinematic Arts Library, University of Southern California, Los Angeles, California.

Public Records

Simon, David, death certificate, September 5, 1924. Bureau of Vital Statistics, Department of Health, Commonwealth of Pennsylvania. Digital image available at ancestry.com.

Simon, Mary, death certificate, August 6, 1933. Bureau of Vital Statistics, Board of Health, State of Florida.

Simon, Samuel, probate files, February 1892. Superior Court, County of Fresno, California. Digital image available at ancestry.com.

Periodicals

Film Bulletin
Film Daily
Harrison's Reports
The Hollywood Reporter
The Jewish Criterion
The Los Angeles Times
Motion Picture Daily
Motion Picture Herald
The Pittsburgh Post-Gazette
The Pittsburgh Press
The Pittsburgh Sun-Telegraph
Showmen's Trade Review
Variety

Websites

The AFI Film Catalog, https://aficatalog.afi.com
www.ancestry.com
The Internet Movie Database, www.imdb.org
Media History Digital Library, www.mediahistory project.org
www.newspapers.com
Pittsburgh Jewish Newspaper Project, https://digitalcollections.library.cmu.edu/portal/collections/pjn/index.jsp
Rauh Jewish Archives, www.jewishfamilieshistory.org
YouTube, www.youtube.com

Index

Numbers in *bold italics* indicate pages with photographs